The Anchor Essay Annual

The Best of

1998

The
Best
of
1998

Edited and with an Introduction by
Phillip Lopate

The Anchor Essay Annual

Anchor Books/Doubleday
New York London Toronto Sydney Auckland

AN ANCHOR BOOK
PUBLISHED BY DOUBLEDAY
a division of Bantam Doubleday Dell Publishing Group, Inc.
1540 Broadway, New York, New York 10036

ANCHOR BOOKS, DOUBLEDAY, and the portrayal of an anchor are
trademarks of Doubleday, a division of Bantam Doubleday Dell
Publishing Group, Inc.

Book design by Cheryl L. Cipriani

Library of Congress Cataloging-in-Publication Data is available from the
publisher upon request.

ISBN 0-385-48414-3
Copyright © 1998 by Phillip Lopate
All Rights Reserved
Printed in the United States of America
First Anchor Books Edition: September 1998

10 9 8 7 6 5 4 3 2 1

Contents

Phillip Lopate

Introduction

This is my second year of editing *The Anchor Essay Annual,* and it feels as though I am finally getting my bearings. If at first, I don't mind admitting, I was overwhelmed by the task, the sheer volume of reading and the need to devise a system for acquiring and organizing materials, by now I am becoming inured to the sensation of being swamped, like a punch-drunk fighter who keeps getting up off the canvas long after his brain is addled.

One factor that both increases my work and delights me is that the essay is unquestionably going through a resurgence. The literary quarterlies, bless their souls, are packed these days with good essays: they had been doing a magnificent job of keeping the form alive in leaner years, and now that there is more interest, journals arrive in the mail with three or more worthy candidates. The mass magazines, the slicks, have opened their pages to essays as well, in the guise of provocative think-pieces and intimate confessions. Beyond that, when I have traveled this past year to various campuses across the country, I have encountered a whole new generation of would-be essay-ists—young people!—who are acquiring MFAs in what is now called "creative nonfiction." This phenomenon has even generated a backlash, sure sign of success, with pundits gravely calling for bulwarks to hold back the unwashed foot soldiers of "creative nonfiction." (Myself, I prefer the more old-fashioned term, literary nonfiction.)

In all this activity, the personal essay is prevalent. Patricia Hampl has called the personal essay "the centerpiece of literary nonfiction" and "the signature genre of the day." Whether or not you agree with that assessment, it is certainly unarguable that aspects of the personal essay have begun to bleed into other, more traditionally impersonal, essay types, as though authors now feel emboldened (or compelled) to appeal to their own experience as testimony, before launching into their main argument.

What is less noticeable, perhaps, is that the influence has also gone the other way: our personal essayists are groping more and more to incorporate other-than-personal subject matter—that is, to address disciplines and arguments that take them beyond the narrowness of self. To speak incessantly about the wounds or triumphs of I and My Family can get pretty tiresome; the trick is to project one's experience on the page in such an enhanced, objectified way that it acquires, or merges with, a larger significance. Drawing upon a specific field of inquiry (religion, politics, history, science, art, etc.) for background is one way of doing that.

In making these selections I have striven to balance the personal and the impersonal, or formal, element in essay-writing—to give both manners a chance to shine. I have also wanted to suggest the various subsets that enrich the essay today, such as memoir piece (Bert O. States, Luc Sante), nature writing (Mary Oliver), travel (André Aciman), feminism (Emily Fox Gordon), music criticism (Edward W. Said), critical theory (Stanley Fish), pop culture (Margaret Talbot). I envision this annual as reflecting the "state of the art" in contemporary essay-writing—an end-of-year bash honoring the most memorable performances. Some guests are up-and-coming, with as-yet unfamiliar names. Others are just whom you might expect, though

ence, rather than interim reports at the end of youth. As the New Memoir becomes more and more taken over by the scene-making methods of the fiction workshop and the deep-image reverberations of contemporary poetry, a "show, don't tell" interdiction falls on it, and it cedes some of its powers of interpretation. The essay becomes a last refuge for analytical prose.

Finally it seems to me, the essay continues to invite mischief. One of our younger essayists, David Lazar, notes, "As a matter of fact, I have, ironically, never trusted anyone who was incapable of 'putting one over,' as though the inability to be obviously untrustworthy at least some of the time bespeaks a moral weakness, or thinness of character." The essayist playfully adjusts the masks of sincerity and irony, welcoming the reader to trust, mistrust, and judge.

no less worthy of inclusion because of that. Indeed, ve
essayists such as Guy Davenport, Edward Hoagland, '
Gornick, Sam Pickering, Joseph Epstein, and Gerald Earl
done so much for the form, year after year, that they dese
be inducted into an Essay Hall of Fame. Inevitably, a few g
cannot appear in person. Each year we seem to lose one o
master practitioners: Murray Kempton, the Senecan ne
perman who leaves us his inimitable war memoir, salt-o
earth humanism in mock-*gravitas,* and J. B. Jackson, the
geographer-essayist who is represented here by a gem, a
covery from the 1950s, since no celebration of the new s
fail to honor the past. There seem to be a goodly assortme
greying heads at the party, for, despite the infusion of yot
voices (David Foster Wallace, Lucy Grealy, Thomas Lynch
essay continues to be a form whose reflective wisdom abou
patterns of life suits the middle-aged and elderly (Hilary
ters, Norman Podhoretz, William Maxwell) so well. F
there are a few foreign visitors (Gilles Deleuze, Carlos
sivais, Robert McLiam Wilson), because any panorama o
essay today must take into consideration the powerful influe
issuing from abroad.

Speaking of Deleuze, there is a tendency for America
throw up their hands in their face of French theory, as thou
were a plot against commonsense. I have had the very
response at times, and much of the critical writing from Fr
continues to irk me as unnecessarily opaque. On the other b
when I come across a particularly thoughtful, stimulating e
ple of the species, I feel the urge to include it, because or
the ancient glories of the essay has been its ability to do phi
phy in a small space. Deleuze is an admittedly condensed,
losophical thinker, but he is no more difficult to follow
Emerson. We ought not dismiss all intellectual writing as "
demic." An intellectual essay can sometimes be an advent
an academic one, never.

The rise of the essay in recent years has undoubtedly b
connected to the fashion for memoir. But memoirs used to
the repositories for deep reflections on a life's worth of exp

The
Anchor
Essay
Annual

The
Best
of

1998

Vivian Gornick

The Princess and the Pea

I learned early that life was either Chekhovian or Shakespearean. In our house there was no contest. My mother lay on a couch, in a half-darkened room, one arm flung across her forehead, the other pressed against her breast. "I'm lonely!" she cried, and from every quarter of the tenement, women, and men also, flapped about, trying to assuage an anguish of the soul they took to be superior. But she turned away, her eyes closed in frantic dissatisfaction. She wanted a solace of the spirit none of them could provide. They were not the right people. No one around her was the right person. There had been only one right person, and now he was dead.

She had elevated love to the status of the holy grail. To find love was not simply to have sexual happiness, it was to achieve a place in the universe. When she married my father, she told me, a cloud of obscurity lifted from her soul. That's how she put it: a cloud of obscurity. Papa was magic: his look, his touch, his understanding. She leaned forward when she got to the end of this sentence. Understanding was the talismanic word. To be understood was everything. Without understanding, she said, *she didn't know she was alive;* with understanding she felt centered and in the world. In my father's presence she responded with a depth she hadn't known she possessed to poetry, politics, music, sex: everything. She closed her eyes dramatically. Everything. When he died, she said, "everything" went with him. The cloud over her soul returned, blacker than ever: now it blotted out the earth. She refused, absolutely refused, to live in the world without understanding.

Papa's understanding was like having the glass slipper fit. The glamor of recognition was magically bestowed. Smart, flirtatious, impassioned, all she had to do was stand there and be adored. The pleasure her intelligent welcome gave my hardworking father when he walked through the door at six in the evening transformed a Bronx tenement apartment into a rich and royal background. His appreciating response brought largeness into the room. Without ever having to leave the kitchen, my mother could impact upon the world.

When my father died she went into a sentimental decline, suffering like a character in a nineteenth-century novel the loss of the man (never-to-be-replaced) who had understood her. His presence had made her life significant. His absence now returned her to sack-cloth and ashes. The depression was profound and, apparently, non-negotiable, persisting undiminished and undiluted for years on end. She could not forget her distinguished loss, her wounded existence, the absolute *rightness* of what had once been hers. Whatever was now being offered, it would not do. Refusal took on a life of its own. Nothing was ever exactly the right thing. No one was ever exactly the right one.

I became my mother's daughter. "I'm lonely!" I cried at twelve; at seventeen; at twenty-eight. A pity, really, as I was compulsively sociable. All I ever wanted to do was talk. Heaven on earth was me in a voluble state of free association. But very young I grew anxious. I was not able to find myself interesting without intelligent response. I required the company of minds attuned to my own. No one around gave me back the words I needed to hear. The ones I did get back isolated me. I was forever telling the children on the block a story that had grown out of something that had just happened at school, in the grocery store, in the building. I'd give them the narration, then I'd sum up, giving them the sentence that delivered the meaning of the story. After that I wanted someone to speak a sentence that would let me know my own had been received. Instead, eager looks evaporated, expressions turned puzzled or hostile and, inevitably, someone said, "Whaddaya mean by that?"

I grew agitated, restless and insulting, permanently aggrieved. "How can you say that!" I cried long before I could vote. "That's the stupidest thing I ever heard." I was beside myself with my mother's sense of deprivation. It was as though I'd been cheated at birth of the Ideal Friend, and now all I could do was register the insufficiency of the one at hand.

I was never going to know what Keats knew before he was twenty-five, that "any set of people is as good as any other." Now *there* was a Shakespearean life. Keats occupied his own experience to such a remarkable degree he needed only the barest of human exchanges to connect with an inner clarity he had himself achieved. For that, almost anyone would do. He lived inside the heaven of a mind absorbed by its own conversation. I would wander for the rest of my life in the purgatory of self-exile, always looking for the right person to talk to.

It was transcendence I was after: the authority of a principled imagination: the redemption of high seriousness. But how was I to get from here to there? I hadn't a clue. This dead end led quickly into high-minded moralizing. I became the only girl on the block who pronounced regularly on the meaning and nature of Love. Real love, true love, right love; love that was passionate and madly sympathetic, providing communion of the deepest sort. You knew *instantly*, I declared categorically, when you were in the presence of love. If you didn't know, it wasn't love. And if it *was*, you were to give yourself over to it without question—whatever the obstacles—because love was the supreme intensity, the significant exaltation. It was the certainty with which I rehearsed this litany—again and again—that marked me forever.

At the same time that I was pontificating about Love, I was a girl who continually daydreamed herself Emma Goldman. In my imagination I was forever up on the stage of a great auditorium, or on a platform out in the street, addressing a crowd of thousands, urging them to revolution. The conviction that one day I would have the eloquence and the vision to move people to such action was my secret thrill. Sometimes I'd feel puzzled about how I would manage life both as an agent of revolution and as a devotee of Love. Inevitably, then, a picture formed itself in the air before me of myself on the stage, my face glowing with purpose, and an adoring man in the audience waiting for me to come down into his arms. That seemed to account adequately for all necessities.

As I passed into adolescence and then into my late teens, this image in my head of myself leading the revolution began, mysteriously, to complicate itself. I knew, of course, that a significant life included real work—work done out in the world—but now I seemed to imagine that an Ideal Partner was necessary in order to do the work. With the right man at my side, I posited, I could do it all. Without the right man . . . But no, that was unthinkable. There would *be* no without the right man. I would have to make certain of that. The emphasis began to shift away from doing the work to finding the right man in order to do the work. Slowly but surely, finding the right man seemed to become the work.

In college, the girls who were my friends were literary. Every one of them identified either with George Eliot's Dorothea Brooke, who takes a pedant for a man of intellect, or with Henry James's Isabel Archer, who sees the evil-hearted Osmond as a man of cultivation. Those who identified with Dorothea were impressed by her prideful devotion to "standards," those who didn't thought her a provincial prig. Those who identified with Isabel adored her for the largeness of her emotional ambition, those who didn't thought her dangerously naive. Either way, my friends and I saw ourselves as variations of one or the other. The seriousness of our concerns lay in our preoccupation with these two fictional women. Their destinies were prototypes of what we imagined our own to be.

None of us questioned the essential situation. The problem in each book was: what happens when the protagonist—beautiful, intelligent, sensitive—mistakes the wrong man for the right man. As a problem, the situation seemed entirely reasonable to all of us. We saw it happening every day of the week. Among ourselves were young women of grace, talent, and beauty attached, or becoming attached, to men—dull in mind or spirit—who were bound to drag them down. The prospect of such a fate haunted all of us. We each shuddered to think that we might become such women, and fall into the hell of a life bound either to a Casaubon or an Osmond. That's how we thought of it: as falling into a life; having to evade something out there, waiting to ensnare us.

Not me, I determined. If I couldn't find the right man, I swore boldly, I'd do without.

For ten years after college I knocked about, in pursuit of the holy grail: Love with a capital L, Work with a capital W. I read, I wrote, I fell into bed. I was married to an artist for ten minutes, I smoked marijuana for five. Lively and animated, I roamed the streets of New York and Europe. Somehow, nothing quite suited. I couldn't figure out how to get down to work, and needless to say I couldn't stumble on the right man. Repeatedly, I'd determine on a course of action; repeatedly, I'd fall back. In time, a great lassitude overcame me. It was as though I'd fallen asleep on my feet, and needed to be awakened.

In my thirties I married a scientist, a man of melancholy temperament. It had taken him eighteen years to complete his dissertation. His difficulty made him poetic in my eyes. He, of course, was remarkably sensitive to my own divided will. During our courtship we walked together by the hour while I discoursed passionately, and with eloquence, on why I could not get to Moscow. His eyes flashed with emotion as I spoke.

"My dear girl!" he would exclaim. "My beautiful, marvelous girl. You are life itself!"

I became the interesting, conflicted personage, and he the intelligent, responsive wife. The arrangement made us both happy. It felt like comradeship. At last, I thought, I had an Ideal Friend.

Gerald was the most understanding man I had ever known. Every day I poured out at him a torrent of dramatic narrative, and every day he nodded along beside me, saying, "In other words . . . ," giving me back myself twice as good as I'd given it to him. Hearing my own words come back at me through his ever-enlarging rhetoric rescued me repeatedly from an irresoluteness I could not conquer. Talking with my husband was as good as sitting down at the typewriter. Better. In conversation with Gerald my thoughts seemed full and consequential. The flow came easily. I opened my mouth to speak and soon everything I had to say was there. I'd smile at him. If it wasn't for you, my smile said, I'd never have had this delightful turn of mind.

Cocooned inside our endless talk, from time to time I'd think, When will you act? Then Gerald and I would go for a walk. I'd take his arm and say, "I've been thinking . . ." He'd turn eagerly toward me. "Yes, dear heart?" his expression said. "What delightful thing have you been thinking?" I'd open my mouth and begin to talk.

Life seemed sweet, larger than it had before. Alone, I had been cramped up inside; now I felt myself breathing freely. I was glad to wake up with my husband beside me. I experienced comfort of the soul, and a way to embrace existence I'd not known before. In this mood we thought it a fine thing to roam about, leave the city, discover the country. We traveled west, and when we reached the California coast rented a bungalow. I remember the first moment I saw that glittering circle of sand, sky, rock and water, and all those glamorous houses gleaming up and down the brilliant mountainside. A wonderful piece of laughter began to grow in me. The world was lovely, radiant, entertaining. I could be happy here. All this deliciousness, and I had a friend in the house.

One morning I woke up desolate. Why, I could not tell.

Nothing had changed. He was the same, I was the same. Just a few weeks before I'd awakened feeling festive. Now I stood in the shower stricken, spots of grief dancing in the air before my eyes, the old loneliness seeping back in.

Who is he? I thought.

He's not the right one, I thought.

If only I had the right one, I thought.

A year later we were divorced.

I was still my mother's daughter. Now she was the negative and I the print, but there we both were. Alone, at last, with: not the right one.

I did not understand, until years after I'd left Gerald, that I was born to find the wrong man, as were Dorothea and Isabel. That's what we were in business for. If this had not been the case, we'd have all—privileged women that we were—found some useful work to do and long forgotten the whole question of the right man. But we did not forget it. We never forgot it. The elusive right man became our obsessive preoccupation. Not finding him was the defining experience.

It is the same with the princess on the pea. She's not after the prince, she's after the pea. That moment when she feels the pea beneath the twenty mattresses, that is *her* moment of definition. It is the very meaning of her journey, why she has traveled so far, what she has come to declare: the dissatisfaction that will keep her life at bay.

So it was with my mother, who spent most of her life sighing for the absent right one. And so it was with me.

We were in thrall to passive longing, all of us—Dorothea and Isabel, my mother and I, the fairytale princess. Longing is what attracted us, what compelled our deepest attention. The essence, indeed, of a Chekhovian life. Think of all those Natashas sighing through three long acts for what is not, and can never be. While one (wrong) man after another listens sympathetically to the recital of a dilemma for which there is no solution.

Gerald and I were Natasha and the Doctor walking in the

woods, forever talking, talking, talking. Behind Natasha's eloquent and enchanting conversation lies a passivity of monumental proportion—for which the Doctor is the perfect foil. His endless listening provides her with necessary illusion, makes her think she's on the move, going somewhere. But it's only a quick fix; after the high comes a great weariness. Inevitably, Natasha and the Doctor must part. They have only been keeping each other company, wasting their equally insufficient intent together. Yet, Natasha turns away in a mood to accuse. The problem, she tells herself angrily, is that he wasn't the right one. I am not such a fool that I will say he was, when he wasn't. If he had been the right one, then I should think and act, be and do.

What we all wanted—Natasha and I, Dorothea and Isabel, my mother and the princess—was to think and act, be and do. But we didn't want it enough. Not wanting it enough, we fell into a petulance that mimicked the act of thinking. We narrowed our eyes and spotted the flaw, pursed our lips and announced imperfection, folded our arms and passed judgment. Judgment always encourages the critical intelligence to dwell on that which is missing, but *passing* judgment makes that which is missing a permanent irritation. Soon enough, through the painful logic of inborn grievance, the irritation becomes a wound, an infliction: a devotion and a destiny.

Thomas Lynch

The Undertaking

Every year I bury a couple hundred of my townspeople. Another two or three dozen I take to the crematory to be burned. I sell caskets, burial vaults, and urns for the ashes. I have a sideline in headstones and monuments. I do flowers on commission.

Apart from the tangibles, I sell the use of my building: eleven thousand square feet, furnished and fixtured with an abundance of pastel and chair rail and crown moldings. The whole lash-up is mortgaged and remortgaged well into the next century. My rolling stock includes a hearse, two Fleetwoods, and a minivan with darkened windows our pricelist calls a service vehicle and everyone in town calls the Dead Wagon.

I used to use the *unit pricing method*—the old package deal. It meant that you had only one number to look at. It was a large number. Now everything is itemized. It's the law. So now there is a long list of items and numbers and italicized disclaimers, something like a menu or the Sears Roebuck Wish Book, and sometimes the federally-mandated options begin to look like cruise control or rear-window defrost. I wear black most of the time, to keep folks in mind of the fact we're not talking

Buicks here. At the bottom of the list there is still a large number.

In a good year the gross is close to a million, five percent of which we hope to call profit. I am the only undertaker in this town. I have a corner on the market.

The market, such as it is, is figured on what is called *the crude death rate*—the number of deaths every year out of every thousand persons.

Here is how it works.

Imagine a large room into which you coax one thousand people. You slam the doors in January, leaving them plenty of food and drink, color TVs, magazines, and condoms. Your sample should have an age distribution heavy on baby boomers and their children—1.2 children per boomer. Every seventh adult is an old-timer, who, if he or she wasn't in this big room, would probably be in Florida or Arizona or a nursing home. You get the idea. The group will include fifteen lawyers, one faith healer, three dozen real-estate agents, a video technician, several licensed counselors, and a Tupperware distributor. The rest will be between jobs, middle managers, ne'er-do-wells, or retired.

Now for the magic part—come late December when you throw open the doors, only 991.6, give or take, will shuffle out upright. Two hundred and sixty will now be selling Tupperware. The other 8.4 have become the crude death rate.

Here's another stat.

Of the 8.4 corpses, two-thirds will have been old-timers, five percent will be children, and the rest (slightly less than 2.5 corpses) will be boomers—realtors and attorneys likely—one of whom was, no doubt, elected to public office during the year. What's more, three will have died of cerebral-vascular or coronary difficulties, two of cancer, one each of vehicular mayhem, diabetes, and domestic violence. The spare change will be by act of God or suicide—most likely the faith healer.

The figure most often and most conspicuously missing from the insurance charts and demographics is the one I call The Big One, which refers to the number of people out of every hundred born who will die. Over the long haul, The Big One hovers right around . . . well, dead nuts on one hundred percent. If this were on the charts, they'd call it *death expectancy* and no one would buy futures of any kind. But it is a useful number and has its lessons. Maybe you will want to figure out what to do with your life. Maybe it will make you feel a certain kinship with the rest of us. Maybe it will make you hysterical. Whatever the implications of a one hundred percent death expectancy, you can calculate how big a town this is and why it produces for me a steady if unpredictable labor.

They die around the clock here, without apparent preference for a day of the week, month of the year; there is no clear favorite in the way of season. Nor does the alignment of the stars, fullness of moon, or liturgical calendar have very much to do with it. The whereabouts are neither here nor there. They go off upright or horizontally in Chevrolets and nursing homes, in bathtubs, on the interstates, in ERs, ORs, BMWs. And while it may be that we assign more equipment or more importance to deaths that create themselves in places marked by initials—ICU being somehow better than Greenbriar Convalescent Home—it is also true that the dead don't care. In this way, the dead I bury and burn are like the dead before them, for whom time and space have become mortally unimportant. This loss of interest is, in fact, one of the first sure signs that something serious is about to happen. The next thing is they quit breathing. At this point, to be sure, *a gunshot wound to the chest* or *shock and trauma* will get more ink than a CVA or ASHD, but no cause of death is any less permanent than the other. Any one will do. The dead don't care.

Nor does *who* much matter, either. To say, "I'm OK, you're OK, and by the way, he's dead!" is, for the living, a kind of comfort.

It is why we drag rivers and comb plane wrecks and bomb sites.

It is why MIA is more painful than DOA.

It is why we have open caskets and all read the obits.

Knowing is better than not knowing, and knowing it is you is terrifically better than knowing it is me. Because once I'm the dead guy, whether you're OK or he's OK won't much interest me. You can all go bag your asses, because the dead don't care.

Of course, the living, bound by their adverbs and their actuarials, still do. Now, there is the difference and why I'm in business. The living are careful and oftentimes caring. The dead are careless, or maybe it's care-less. Either way, they don't care. These are unremarkable and verifiable truths.

My former mother-in-law, herself an unremarkable and verifiable truth, was always fond of holding forth with Cagneyesque bravado—to wit: "When I'm dead, just throw me in a box and throw me in a hole." But whenever I would remind her that we did substantially that with everyone, the woman would grow sullen and a little cranky.

Later, over meatloaf and green beans, she would invariably give out with: "When I'm dead just cremate me and scatter the ashes."

My former mother-in-law was trying to make carelessness sound like fearlessness. The kids would stop eating and look at each other. The kids' mother would plead, "Oh Mom, don't talk like that." I'd take out my lighter and begin to play with it.

In the same way, the priest that married me to this woman's daughter—a man who loved golf and gold ciboria and vestments made of Irish linen; a man who drove a great black sedan with a wine-red interior and who always had his eye on the cardinal's job—this same fellow, leaving the cemetery one day, felt called upon to instruct me thus: "No bronze coffin for me. No sir! No orchids or roses or limousines. The plain pine box is the one I want, a quiet Low Mass and the pauper's grave. No pomp and circumstance."

He wanted, he explained, to be an example of simplicity, of prudence, of piety and austerity—all priestly and, apparently, Christian virtues. When I told him that he needn't wait, that he could begin his ministry of good example even today, that he could quit the country club and do his hacking at the public links and trade his brougham for a used Chevette; that free of his Florsheims and cashmeres and prime ribs, free of his bingo nights and building funds, he could become, for Christ's sake, the very incarnation of Francis himself, or Anthony of Padua; when I said, in fact, that I would be willing to assist him in this, that I would gladly distribute his savings and credit cards among the worthy poor of the parish, and that I would, when the sad duty called, bury him for free in the manner he would have, by then, become accustomed to; when I told your man these things, he said nothing at all, but turned his wild eye on me in the way that the cleric must have looked on Sweeney years ago, before he cursed him, irreversibly, into a bird.

What I was trying to tell the fellow was, of course, that being a dead saint is no more worthwhile than being a dead philodendron or a dead angelfish. Living is the rub, and always has been. Living saints still feel the flames and stigmata of this vale of tears, the ache of chastity and the pangs of conscience. Once dead, they let their relics do the legwork, because, as I was trying to tell this priest, the dead don't care.

Only the living care.

And I am sorry to be repeating myself, but this is the central fact of my business—that there is nothing, once you are dead, that can be done *to you* or *for you* or *with you* or *about you* that will do you any good or any harm; that any damage or decency we do accrues to the living, to whom your death happens, if it really happens to anyone. The living have to live with it. You don't. Theirs is the grief or gladness your death brings. Theirs is the loss or gain of it. Theirs is the pain and the pleasure of memory. Theirs is the invoice for services rendered and theirs is the check in the mail for its payment.

And there is the truth, abundantly self-evident, that seems, now that I think of it, the one most elusive to the old in-laws, the parish priest, and to perfect strangers who are forever accosting me in barber-shops and cocktail parties and parent-teacher conferences, hell-bent or duty-bound to let me in on what it is they want done with them when they are dead.

Give it a rest is the thing I say.

Once you are dead, put your feet up, call it a day, and let the husband or the missus or the kids or a sibling decide whether you are to be buried or burned or blown out of a cannon or left to dry out in a ditch somewhere. It's not your day to watch it, because the dead don't care.

Another reason people are always rehearsing their obsequies with me has to do with the fear of death that anyone in their right mind has. It is healthy. It keeps us from playing in traffic. I say it's a thing we should pass on to the kids.

There is a belief—widespread among the women I've dated, local Rotarians, and friends of my children—that I, being the undertaker here, have some irregular fascination with, special interest in, inside information about, even attachment to, *the dead.* They assume, these people, some perhaps for defensible reasons, that I want their bodies.

It is an interesting concept.

But here is the truth.

Being dead is one—the worst, the last—but only one in a series of calamities that afflicts our own and several other species. The list may include, but is not limited to, gingivitis, bowel obstruction, contested divorce, tax audit, spiritual vexation, cash flow problems, political upheaval, and on and on and on some more. There is no shortage of misery. And I am no more attracted to the dead than the dentist is to your bad gums, the doctor to your rotten innards, or the accountant to your sloppy expense records. I have no more stomach for misery than the banker or the lawyer, the pastor or the politico—because misery is careless and is everywhere. Misery is the bad check, the ex-spouse, the mob in the street, and the IRS—who, like the dead, feel nothing and, like the dead, *don't care.*

Which is not to say that the dead do not matter.

They do. They do. Of course they do.

Last Monday morning Milo Hornsby died. Mrs. Hornsby called at 2 A.M. to say that Milo had *expired* and would I take care of it, as if his condition were like any other that could be renewed or somehow improved upon. At 2 A.M., yanked from my REM sleep, I am thinking, put a quarter into Milo and call me in the morning. But Milo is dead. In a moment, in a twinkling, Milo has slipped irretrievably out of our reach, beyond Mrs. Hornsby and the children, beyond the women at the laundromat he owned, beyond his comrades at the Legion Hall, the Grand Master of the Masonic Lodge, his pastor at First Baptist, beyond the mailman, zoning board, town council, and Chamber of Commerce; beyond us all, and any treachery or any kindness we had in mind for him.

Milo is dead.

X's on his eyes, lights out, curtains.

Helpless, harmless.

Milo's dead.

Which is why I do not haul to my senses, coffee and quick shave, Homburg and great coat, warm up the Dead Wagon, and make for the freeway in the early o'clock for Milo's sake. Milo doesn't have any sake anymore. I go for her—for she who has become, in the same moment and the same twinkling, like water to ice, the Widow Hornsby. I go for her—because she still can cry and care and pray and pay my bill.

The hospital that Milo died in is state-of-the-art. There are signs on every door declaring a part or a process or bodily function. I like to think that, taken together, the words would add up to The Human Condition, but they never do. What's left of Milo, the remains, are in the basement, between SHIPPING & RECEIVING and LAUNDRY ROOM. Milo would like that if he were still liking things. Milo's room is called PATHOLOGY.

The medical-technical parlance of death emphasizes disorder.

We are forever dying of failures, of anomalies, of insufficiencies, of dysfunctions, arrests, accidents. These are either chronic or acute. The language of death certificates—Milo's says "Cardiopulmonary Failure"—is like the language of weakness. Likewise, Mrs. Hornsby, in her grief, will be said to be breaking down or falling apart or going to pieces, as if there were something structurally awry with her. It is as if death and grief were not part of The Order of Things, as if Milo's failure and his widow's weeping were, or ought to be, sources of embarrassment. "Doing well" for Mrs. Hornsby would mean that she is bearing up, weathering the storm, or being strong for the children. We have willing pharmacists to help her with this. Of course, for Milo, doing well would mean he was back upstairs, holding his own, keeping the meters and monitors bleeping.

But Milo is downstairs, between SHIPPING & RECEIVING and LAUNDRY ROOM, in a stainless-steel drawer, wrapped in white plastic top to toe, and—because of his small head, wide shoulders, ponderous belly, and skinny legs, and the trailing white binding cord from his ankles and toe tag—he looks, for all the world, like a larger than life-size sperm.

I sign for him and get him out of there. At some level, I am still thinking Milo gives a shit, which by now, of course, we all know he doesn't—because the dead don't care.

Back at the funeral home, upstairs in the embalming room, behind a door marked PRIVATE, Milo Hornsby is floating on a porcelain table under florescent lights. Unwrapped, outstretched, Milo is beginning to look a little more like himself—eyes wide open, mouth agape, returning to our gravity. I shave him, close his eyes, his mouth. We call this *setting the features*. These are the features—eyes and mouth—that will never look the way they would have looked in life when they were always opening, closing, focusing, signaling, telling us something. In death, what they tell us is that they will not be doing anything anymore. The last detail to be managed is Milo's hands—one folded over the other, over the umbilicus, in an attitude of ease, of repose, of retirement.

They will not be doing anything anymore, either.

I wash his hands before positioning them.

When my wife moved out some years ago, the children stayed here, as did the dirty laundry. It was big news in a small town. There was the gossip and the goodwill that places like this are famous for. And while there was plenty of talk, no one knew exactly what to say to me. They felt helpless, I suppose. So they brought casseroles and beef stews, took the kids out to the movies or canoeing, brought their younger sisters around to visit me. What Milo did was send his laundry van around twice a week for two months, until I found a housekeeper. Milo would pick up five loads in the morning and return them by lunchtime, fresh and folded. I never asked him to do this. I hardly knew him. I had never been in his home or his laundromat. His wife had never known my wife. His children were too old to play with my children.

After my housekeeper was installed, I went to thank Milo and pay the bill. The invoices detailed the number of loads, the washers and the dryers, detergent, bleaches, fabric softeners. I think the total came to sixty dollars. When I asked Milo what the charges were for pick-up and delivery, for stacking and folding and sorting by size, for saving my life and the lives of my children, for keeping us in clean clothes and towels and bed linen, "Never mind that" is what Milo said. "One hand washes the other."

I place Milo's right hand over his left hand, then try the other way. Then back again. Then I decide that it doesn't matter. One hand washes the other either way.

The embalming takes me about two hours.

It is daylight by the time I am done.

Every Monday morning, Ernest Fuller comes to my office. He was damaged in some profound way in Korea. The details of his damage are unknown to the locals. Ernest Fuller has no limp or anything missing so everyone thinks it was something he saw in Korea that left him a little simple, occasionally perplexed, the type to draw rein abruptly in his day-long walks, to consider the meaning of litter, pausing over bottle caps and gum wrappers. Ernest Fuller has a nervous smile and a dead-fish handshake. He wears a baseball cap and thick eyeglasses. Every Sunday night Ernest goes to the supermarket and buys up the tabloids at the checkout stands with headlines that usually involve Siamese twins or movie stars or UFOs. Ernest is a speed reader and a math whiz but because of his damage, he has never held a job and never applied for one. Every Monday morning, Ernest brings me clippings of stories under headlines like: 601 LB MAN FALLS THRU COFFIN—A GRAVE SITUATION or EMBALMER FOR THE STARS SAYS ELVIS IS FOREVER. The Monday morning Milo Hornsby died, Ernest's clipping had to do with an urn full of ashes, somewhere in East Anglia, that made grunting and groaning noises, that whistled sometimes, and that was expected to begin talking. Certain scientists in England could make no sense of it. They had run several tests. The ashes' widow, however, left with nine children and no estate, is convinced that her dearly beloved and greatly reduced husband is trying to give her winning numbers for the lottery. "Jacky would never leave us without good prospects," she says. "He loved his family more than anything." There is a picture of the two of them, the widow and the urn, the living and the dead, flesh and bronze, the Victrola and the Victrola's dog. She has her ear cocked, waiting.

We are always waiting. Waiting for some good word or the winning numbers. Waiting for a sign or wonder, some signal from our dear dead that the dead still care. We are gladdened when they do outstanding things, when they arise from their graves or fall through their caskets or speak to us in our waking dreams. It pleases us no end, as if the dead still cared, had agendas, were yet alive.

But the sad and well-known fact of the matter is that most of us will stay in our caskets and be dead a long time, and that our urns and graves will never make a sound. Our reason and requiems, our headstones or High Masses, will neither get us in nor keep us out of heaven. The meaning of our lives, and the memories of them, belong to the living, just as our funerals do. Whatever being the dead have now, they have by the living's faith alone.

We heat graves here for winter burials, as a kind of foreplay before digging in, to loosen the frost's hold on the ground before the sexton and his backhoe do the opening. We buried Milo in the ground on Wednesday. The mercy is that what we buried there, in an oak casket, just under the frost line, had ceased to be Milo. Milo had become the idea of himself, a permanent fixture of the third person and past tense, his widow's loss of appetite and trouble sleeping, the absence in places where we look for him, our habits of him breaking, our phantom limb, our one hand washing the other.

Francine Prose

The Old Morgue

My father was a pathologist. For most of his professional career—that is, for all of my early life—he worked in the autopsy rooms and laboratories of the Bellevue Hospital Mortuary.

The Old Morgue, people call it now. And whenever the Old Morgue is mentioned, a passionate nostalgia shines (a little crazily) in the eyes of those who still remember the beautiful gloomy brick building (built near the turn of the century by McKim, Mead and White) that's been replaced by the "new" Bellevue's glass and steel.

The Old Morgue had stone staircases, wrought iron railings, tiled floors, dark halls, and the atmosphere of an antiquarian medical establishment—part torture chamber, part charnel house, part research laboratory—so brilliantly captured in David Lynch's film version of *The Elephant Man*. In my memory, the Old Morgue evokes those shadowy group portraits of distinguished scientists performing anatomical dissections, arranged with formal ceremony around a flayed cadaver painted with the esthetic high gloss of a Dutch Master *nature morte*.

The autopsy room was enormous—cavernous, people say—with twenty-foot ceilings, windows reaching from roof to floor, and, high above, a skylight that cast sheets of dusty light onto the doctors, the assistants, the students gathered round the gleaming chrome tables. For all the disturbing tools of the trade—the hoses, scalpels, saws, the scales for weighing organs—the room had the classical elegance of an old-fashioned hotel lobby in which the dead might rest for a while until their rooms were ready.

The morgue was my father's office—where he went every day to work. It was where my mother took me after ballet lessons so he could drive us home to Brooklyn. On school holidays, I dressed up so he could show me off to his colleagues and then find me a quiet corner of his lab where I could read until lunch. I liked going with him to his job. I never thought much about the beauty of the Old Morgue, or its strangeness, or the strangeness of growing up in a household in which dinner-table conversation concerned the most fascinating cases that had come down for autopsy that day.

Most everyone's childhood seems normal to them, and everyone's childhood marks them. Like army brats, like diplomats' kids, like the offspring of Holocaust survivors and (so I'm told) suicides, the children of pathologists recognize each other. Two of my friends are pathologist's daughters; we speak a common language. Last week, confessing to one that I'd binged on plained—disgustedly, unthinkingly—that the layer of fat beneath the skin was "just like every goddamn autopsy you've ever seen." She laughed, and then said, "I hope you know not to say things like that to most people."

This fall, at a dinner party in Manhattan, I met a writer, a woman whose mother worked with my father; both were pathologists at Bellevue. As the other guests put down their forks and looked on, faintly appalled, we reminisced nostalgically about growing up in the Old Morgue. We discussed our shared fascination with the morgue employees known as dieners. German for "servants," the word had always made us think of Dr. Frankenstein's trusty helper, Igor. Though they were usually busy with the physical work of the autopsy room—sawing through the breast bone and skull, sometimes making the Y-shaped incision—the dieners knew the best stories (accounts of the more peculiar cases that had come into their provenance) and took time to tell them, like fairy tales, to the two little girls waiting for their parents to finish work and take them home.

We talked about how you always knew you were getting close to the morgue when you heard the keening, asthmatic whine of the dieners' electric saws . . . And for just a moment, that high-pitched buzz seemed more immediate and more real than the genteel clink of silver as the other guests bravely returned to their meals.

Forensic and clinical pathologists are said to be different breeds. Articulate and extroverted, the forensic scientist (who deals with suspicious, violent, or accidental death) is drawn to popping flash bulbs and adversarial courtroom situations, while the stereotypical pathologist (whose patients are more likely to have died of organic disease) is an eccentric loner without the minimal social skills to interact with the living. But until 1961, when the New York City Medical Examiner's Office traded the Victorian gloom of Bellevue for its own faux-Bauhaus quarters on 30th Street and First Avenue, the forensic pathologists shared the Old Morgue with clinical pathologists, like my father.

Indeed, the history of pathology at Bellevue is inseparable from that of the Medical Examiner's office, established in 1917. (Previously, the city coroner was rarely a physician, which is still not a job requirement in many areas of the country, where the county coroner may be a mortician or a moonlighting tow-truck driver.) Pathologists reverentially recite the names of the first ME's—Norris, Gonzales, Helpern—like a royal line of succession dating back to the era when the morgue was known as the deadhouse.

The Old Morgue had no air-conditioning. From the safe distance of decades, my father's former colleagues take pride in having braved working conditions that no one would stand for today. No young pathologist would consider doing those long postmortems in the stifling summer heat, when the smell of the autopsy room, barely cloaked by disinfectant, permeated the whole building; you took it home in your clothes.

The doctors at the morgue worked hard: long hours for little pay, often for the loftiest and most idealistic of reasons. "More than any other specialty, pathologists teach other doctors," says Marvin Kuschner, who left Bellevue to become dean of SUNY-Stony Brook Medical School. "And my generation was inspired by *Arrowsmith*, by *The Microbe Hunters*. We all wanted to save the world and find the cure for cancer." Pathologists have a broader knowledge of the science of medicine than their counterparts in other fields; they know who the good diagnosticians are, which surgeons make fatal mistakes.

No one becomes a pathologist for the money. Most have comparatively low-paying university appointments, and though it's possible to supplement an academic salary with a high-volume business reading slides of biopsies and cervical Pap smears, still the sum is a fraction of the income of the surgeon or orthopedist. Medical examiners—city or state employees—receive even lower salaries, for which they are obliged to contend with unsympathetic reporters and merciless political pressure: the unscientific agendae of the government and the police. One way you can tell an honest ME, they say, is that he's probably been fired. And no one goes into the field for the glory: pathologists don't tend to have grateful patients passing around their business cards at Park Avenue dinner parties.

Pathologists speak unashamedly of their work as a vocation, a calling, and—with tender care and respect—of their patients, the dead. ("We have to learn to talk to our patients as much as an internist must talk to living patients," says Michael Baden, the outspoken former New York City Medical Examiner now serving as Director of the Forensic Unit of the New York State Police. "A dead person can't tell us where it hurts. But we can figure it out.")

And yet for all the seriousness with which the doctors took their work, the Old Morgue was an oddly jolly place, with its camaraderie, its in-jokes, its characters and legends. Everyone knew the story of the Irish politician whose body was left by the dieners on a table overnight; by morning his nose had been devoured by roaches or rats. The problem was solved when an artistic doctor fashioned a new nose of putty—tinted green to match the skin color produced by the dead man's cirrhotic liver. But the embalming process blanched the skin, leaving the deceased with a green nose at his open-casket Irish wake.

I remember hearing about the daper pathologist who did autopsies in an elegant suit with a cornflower in his lapel and who scrawled obscenities on the walls and blackboards. About the doctor with the eerie booming laugh who had his mother-in-law exhumed to prove that his wife had poisoned her—and was doing the same to him. The withdrawn medical examiner who played handball against his office walls at midnight; the pathologist who taught his students these precious home truths: "Burial is just long-term storage" and "Maggots are your friends." (In fact, human DNA and evidence of drug use can be obtained from maggots who have skeletonized a corpse.) The doctor who procured human brains for medical students and committed suicide when this service he'd provided gratis was exposed by the press.

After autopsy, the organs of the deceased are put in a bag and sewn up inside the corpse; still, one hears rumors about souvenir-taking. Officially, JFK's brain is missing, though Baden, who examined the Kennedy autopsy findings for the Congressional Select Committee on Assassinations, has an elaborate theory positing that Robert Kennedy safeguarded the tissue removed from his brother's body and restored it to the coffin just before burial. Trotsky's brain has never been found, while Einstein's surfaced in Illinois in the possession of a former Princeton neuropathologist planning to write a paper on the physiology of genius.

One Bellevue veteran recounts meeting, on the street, a colleague who opened a package wrapped in newspaper and showed him a human heart. My friend's pathologist-father brought home a heart in a Kentucky Fried Chicken bucket and dumped it into the bathroom sink for an impromptu anatomy lesson. Another friend was nearly dismissed from her Upper

East Side private girls' school when her fellow students found, in her locker, a foetus that her mother had given her to bring to biology class.

My father never brought keepsakes from the morgue home to us. And yet he—readily, eagerly—took me along to the morgue. When I was fourteen, during the summer between my freshman and sophomore years of high school, he got me a summer job as an assistant in a chemistry lab next door to the autopsy room.

Only lately, as the mother of teenagers near the age that I was then, have I begun to wonder: *What in the world was he thinking?* Most likely, it seemed perfectly normal to employ his daughter in the family business. (Recently, his best friend told me that he'd got his son a summer job driving the truck that picked up bodies for the Long Island Medical Examiner.)

The Old Morgue was definitely hardball. It had a heavily macho ambiance, a gum-chewing, cigar-smoking rough and tumble. "There were certain ragged edges to the performance," admits one veteran.

"Bellevue fostered a great brotherhood," says Renate Dische, a pediatric pathologist. "People who worked there have a mutual bond. It was a tough environment. The first week I got there, it was summer, hot as blazes. And there was terrific excitement: they'd found a body in a steamer trunk. It was like the good old days in the 1920s! Everyone was running around, taking pictures of the trunk open, the trunk closed. Inside was this plug-ugly guy curled up in foetal position. Some loan shark who had lent money to a poor artist."

I don't imagine that my father worried much about exposing me to the teeming activity of a workplace in which twenty autopsies might be going at once, far more in cases of disaster. (I remember him working through the night after two planes collided over downtown Brooklyn.) Nor do I think he was greatly concerned about any psychic damage that might result from my intimate acquaintance with mortuary life.

But what about the real dangers? "I always felt there was

TB on the *staircases* at Bellevue," says Renate Dische. "And the staff was careless about tuberculosis. So quite a few doctors came down with TB and had to go to sanitariums." (On vacation in the Adirondacks, my father took us to see the former TB hospital at Saranac Lake, a marvelously creepy cluster of buildings surrounded by porches on which the sick were dosed with sunlight and fresh air.)

Hepatitis was also a problem, as were the flies which swarmed in whenever the tall windows were opened to relieve the stifling heat—flies so fat and preoccupied that, one doctor recalls, "you could take a scalpel and cut right through them as they ate off the bodies." Then there was the oppressive odor that permeated everything. People warned me: Wait till they bring in a floater, a body that's been in the water. I couldn't imagine anything worse than the normal smell, but on the day a floater came in, I knew at once what had happened—and that I'd been correctly warned.

In the basement was an embalming school, and beneath that the tunnels through which bodies were transported; the tunnels were home to packs of wild cats installed to control the rat population and to an underground mini-society of the homeless, even then. Upstairs, the quotidian routines of the mortuary were regulated by disgruntled city employees like the elevator operator who punished impatient interns by stopping the car between floors and making them jump or climb; when he died, the staff attended his autopsy to make sure he was really dead.

I don't believe my father had any particular pedagogical or philosophical interest in exposing me to the harsh fact of death. Nor was he careless about my safety; he was, if anything, overprotective. I think he believed the slim risk was worth it because he was fervently hoping—as he continued to hope long after I'd published several novels—that I would be drawn to his profession, that I would become a doctor.

In fact, I enjoyed my job in the lab, mostly washing glassware. I liked my boss, a biochemist who hoped to prove experimentally, by analyzing the urine of schizophrenics, that a percentage of the patients in the Psychiatric Building across 29th

Stanley Fish

Boutique Multiculturalism, or Why Liberals Are Incapable of Thinking About Hate Speech

1. MULTICULTURALISM DOES NOT EXIST

Multiculturalism comes in at least two versions, boutique multiculturalism and strong multiculturalism. Boutique multiculturalism is the multiculturalism of ethnic restaurants, weekend festivals, and high profile flirtations with the other in the manner satirized by Tom Wolfe under the rubric of "radical chic."* Boutique multiculturalism is characterized by its superficial or cosmetic relationship to the objects of its affection. Boutique multiculturalists admire or appreciate or enjoy or sympathize with or (at the very least) "recognize the legitimacy of" the traditions of cultures other than their own; but boutique multiculturalists will always stop short of approving other cultures at a point where some value at their center generates an act that offends against the canons of civilized decency as they have been either declared or assumed. The death sentence under which Salman Rushdie now lives is an obvious and perspicuous example, although it is an example so extreme that it might be better to begin with a few

---

* See Tom Wolfe, *Radical Chic and Mau-mauing the Flak Catchers* (New York, 1970).

that are less dramatic. A boutique multiculturalist may find something of value in rap music and patronize (pun intended) soul-food restaurants, but he will be uneasy about affirmative action and downright hostile to an afrocentrist curriculum. A boutique multiculturalist may enjoy watching Native American religious ceremonies and insist that they be freely allowed to occur, but he will balk if those ceremonies include animal sacrifice or the use of a controlled substance.° A boutique multiculturalist may acknowledge the diversity of opinions about abortion, but he is likely to find something illegitimate in the actions of abortion opponents who block the entrance to clinics and subject the women who approach them to verbal assaults. A boutique multiculturalist may honor the tenets of religions other than his own, but he will draw the line when the adherents of a religion engage in the practice of polygamy.

In each of these cases (and in the many analogous cases that could be instanced) the boutique multiculturalist resists the force of culture he appreciates at precisely the point at which it matters most to its strongly committed members: the point at which the African American tries to make the content of his culture the content of his children's education, the point at which a Native American wants to practice his religion as its ancient rituals direct him to, the point at which antiabortionists directly confront the evil that they believe is destroying the moral fiber of the country, the point at which Mormons seek to be faithful to the word and practices of their prophets and elders.

Another way to put this is to say that a boutique multiculturalist does not and cannot take seriously the core values of the cultures he tolerates. The reason he cannot is that he does not see those values as truly "core" but as overlays on a substratum of essential humanity. That is the true core, and the differences that mark us externally—differences in language, clothing, religious practices, race, gender, class, and so on—are for the bou-

---

° See *Employment Division, Department of Human Resources of Oregon et al.* v. *Smith et al.*, 494 U.S. 872 (1990), in which Native Americans were denied exception for the religious use of peyote.

tique multiculturalist no more than what Milton calls in his *Are-opagitica* "moderat varieties and brotherly dissimilitudes that are not vastly disproportionall."* We may dress differently, speak differently, woo differently, worship or not worship differently, but underneath (or so the argument goes) there is something we all share (or that shares us) and that something constitutes the core of our identities. Those who follow the practices of their local culture to the point of failing to respect the practices of other cultures—by calling for the death of an author whose writings denigrate a religion or by seeking to suppress pornography because it is offensive to a gender—have simply mistaken who they are by identifying with what is finally only an *accidental* aspect of their beings.

The essential boutique multiculturalist point is articulated concisely by Steven C. Rockefeller: "Our universal identity as human beings is our primary identity and is more fundamental than any particular identity, whether it be a matter of citizenship, gender, race, or ethnic origin."** Taking pleasure in one's "particular identity" is perfectly all right so long as when the pinch comes, and a question of basic allegiance arises, it is one's universal identity that is affirmed, for as "important as respect for diversity is in multicultural democratic societies, ethnic identity is not the foundation of recognition of equal value and the related idea of equal rights" ("C," p. 88). That is to say, we have rights, not as men or women or Jews or Christians or blacks or Asians, but as human beings, and what makes a human being a human being is not the particular choices he or she makes but the capacity for choice itself, and it is this capacity rather than any of its actualizations that must be protected.

It follows then that while any particular choice can be pursued at the individual's pleasure, it cannot be pursued to the point at which it interferes with or prescribes or proscribes the

---

* John Milton, *Areopagitica,* in *The Prose of John Milton,* ed. J. Max Patrick (1644; Garden City, N.Y., 1967), p. 322.
** Steven C. Rockefeller, "Comment," in *Multiculturalism and "The Politics of Recognition": An Essay,* ed. Amy Gutmann (Princeton, N.J., 1992), p. 88; hereafter abbreviated "C."

choices of other individuals. (This is of course a reformulation of J. S. Mill's "harm principle" in *On Liberty*.) One may practice one's religion, even if it is devil worship, in any manner one likes, but one may not practice one's religion to the extent of seeking to prevent others from practicing theirs by, say, suppressing their sacred texts, or jailing their ministers. Women may rightly insist that they receive equal pay for equal work, but they cannot rightfully insist that they be given extra compensation or preferential treatment just because they are women. One may choose either to read or to disdain pornography, but one who believes in pornography's liberatory effects cannot compel others to read it, and one who believes that pornography corrupts cannot forbid others to publish it.

Of course it is just those two actions (or some versions of them) that pro- and antipornography forces will most want to take since they flow logically from the beliefs of the respective parties and will be seen by those parties as positive moral requirements. This is what I meant earlier when I pointed out that the boutique multiculturalist will withhold approval of a particular culture's practices at the point at which they matter most to its strongly committed members: a deeply religious person is precisely that, *deeply* religious, and the survival and propagation of his faith is not for him an incidental (and bracketable) matter, but an essential matter, and essential too in his view for those who have fallen under the sway of false faiths. To tell such a person that while his convictions may be held he must stop short of fully implementing them is to tell him that his vision of the good is either something he must keep to himself or something he must offer with a diffidence that might characterize his offer of canapés at a cocktail party.* Rockefeller might say that "respect for the individual is understood to involve not only respect for . . . universal human potential . . . but also re-

---

* Some political theorists go so far as to insist, not merely that religious reasons be disallowed in the public forum, but that citizens should not advocate or vote for any position unless their motives are "adequately secular" (Robert Audi, "The Separation of Church and State and the Obligations of Citizenship," *Philosophy and Public Affairs* 18 [Summer 1989]: 280). See also the full discussion of the question in Kent Greenawalt, *Private Consciences and Public Reasons* (Oxford, 1995).

spect for . . . the different cultural forms in and through which individuals actualize their humanity" ("C," p. 87), but it is clear from his commentary that the latter respect will be superficial precisely in the measure that the cultural forms that are its object have themselves been judged to be superficial, that is, not intrinsic to universal identity.

The politics generated by views like Rockefeller's has been called by Charles Taylor "a politics of equal dignity." The politics of equal dignity, Taylor explains, ascribes to everyone "an identical basket of rights and immunities," identical because it is limited to that aspect of everyone that is assumed to be universally the same, namely, "our status as rational agents," agents defined by a shared potential for deliberative reason.* The idea is that so long as that potential is protected by law, particular forms of its realization—cultural traditions, religious dogmas, ethnic allegiances—can be left to make their way or fail to make their way in the to-and-fro of marketplace debate. A tradition may die, a religion may languish, an ethnic community may fail to secure representation in the classroom or the boardroom, but these consequences are of less moment and concern than the integrity of the process that generates them, a process that values deliberation over the results of deliberation, results that are, from the perspective of this politics, indifferent.**

Results or outcomes are not at all indifferent in another politics, named by Taylor, the "politics of difference" ("PR," p. 38). The politics of difference, as Taylor explains it, does not merely allow traditions a run for their money; it is committed to their flourishing. If the politics of equal dignity subordinates local cultural values to the universal value of free rational choice, the politics of difference names as its preferred value

---

* Charles Taylor, "The Politics of Recognition," in *Multiculturalism and "The Politics of Recognition,"* pp. 38, 41; hereafter abbreviated "PR."

** John Rawls put it this way: "The state is not to do anything that makes it more likely that individuals accept any particular conception rather than another" (John Rawls, *Political Liberalism* [New York, 1993], p. 193). Rawls acknowledges that "some conceptions will die out and others survive only barely," but this, he says, is inevitable because "no society can include within itself all forms of life" (p. 197). (A statement made with all the complacency of someone who knows that his form of life will certainly be included in his society.)

the active fostering of the unique distinctiveness of particular cultures. It is that distinctiveness rather than any general capacity of which it is an actualization that is cherished and protected by this politics. Whereas the politics of equal dignity "focuses on what is the same in all" and regards particularity as icing on a basically homogeneous cake, the politics of difference asks us "to recognize and even foster particularity" as a first principle ("PR," p. 43).

In practical terms, fostering particularity requires that we make special adjustments to the special requirements of distinctive groups, for if we refuse such adjustments in the name of some baseline measure of rational potential, we weaken the distinctiveness whose recognition is our chief obligation. "Where the politics of universal dignity fought for forms of nondiscrimination that were quite 'blind' to the ways in which citizens differ, the politics of difference often redefines nondiscrimination as requiring that we make these distinctions the basis of differential treatment" ("PR," p. 39). It is the politics of difference that gives us campus speech codes (like Stanford's before it was struck down) that judicialize racist epithets directed against minorities but do not consider epithets (honkey, redneck, whitey) directed against Caucasian males a form of racism (on the reasoning that racism is defined as hostility plus power rather than as mere hostility). It is the politics of difference that leads to the establishment of schools for young black males in our inner cities (on the reasoning that the maintenance of cultural and gender homogeneity will bolster confidence and stimulate learning). It is the politics of difference that produces demands by blacks, Asians, and Native Americans that they be portrayed in films and plays by actors who are themselves blacks, Asians, and Native Americans. It is the politics of difference that asks for proportional representation of various cultural traditions in the classroom and in faculty hiring. The politics of difference is the equivalent of an endangered species act for human beings, where the species to be protected are not owls and snail darters, but Arabs, Jews, homosexuals, Chicanos, Italian Americans, and on and on and on.

The politics of difference is what I mean by strong multiculturalism. It is strong because it values difference in and for itself rather than as a manifestation of something more basically constitutive. Whereas the boutique multiculturalist will accord a superficial respect to cultures other than his own, a respect he will withdraw when he finds the practices of a culture irrational or inhumane, a strong multiculturalist will want to accord a *deep* respect to all cultures at their core, for he believes that each has the right to form its own identity and nourish its own sense of what is rational and humane. For the strong multiculturalist the first principle is not rationality or some other supracultural universal, but tolerance.

But the trouble with stipulating tolerance as your first principle is that you cannot possibly be faithful to it because sooner or later the culture whose core values you are tolerating will reveal itself to be intolerant at that same core; that is, the distinctiveness that marks it as unique and self-defining will resist the appeal of moderation or incorporation into a larger whole. Confronted with a demand that it surrender its viewpoint or enlarge it to include the practices of its natural enemies—other religions, other races, other genders, other classes—a beleaguered culture will fight back with everything from discriminatory legislation to violence.

At this point the strong multiculturalist faces a dilemma: either he stretches his toleration so that it extends to the intolerance residing at the heart of a culture he would honor, in which case tolerance is no longer his guiding principle, or he condemns the core intolerance of that culture (recoiling in horror when Khomeini calls for the death of Rushdie), in which case he is no longer according it respect at the point where its distinctiveness is most obviously at stake. Typically, the strong multiculturalist will grab the second handle of this dilemma (usually in the name of some supracultural universal now seen to have been hiding up his sleeve from the beginning) and thereby reveal himself not to be a strong multiculturalist at all. Indeed it turns out that strong multiculturalism is not a distinct position but a somewhat deeper instance of the shallow category of boutique multiculturalism.

To be sure, there will still be a difference, but it will be a difference in degree. When the novelist Paul Theroux encounters a Pakistani with an advanced degree in science who nevertheless declares " 'Rushdie must die,' " he responds in true boutique multiculturalist fashion by setting him "straight" and informing him (as if he were a child) that his are "ignorant and barbarous sentiments."* (I bet that really convinced him!) Contrast this with M. M. Slaughter, a strong multiculturalist who, in the place of name calling, offers an explanation of why an educated Muslim whose sense of identity "is inseparable from the community of believers" might think himself mortally wounded by something written in a book. For Slaughter, the issue is properly understood, not as a simple contrast between civilization and barbarity, but as a tension between "essentialist ideologies that inevitably and irreconcilably conflict. . . . The concept of the autonomous self requires the free speech principle; the socially situated self of Islamic society necessarily rejects free speech in favor of prohibitions against insult and defamation." Yet even while she elaborates the point, Slaughter declines to extend her act of sympathetic understanding into a statement of approval, and she is careful to declare at the beginning of her essay that "the placing of a bounty on Rushdie's head" is "a terroristic act."** Slaughter's judgement, in short, is finally not all that different from Theroux's, although it comes accompanied by an analysis the novelist has no interest in making. Both Theroux and Slaughter—one of which sees the *fatwa* as an instance of fanaticism bordering on insanity, while the other pushes through to a comprehension of the system of thought in which the *fatwa* might constitute a moral obligation—stop far short of going all the way, that is, of saying, with Theroux's Pakistani, "Rushdie must die."

In the end neither the boutique multiculturalist nor the strong multiculturalist is able to come to terms with difference,

---

* Paul Theroux, letter to Salman Rushdie, in *The Rushdie Letters: Freedom to Speak, Freedom to Write,* ed. Steve MacDonogh (Lincoln, Nebr., 1993), p. 33.
** M. M. Slaughter, "The Salman Rushdie Affair: Apostasy, Honor, and Freedom of Speech," *Virginia Law Review* 79 (Feb. 1993): 198, 156, 155, 154.

although their inabilities are asymmetrical. The boutique multiculturalist does not take difference seriously because its marks (quaint clothing, atonal music, curious table manners) are for him matters of lifestyle, and as such they should not be allowed to overwhelm the substratum of rationality that makes us all brothers and sisters under the skin. The strong multiculturalist takes difference so seriously as a general principle that he cannot take any *particular* difference seriously, cannot allow its imperatives their full realization in a political program, for their full realization would inevitably involve the suppression of difference. The only way out for the would-be strong multiculturalist is to speak not for difference in general but for *a* difference, that is for the imperatives of a distinctive culture even when they impinge on the freedom of some other distinctive culture.

But if he did that the strong multiculturalist would no longer be faithful to his general principle. Instead he would have become a "really strong" multiculturalist, someone whose commitment to respecting a culture was so strong that he will stay its course no matter what; but that would mean that he wasn't a multiculturalist at all since if he sticks with the distinctiveness of a culture even at the point where it expresses itself in a determination to stamp out the distinctiveness of some other culture, he will have become (what I think every one of us always is) a uniculturalist. It may at first seem counterintuitive, but given the alternative modes of multiculturalism—boutique multiculturalism, which honors diversity only in its most superficial aspects because its deeper loyalty is to a universal potential for rational choice; strong multiculturalism, which honors diversity in general but cannot honor a particular instance of diversity insofar as it refuses (as it always will) to be generous in its turn; and really strong multiculturalism, which goes to the wall with a particular instance of diversity and is therefore not multiculturalism at all—no one could possibly *be* a multiculturalist in any interesting and coherent sense.°

° For evidence I might point to *Multiculturalism: A Critical Reader*, ed. David Theo Goldberg (Cambridge, Mass., 1994), a volume in which the contributors

2. MULTICULTURALISM
AS DEMOGRAPHIC FACT

The reason that this will sound counterintuitive is that multiculturalism and its discontents are all people are talking about these days. Is everyone arguing about something that doesn't exist? An answer to that question will require a fresh beginning to our analysis and the introduction of a new distinction between multiculturalism as a philosophical problem and multiculturalism as a demographic fact. Multiculturalism as a philosophical problem is what we've been wrestling with in the preceding passages with results not unlike those achieved (if that is the word) by Milton's fallen angels who try to reason about fate, foreknowledge, and free will and find themselves "in wandering mazes lost."°° We too become lost in mazes if we think of multiculturalism as an abstract concept that we are called upon either to affirm or reject. But if we think of multiculturalism as a demographic fact—the fact that in the United States today many cultural traditions flourish and make claims on those who

---

wrestle unsuccessfully with the conundrums I have been explicating. Some of the essays urge something called critical multiculturalism, which Peter McLaren glosses as the "task of transforming the social, cultural, and institutional relations in which meanings are generated" (Peter McLaren, "White Terror and Oppositional Agency: Towards a Critical Multiculturalism," p. 53). This is to be done in the service and name of heterogeneity (see Goldberg, "Introduction: Multicultural Conditions," pp. 25–31), but just where is heterogeneity to be located? Whose heterogeneity (read "difference") is it? If it is located somewhere, then it is not heterogeneity. If it is located everywhere, then it is universalist liberalism all over again, and the supposed enemy has been embraced.

The Chicago Cultural Studies Group tries to finesse this dilemma by urging full disclosure. One should "indicate the goal of one's knowledge production" and thereby "disrupt one's claim to academic authority and authorial self-mastery" (Chicago Cultural Studies Group, "Critical Multiculturalism," *Critical Inquiry* 18 [Spring 1992]: 549; rpt. in *Multiculturalism*, pp. 114–39). But by now this gesture *is* a claim to authority and signifies mastery and control even as they are disowned in search of a "better standpoint for substantive critique" (p. 549). The authors can only conclude that "a genuinely critical multiculturalism cannot be brought about by good will or by theory, but requires institutions, genres, and media that do not yet exist" (p. 553). They never will.

°° Milton, *Paradise Lost*, in *John Milton*, ed. Stephen Orgel and Jonathan Goldberg (Oxford, 1990), bk. 2, l. 561, p. 389.

identify with them—the impulse either to affirm or reject it begins to look rather silly; saying yes or no to multiculturalism seems to make about as much sense as saying yes or no to history, which will keep on rolling along irrespective of the judgement you pass on it.

Not that there is nothing to say once you have recognized that multiculturalism is a demographic fact; it is just that what you say will have more to do with the defusing of potential crises than the solving of conceptual puzzles. We may never be able to reconcile the claims of difference and community in a satisfactory formula, but we may be able to figure out a way for *these* differences to occupy the civic and political space of *this* community without coming to blows. "All societies," Taylor observes, "are becoming increasingly multicultural"; as a result, "substantial numbers of people who are citizens" of a particular country are also members of a culture "that calls into question" that country's "philosophical boundaries" ("PR," p. 63). What we "are going to need . . . in years to come," Taylor predicts, is some "inspired adhoccery."*

I want to take the phrase "inspired adhoccery" seriously. What it means is that the solutions to particular problems will be found by regarding each situation-of-crisis as an opportunity for improvisation and not as an occasion for the application of rules and principles (although the invoking and the recharacterizing of rules and principles will often be components of the improvisation). Any solution devised in this manner is likely to be temporary—that is what *ad hoc* means—and when a new set of problems has outstripped its efficacy, it will be time to improvise again. It follows then that definitions of multiculturalism will be beside the point, for multiculturalism will not be one thing, but many things, and the many things it will be will weigh differently in different sectors of the society. In some sectors multiculturalism will take care of itself, in others its problematic will hardly register, and in others it will be a "problem" that must be confronted.

---

* Taylor, "The Rushdie Controversy," *Public Culture* 2 (Fall 1989): 121.

It will not, however, typically be a philosophical or theoretical problem. Multiculturalism in the workforce? Projections of demographic patterns indicate that in the foreseeable future the workforce will be largely made up of women and minorities; accordingly, corporations have already begun to change their recruiting patterns. It is clear, Corning CEO James Houghton has said, that no company can afford a predominantly white, male workforce. Neither can a company afford a workplace driven by racial and ethnic tensions; and therefore the same bottom line consideration that is altering hiring and promotion policies is also mandating sensitivity programs, a more consultative organizational structure, and decentered management. In short, for the business world it's multiculturalism or die.

The same formula applies for different reasons to colleges and universities. When the college population was relatively small and homogeneous it was a matter of neither concern nor surprise that the range of cultural materials studied was restricted to the books produced by earlier generations of that same homogeneous population; but when the GI bill brought many to college who would otherwise not have thought to go, and when some of those newly introduced to the academy found that they liked it and decided to stay on as faculty members, and when the rising tide of feminist consciousness led women to no longer be willing to sacrifice their careers to the ambitions of their husbands, and when a college degree became a prerequisite for employment opportunities previously open to high school graduates, and when immigration after the Korean and Vietnam Wars added large numbers of motivated students to a growing cultural mix, and when pride in ethnic traditions (stimulated in part by the extraordinary impact of the television miniseries *Roots*) weakened the appeal of the "melting pot" ideal, the pressures to include new materials in the classroom and to ask that they be taught by members of the cultures or subcultures from which they were drawn seemed to come from all directions. Although multiculturalism is sometimes characterized as a conscious strategy devised by insurgent political groups desirous of capturing America's cultural space so that it can be turned over to alien ideas, in fact it is a development that was planned by no one. As an effect it was decidedly overdetermined, and now that it is here those who wish to turn the clock back will find themselves increasingly frustrated.

To be sure there will always remain a few colleges (like Hillsdale in Michigan) that set themselves up as the brave defenders of the beachheads others have ignominiously abandoned, but by and large, at least in the world of education, multiculturalism is a baseline condition rather than an option one can be either for or against. Indeed in many facets of American life there is no multiculturalism issue despite the fact that it is endlessly debated by pundits who pronounce on the meaning of democracy, the content of universal rights, the nature of community, the primacy of the individual, and so on. These mind-numbing abstractions may be the official currency of academic discussion, but they do not point us to what is really at stake in the large social and economic dislocations to which they are an inadequate (and even irrelevant) response. In and of themselves they do no genuine work and insofar as they do any work it is in the service of the adhoccery to which they are rhetorically opposed.

I would not be misunderstood as recommending adhoccery; my point, rather, is that adhoccery will be what is going on despite the fact that the issues will be framed as if they were matters of principle and were available to a principled resolution. As we have seen, there are principles aplenty—autonomy, respect, toleration, equality—but when they are put into play by sophisticated intelligences the result is not resolution but a sharpened sense of the blind alleys into which they lead us. Here, for example, is Amy Gutmann asking a series of questions to which she apparently thinks there are answers:

> Should a liberal democratic society respect those cultures whose attitudes of ethnic or racial superiority
> . . . are antagonistic to other cultures? If so, how can

respect for a culture of ethnic or racial superiority be reconciled with the commitment to treating all people as equals? If a liberal democracy need not or should not respect such "supremacist" cultures, even if those cultures are highly valued by many among the disadvantaged, what precisely are the moral limits on the legitimate demand for political recognition of particular cultures?*

You will recognize in these questions the interlocking quandaries that led me to conclude that multiculturalism is an incoherent concept that cannot be meaningfully either affirmed or rejected. But this is not Gutmann's conclusion. In good liberal-rationalist fashion, she regards the difficulties she uncovers as spurs to a greater conceptual effort, and she sets herself the task of coming up with a formulation that will rescue us from a world of entrenched "political battlefields" and point the way to "mutually respectful communities of substantial, sometimes even fundamental, intellectual disagreement" ("I," p. 20). What is remarkable about this statement is its reproduction of the dilemmas it claims to resolve and the determined (if unintentional) evasion of the difficulties these dilemmas present. The vocabulary will not stand up to even the most obvious lines of interrogation. How respectful can one be of "fundamental" differences? If the difference is fundamental—that is, touches basic beliefs and commitments—how can you respect it without *dis*respecting your own beliefs and commitments? And on the other side, do you really show respect for a view by tolerating it, as you might tolerate the buzzing of a fly? Or do you show respect when you take it seriously enough to oppose it, root and branch?

It is these and related questions that Gutmann begs and even hides from herself by inserting the word "intellectual" between "fundamental" and "disagreement." What "intellectual"

---

* Gutmann, introduction, *Multiculturalism and "The Politics of Recognition,"* p. 5; hereafter abbreviated "I."

does is limit disagreement to matters that can be debated within the decorums of Enlightenment rationalism. Fiercer disagreements, disagreements marked by the refusal of either party to listen to reason, are placed beyond the pale where, presumably, they occupy the status of monstrosities, both above and below our notice (above our notice when they are disagreements over matters of religion, below our notice when they are disagreements between groups that want, not to talk to one another, but to exterminate one another). As a result, the category of the fundamental has been reconfigured—indeed, stood on its head—so as to exclude conflicts between deeply antithetical positions; that is, to exclude conflicts that are, in fact, fundamental.

The sleight of hand involved here is nicely illustrated by Gutmann's example of a disagreement that she says can be pursued in the context of mutual respect, the disagreement between the pro-choice and pro-life parties in the abortion debate. It is an example that tells against the principle it supposedly supports; for as everyone knows strong pro-life advocates regard pro-choicers as either murderers or supporters of murderers, while in the eyes of pro-choicers, pro-life advocates are determined to deprive women of the right to control their own bodies. The disagreement between them is anything but intellectual because it is so obviously fundamental. In an intellectual disagreement the parties can talk to one another because they share a set of basic assumptions; but in a fundamental disagreement, basic assumptions are precisely what is in dispute. You can either have fundamental or you can have intellectual, but you can't have both, and if, like Gutmann, you privilege intellectual, you have not honored the level of fundamental disagreement, you have evaded it.

3 . HATE SPEECH

Gutmann does it again when she turns to the vexed issue of campus hate speech. Here the question is, How can we have a community of mutually respectful cultures when it is a practice in some cultures to vilify the members of others?° It looks like an intractable problem, but Gutmann solves it, she thinks, by distinguishing between differences one respects and differences one tolerates. You respect a difference when you see it as a candidate for serious moral debate; it has a point even though it is not your point; but some differences are asserted so irrationally that debate is foreclosed, and those differences, while they must be tolerated in a free society, must also be denounced by all right-thinking persons. Hate speech—speech directed against women, Jews, blacks, and gays—falls into the second category; it is "indefensible on moral and empirical grounds" ("I," p. 23).

This seems neat and satisfying until one realizes that the "moral and empirical grounds" on the basis of which the arguments of certain speakers are judged "indefensible" have not been elaborated. Rather, they are simply presupposed, and presupposed too is their normative status. In effect Gutmann is saying, "well, everybody knows that some assertions just aren't worth taking seriously." This is the result of withdrawing the offending opinions from the circle of rationality: a blind eye is turned toward the impact they might have on the world by assuming—without any empirical evidence whatsoever—that

---

° This is a standard question in discussions of multiculturalism from a liberal perspective. Will Kymlicka asks it in *Multicultural Citizenship* (Oxford, 1995): "How should liberals respond to illiberal cultures?" (p. 94). His answer is that since liberals should eschew illiberal practices, they "should not prevent illiberal nations from maintaining their societal culture, but should promote the liberalization of these cultures" (pp. 94–95). In other words, respect the culture by trying to change it. In his inability to see the contradiction between maintaining a tradition and setting out to soften it and blur its edges, Kymlicka enacts the dilemmas traced out in the first part of this essay. He is trying to be a strong multiculturalist but turns boutique when the going gets tough. He would reply that by "promote" he means persuade rather than impose and that rational persuasion is always an appropriate decorum. "Hence liberal reformers inside the culture should seek to promote their liberal principles through reason or example, and liberals outside should lend their support to any efforts the group makes to liberalize their culture" (p. 168). The key word is "reason," which for Kymlicka, as for Rockefeller, is a standard that crosses cultural boundaries and will be recognized by all parties (except those that are nuts). But reasons of the kind liberals recognize—abstract, universal, transhistorical—are precisely what the members of many so-called illiberal cultures reject. The application of "reason" in an effort to persuade is not the opposite of imposition but a version of it.

they will have none, that only crazy people will listen to crazy
talk. With that assumption in place—and it is in place before
she begins—the community of mutually respectful disputants
has been safely constituted by the simple strategy of exiling
anything that might disturb it. No wonder that within its con-
fines disputants exercise mutual respect, since mutuality (of an
extremely pallid kind) has been guaranteed in advance, as problems are solved by being defined out of existence.* Once hate
speech—a designation its producers would resist—has been la-
belled "radically implausible" ("I," p. 22) (and plausibility is
added to the abstractions whose essentialist shape Gutmann
blithely assumes), it is no more threatening than a belch or a
fart: something disagreeable, to be sure, but something we can
live with, especially since the category of the "we" has been
restricted to those who already see things as Gutmann does.

In the end, the distinction between what is to be respected
and what is tolerated turns out to be a device for elevating the
decorum of academic dinner parties to the status of discourse

---

* Rawls makes essentially the same move in *Political Liberalism* when he acknowledges that "prejudice and bias, self and group interest, blindness and willfulness,
play their all too familiar part in political life," but he insists that these "sources of
unreasonable disagreement stand in marked contrast to those compatible with everyone's being fully reasonable" (p. 58). One must ask how the contrast gets
marked. And the answer is from the perspective of a predecision to confine reasonable disagreements to those engaged in by coolly deliberative persons. The irony is
that "prejudice," "bias," "blindness," and "willfulness" are instances of name calling, just the kind of activity Rawls wants to avoid. These words stigmatize certain
kinds of argument in advance and remove them peremptorily from the arena of
appropriate conversation. Susan Mendus neatly illustrates the strategy in a single
brief sentence: "Prejudice and bigotry, not moral disapproval, are the hallmarks of
racism" (Susan Mendus, *Toleration and the Limits of Liberalism* [Atlantic Highlands, N.J., 1989], p. 15). The assertion is that racists (another instance of name
calling) have no arguments, only primitive biases. The assertion works if you accept
its first (unstated) premise: only arguments that are abstract and universal are really
arguments; all others are mere prejudice. This leaves the field of "moral disputa-
tion" to those who have already rejected as accidental or regrettable any affiliations
or commitments based on race or ethnicity. Moral dispute will then go on in the
same sanitized forum marked out by Gutmann's distinction between views you
tolerate (but don't deign to argue with) and views you respect. The alternative
would be to see that prejudice—that is, partiality—is a feature of any moral position, including the liberal one championed by Gutmann, Rawls, and Mendus, and
that what you want to say about those who devalue persons on the basis of race is
not that they are outside the arena of moral debate but that theirs is a morality you
think wrong, evil, and dangerous (provided of course that that is what you think).

universals while consigning alternate decorums to the dustbin of the hopelessly vulgar. In the expanded edition of the volume she edits, Gutmann is joined by Jürgen Habermas, who declines to admit religious fundamentalists into his constitutional republic because they "claim *exclusiveness* for a privileged way of life" and are therefore unfit for entry into "a civilized debate . . . in which one party can recognize the other parties as co-combatants in the search for authentic truths."* Of course, religious fundamentalists begin with the conclusion that the truths they hold are already authentic, but that is precisely why they will be denied entry to the ideal-speech seminar when it is convened. (I hear you knocking but you can't come in.) Fundamentalists and hate speakers might seem an odd couple; what links them and makes them candidates for peremptory exclusion is a refusal to respect the boundaries between what one can and cannot say in the liberal public forum. (You can't say kike and you can't say God.) Although the enemies named by Gutmann and Habermas are different, they are dispatched in the same way, not by being defeated in combat, but by being declared ineligible before the fight begins.

The result is the kind of "civilized" conversation dear to the hearts of academic liberals who believe, on the model of the world-as-philosophy-seminar, that any differences between "rational" persons can be talked through. It is finally a faith in talk—in what liberals call open and inclusive dialogue—that underwrites a program like Gutmann's. But the dialogue is not really open at all, as we can see when she sets down the requirements for entry:

---

* Jürgen Habermas, "Struggles for Recognition in the Democratic Constitutional State," in *Multiculturalism: Examining the Politics of Recognition,* ed. Gutmann (Princeton, N.J., 1994), p. 133; emphasis mine. As Larry Alexander points out, "An actual dialogue test is, in effect, a requirement of unanimity." That is, participants must already agree as to what is appropriate and what is not; but agreement is supposedly the goal of the dialogue and if it is made a requirement for entry (in the manner of Gutmann and Habermas) the goal has been reached in advance by rigging the context. Success is then assured, but it is empty because impediments to it have been exiled in advance even though they surely exist in the world (Larry Alexander, "Liberalism, Religion, and the Unity of Epistemology," *San Diego Law Review* 30 [Fall 1993]: 782).

> Mutual respect requires a widespread willingness and
> ability to articulate our disagreements, to defend them
> before people with whom we disagree, to discern the
> difference between respectable and disrespectable
> agreement, and to be open to changing our own minds
> when faced with well-reasoned criticism. ["I," p. 24]

Words like "widespread" and "open" suggest a forensic table to
which all are invited, but between them is the clause that gives
the lie to the apparent liberality—"to discern the difference
between respectable and disrespectable disagreement"—which
means of course to decide in advance which views will be heard
and which will be dismissed. It is a strange openness indeed that
is defined by what it peremptorily excludes.

It is not my intention, however, to fault Gutmann for not
being open enough. Quite the reverse. It is her desire to be
open that is the problem because it prevents her from taking the
true measure of what she recognizes as an evil. If you wish to
strike a blow against beliefs you think pernicious and "fraught
with death" (the phrase is Oliver Wendell Holmes's in *Abrams
v. United States)*° you will have to do something more than
exclaim, "I exclude you from my community of mutual respect."
That kind of exclusion will be no blow to an agenda whose
proponents are not interested in being respected but in tri-
umphing. Banishing hate speakers from your little conversation
leaves them all the freer to pursue their deadly work in the dark
corners from which you have averted your fastidious eyes. Gutmann's instinct to exclude is the right one; it is just that her
gesture of exclusion is too tame—it amounts to little more than
holding her nose in disgust—and falls far short of wounding the
enemy at its heart. A deeper wound will only be inflicted by
methods and weapons her liberalism disdains: by acts of un-
generosity, intolerance, perhaps even repression, by acts that
respond to evil not by tolerating it—in the hope that its energies
will simply dissipate in the face of scorn—but by trying to stamp

---

° *Abrams* v. *United States*, 250 U.S. 616 (1919).

it out. This is a lesson liberalism will never learn; it is the lesson liberalism is *pledged* never to learn because underlying liberal thought is the assumption that, given world enough and time (and so long as embarrassing "outlaws" have been discounted in advance), difference and conflict can always be resolved by rational deliberation, defined of course by those who have been excluded from it.

I remarked earlier that producers of what is called hate speech would not accept that description of their words, words they would hear as both rational and true. In arguments like Gutmann's and Habermas's, rationality is a single thing whose protocols can be recognized and accepted by persons of varying and opposing beliefs. In this model (as in Rockefeller's) differences are superficial, and those who base political and social judgements on them are labeled irrational. But if rationality is always differential, always an engine of exclusion and boundary making, the opposition is never between the rational and the irrational but between opposing rationalities, each of which is equally, but differently, intolerant. This leads to the perhaps startling but inevitable conclusion that hate speech is rational and that its nature as a problem must be rethought. Indeed, it is only when hate speech is characterized as irrational that the label "problem" seems appropriate to it, and also comforting, because a problem is something that can be treated, either by benign neglect (don't worry, it's a fringe phenomenon that will never catch on), or by education and dialogue (the answer to hate speech is more speech: remember Theroux and the Pakistani), or, in a darker view of the matter, by quarantine and excommunication (you have a disease and while we won't exterminate you, neither will we have anything to do with you). This is the entire spectrum of remedies in the liberal pharmacy, which can only regard hate speech as something we can live with or something we can cure or something we can't cure but can avoid by refusing to join a militia.

It is in relation to this spectrum that speech codes seem obviously counterproductive, either because they are an overstrong response to a minor irritant, or because they stand in the way of the dialogue that will lead to health, or because they will only reinforce the paranoia that produced the problem in the first place. Everything changes, however, once hate speech is seen, not as evidence of some cognitive confusion or as a moral anomaly, but as the expression of a morality you despise, that is, as what *your* enemy (not the universal enemy) says.° If you think of hate speech as evidence of moral or cognitive confusion you will try to clean the confusion up by the application of good reasons; but if you think that hate speakers rather than being confused are simply wrong—they reason well enough but their reasons are anchored in beliefs (about racial characteristics, sexual norms, and so on) you abhor—you will not place your faith in argument but look for something stronger.°° The difference between seeing hate speech as a problem and seeing it as what your enemy says is that in response to a "problem" you think in terms of therapy and ask of any proposal, Will it eliminate the pathology? whereas in response to what your enemy says you think in terms of strategy and ask of any proposal, Will it retard the growth of the evil I loathe and fear?

The advantage of this shift is that it asks a real question to which there can be a variety of nuanced answers. When you ask,

---

° Liberalism requires a universal enemy so that its procedures of inclusion and exclusion can be implemented in the name of everyone. If, however, there is no universal enemy but only enemies (mine or yours), procedures will always be invoked in the name of some and against some others. The unavailability of a universal enemy is something liberal thinkers are always running up against. They respond typically either by just stipulating someone's enemy as universal (as Gutmann does) or by giving up the attempt to identify an enemy and regarding everyone as potentially persuadable to the appropriate liberal views. (This might be thought of as sentimental or sappy multiculturalism.) See on these points Ellen Rooney, *Seductive Reasoning: Pluralism as the Problematic of Contemporary Literary Theory* (Ithaca, N.Y., 1989), especially her discussion of the theoretical dream of general persuasion.

°° Since Gutmann identifies virtue with the capacity for rational deliberation, she will assume that hate speakers are deficient reasoners, but in fact they will often have cognitive abilities as strong as anyone's, and they will be able to answer reason with reason. As Richard Rorty has put it in the context of the familiar demand that we be able to prove to a Nazi that he is wrong, "attempts at showing the philosophically sophisticated Nazi that he is caught in a logical . . . self-contradiction will simply impel him to construct . . . redescriptions of the presuppositions of the charge of contradiction" (Richard Rorty, "Truth and Freedom: A Reply to Thomas McCarthy," *Critical Inquiry* 16 [Spring 1990]: 637).

as liberals always do, Will speech codes dispel racism and re-move prejudice from the hearts of those who now display it? the answer can only be no, which, I would say, points not to the inadequacy of speech codes but to the inadequacy of the ques-tion. The demand that speech codes dispel racism trades on the knowledge (which I share with antiregulation liberals) that rac-ism cannot be altered by external forces; it is not that kind of thing. But the fact that it is not that kind of thing does not mean that there is nothing to be done; it merely means that whatever we do will stop short of rooting out racism at its source (as we might succeed in doing if it were a disease and not a way of thinking) and that the best we can hope for is a succession of tactical victories in which the enemy is weakened, discomforted, embarrassed, deprived of political power, and on occasion routed. (My phrase "the enemy" might suggest that I was refer-ring to everyone's enemy and slipping back into a liberal univer-salism in which anomalous monsters are clearly labeled and known to everyone; but my use of the phrase marks the point at which I come out behind the arras of analysis and declare my own position, which rests not on the judgement that racism doesn't make any sense [it makes perfect sense if that's the way you think] but that it makes a sense I despise. I am now reach-ing out to readers who are on my side and saying if you want to win—and who doesn't?—do this.)

This, however, is not a small basket of hopes, and what's more the hopes are realizable. If you think of speech codes, not as a magic bullet capable of definitive resolution, but as a possi-ble component of a provisional strategy, you no longer have to debate them in all-or-nothing terms. You can ask if in this situa-tion, at this time and in this place, it would be reasonable to deploy them in the service of your agenda (which, again, is not to eliminate racism but to harass and discomfort racists). The answer will often be no, and, in fact, that is my usual answer; for in most cases speech codes will cause more problems than they solve, and, all things considered, it will often be the better part of wisdom to tolerate the sound of hate and murmur something about sticks and stones and the value of free expression. At that moment you will be talking like a liberal, but there's nothing wrong with that as long as you don't take your liberalism too seriously and don't hew to it as a matter of principle.* Just as speech codes become thinkable once they are no longer asked to do impossible things, so do liberal platitudes become usable when all you want from the is a way of marking time between the battles you think you can win. Switching back and forth between talking like a liberal and engaging in distinctly illiberal actions is something we all do anyway; it is the essence of adhoccery. Perhaps if we did it with less anxiety, we might do it better. We might even be inspired.

---

* One way of characterizing this essay would be as an attack on principle, or, more precisely, "neutral principle" as it is commonly sought in legal and social contexts. A neutral principle is one you would be willing to apply no matter what the circumstances or the interests involved. The trouble with a neutral principle is that either so much content has been eliminated on the way to formulating it that it is empty, or that it retains the content of an agenda that will now be able to present itself politically and rhetorically as universal. Liberalism of the kind urged by Gutmann, Rawls, Kymlicka, Rockefeller, and Mendus displays both these liabilities, liabilities that are really advantages to a position that will not or cannot face its contradictions.

The alternative to the neutral principle is a real principle, a principle rooted in a moral conviction (of which racism, sexism, and homophobia would be examples) that you either accept or reject. From the vantage point of a real principle, you don't say to your enemy, "you're not respecting the decorum of enlightened argument"; you say, "you are wrong." Lauren Berlant and Michael Warner report that there is "no rhetoric available in the national media to throw the right into a . . . defensive ambivalence" (Lauren Berlant and Michael Warner, "Introduction to 'Critical Multiculturalism,'" in *Multiculturalism*, p. 111). If this is true it is because Berlant and Warner, like other liberals and leftists, agree to play in the arena of principle marked out by universals like "free inquiry, open intellectual discussion, and respect for individuals" (ibid.). In this arena they will always lose because those words, as currently deployed, rule out in advance the agendas they might wish to promote. What they should do is not fight over title to that vocabulary, but just drop it and say that those who currently wrap themselves in it are wrong and dangerous.

On the question of principle and what I term its immorality, see Stanley Fish, "At the Federalist Society," *Howard Law Journal* 39 (Spring 1996), and the excellent discussion in Alexander and Ken Kress, "Against Legal Principles," *Law and Interpretation: Essays in Legal Philosophy*, ed. Andrei Marmor (Oxford, 1995), pp. 279–327. See especially page 325, where the authors observe that since arguments of principle require officials systematically to disregard both their own moral convictions and the moral convictions of those they disagree with, "they must do what is unjust from everyone's perspective." Their conclusion is mine: "Surely this is a perverse requirement."

Mary Oliver

Sister Turtle

For some years now I have eaten almost no meat. Though, occasionally, I crave it. It is a continually interesting subject of deep ambiguity. The poet Shelley believed his body would at last be the total and docile servant of his intellect if he ate nothing but leaves and fruit—and I am devoted to Shelley. But I am devoted to Nature too, and to consider Nature without this appetite—this other-creature-consuming appetite—is to look with shut eyes upon the miraculous interchange that makes things work—that causes one thing to nurture another—that creates the future out of the past. Still, in my personal life, I am often stricken with a wish to be *beyond all that.* I am burdened with anxiety. Anxiety for the lamb with his bitter future, anxiety for my own body, and, not least, anxiety for my own soul. You can fool a lot of yourself but you can't fool the soul. That worrier.

At the edge of the land lie the watery palaces—the ocean shore, the salt marsh, the black-bellied pond. And in them and upon them: clams, mussels, fish of all shapes and sizes, snails, turtles, frogs, eels, crabs, lobsters, worms, all crawling and diving and squirming among the cattails, sea rocks, seaweeds, sea-pickles, *spartina,* lamb's quarters, sour grass, arrowhead, mallow. Something eats each of these, each of these eats something else. This is our world. The orange mussel has a blue-black fringe along its body, and a heart and a lung, and a stomach. The scallop as it snaps its way through the water, when the east wind blows, gazes around with its dozens of pale blue eyes. The clam, sensing the presence of your hands, or the approach of the iron tine, presses deeper into the sand. Just where does self-awareness begin and end? With the June bug? With the shining, task-ridden ant? With the little cloud of gnats that hovers over the pond? I am one of those who has no trouble imagining the sentient lives of trees, of their leaves in some fashion communicating or of the massy trunks and heavy branches knowing it is I who have come, as I always come, each morning, to walk beneath them, glad to be alive and glad to be there.

All this, as prelude to the turtles.

I I

They come, lumbering, from the many ponds. They dare the dangers of path, dogs, the highway, the accumulating heat that their bodies cannot regulate, or the equally stunning, always possible, cold.

Take one, then. She has reached the edge of the road, now she slogs up the impossible hill. When she slides back she rests for a while then trundles forward again. Emerging wet from the glittering caves of the pond, she travels in a coat of glass and dust. Where the sand clings thickly the mosquitoes, that hover about her like a gray veil, are frustrated. Not about her eyes, though, for as she blinks the sand falls; so at her tough, old face-skin those winged needles hang until their bodies fill, like tiny vials, with her bright blood. Each of the turtles is a female, and gravid, and looking for a place to dig her nest; each of the mosquitoes is a female also who cannot, without one blood meal, lay her own fertile eggs upon the surface of some quiet pond.

Once, in spring, I saw the rhapsodic prelude to this enterprise of nest-building: two huge snapping turtles coupling. As they floated on the surface of the pond their occasional motions set them tumbling and heaving over and around again and yet again. The male's front feet gripped the edge of the female's shell, as he pressed his massive body tightly against hers. For most of the afternoon they floated so, like a floundered craft—splashing and drifting through the murky water, or hanging motionless among the rising carpets of the pond lilies.

On these first hot days of summer, anywhere along the edges of these ponds or on the slopes of the dunes, I come upon the traveling turtles. I am glad to see them and sorry at the same time—my presence may be a disturbance that sends them back to the ponds before the egg-laying has been accomplished, and what help is this to the world? Sometimes they will make the attempt again, sometimes they will not. If not, the eggs will dissolve back into other substances, inside their bodies.

There are other interruptors, far craftier than I. Whether the turtles come through sunlight or, as is more likely, under the moon's cool but sufficient light, raccoons follow. The turtles are scarcely done, scarcely gone, before the raccoons set their noses to the ground, and sniff, and discover, and dig, and devour, with rapacious and happy satisfaction.

And still, every year, there are turtles enough in the ponds.

As there are raccoons enough, sleeping the afternoons away high in the leafy trees.

One April morning I came upon a snapping turtle shell at the edge of Pasture Pond, tugged from the water, I imagine, by these same raccoons. Front to back, it measured more than 30 inches. Later I found leg bones nearby, also claws, and scutes, as they are called—the individual shingles that cover the raw bone of the shell. Perhaps the old giant died during some hard winter, frozen first at the edges and then thoroughly, in some too-shallow cove. Or perhaps it died simply in the amplitude of time itself—turtles like other reptiles never stop growing, which makes for interesting imagined phenomena, if one's inclination is to the bizarre. But the usual is news enough. The adult snapping turtle can weigh 90 pounds, is omnivorous, and may live for decades. Or, to put it another way, who knows? The shell I found that April morning was larger than any of my field guides indicates is likely, or even possible.

III

I saw the tracks immediately—they swirled back and forth across the shuffled sand of the path. They seemed the design of indecision, but I am not sure. In three places a little digging had taken place. A false nest? A foot giving a swipe or two of practice motion? A false visual clue for the predator to come?

I leashed my two dogs and looked searchingly until I saw her, at one edge of the path, motionless and sand-spattered. Already she was in the nest—or, more likely, leaving it. For she will dig through the sand until she all but vanishes—sometimes until there is nothing visible but the top of her head. Then, when the nesting is done, she thrusts the front part of her body upward so that she is positioned almost vertically—like a big pie-pan on edge. Beneath her, as she heaves upward, the sand falls into the cavity of the nest, upon the heaped, round eggs.

She sees me, and does not move. The eyes, though they throw small light, are deeply alive and watchful. If she had to die in this hour and for this enterprise she would, without hesitation. She would slide from life into death, still with that pin of light in each uncordial eye, intense and as loyal to the pumping of breath as anything in this world.

When our eyes meet, what can pass between us? She sees me as a danger, and she is right. If I come any closer she will dismiss me peacefully if she can by retracting into her shell. But this is difficult, her bulky body will not fit entirely inside the recesses of that bony hut. She retreats, but still her head is outside, and a portion of each leg. She might hiss, or she might not. She might open the mighty beak of her mouth to give warning, and I might stare a moment into the clean, pale, glossy tunnel of her inner mouth, with its tag of tongue, before that head, that unexpected long neck flashes out—flashes, I say—and strikes me, hand or foot. She is snake-swift and accurate, and can bite cleanly through a stick three inches thick. Many a dog walks lame from such an encounter. I keep my dogs leashed, and walk on. We turn the corner and vanish under the trees. It is five a.m.; for me, the beginning of the day—for her, the end of the long night.

Of appetite—of my own appetite—I recognize this: it flashes up, quicker than thought; it cannot be exiled; it can be held on leash, but only barely. Once, on an October day, as I was crossing a field, a red-tailed hawk rattled up from the ground. In the grass lay a pheasant, its breast already opened, only a little of the red, felt-like meat stripped away. It simply flew into my mind—that the pheasant, thus discovered, was to be *my* dinner! I swear, I felt the sweet prick of luck! Only secondly did I interrupt myself, and glance at the hawk, and walk on. Good for me! But I know how sparkling was the push of my own appetite. I am no fool, no sentimentalist. I know that appetite is one of the gods, with a rough and savage face, but a god all the same.

Teilhard de Chardin says somewhere that man's most agonizing spiritual dilemma is his necessity for food, with its unavoidable attachments to suffering. Who would disagree.

A few years ago I heard a lecture about the Whitney family, especially about Gloria Vanderbilt Whitney, whose patronage established the museum of that name in New York City. The talk was given by Mrs. Whitney's granddaughter, and she used a fine phrase when speaking of her family—of their sense of "inherited responsibility"—to do, of course, with received wealth and a sense of using it for public good. Ah! Quickly I slipped this phrase from the air and put it into my own pocket!

For it is precisely how I feel, who have inherited not measurable wealth but, as we all do who care for it, that immeasurable fund of thoughts and ideas, from writers and thinkers long gone into the ground—and, inseparable from those wisdoms because *demanded* by them, the responsibility to live thoughtfully and intelligently. To enjoy, to question—never to assume, or trample. Thus the great ones (*my* great ones, who may not be the same as *your* great ones) have taught me—to observe with passion, to think with patience, to live always care-ingly.

So here I am, walking on down the sandy path, with my wild body, with the inherited devotions of curiosity and respect. The moment is full of such exquisite interest as Fabre or Flaubert would have been utterly alive to. Yes, it is a din of voices that I hear, and they do not all say the same thing. But the fit of thoughtfulness unites them.

Who are they? For me they are Shelley, and Fabre, and Wordsworth—the young Wordsworth—and Barbara Ward, and Blake, and Basho, Maeterlinck and Jastrow, and sweetest Emerson, and Carson, and Aldo Leopold. Forebears, models, spirits whose influence and teachings I am now inseparable from, and forever grateful for. I go nowhere, I arrive nowhere, without them. With them I live my life, with them I enter the event, I mold the meditation, I keep if I can some essence of the hour, even as it slips away. And I do not accomplish this alert and loving confrontation by myself and alone, but through terrifying and continual effort, and with this innumerable, fortifying company; bright as stars in the heaven of my mind.

Were they seed-eaters? Were they meat-eaters? Not the point. They were dreamers, and imaginers, and declarers; they lived looking and looking and looking, seeing the apparent and beyond the apparent, wondering, allowing for uncertainty, also grace, easy-going here, ferociously unmoveable there; they were thoughtful. A few voices, strict and punctilious, like Shelley's, like Thoreau's, cry out: *Change! Change!* But most don't say that; they simply say: Be what you are, of the earth, but a dreamer too. Teilhard de Chardin was not talking about how to escape anguish, but about how to live with it.

I V

I went back, toward evening, and dug in the sand to the depth of nine inches more or less, and found nothing. There, a few unbroken roots told me the turtle's paddle-shaped feet had gone no farther down. There, as I imagine it, she had shifted the angle of her digging. Perhaps she rested first. Then she began again her sweep-shoving, digging a smaller chamber opening from the original, but narrower, a *sanctum,* to the front of the first. When she was done, a short fleshy tube descended from her body and reached to this chamber, where the expelled eggs piled up rapidly on the nest of sand.

Into this passage I dug, until my fingers felt the first of the eggs—round, slightly soft—then I began to feel more, and I began to remove them. There were twenty-seven, smaller than ping-pong balls which they somewhat resembled. They were not altogether opaque, but cast a slightly yellow interior light. I placed thirteen in my pocket, carefully, and replaced fourteen in the nest, repacked the nest with sand, and swept from the surface all sign of my digging.

I scrambled them. They were a meal. Not too wonderful, not too bad. Rich, substantial. I could not crack the shells, but had to make a knife-slit to enter into each bright chamber. The yolks were large, the white-of-the-egg scant; the little fertility knot, the bud of the new turtle, was no more apparent than it is in a fertile chicken's egg. There was, in the fabric of the eggs scrambled, a sense of fiber, a tactility, as though a sprinkle of cornmeal had been tossed in, and had not quite dissolved. I imagined it as the building material of the shell. The eggs were small enough that thirteen made no greedy portion. I ate them all, with attention, whimsy, devotion, and respect.

The next morning I went back to the path. I wanted to see how the nest-place was after one sheet of darkness had gone over it. None of the other prowlers—raccoons, that is—had discovered it. By end of summer, under the provisions of good fortune, the hatchlings, fourteen of them, would rise through

the sand. Hardly pausing to consider the world which so suddenly appeared around them, they would turn unerringly
toward the dark and rich theatre of the nearest pond, would
hasten to its edge, and dive in.

Now, in the last hot days of June, I see no more turtles on
the paths, nor even their curvaceous wandering trails over the
dunes. Now the heat brings forth other buddings and advance-
ments. Almost overnight the honey-locust trees have let down
their many tassels of blossoms, small white flasks filled with the
sweetest honey. I gather handfuls and, for a second, hold them
against my face. The fringes of paradise: summer on earth.
They, too, will nourish me. Last week I ate the eggs of the
turtle, like little golden suns; today, the honey-locust blossoms,
in batter, will make the finest crepes of the most common pan-
cakes. My body, which must be fed, will be well-fed. The hawk,
in the pale pink evening, went back to the body of the pheasant.
The turtle lay a long time on the bottom of the pond, resting.
Then she turned, her eyes upon some flickering nearby as, without terror, without sorrow, but in the voracious arms of the first
of the earth's gods, she did what she must, she did what all must
do. All things are meltable, and replaceable. Not at this moment, but soon enough, we are lambs and we are leaves, and we
are stars, and the shining, mysterious pond water itself.

Carlos Monsivais

Identity Hour, or What Photos Would You Take of the Endless City? (From a Guide to Mexico City)

Visually, Mexico City signifies above all else the superabundance of people. You could, of course, turn away from this most palpable of facts towards abstraction, and photograph desolate dawns, or foreground the aesthetic dimension of walls and squares, even rediscover the perfection of solitude. But in the capital, the multitude that accosts the multitude imposes itself like a permanent obsession. It is the unavoidable theme present in the tactics that everyone, whether they admit it or not, adopts to find and ensconce themselves in even the smallest places the city allows. Intimacy is by permission only, the "poetic licence" that allows you momentarily to forget those around you—never more than an inch away—who make of urban vitality a relentless grind.

Turmoil is the repose of the city-dwellers, a whirlwind set in motion by secret harmonies and lack of public resources. How can one describe Mexico City today? Mass overcrowding and the shame at feeling no shame; the unmeasurable space, where almost everything is possible, because everything works thanks only to what we call a "miracle"—which is no more than the meeting-place of work, technology and chance. These are the most frequent images of the capital city:

- multitudes on the Underground (where almost six million travellers a day are crammed, making space for the very idea of space);

- multitudes taking their entrance exam in the University Football Stadium;

- the "Marfas" (Mazahua peasant women) selling whatever they can in the streets, resisting police harassment while training their countless kids;

- the underground economy that overflows on to the pavements, making popular marketplaces of the streets. At traffic lights young men and women overwhelm drivers attempting to sell Kleenex, kitchenware, toys, tricks. The vulnerability is so extreme that it becomes artistic, and a young boy makes fire—swallowing it and throwing it up—the axis of his gastronomy;

- mansions built like safes, with guard dogs and private police;

- masked wrestlers, the tutelary gods of the new Teotihuacán of the ring;

- the *Templo Mayor:* Indian grandeur;

- *"Piñatas"* containing all the most important traditional figures: the Devil, the Nahual, Ninja Turtles, Batman, Penguin . . . ;

- the Basilica of Guadalupe;

- the swarm of cars. Suddenly it feels as if all the cars on earth were held up right here, the traffic jam having now become second nature to the species hoping to arrive late at the Last Judgement. Between four and six o'clock in the morning there is some respite, the species seems drowsy . . . but suddenly everything moves on again, the advance cannot be stopped. And in the traffic jam, the automobile becomes a prison on wheels, the cubicle where you can study Radio in the University of Tranquillity;

- the flat rooftops, which are the continuation of agrarian life by other means, the natural extension of the farm, the redoubt of Agrarian Reform. Evocations and needs are concentrated on the rooftops. There are goats and hens, and people shout at the helicopters because they frighten the cows and the farmers milking them. Clothes hang there like harvested maize. There are rooms containing families who reproduce and never quite seem to fit. Sons and grandsons come and go, while godparents stay for months, and the room grows, so to speak, eventually to contain the whole village from which its first migrant came;

- the contrasts between rich and poor, the constant antagonism between the shadow of opulence and the formalities of misery;

- the street gangs, less violent than elsewhere, seduced by their own appearance, but somewhat uncomfortable because no one really notices them in the crowd. The street gangs use an international alphabet picked up in the streets of Los Angeles, fence off their territories with graffiti, and show off the aerial prowess of punk hairstyles secure in the knowledge that they are also ancestral, because they really copied them off Emperor Cuauhtemoc. They listen to heavy metal, use drugs, thinner and cement, destroy themselves, let themselves be photographed in poses they wish were menacing, accept parts as extras in apocalyptic films, feel regret for their street-gang life, and spend the rest of their lives evoking it with secret and public pleasure.

The images are few. One could add the Museum of Anthropology, the Zócalo at any time (day or night), the Cathedral and, perhaps (risking the photographer), a scene of violence in which police beat up street vendors, or arrest youngsters, pick them up by the hair, or swear that they have not beaten anyone. The typical repertoire is now complete, and if I do not include the *mariachis* of Plaza Garibaldi, it is because this text does not come with musical accompaniment. Mexico: another great Latin American city, with its seemingly uncontrollable growth, its irresponsible love of modernity made visible in skyscrapers, malls, fashion shows, spectacles, exclusive restaurants, motorways, cellular phones. Chaos displays its aesthetic offerings, and next to the pyramids of Teotihuacán, the baroque altars, and the more wealthy and elegant districts, the popular city offers its rituals.

ON THE CAUSES FOR PRIDE THAT
(SHOULD) MAKE ONE SHIVER

It was written I should be loyal to the nightmare of my
    choice.
—Joseph Conrad, *Heart of Darkness*

Where has that chauvinism of old gone for which, as the saying goes, "There is nowhere like Mexico"? Not far, of course: it has returned as a chauvinism expressed in the language of catastrophe and demography. I will now enumerate the points of pride (psychological compensation):

- Mexico City is the most populated city in the world (the Super-Calcutta!);

- Mexico City is the most polluted city on the planet, whose population, however, does not seem to want to move (the laboratory of the extinction of the species);

- Mexico City is the place where it would be impossible for anything to fail due to a lack of audience. There is public aplenty. In the capital, to counterbalance the lack of clear skies, there are more than enough inhabitants, spectators, car-owners, pedestrians;

- Mexico City is the place where the unlivable has its rewards, the first of which has been to endow survival with a new status.

What makes for an apocalyptic turn of mind? As far as I can see, the opposite of what may be found in Mexico City. Few people actually leave this place whose vital statistics (which tend, for the most part, to be short of the mark) everyone invents at their pleasure. This is because, since it is a secular city after all, very few take seriously the predicted end of the world—at least, of *this* world. So what are the retentive powers of a megalopolis which, without a doubt, has reached its historic limit? And how do we reconcile this sense of having reached a limit with the medium- and long-term plans of every city-dweller? Is it only centralist anxiety that determines the intensity of the city's hold? For many, Mexico City's major charm is precisely its (true and false) "apocalyptic" condition. Here is the first megalopolis to fall victim to its own excess. And how fascinating are all the biblical prophecies, the dismal statistics and the personal experiences chosen for catastrophic effect! The main topic of conversation at gatherings is whether we are actually living the disaster to come or among its ruins; and when collective humour describes cityscapes, it does so with all the enthusiasm of a witness sitting in the front row at the Last Judgement: "How awful, three hours in the car just to go two kilometres!" "Did you hear about those people who collapsed in the street because of the pollution?" "In some places there is no more water left." "Three million homes must be built, just for a start. . . ."

The same grandiose explanation is always offered: despite the disasters, twenty million people *cannot leave Mexico City or the Valley of Mexico, because there is nowhere else they want to go; there is nowhere else, really, that they can go.* Such resignation engenders the "aesthetic of multitudes". Centralism lies at the origins of this phenomenon, as does the supreme concentration of powers—which, nevertheless, has certain advantages, the first of which is the identification of liberty and tolerance: "I don't feel like making moral judgements because then I'd have to deal with my neighbors." Tradition is destroyed by the squeeze, the replacement of the extended family by the nuclear family, the wish for extreme individualization that accompanies anomie, the degree of cultural development, the lack of democratic values that would oblige people to—at least minimally—democratize their lives. "What should be abolished" gradually becomes "what I don't like."

To stay in Mexico City is to confront the risks of pollution, ozone, thermic inversion, lead poisoning, violence, the rat race, and the lack of individual meaning. To leave it is to lose the formative and informative advantages of extreme concentration, the experiences of modernity (or postmodernity) that growth and the ungovernability of certain zones due to massification bring. The majority of people, although they may deny it with their complaints and promises to flee, are happy to stay, and stand by the only reasons offered them by hope: "It will get better somehow." "The worst never comes." "We'll have time to leave before the disaster strikes." Indeed, the excuses eventually become one: outside the city it's all the same, or worse. Can there now really be any escape from urban violence, overpopulation, industrial waste, the greenhouse effect?

Writers are among the most sceptical. There are no anti-utopias; the city does not represent a great oppressive weight (this is still located in the provinces) but, rather, possible liberty, and in practice, nothing could be further from the spirit of the capital city than the prophecies contained in Carlos Fuentes's novel *Christopher Unborn* and his short story "Andrés Aparicio" in *Burnt Water*. According to Fuentes, the city has reached its limits. One of his characters reflects:

> He was ashamed that a nation of churches and pyra-
> mids built for all eternity ended up becoming one with
> the cardboard, shitty city. They boxed him in, suffo-
> cated him, took his sun and air away, his senses of
> vision and smell.

Even the world of *Christopher Unborn* (one of ecological, polit-ical, social and linguistic desolation) is invaded by fun ("relajo"). In the end, although the catastrophe may be very real, catastro-phism is the celebration of the incredulous in which irresponsi-bility mixes with resignation and hope, and where—not such a secret doctrine in Mexico City—the sensations associated with the end of the world spread: the overcrowding is hell, and the apotheosis is crowds that consume all the air and water, and are so numerous that they seem to float on the earth. Confidence becomes one with resignation, cynicism and patience: the apocalyptic city is populated with radical optimists.

In practice, optimism wins out. In the last instance, the advantages seem greater than the horrors. And the result is: *Mexico, the post-apocalyptic city.* The worst has already happened (and the worst is the monstrous population whose growth nothing can stop); nevertheless, the city functions in a way the majority cannot explain, while everyone takes from the resulting chaos the visual and vital rewards they need and which, in a way, compensate for whatever makes life unlivable. Love and hate come together in the vitality of a city that produces spectacles as it goes along: the commerce that invades the pavements, the infinity of architectonic styles, the "street theatre" of the ten million people a day who move about the city, through the Underground system, on buses, motorbikes, bicycles, in lorries and cars. However, the all-star performance is given by the loss of fear at being ridiculed in a society which, not too long ago, was so subjugated by what "others might think". Never-ending mixture also has its aesthetic dimension, and next to the pyramids of Teotihuacán, the baroque altars and the more wealthy and elegant districts, the popular city projects the most favoured—and the most brutally massified—version of the century that is to come.

Bert O. States

My Slight Stoop: A Remembrance

I was born on my sister's tenth birthday, August 8, 1929, at ten A.M., or thereabout, and in one way or another that has been the axial date of both our lives. For one thing, there were no other brothers and sisters to dilute our closeness, and we were far enough apart to miss the usual filial rivalries. But I think the most important thing was that the interval between us was a full decade, to the day. So as a result of these three factors alone we were drawn together, as it were, by the preciseness of our apartness. Of course I have no notion of what life might have been like had I been born on August 5th or November 21st or, say, seven years after her, instead of ten. But I am enough of a determinist to believe that small things eventually make incremental differences, and that each moment is a beginning from which no other future could possibly have ensued but the one that does. For example, it has always struck me that the single most consequential event of my life, in terms of pure yield, was my part-time job as a waiter in the freshman women's dining hall at Penn State in 1948, from which my own family eventually "ensued." I suppose you could argue that the *real* date was my coming to Penn State in the first place, or something even earlier, or not a date at all but my family not having enough money for me *not* to work, or my *not* being killed in a camping accident, had there been one, say, at McGees Mills in 1943, or finally just being born in the first place. All of this may be true, but it is somehow *endlessly* beside the point. Clearly, my life changed radically because I waited tables at Atherton Hall in 1948. Anyway, the idea is that unlike other pairs of sibling birthdays, which go leapfrogging asymmetrically through the years, my sister's and mine were perfectly synchronized, like the orbits of double stars, and could be chronicled on the same "binocular" scale: on the day I was ten she was twenty; on the day she was thirty-five I was twenty-five, and so on. So there was always something distantly mystical about "our" birthday, and I can't recount the number of times when a smile of disbelief came over the faces of people on first hearing about it; it was as if they'd been told that the cinema projector was invented, of all people, by the Lumière brothers (which it was). So the day belonged equally to both of us, wherever we were, and as a result we had all the advantages of identical twins and none of what I imagine must be the disadvantages.

And there are even subtler effects, including a certain factor of maternalism on my sister's part that inevitably blurred the distinction between her and my mother. I arrived on my sister's tenth birthday; therefore, her birthday must have had something to do with my arrival. Her birthday gave birth to me, as it were. In fact, for some time I was referred to as her birthday present, and in the lean "teen" years I cashed in on this by simply tying a bow around my head and presenting myself as a gift. So there is also the maternal side of it, and the reason why my mother and my sister were the co-figures of authority in my life. I can't blame that entirely on the 8th of August, but that is where it begins, and of course everyone in the family promoted what was really this calendrical roll of the dice into a kind of family myth.

Another factor was that my father was a railroader and for the better part of my growing up years spent three to four days a week as a trainman on the passenger run between Buffalo and

Pittsburgh. So he was an intermittent figure in my life to whom, I'm afraid, I did not do justice as an only son. I have many memories of him, most of them good or satisfactory, none really negative. He rarely scolded me or got angry, mainly, I suspect, because he was a sufficient stranger in the house to feel uncomfortable disciplining me. I was, he must have thought, my mother's son. And I can see how that must have been difficult for him.

I suspect this; I don't know it for a fact because we never talked about such things and my father kept his emotions to himself. I also suspect that he must have felt at times that there was a slightly conspiratorial atmosphere in the household, owing not only to his status as the itinerant provider but to its being run by two very strong women who did pretty much as they pleased. Finally, though I didn't learn it until much later, there were problems in the marriage, but that is a matter I don't care to get into here. For the most part, my father simply took for granted what was done to or in the house in his absence—or in his presence, for that matter—and he regularly came home to what must have been some difficult adjustments. For example, I know it disturbed him very much that my mother subscribed to expensive glossy magazines like *Architectural Digest, Harper's Bazaar, House and Garden,* and *Country Home,* along with dozens of others that were arranged, much as they might be at a dentist's office, in two neat rows down the sides of a huge new Formica coffee table that had cost the price of several months' rent. In those days, subscriptions were pedaled door to door by cheerful salesmen who knew exactly how to be nice. ("Good morning, Mrs. States. How is your father doing?") My mother knew all of them by name and since she loved nothing more than to be surrounded by pictures of beautiful things—the things themselves (beyond incidental accessories) being out of her reach—she was an easy touch for anyone selling an attractive product on a liberal installment plan.

So my father's complaints, when he made them, were feeble and tentative at best, or laced with almost imperceptible irony ("Oh, isn't that a new coffee table?"), and who can say what his thoughts must have been as he watched his salary being deviated into books filled with the colorful homes and gardens of the wealthy, to objets d'art like copper wall lavaboes, travertine busts of Eros, various pewter guinea hens and quail, and capacious ceramic ashtrays—or to educational "investments" like encyclopedias and, at one extravagant point, a complete set of the Harvard Classics (shelved in a dark mahogany bookcase) that was certainly never read and the bookcase almost never opened except when my mother hid money in it and then forgot in which of the fifty volumes she had put it. What had attracted her in the first place of course was the bookcase itself (though the word Harvard probably helped), that is to say an elegant piece of furniture which came in four rectangular units (the two matching shelf boxes, a foot pedestal and a veneer top) and had two up-lifting glass doors (with discreet brass knobs) that slid back into the case for easy access; and behind the glass you could see the two rows of blue linen spines of the books with all the titles embossed in gold. This bookcase stood prominently in the living room or hallway of whatever duplex we rented (we never owned a house), until my mother went to live with my sister in California after Dad died. At that point the books, most of them still unopened, were stored in cardboard boxes, along with everything else she owned, in Kendra's warehouse in Punxsutawney. The veneer of the bookcase itself had long since buckled and split open and its legs were scarred and chipped by innumerable collisions with the bumper of mother's Hoover, and I'm not sure what ever happened to it. I remember going to Kendra's some years later on a trip from State College to settle the account. It was a huge high-ceilinged hall of a room with every unit of storage stacked as high and efficiently as possible and separated from others by those dirty padded blankets they use in moving vans. I'm not sure where everything ended up. The sofa and chairs, and probably the Formica coffee table, were given immediately to Mother's next-door neighbor, Esther Nicewonger, in her departure for California, and apart from some valuable personal effects the rest was sold to Mr. Kendra for a price that conveniently just covered the storage bill. The

Harvard Classics, however, came into my possession, and I remember making periodic searches for two dollars Mother was said to have lost to one of the volumes. It wasn't the money of course; it was the evidence of her personality I was hoping to find.

I can't say that my father was henpecked; his authority was simply compromised by his double life and by the intimacy of a family that carved its way more or less without him through the years during and after the Depression. Looking back, I have the impression that he lived two separate lives, a little like Alec Guinness in *The Captain's Paradise.* It wasn't that the life at home was bad or intolerable. When he was home he was never excluded and I don't remember any serious quarrels beyond occasional loud words coming up from the kitchen at night through the floor register of my bedroom. But Dad did cheerfully whatever he was asked, and this amounted mainly to running errands and taking us all for a "ride" to the States farm (owned by his elder brother) in Sprankles Mills on Sundays.

It was, I imagine, my mother (or my mother and sister ganging up on him) who convinced him one afternoon in my fifteenth year that it was his duty, and the proper time, to explain sex to me. So the two of us suddenly got in his blue Dodge, for no announced reason, and drove out the Indiana hill road, he silent and ominous, I simply curious about why we were out for a ride and *not* going to a store, and finally after a brief warm-up ("How old are you now, Buddy?"), he said something to the effect that I should be nice to girls. And I thought, *Here it comes!* And, within another sentence or so, without transition, he suddenly blurted out that I should keep my Jasper in my pants.

"You know what I mean?" he said.

I'm sure I nodded.

"Don't be dunking the noodle, Buddy," he added, patting my knee. "Don't be dunking the old noodle. You do know what I mean?"

"Ummm."

"That's very important. *Very* important. Girls are very

very. . . . You have to be very careful. You can get in a lot of trouble." Pause. "Yes-siree-Bob. A lot of trouble." And he clicked his cheek with his tongue, as he always did when he had made a point.

My father, incidentally, came of solid farm stock and he had, in addition to an alert ear for sexual irony, an arsenal of sly euphemisms and metaphors I didn't appreciate until long after his death, some of the more colorful ones having to do with farting. (I've always liked to think that he learned these wonderful idioms when he was working as a roustabout for Cole Bros. Circus, a shadowy part of his life before he married my mother.) I suppose he had more to say that afternoon than I am recalling now, but I rather doubt he wanted to get into the biology part. Anyway, it wasn't hard to see that he was very nervous and aiming somewhere between a token lecture and a conspiracy of fellow males. And that was his way. I wasn't sure what my role was so I played the quiet listener and for the most part only grunted and looked out the window. The truth is, it was the silence of guilt, in thought though not in deed, for, even as he spoke, I was carrying in my wallet a single just-in-case-it-ever-happens Trojan rubber, its frayed collar by now peeping through the worn foil wrap, which I had snitched from the contraceptive drawer of Feicht's drug store one evening after hours when Indian Long and I were mopping the floor, as we did twice a week for seventy-five cents and all the ice cream and peanuts we could eat. At any rate, when our "talk" was over there was this air of relief in the car; something had been gotten through and, duty done, my father became jovial and began to whistle tunelessly, a trait I later realized I had picked up from him. I have visions of Mother getting him alone that same day and asking, "Well, did you tell him?" and Bert saying, "Of course I told him," pumped up, as he so rarely had the chance to be, by the achievement.

So that was one Memorable Moment with my father. Actually, it was my second "official" exposure to sexual instruction. The first, a year or two earlier, was the pamphlet sent from DuBois (twenty miles northeast of Punxsutawney) by my Aunt

Tina to "brother Bert and Helma" (my mother). Tina was an
unmarried schoolteacher who lived figuratively and (almost) literally in the shadow of the Presbyterian church and she was the
only college graduate in the family, on either side. Periodically,
she would send news and advice from DuBois in the form of
short two- or three-page letters on rose stationery with a small
Jesus in the upper left corner looking skyward radiantly (in profile) from a florally entwined bower, and almost invariably there
was a newspaper clipping having to do with one of her many
church groups doing something beneficial. Once you got past
the religion Tina was a kind and well-meaning lady, deservedly
the shepherdess and chief historian of the States clan (my
mother's side of the family is another matter), and we all liked
to keep alive a rumor that she had once had an affair, hardly
including sex, with a nameless man from Pittsburgh whom she
had almost married. This of course was hearsay, pure wishful
thinking. Anyway, Tina felt it her place to send little encyclicals
now and then reminding my parents (and the parents of other
branches of the States and Ross families living in Williamsport,
Reynoldsville, Buffalo and Iowa) of certain rites of passage pertaining to "the children." This particular pamphlet (I draw a
blank on the title) probably came separately from her church
bulletins in a larger envelope, and probably with a brief note
like "Thought the enclosed, dist. by the W. Pa. Council of Boys'
Clubs, might be appropriate for B. Jr." At least that would be in
keeping with the frugality of her communications (I don't know
that there *was* a Council of Boys' Clubs in Western Pennsylvania; but if there were Tina would know all about it). At any rate,
it was simply given to me by my mother, without preamble, to
"look over." It was a two-staple, surreptitious-looking affair of
perhaps fifteen pages in large type that reminded me immediately of the dirty books that I was now and then fortunate
enough to intercept as they made their way through the junior
high underground.

The pamphlet was of course devoted to the topic of self-
abuse. But the only thing I remember about it is a priceless
cartoon of four panels in which (1) a healthy knickered young

boy and his dog are bounding in full joy across the world, schoolbooks flying behind him on a belted leash; in (2) we see him puffing slightly as he continues to run, having fallen behind others in his class (represented on the right-hand frame by a single sneakered leg kicking up dust); in (3) he is having real difficulty, throwing off exaggerated beads of sweat, like the characters in Mary Worth; at (4) he is virtually reduced to a crawl, bookless, dogless, all hunched over and hyperventilating, his rib cage visible from a loss of weight, and judging by the X's that had replaced his eyes in panel 3 he was going blind as well. And all because, as my father would say, he had been yanking his noodle-dandy on the side. I read it, there in the living room, in irrepressible shame (it had come *far* too late). But nothing more was said, and the pamphlet was very quickly withdrawn from view, and that's the last I saw of it—or heard about the topic. The matter was left, so to speak, in my hands, and the only consequence was that my guilt soared tenfold and I became much more circumspect about when and where I gave in to the demon. There are a lot of memories I would cheerfully erase but the pamphlet episode isn't one of them, and it would have been a find beyond all value to have discovered it years later in one of my searches of the Harvard Classics, tucked perhaps into the pages of Gibbon's *Decline and Fall.*

One of my chores was to take my father's lunch to the station when the noon passenger train came through town twice a week out of Pittsburgh and then, coming back, out of Buffalo. My mother usually packed a couple of thick bologna sandwiches, or, if it was a Monday, leftover chicken (wrapped in stiff wax paper), a dessert and a piece of fruit in a brown bag, and I delivered it and spent the odd minutes with Dad while he set out the warning flare, boarded the passengers, and waited for the whistle to depart. What news I had was exhausted in a few sentences, and of course he had very little to share with me because his life on the road had nothing to do with anything I was remotely interested in. But he appreciated the time and he always gave me a dime or a quarter and wanted to introduce me to the train crew. To this day I see him as standing on the bottom step of the boarding platform in his dark blue uniform, waving as the train gathered speed out of the station. Then, even before it was out of sight, I cut lickety-split down Farmer's Alley, through Barkley Square, and back into my own interrupted world, always, I am sorry to say, with the impression that I had lost valuable free time.

My father of course wanted me to pursue a career on the railroad. He had only a fifth-grade education, and my mother a fourth, or maybe it was the other way around. But my own education, to which he submitted at the cost of a good part of his unsteady earnings (on his retirement from the B&O on account of poor health, he became a car salesman for Altman's garage), was a major cause of the unreachability between us. For example, there was the afternoon on our front porch on Liberty Street when he and I were sitting alone. With my family I had come home from graduate school at Penn State. And he asked me, in an effort to make conversation, and to understand what I was doing, "What are you studying, Buddy?"

"English," I said.

In the silence I could hear his frustration. Then with a controlled anxiety in his voice that hovered somewhere between irony and real confusion, he said, "Don't you know enough English?" And I said something stupid, and suddenly it seemed stupid to be studying English. How could I tell him, by way of explanation, that I was taking entire courses on single poets, that I wrote long papers on dead people whose names he had never heard, all this while living on a ridiculous salary provided largely by Nancy's part-time job at the drug store in State College? This was simply beyond the vale of his understanding, especially when there were ample openings on the railroad for a bright young fellow willing to work his way up. So there we sat, continents apart, and slipping even further.

Finally, I must speak of my grandfather, my mother's father. Danny lived with us about twenty years, from the death of his wife to the end of his life in 1956. He was a strong muscular Swede, almost bald, who had left "the old country" at twenty-one and had never returned. The story is that he went to England for a weekend, got very drunk, and got on a boat to America, and never came back. I am not sure the story is any truer than the one about Tina's "secret beau" because even though Danny liked his whiskey it doesn't sound like his style to leave his mother Botilda unattended there in Sweden. There must have been an arrangement or plan of some sort. Anyway, he settled in Rossiter, a village outside of Punxsutawney, where he was a blacksmith for the mines, and when he moved into town with us he was a blacksmith for the railroad or for the brewery. (There are no records, and I have no idea why either would need a blacksmith, but a blacksmith he was.) Toward the end of his life Danny gradually became poor-sighted and wore glasses with extremely thick lenses, giving his right eye, especially, a huge cyclopean effect. He smoked a pipe incessantly, or rather kept it in his mouth incessantly, and after his retirement he sat in a chair on the front porch during the day and in a special chair in the living room at night where he smoked and listened to Lowell Thomas. Every so often, when she was doing the dinner dishes, my mother would come up to him, drying her hands on her apron, lean over the chair close to his ear (he was also hard-of-hearing) and say, "How are you, Danny?" and he would say, "Oh, I'm fine," whether he was fine or not. And she would kiss his bald forehead.

Then she would ask, "Do you want another piece of pie?" whether we had had pie or not.

"Yes," he would say.

"Now?"

"Oh no."

"Tomorrow?"

"Tomorrow'll be fine."

It never varied. It was always the same routine. And years later, when I was directing Beckett's *Waiting for Godot* at the University of Pittsburgh this ritual came to me in an odd flashback during rehearsal one night. There is no explaining it properly, but between the play and the memory something fell into place that I couldn't name. Suddenly, everything gave away to this picture of Danny, at eighty, sitting in his chair and my

mother leaning over him, with infinite love, and trying to bring
him out of the past and out of the rapidly gathering dark. And I
think what was so terrible is that I had seen this scene for so
long that I had looked straight through it, without understanding what it was all about.

Gradually his sight got worse, but he could still see well
enough to play cards. And it was my job on Sundays to walk him
to the Eagles Club, which was about six residential blocks from
our house through the park to Barkley Square on Main Street;
then I would go on to the Sunday matinee at the Jefferson
Theater and I'd pick him up after the movie at four. Most of the
time, I was admitted to the card room, if the bartender on duty
knew who I was (otherwise I sat in the lobby), and I'd wait there
in the gloom until the last game was finished. What I remember
most is that Danny sat there at a round felt table with three or
four now faceless men in a captain's chair, one eye squinted
shut and the cards fanned close to his "good" eye, a small bead
of saliva gathering under the bowl of his pipe. The room was
gray with smoke and the odor of stale draft beer seeped out of
everything and you could still smell it on your clothes when you
got outside.

I was eleven at the time, and I know this only because on
the most memorable of these Sundays I went to see a new
movie called *Swiss Family Robinson* with Thomas Mitchell and
Freddy Bartholomew and looking it up in my *Movie Guide* just
now I see that it came out in 1940. So I was eleven, and in
seventh grade. This is one of those few movies I never want to
see a second time (as, alas, I recently did another old favorite,
Gunga Din) because its value depends strictly on its place in my
life at that time. Now I would probably find it naive or technically flawed or overacted—like *Gunga Din*—and another beautiful thing would unnecessarily be spoiled. No, it belongs to my
"Romantic" period, to the era in which I read Robert Louis
Stevenson and Albert Payson Terhune and I buried treasure
(often fifteen or twenty cents) in the woods across the Mahoning Creek behind our house in one of the small metal boxes my
father's razors came in. My main motive for burying the trea-

sure in the first place was the excuse to make the map; and though I knew perfectly well where the treasure was located, it was necessary to make a complete map of the area, to show (in little houselike boxes) where the Hueys and the Scavas and the Eberharts lived (though the location of their houses had nothing to do with getting to the "X" where the treasure was hidden), and where the Penn Street truss bridge crossed the Mahoning, the location of the Punxsy beef slaughterhouse, Harmon field, the B R & P railroad tracks, and so on. Then I would fray the edges of the construction paper to make it look as if the map had been carried around in the vest pocket of a pirate. And I would hide the map in a cigar box behind a ceiling beam in the cellar. This is the same period in which I used to copy out medieval maps of the Atlantic Ocean with sea serpents swimming in great roller-coaster coils through scalloped waters, cherubim with their cheeks spraying wind that drove potbellied schooners across the perilous unknown seas. This is the same journey that the Robinson family had made which to me was the ultimate escape to Paradise, and it all came to perfection in the magnificent tree house that protected them from the island's many dangers.

There are few things as desolating as coming out of a Sunday matinee to begin with, but stepping into the harsh afternoon sun after this experience left me with an ugly sense of something all wrong at the core of life. All the way back to the Eagles I could think only of that tree house which had even surpassed the splendor of the drawing I envied so much in my own copy of the book. *Why wasn't it possible to live like that?* And to make matters worse, as I walked along the memory kept slipping away in the glare and ubiquity of reality, and when I got inside the Eagles and sat down in the dark cavern of the card room, with the ceiling fan clanking, and waited for the game to end, everything seemed saturated with emptiness. I did not understand what had taken place between the movie and that moment; but it seemed to me that a secret and unalterable sadness had divulged itself in the world. Something that was always there but unseen and unfelt except at certain moments. This was my first recollection of an experience I was to have over and over, particularly on Sundays, and years later when I had taken a philosophy course at Penn State I actually gave it a name, inspired, I must admit, by Proust's passage about the "asymmetrical Saturday": I called it "the existential Sunday."

As if to confirm this "fact of life," there was even a song that was popular about that time called "Gloomy Sunday," and one verse went

> Sundays are gloomy, with shadows I spend it all.
> My heart and I have decided to end it all.

I never thought seriously about ending it all, but I can understand why Sunday would be the day to do it, if you were at all inclined that way. The thing about Sundays was, and still is, the complete suspension of the laws governing daily life. Everything is half dead on Sunday ("Sunday is viscous, with torpor I spend it all . . ."). Sunday was a hollow parenthesis in the week, a day whose festivity was compromised by church in the morning, homework in the evening, and the long shadow of the school week ahead (including math with Miss Coleman and Latin with Miss Brown). Sunday was a solemn preparation for the descent into Monday. There was simply something wrong about Sunday, and I blamed most of it on God.

A few years later when I had moved onto the main campus I used to hitchhike to Punxsutawney on weekends and then back to State College on Sunday and I got to Jordan Hall late in the afternoon. I didn't at all like life at Penn State in the first year (my junior year really) because I had a girlfriend back home and every weekend I went home, snow or rain, a seventy-mile hitch across the Allegheny Mountains. As a consequence, my return on Sunday was the low point in the week, and it was just like a prolonged emergence from the matinee into reality. My room was on the fourth and top floor where the walls sloped into the ceiling, mansard style, and the only sources of natural light were two thin dormer windows with deep sills on which my roommate and I piled our books. When I opened the door this same lugubrious emptiness always overcame me. There were the two single beds, the two facing desks and two desk chairs, two reading chairs, two lamps, two closets, two ashtrays, two of everything, just as I had left them (my roommate always got in later in the afternoon), and the waning sunlight slashed into the room onto the throw rug and up across the beds, illuminating everything with this terrifying indifference. I imagined the room to be expecting me, as if everything in it had conspired to be alertly itself when I opened the door, like people hushed together for a surprise party. All of the things sat there in their places smirking at the inevitability of my return: "Welcome home! We're still here, just as you left us." So it seemed to me the weekend had simply been short-circuited and I hadn't left at all but had only gone down the hallway to the bathroom, and all the rest of it was a false memory. This is how the idea of the existential Sunday was born, one of the gloomier fruits of my education.

"What are you studying, Buddy?"

"I'm studying existentialism."

"I see."

But it was my mother who ran the family and it was my sister who ran my mother—on most matters, though not by any means all. And they had some colossal fights. In addition to her intelligence, my sister was also overwhelmingly convincing. It was my sister who began the campaign for my going to college and it was Mimi, my mother, who passed the decision on to Bert, my father, whose dream of my following in his steps ended in the fall of 1946. I must add that this was in no way a coercion on my sister's part, but a mutual understanding and a realization, somewhat new in the world in those days, that an education was the only ticket out of town, unless you went to work in a factory in Buffalo or Cleveland. The new undergraduate center in DuBois had just opened and the veterans were coming back on the GI Bill, and it was suddenly an ideal time to think the unthinkable. And thus began ten additional years of education, interrupted by two years in the army. In 1989 my sister presented me with a thick volume of family photographs, beginning with our great-grandparents (including Botilda Hellberg) and coming up to our own generation. Each photo was identified and amply documented to the best of her memory, and her introduction began with these words: "When you came into my life on my very own tenth birthday, it was required of me that I keep track of you. This pictorial manuscript is my own version of your track record."

And that was my sister Lois, the organizer and attendant of the family fortunes, especially my own. In an odd way, she assumed the role vacated by Tina, who died in a Clarion sanitarium following eighteen voiceless months in a coma, staring straight at the wall from a wheelchair, according to Aunt Winifred (Ross) who tended her. I have never known anyone, besides Tina, who "kept track" of everybody on the family tree as carefully as Lois did. She was far more interested in the lives of those around her, even those that touched hers only casually, if at all, than she seemed to be in her own, and she liked nothing more than a good story or an anecdote about someone, it didn't matter who, to whom something interesting had happened. And she would always ask for follow-up stories when we had our usual phone conversations on Saturday morning following our move to California ("Have you heard any more about—your friend, what's his name?"). It was a joy to tell her these stories because I had the sense that she lived them in somewhat the way that my mother lived the photos in her magazines, and the telling was always punctuated by her "Ohhh!"s or her laughter or sympathy, as the case required. Where her own pain is concerned she was, like my grandfather, virtually Stoic and when her eyesight was all but erased by macular degeneration she immediately plunged into active membership in the White Cane Gang, and the activities of the "visually impaired." She wore her blindness like a badge, or as she would put it, she got all the mileage possible out of it.

From the time I was fifteen until my own family moved to California in 1978, our relationship, except for annual visits, consisted of phone calls and letters. On one of my recent visits to Monterey we were sitting in the living room. Then she got up, went into the bedroom and presently came back with a 10″ × 12″ box perhaps six inches high.

"These may interest you," she said in a husky whisper, putting the box in my lap.

My sister, to put it generously, was a large woman (like my mother), age seventy-three at this point, afflicted not only by the macular degeneration but also by diabetes, severe leg cramps, hypertension, swollen feet, obesity, and a deathly fear of losing a limb to gangrene, as had our mother and her mother before her.

"What's this?" I asked.

"These are your letters," she said. And there (apparently) were all the letters I had written her beginning in the mid-nineteen forties when I was a senior in high school and she was twenty-six and a medical secretary in Ontario, California. "You ought to have them."

I didn't know what to say. "Well, they're really yours."

"I can't read them anymore, and you can. You should. There you are. *There* you are!" And she slapped her knees as she sat down. "You can watch yourself growing up."

"Well, I don't know that I want to do that," I said. "Once is enough." I suddenly felt very strange. The prospect of reading my own letters seemed to me about as interesting as hearing one of my lectures played back on a tape recorder. In fact, just having the letters there on my lap aroused a vaguely ominous feeling of being confronted with something I had "done." I was also astonished at the size of the stack and at the idea that she had patiently collected the letters, saved them in the order of their arrival, from the very beginning of our correspondence.

"Well thanks," I said. It was a flat moment and I was aware that she wanted it to be a big moment, but I could think of no way to manufacture any delight or even a sincere thank you.

"Oh come on," she said with some indignation, "surely you're curious."

"Not very."

"Not a little?"

"Well . . . . I'd rather read someone else's letters. Yours."

"Oh, you're so damned unsentimental."

"Only about some things," I said, now really on the defense. "I'm not sure I would like myself."

"This is your history, for god's sake, right there in your lap—or a big part of it."

And then we got into a minor skirmish on the general theme of my "objectivity." It shortly broadened to why I don't go to my high school reunions, or go back to Punxsutawney, and so on. My coolness, I must confess, was also based on even more urgent concerns, for I realized that if I wasn't careful I'd shortly be asked to read one, if not several, letters aloud to her, and to whoever else was in the room, and that would have been a debacle. But I dodged that bullet at some cost and she remained, I suppose, permanently (if she thought about it again) disappointed that I took so little interest in my "own past." It so happens that I opened the box just a moment ago—it is now late 1995—in order to find out when the series began because I hadn't really looked at the contents. Maybe my point of view will be clearer if I quote the first paragraph of the earliest letter, which I have just perused and which lives down to my expectations. It is dated March 12, 1946, from Punxsutawney, Penna., written (by hand) only a few weeks after Lois had left Punxsutawney for California—forever, as it turned out.

> Hi Sis,
>
> It's strange, indeed, writing to you so far off. I don't quite know how to begin. I could start out with the old "How are you?" routine, but that's just commonplace and I mustn't forget, I'm not writing to a commonplace gal! right?
>
> I hope you are feeling allright. If you're not, I can only say that you'll become acclimatized—I hope!

That is painful. I thought about not including it but decided in the end that it was crucial "evidence." For what I want to say would be meaningless without that little fragment of my past. I can only assume that I got better as the series went on, or at least had better control of the march of ideas and sentiments down the page; on the other hand, this letter may be the most innocent and uncontaminated of the lot. I will probably never know because the thought of stumbling through this history of enthusiasms, discoveries, world-weariness and existential Sundayism is simply too disturbing to think about. Kierkegaard once said—"Here he goes," my sister would say at this point—that the ironical thing about life is that you live it by going forward but you understand it by going back over it. Well, yes and no. It is one thing to try to understand life, even by going back over it in your memory and thoughts about what it may have amounted to. It is another thing to return to the artifacts you cast out while you were living it, to see that what you took as your own spontaneity was an infinite series of conventional choices or unconscious adaptations of attitudes, fears and intolerances that are shared by almost everyone. It's one thing to look at an old photograph of yourself, another to read the record of what went on in your head. The box of letters is probably the most complete record of my personal mental life that exists. I get a spasm of self-allergy just thinking about all the convictions and genuinely sincere beliefs that must be waiting there in these pages as the new world of college, then the army, my first trip overseas, then graduate school, and finally university employment, opens up new avenues of experience.

In literary studies there is an honorable endeavor in which scholars use various techniques for identifying the "hand" of an author through stylistic devices. If you want to know whether Shakespeare wrote a certain play or poem, or passage in a play he *didn't* write, you can submit it to an analysis of such things as frequency and kinds of metaphors, the recurrence of words in the known Shakespearean vocabulary, tendencies to use various figures of speech, things like catalogues, anatomies, or certain organizational devices, sentence patterns, word inversions, and so on. (How many times, for instance, does the figure hendiadys or zeugma appear?) In its way, it is the literary equivalent of finger printing or DNA analysis. This becomes more interesting when you consider that what one is really uncovering is evidence of individuality, of the "genetic" stamp through which a particular mind unthinkingly speaks itself, since style, good or bad, is something that expresses itself independently of conscious will. Style is really what you don't know about yourself.

For example, I recall a colleague saying to me one day, very pleasantly, that he missed seeing me on campus (I had been on leave); more specifically he missed seeing (I think it went) that "shock of grey hair and that slight stoop." This went through me like a meat hook. Stoop? What is this about a stoop? I thought. No one had told me about a stoop. Jesus, I'd been going through life with a slight stoop. I can be *identified* by my stoop, a sort of walking parenthesis—topped by a "shock of grey hair." I've never forgotten it and when I happen to think of it in public I straighten up to a point that must strike others, if they noticed, as an unnatural rigidity, as if I'd just had a cramp, but before I have gone half a block I have fallen back into my emblematic stoop. And invariably, this recalls the myriad of instances in which my mother would sneak up behind me, put her large hands on my shoulders and pry them backwards with her thumbs in my spine, as if I were one of those rabbit carcasses I can still see her splaying during the hunting seasons when we lived in Albion: "Keep your shoulders back, Buddy. Don't slouch." So there was the evidence, early and late, that the stoop had developed into a lifelong characteristic I knew nothing about. And when you compound my stoop with innumerable other gestural or physical habits I *still* know nothing about—it just seems better not to think about it.

So there is something about style that is the most personal of personal things. In a certain sense, it should be left to itself, unremarked upon, like the habits of the body, and taken for what it is: an overall unconscious manner of self-presentation. What a nasty thing, for example, to say to someone, "Do you realize how often you say, 'I'll wager that—'?" or "Why do you always flick your nose with your knuckle?" Or, had my friend (who meant to pay me a compliment) said, "Did you know you walked with a slight stoop?" These are subcutaneous matters. No one likes to have involuntary habits pointed out—unless, of course, you say something borrowed from the language of lovers, like "You have such a cute way of raising your eyebrow," or "I've always loved your snicker!"

Now then, to come back to my letter of March 12, 1946, which is probably the earliest surviving letter in my "hand," consider the evidence for authorship. Take the opening sentences: "It's strange, indeed, writing to you so far off. I don't quite know how to begin." Once past the sense itself (what there is of it), what leaps out at me first is the word "indeed." Even now, reporting all this "objectively," I wince. Here it is, 1946, I'm a senior in high school, the feature editor of *The Hilights*, winner of a state prize for high school feature writing, and my letter is no sooner under way than out pops this "indeed," like a pimple, and it is followed in the shadow of the same sentence by a "quite"—two affectations I had picked up god knows where, and to this day I have to be constantly on the lookout for them because they are always poised ready to pounce into my prose by way of making a point stronger that doesn't need to be made stronger: indeed, a point that would be stronger if no attempt were made to make it stronger! (For example, how much better, how much *more* powerful, is: "It's strange writing to you so far off. I don't know how to begin," or leaving out the "I don't know how to begin" altogether, since all it is doing is gathering dust. Which would leave only one error in grammar, but at least it's off and running.) "Indeed" and "quite" are what linguists call emphatics and an addiction to emphatics is the equivalent of constantly waving your hands while you talk, or peppering your speech with "you knows" and "likes," or flicking your nose with your knuckle, or walking with a slight stoop. It isn't really that I *dislike* what I am, or have become; it's mainly that there is this part of the self that one has nothing to do with choosing, and that somehow *what one is* and how one behaves seem more visible in these unchosen stylistic details, these excesses, these innocent gestures that degenerate, if not tended, into proclivities and thence into self-caricature. So I encounter this "indeed" and this "quite"—thereby, in a weary attempt to escape the "commonplace" falling straight into it (and how *badly* the stylist who wrote this letter *detests* the commonplace!)—and I see the genesis of a tic that couldn't have been more than one or two years old at the time, now well into its metastasis. Moreover, if I dug into the stack an inch or so down I would encounter, in addition to more indeeds and quites, such things as my absolute conviction (three or four years later) that gloomy-Sunday Schopenhauer had said all that was necessary to say about "the human condition"—Christ! The *human condition!*—that Plato failed completely to understand the artist, and that Zola was the greatest novelist who ever lived (including, of course, all the novelists I hadn't read). All of this I imparted to my sister in copious outpourings of passionate prose, aided and abetted by platoons of indeeds and quites and hyperbolic exclusionary constructions like "If there's one thing I can't stand it's. . . ." or "You *must* read Albert Camus's *Plague*. It's *the* finest novel of the post-war period!" (I even gave her a copy of the Modern Library edition one Christmas: can you imagine giving someone *The Plague* for Christmas!) All of this is there in the box, waiting for me, like my furniture at 406 Jordan Hall in the shank of a sunny Sunday afternoon. "Read me. I dare you!"

It's not that this is such a bad trait in anyone (the point is really: how could it be otherwise?), but that I was in college, the first member of the family, apart from Tina, to do so, and it was largely at my sister's urging that I was there at all. And what I didn't know at the time and found out only later on the evening of a horrific fight over my low opinion of psychoanalysis, is that she had wanted to go to college herself and that she resented my being able to go without the least understanding of what it had cost the family. So I was growing up, meaning that I was digesting the wisdom of the world in four-credit units. History was a bore because it etched away everything but the parade of facts ("Sumerian civilization was predominantly agricultural and was therefore skilled in the building of canals and developing effective systems of irrigation"); economics and political science were abstract beyond bearing, allowing nothing erratic to intrude into the organizational chart of governance (What had I to do with initiative, referendum, and recall?), math was outrageously peopleless, and as a consequence I got D's in all these courses, passing only through the generosity of my professors.

So, from my standpoint, the box of letters is primarily a compendium of tics, large and small. To anyone else, the letters would be "quite" normal or boring or "commonplace." To my sister, who read and re-read them, kept track of them, and put them lovingly in order over a forty-year period, they were a valued possession, tendered to me finally in her blindness within a year of her death for my proper Kierkegaardian self-understanding. To me, who cannot see the forest for the trees, they are a revelation of a fact I would prefer not to confront. The letter of March 12, 1946, and all its kindred to follow, was written with an absence of a certain understanding that has only remotely to do with my own fallibility as a person. Each episode described as yet had no sequel, no result; it was necessarily written from the standpoint of ignorance and in-betweenness, as all letters. I suppose, are. Thus there is a real inevitability about letters that are re-read: they have the mark of fossils trapped in the tree gum of their own nearsightedness. To put it perhaps too morbidly, the box reminds me of the scene in Mann's *Magic Mountain*—"Here he goes again!"—in which Hans Castorp first sees an X-ray of his own hand. The flesh had fallen away into a blurred mist and he saw the skeleton nesting like a grey armature within. "With prophetic eyes," Mann writes (I have the book open), "he gazed at this familiar part of his own body, and for the first time in his life he understood that he would die."

What a stunner! I couldn't really expect anyone else to understand what this has to do with the slight stoop, the indeeds and quites, and the box of letters. Not to mention the train lunches and the dawning that afternoon in the Eagles card room. It isn't the dying, though I suppose that's the bottom line of it all. Yes! It *is* the dying—but not in the sense of not *having*, or *no longer* having, but of never having had, because you can never understand what "I'm fine," and "Tomorrow'll be fine," and "Don't be dunking the noodle, Buddy," really meant *then, as the words were spoken!* You find out about it all afterwards, in a sudden convulsion of realization. Pop, there it is. And of course it's already over.

Here is what it is like. I used to play a time game while driving along the highway. The idea is to try to envision the scene in which I arrive at my destination. This occurred most often when I was traveling from Santa Barbara to Monterey for a weekend with my sister, a trip Nancy and I have taken over thirty times in the last fifteen years. I have had every thought and daydream imaginable on that dry tedious stretch of 101 between Paso Robles and the Spreckles cutoff. But sometimes, when Nancy is asleep and having run out of diversions and finding myself in a transcendental mood, I would try to erase the time that would lapse between, say, the river bend at King City or the Gonzales water tower and the moment I walk in the front door at Crescent Circle in Monterey. And then I imagine myself doing just that.

It makes no difference whether I'm a few minutes late or early in arriving; accurate timing isn't a factor, but it does help to target your entrance around a likely window of time because the game is all about condensing two times into one. The important thing is to think undividedly about the moment that will occur around, say, five o'clock, to seal it in a vacuum of deep concentration, isolated from the rest of the here-and-now—in short to teleport my self psychically into a more or less certain future moment (fortune permitting), to see the details of the sagging brick porch, to smell the damp odor of the oak leaves mulching on the garage roof; my sister and Mel (her husband) coming out of the faded persimmon-colored door (with the dolphin knocker we gave them), her arms open ("Welllll, here you are, my brother!" in that soft slow voice), then the hug and the kiss; then the look of the living room, item by item, the Indian rugs on the walls, the arrangement of the furniture, the crack in the fireplace wall that will never get fixed, the storyteller and kachina dolls in the sideboard niche, our mother's green crystal lamp (from the very era of the Formica coffee table!)—all the appointments of my sister's house as I have known them for so many years—and then to imprint that "negative" in my mind and keep it alive for the matching positive that would occur when time has run its course, I get out of the car, go down the walk under the oak and experience the full Match as my bracketed projection and the reality are fused—"Welllll, here you are, my brother!"—into a Supermoment.

That's the idea, but of course it never worked out. The main problem is that you can't retain the projected arrival scene in the mint condition necessary for the Match with the real arrival. It fades the moment you think of something else, and even to try to keep it alive and vibrant between Gonzales and Crescent Circle at sixty-five miles an hour is unsafe, to say the least. So it slips, like every other thought, into the past where it can be reclaimed only as a "then," as an artifact of time, never as trapped in the instant of its own conception in real experience. The most that comes of it (if I succeed in remembering the experiment at all by the time I get there) is a vaguely umbilical demonstration that time does indeed lapse, that every moment is mysteriously eaten by its progeny, and that inevitably the moment in which my consciousness finally blinks out and is swallowed in Time's belly, will be a direct continuation of this very Now in which I write these words, even as this Now is directly attached to an infinite chain of once Nows (now Thens) that stretch backward in the other direction—back to Gonzales, San Luis Obispo, back to Santa Barbara, to yesterday, last year, to Ithaca, Pittsburgh, New Haven, Saratoga, Penn State and Korea, and on back through the yesteryears to Punxsutawney and my first awareness of the world, whatever that may have been.

In short, this moment, any moment, is made of every other moment, and you have the impression, so hitched is one moment into another, so indivisible, so *close* are they as they unfold through each other, that you *should* be able to walk backward in time on a path of moments to the beginning, if you could only convert time into little steppingstones about the size of your mind's feet. But of course moments, finally, don't really exist; they are known only by what has taken place in them, just as we know space only by objects that occupy it.

So the letters had come back to me as an unforeseen closure of all these times, a Supermoment, if you will, unintentionally achieved. "You might find these interesting," she said. And I do, god knows I do—insidiously interesting. Not for their "youthful" contents, or their forgivable "quite"s and "indeed"s and positions taken on this and that, but for the single overwhelming truth of their all coming back at once in the coffin of this simple cardboard box. I had not anticipated this. I did not know how to deal with it. It occurred to me at one point that I might read the letters in reverse order, like a home movie run backward. But it would come to the same thing: they would always be the enigma of an absence, a set of Harvard Classics in which there was no two dollars secreted away toward some small household extravagance. Even if I began at the end and worked my way to the March 16 letter, it would be moving forward into the same future, in the very same sense in which physicists audaciously claim that time only *seems* to move in one direction through the vanity of human consciousness. So time is what you can never have: there is only the *passing* of time, its constant disappearance in its own progress—a terrible terrible enigma—and to think back on it now, a year after her death, is to relive the nostalgia for my impossible tree house, which became, in time, nostalgia for her and for the others, now long gone, who once constituted a family of sorts that began moving apart at about the time I wrote the first letter.

Joseph Epstein

Grow Up, Why Dontcha?

Early in *A Dragon Apparent,* Norman Lewis tells about his travels in Indo-China and his encounter with the religion of Cao-Daism, in which, as he writes, "the best years of one's life are its concluding decades." In Cao-Daism "the dejection that encroaching age stamps so often in the Western face—the melancholy sense of having outlived one's usefulness—[is] replaced . . . with a complacency of spirit and a prestige that increases automatically with the years." The older one gets in this religion, at least if one wishes to rise in its hierarchy, the greater the number of abstentions one is asked to make. But, as an elderly adherent explains to Norman Lewis, the older one is, the better one is able to abstain from the pleasures of the flesh, and besides, as Lewis concludes, "the turn of the screw was put on gently, so that by the time you had to give things up for the Kingdom of God, you were pretty well ready to give them up anyway. It was all so humane."

It also sounds so true to human development, if not to human nature—and very un-American, if not un-Western. In America, we cling to our pleasures, feeling chagrin as each diminishes in intensity, falls away, or disappears altogether. The name of the longed-for but never-discovered secret of life is youth, perpetual youth. Through diet, exercise, cosmetic surgery, or all combined, we ardently seek it. The means may differ but the end is always the same: how to stay young, how to avoid growing old. Everyone has felt the lure of remaining young. I know I have.

Impossible of achievement, the quest is inevitably frustrated; for youth, though it can sometimes be prolonged a bit, cannot really be maintained much beyond its normal span. Trying to do so is a game that can't be won, a mug's game. Not that this stops vast numbers of people from playing, as witness the crowds at gyms and jogging tracks. "Fitness is about sex and immortality," Wilfred Sheed has written. "By toning up the system, you can prolong youth, just about finesse middle age, and then, when the time comes, go straight into senility." Or, I suppose, be in near perfect shape just in time for death.

One would have thought that everyone had figured this out by now. But the emphasis on youthfulness and the terror of old age in American culture, if anything, seem to have grown greater. Not long ago I came across the expression "the leprosy of old age," an all-too-vivid phrase that just now reflects much ghastly truth. No one wishes to succumb to old age any earlier than is absolutely required, though those of us fortunate enough to achieve our eighties will finally have to do so.

In the meanwhile, the relentless pursuit of youthfulness combined with the fear of old age has done great damage to an early ideal of mine—the ideal of the grown-up. To set aside childish things, to ascend to grown-upness, to arrive at adulthood—this, from my earliest years, was my aspiration, the name of my desire. I could not grow up fast enough. And then, lo, when I had finally done so, the notion of being grown-up, or at any rate of acting the grown-up, seemed, *poof,* to have disappeared, shot down from the deck of the good ship *Zeitgeist.*

Among my strongest early memories are a number of incidents in which I found myself struggling, with genuine though hopeless determination, against being treated as a child. Since I was in fact a child, in certain instances a very young child, I wonder if, as they say in both the therapist's office and the quilt maker's studio, a pattern doesn't begin to emerge.

The first memory is a series of connected incidents in which I am being put to bed well before I am prepared to depart the scene. In one room is not so much terrifying as damnably boring darkness; in the other, amusing radio shows, adults, conversation, pleasing company. The reasonableness of this arrangement, in which I must go to bed earlier than everyone else simply because I am the youngest and the smallest, never came near to being persuasive to me. Unlike the Proust kid, I didn't yearn for my mother. I wanted, instead, more action.

Mine was the last generation of males in this country that had to earn its long pants, or at least had to wait until a certain age to wear them. Between short and long pants came those dopey pants called knickers. Knickers stopped and bagged at the knee and were worn with long, usually thick socks that never stayed up. Jeans were not then an alternative: dungarees were something farmers wore and Levi Strauss & Company had not yet turned its marketing attentions east or even middlewest. Knickers, then, were all a boy could wear until at some official agreed-upon time—age nine? ten?—he was allowed a pair of long pants, usually to be worn on special occasions.

When I was six years old, my father told me that he was going to take me with him to his tailor to have a suit made for me. I thought, with great delight, that I had beaten the clock. Young as I was, going up in the elevator to the tailor's in his building on Wabash Avenue in the Loop, I sensed that I was taking part in something like a genuine *rite de passage*.

The masculine atmosphere of the tailor's shop reinforced the feeling: lots of cigar smoke, thick bolts of richly textured cloth set out on high tables, much business talk. My father let me choose my own material; and, as I recall, I did not disgrace myself. Now I am standing before a three-way mirror, and one of the tailors, a man with a strong foreign accent, is draping material over me, his mouth full of pins, which doesn't stop him from talking with my father. I inquire whether it would be pos-

I was lucky, I think, that the draft was still intact. The draft gave young men another two years to think about what they wanted to do with their lives. It also introduced them to a wider America than they may have hitherto known, locked as most Americans are behind their own ethnic and social-class walls. And, for me, another thing that the draft did was make me hungry for civilian—which is to say, adult—life.

Philip Larkin must have shared some of these sentiments. "It was that verse about becoming again as a little child that caused the first sharp waning of my Christian sympathies," he wrote. "If the Kingdom of Heaven could be entered only by those fulfilling such a condition I knew I should be unhappy there." Larkin wrote this in a review of a volume of the Opies' extensive study of children and their folklore. "It was not the prospect of being deprived of money, keys, wallet, letters, books, long-playing records, drinks, the opposite sex, and other solaces of adulthood that upset me," Larkin continued, "but having to put up indefinitely with the company of other children, their noise, their nastiness, their boasting, their back-answers, their cruelty, their silliness."

I don't share Larkin's contempt for children—"the little scum," as Hesketh Pearson once called them—reserving mine for people of adult age who prefer to carry themselves as children. Recently I was reading along in a most interesting book, *The Anatomy of Disgust* by William Ian Miller, full of admiration for its author's erudition and literary power, when he, to illustrate a point about the contempt not infrequently found among members of different social classes, related an encounter between himself and a stonemason he had hired to do some work on his house in Ann Arbor. When Miller "rode up on [his] bicycle, backpack on [his] back" to say hello, he sensed the mason's contempt for him. "He a teacher?" the man asked Miller's wife. Miller remarks that the man straightaway saw him as "a feminized male," from which perception his contempt flowed.

I have to add, though a sometime university teacher myself, as soon as Miller rode up on that bike wearing that backpack, I, too, felt an involuntary touch of contempt for him. It is the backpack, not the bike, that did it. I assume that Miller, a full professor at the University of Michigan Law School, must be no younger than in his forties, perhaps older. Yet here he is boppin' around in what is essentially the garb of a student. In doing so, he seeks, I take it, a kind of agelessness—an agelessness, for all I know, he may very well feel. Somehow, however earnest he may be about his status as husband, father, teacher, he still wants to seem youthful. Had he returned home in suit or jacket and tie, my guess is that the mason would not have seemed in the least contemptuous of him. I know I wouldn't have. I don't even require a jacket and tie. But I cannot bear that backpack on anyone over twenty-five.

One of the divisions of the contemporary world is between those who are prepared to dress (roughly) their age and those who see clothes a means to fight off age. At my university, there are now tenured professors teaching in deliberately un-laced gym shoes. I know of associate deans who never wear neckties. Others—balding, paunchy, droopy-lidded—have not had a fabric other than denim touch their hindquarters for decades. They, poor dears, believe they are staying young.

Clothes have played a large part in bringing about the drift away from grown-up to youth culture. In part, dress in America—and not America alone—has changed owing to an increase in informality across the board in contemporary life. As a boy, I have no memory of my father or any of his friends owning any casual clothes. They wore suits everywhere, even sitting around on a Sunday afternoon; they never left the house without a serious hat. Men now dress, much of the time, like boys, in jeans, sport shirts, gym shoes, the ubiquitous baseball cap. Meanwhile, little girls dress like grown women, in short shorts, bikinis, platform shoes—sexy is the reigning theme. The result is to erase the line between the youthful and the mature, though it doesn't really work. Instead it gives a tone of formlessness to the society that adopts it.

Why should I care about any of this? Is it my business if people wish to appear younger than their true age? If seeming youthful is pleasing to them, why not wish these people God-speed, however hopeless their endeavor? I really ought to be more tolerant. But, alas, I cannot.

The United States, if not the Western world, has been on a great youth binge for at least thirty or forty years now. My guess is that the adulation of youth, as an American phenomenon, began with the election to the presidency of John F. Kennedy. Suddenly, "to be young was very heaven!" At forty-two, Kennedy was the youngest man ever elected president. He was the first president not to wear a hat. He had an athletic build, a beautiful wife, and a low hairline. (We would subsequently learn that he had Addison's disease, a bad back, and other painful injuries to what was essentially an old man's body.) The unspoken part of Kennedy-inspired youth worship was a reduction in admiration for anyone older. To be beyond, say, fifty, was, not much question about it, to be a little out of it. "As we grow older," wrote Gerald Murphy, the friend of F. Scott Fitzgerald, "we must guard against a feeling of lowered consequence."

The student uprisings later in the decade of the sixties set the lock—a sort of aortic clamp—on this. To be young then was not only desirable, it was required as a bona fides of one's integrity and honor. No one over thirty was to be trusted—this was one of the shibboleths of the day—for it was assumed that anyone beyond that age had already made too many compromises, was already too greatly swept up by something called the system, was too much implicated in the way things were. Perhaps at no other time in history was being young felt to be more desirable.

Teaching college students in the 1970s and 1980s, I sensed among many of them what I used to think of as sixties envy. And, of course, in our own day one still sees what are essentially 1960s characters, now in their fifties, walking the streets, tie-dyed, long-haired, sadly sandaled, neither grateful nor dead, waiting for a bus to the past.

The cult of youthfulness may be the principal legacy of the 1960s. And this cult—more like a national craze—allows a very wide berth for youthfulness. Today one would not think to say that no one over thirty is to be trusted; that sentiment has been replaced by the notion that no one under forty needs to get serious. One of the curious qualities I have noticed about recent generations is the absence of any indecent hurry to get started in life.

Consider two successful television shows, *Seinfeld* and *Friends,* where one encounters precisely the kind of perpetual adolescent I have been attempting to describe. Played for laughs, the indecisiveness of the characters in both shows results in a richly comic narcissism, with no one having anything like a center to his or her life and with the notion of adulthood existing in the dim distance, an unreachable utopia. On one of the *Seinfeld* episodes the hopelessly selfish character George Costanza is about to enter into an affair with a married woman. "An affair!" he exclaims. "It's like stockings and martinis and William Holden. It's so adult!" Poor Georgie.

To turn to another George, in *Angel in the Whirlwind,* his history of the American Revolutionary War, Benson Bobrick remarks that "by the time he was sixteen, George [Washington] appeared in every respect an adult." Marcus Cunliffe, in his book on Washington, reinforces the point, saying of Washington that he lived at Ferry Farm with his mother, "leaving childhood behind and entering the short period of youth that in colonial times so often merged with adult life."

William Osler, the great physician, widened the point by asserting "the comparative uselessness of men above forty years of age." Osler added: "Take the sum of human achievement in action, in science, in art, in literature—subtract the work of men above forty, and, while we would miss great treasures, even priceless treasures, we would practically be where we are today."

In 1932 there was a best-seller titled *Life Begins at Forty* by Walter B. Pitkin. I never read it, but I take it that its message was that one needn't feel old at age forty, that many opportunities still existed at that hoary age—occupational, financial, romantic—and that life was scarcely over. It was, friends, just beginning.

Today that title seems quaint. Many people, far from feeling old at forty, haven't really begun their lives at all. Before forty, there is graduate school, general fooling around, possibly professional school, maybe a change in one's career choice, a late marriage, having a child at thirty-eight or thereabouts. This is how, I believe, lots of people nowadays view things. And, of course, some people wait to begin their lives till fifty or beyond—wait, in some cases perhaps, for the next life.

Oddly, this phenomenon seems most often to strike the especially bright. Because they are so bright, the world seems a sea of possibilities to them. I see this among a handful of my former students. One among them, who can write and who knows computer technology, began, soon after college, working for a large consulting firm. Then he ran a business of his own, went to law school, clerked for a well-placed and famous judge, decided not to practice law, joined a firm of European consultants, and wrote a book. What he will do next I cannot say. When he wrote to tell me that he had decided the law was not for him, I replied that I understood but that he was not to ask me for a recommendation to medical school.

The phrase "the despair of possibility" is Kierkegaard's. The brilliantly gloomy Dane knew that one can as easily drown in the sea of possibility as in the swamp of necessity. In *The Sickness unto Death,* he wrote:

> Nor is it merely due to lack of strength when the soul goes astray in possibility—at least this is not to be understood as people commonly understand it. What really is lacking is the power to obey, to submit to the necessary in oneself, to what may be called one's limit. Therefore the misfortune does not consist in the fact that such a self did not amount to anything in the world: no, the misfortune is that the man did not become aware of himself, aware that the self he is, is a perfectly defined something, and so is the necessary. On the contrary, he lost himself, owing to the fact that this self was seen fantastically reflected in the possible.

So it seems with people who wish endlessly to be young, to avoid responsibility, to avoid committing themselves to anything definite, lest other doors close on them. These people remain in a perpetual state of development. As with some movies that never get made, their lives, like the movie scripts, reside in what the kids on the coast call "development hell." And hell it must be, always waiting for life to begin, thinking in the spiritual tense known as the future permanent.

Some people are in jobs where not to seem young can work to their detriment. A few years ago I wrote a screenplay for a decent and likeable producer who one morning, over the phone, told me it was his birthday. When I congratulated him, he said that it wasn't altogether a celebratory occasion. He was now forty-one, and forty-one was, for Hollywood, a bit long in the tooth—unless, of course, one had a few large commercial or artistic triumphs to one's credit, which he, till now, didn't have. In Hollywood, apparently, life can be over at forty.

The point seems to be confirmed in movies of the past few decades. The number of roles for grown-ups in the movies has been very small—minuscule, even. Looking at the male side only, the actors of the 1940s and 1950s had a maturity that is absent from the actors of today. Roles were written that called for a certain grown-upness that no longer exists among us. Take Clark Gable, Gary Cooper, Humphrey Bogart, Gregory Peck, Ray Milland, Walter Pidgeon—grown-ups all. Or consider Spencer Tracy: even when young, he didn't seem young. These were men who could wear suits, not look laughable in hats. There were even parts for older gents: Lionel Barrymore, Adolphe Menjou, Walter Huston, Claude Rains. Male movie stars of our own day—Robert Redford, Al Pacino, Tom Cruise, Harrison Ford, Tom Hanks—are all, in their movie personas, essentially boys, never to be thought of as beyond their late thirties. (Redford is, in fact, sixty.) To be beyond one's late thirties, in the world projected by Hollywood, is to become a quite different persona, one, at least on the screen, strictly non grata.

Some people cannot help but think of themselves as young. W. H. Auden claimed that he always thought himself the

William Maxwell

Nearing 90

Out of the corner of my eye I see my 90th birthday approaching. It is one year and six months away. How long after that will I be the person I am now?

I don't yet need a cane but I have a feeling that my table manners have deteriorated. My posture is what you'd expect of someone addicted to sitting in front of a typewriter, but it was always that way. "Stand up straight," my father would say to me. "You're all bent over like an old man." It didn't bother me then and it doesn't now, though I agree that an erect carriage is a pleasure to see, in someone of any age.

I have regrets but there are not very many of them and, fortunately, I forget what they are. I forget names too, but it is not yet serious. What I am trying to remember and can't, quite often my wife will remember. And vice versa. She is in and out during the day but I know she will be home when evening comes, and so I am never lonely. Long ago, a neighbor in the country, looking at our flower garden, said, "Children and roses reflect their care." This is true of the very old as well.

Though there have been a great many changes in the world since I came into it on August 16, 1908, I try not to deplore. It is not constructive and there is no point in discouraging the young by invidious comparisons to the way things used to be.

I am not—I think I am not—afraid of dying. When I was 17 I worked on a farm in southern Wisconsin, near Portage. It was no ordinary farm and not much serious farming was done there, but it had the look of a place that had been lived in, and loved, for a good long time. I was no more energetic than most adolescents but the family forgave my failures and shortcomings and simply took me in, let me be one of them. The farm had come down in that family through several generations, to a woman who was so alive that everything and everybody seemed to revolve around her personality. She lived well into her 90's and then one day told her oldest daughter that she didn't want to live anymore, that she was tired. Though I was not present but only heard about it in a letter, this remark reconciled me to my own inevitable extinction. I could believe that enough is enough.

Because I actively enjoy sleeping, dreams, the unexplainable dialogues that take place in my head as I am drifting off, all that, I tell myself that lying down to an afternoon nap that goes on and on through eternity is not something to be concerned about. What spoils this pleasant fancy is the recollection that when people are dead they don't read books. This I find unbearable. No Tolstoy, no Chekhov, no Elizabeth Bowen, no Keats, no Rilke. One might as well be—

Before I am ready to call it quits I would like to reread every book I have ever deeply enjoyed, beginning with Jane Austen and Isaac Babel and Sybille Bedford's *The Sudden View* and going through shelf after shelf of the bookcases, until I arrive at the autobiographies of William Butler Yeats. As it is, I read a great deal of the time. I am harder to please, though. I see flaws in masterpieces. Conrad indulging in rhetoric when he would do better to get on with it. I would read all day long and well into the night if there were no other claims on my time. Appointments with doctors, with the dentist. The monthly bank statement. Income tax returns. And because I don't want to turn

into a monster, people. Afternoon tea with X, dinner with the
Y's. Our social life would be a good deal more active than it is if
more than half of those I care about hadn't passed over to the
other side. However, I remember them. I remember them
more, and more vividly, the older I get.

I did not wholly escape the amnesia that overtakes children around the age of 6 but I carried along with me more of
my childhood than, I think, most people do. Once, after dinner,
my father hitched up the horse and took my mother and me for
a sleigh ride. The winter stars were very bright. The sleigh bells
made a lovely sound. I was bundled up to the nose, between my
father and mother, where nothing, not even the cold, could get
at me. The very perfection of happiness.

At something like the same age, I went for a ride, again
with my father and mother, on a riverboat at Havana, Ill. It was
a side-wheeler and the decks were screened, I suppose as protection against the mosquitoes. Across eight decades the name
of the steamboat comes back to me—the *Eastland*—bringing
with it the context of disaster. A year later, at the dock in Chicago, too many of the passengers crowded on one side, waving
goodbye, and it rolled over and sank. Trapped by the screens
everywhere, a great many people lost their lives. The fact that I
had been on this very steamboat, that I had escaped from a
watery grave, I continued to remember all through my childhood.

I have liked remembering almost as much as I have liked
living. But now it is different, I have to be careful. I can ruin a
night's sleep by suddenly, in the dark, thinking about some particular time in my life. Before I can stop myself it is as if I had
driven a mine shaft down through layers and layers of the past
and must explore, relive, remember, reconsider, until daylight
delivers me.

I have not forgotten the pleasure, when our children were
very young, of hoisting them onto my shoulders when their legs
gave out. Of reading to them at bedtime. Of studying their beautiful faces. But that was more than 30 years ago. I admire the
way that, as adults, they have taken hold of life, and I am glad

that they are not materialistic, but there is little or nothing I can do for them at this point, except write a little fable to put in their Christmas stocking. Our grandchild is too young to respond to any beguiling but his mother's and father's. It will be touch-and-go whether I live long enough for us to enjoy being in each other's company.

"Are you writing?" people ask—out of politeness, undoubtedly. And I say, "Nothing very much." The truth but not the whole truth—which is that I seem to have lost touch with the place that stories and novels come from. I have no idea why.

I still like making sentences.

Every now and then, in my waking moments, and especially when I am in the country, I stand and look hard at everything.

Emily Fox Gordon

Faculty Wife

They're nearly gone now, victims of attrition and destruction of habitat. The sociology of academic life may never record their dwindling and extinction.

I speak of the faculty wives of my mother's generation. Rare as they have become, I still spot them occasionally. That near-elderly woman I see on my walks, for example, out in the swampy fields gathering grasses; there is a diffuse benevolence in her aspect that marks her. And the museum docent leading a group of grade school children through the Gainsboroughs; surely she's one too. "Children," she whispers, leaning down to address them intimately, draping her arms around the necks of two representatives, "just look at the lady's shoulders. Aren't they just like two scoops of vanilla ice cream?"

I. THE KANGAS

Once at age ten, on my way home from school, I stood watching as two dogs mated in Mrs. B's yard. Neither of these belonged to anybody I knew—they were members of a pack of yellow, dingo-like dogs that roamed our small New England college town in those unregulated days. As I stood, ashamed and riveted, the strap of my bookbag cutting into my shoulder, watching the conjoined vibrating of these curs, Mrs. B emerged from the door of her house and padded out to join me. Mrs. B was a small woman who wore her glasses on a velveteen rope around her neck, walked on the balls of her feet and hummed airs from Mozart. "Isn't it fascinating!" she stage-whispered as she joined me, taking my arm while the glazed-eyed dogs shuddered to stillness and decoupled, the female, once released, twisting to snarl and snap at the male.

Mrs. B was insufferable, but she was happy and virtuous. She belonged to the subspecies of faculty wife that I've privately named the Kangas, after the intrusively maternal kangaroo in *Winnie the Pooh*. They were the super-competent elite. Their gardens spewed healthy produce; their homemade bread rose high and evenly pocked, their children were born gifted and raised according to psychoanalytically sound principles which the Kangas felt no compunctions about applying to the children of others whenever possible. That was what Mrs. B was doing on that fall afternoon when she mortified me so; she was demonstrating that I need feel no shame about my curiosity. She was commending to me an attitude of appreciative detachment toward all the processes of nature. Instead, of course, she opened up to me the true depth of my shame, acquainted me with the reek of my own horrified arousal. I will always associate that experience with the sulphurous smell of the egg-salad sandwich remnant lying smashed in the bottom of my bookbag.

Did she consider me capable of the detachment she modelled for me? Or was she deliberately shaming me? I remember her profile as we watched the dogs hump, the enlightened elevation of her chin, her lower lip slightly pursed. She lacked only a pair of opera glasses.

The Kanga households were a grid of interlocking fiefdoms circling the college campus. Their shaggy backyard gardens abutted one another, brandishing sunflowers and booby-trapped with monstrous zuchini marrows in August, still bearing frost-blighted brussels sprouts in October. My brother and I tromped a zigzag path through those gardens like bear cubs, foraging for tomatoes and beans.

On my way to school I heard snatches of violin and flute, also the whirr and thump of the kiln in Mrs. R's mudroom. I saw the sparks of Mrs. L's blowtorch as she worked in the garage she had converted into a sculptor's studio. And silent work was going on all around me; in the long spaces of school day afternoons sestinas and novellas were being composed.

This was the era of the Feminine Mystique, of women languishing in suburban isolation, manifesting their unhappiness somatically with ulcers and rashes. But Kangas (a demographically insignificant group, I'm sure, a tiny powerless elite) seemed immune to the general malaise. They were a vigorous bunch, highly educated and accomplished. Their musical consorts, book discussion groups, charitable and political activities all served to confirm these women in their conviction that their lives were beautiful and useful, even if their work was unpaid.

The Kangas consciously resisted the domestic cleanliness obsession which gripped American women in the fifties. The big Victorian houses they rented from the college were cluttered with evidence of their enthusiasms. Unwieldy arrangements of dried flowers spilled out of giant hand-thrown pots; surfaces were littered with childrens' collections of seashells and butterflies. Sometimes a harp or a loom occupied a corner of the living room. With Kangas, the rule was accretion; where they nested, culture thickened and deepened. Unpressed by the mold of employment, they grew into all the eccentric spaces of their differently cultivated leisure.

At the top of Kanga society was a select group of the older wives, the permanent staff of the Women's Exchange, a consignment shop which supported the local Visiting Nurses' Association. These were Kangas of an earlier generation, less educated than the post-war faculty wives and even more tightly bonded as a group. I spent many hours at the Exchange while my mother worked there as a volunteer; I remember lying on my back in a litter of snowsuits in the back room, inhaling dry cleaning fumes and staring up at a buzzing, blinking fluorescent light. I listened, on and off, to the conversation between the women working there. Sometimes they would exclaim over the quality of a new consignment—a clutch of the Rudolph girls' cashmere sweaters, perhaps, in six pastel shades, never worn—and their voices would lower and hover together deploringly as they allowed themselves the pleasure of touching the soft wool. Or they would speak more softly yet—this was always my cue to listen hard—about failed marriages, illnesses, birth defects. The older wives were amateur eugenicists, shrewd judges of the health and viability of newborns. Often I heard them speak about "good" and "bad" faces, and when a local doctor's daughter dropped dead at age nineteen of an undiagnosed heart ailment they all swore that they had privately predicted it.

The most benign of the Kangas was my parents' friend M. She was a big, soft woman with a heap of disordered hair worn in an outsize twist. Her voice was more than musical; she was the only person I've ever known who consistently sang her speech.

M's house was full of dhurries, woven baskets, brass bowls, batik hangings, things commonplace enough nowadays, but exotic then. Here I'm reminded of an interesting generalization I can make about the faculty wives of my youth: their tastes and interests were culturally prophetic. As I've grown up and then older I've watched various customs and items of cuisine and decoration favored by my mother and her friends which were odd and singular at the time become trendy and widely disseminated. The Kangas grew their own herbs, ground their own coffee, cut up their own chickens and cooked them in olive oil, drank wine with meals, made sure that their children's diets included fiber, or "roughage" as they called it, inquired about the availability of endive at the A&P. They favored earth colors and matte surfaces. Now that I find these provisions and proclivities all around me it's as if my mother had been writ large and faint upon the culture.

M was a Californian exiled in a cold New England town where her expansiveness of spirit could never quite find room. The other Kangas viewed her enthusiasms—during a Polynesian phase she hosted a cocktail party in a grass skirt and a lei—with affectionate irony. I was grateful to her because she was kind to me in a way I could have found acceptable only in somebody whose air of breezy dissociation made her incapable of intrusiveness. Once when she was giving me a ride somewhere in her big rattling station wagon, she began to muse about me and my prospects. "How wonderful," she sang, "to get taller and stronger and just grow out of all the misunderstandings and fears. How wonderful to have all that time and to know that things will get better and better." She gestured extravagantly, but she kept her shining eyes turned forward toward the road and toward a vague and glorious vision of me and the transforming future. I felt a slight mortification at being reminded that for me there was nowhere to go but up. Even so, as she spoke I began to feel buoyed, like a grounded ship slowly lifted by the tide. She had good will by the gallon, and the impersonal banality of what she said served to dilute it enough so that I could absorb it.

In those days I was busy with a complicated internal project; at the same time I was trying to assimilate my mother's aesthetic (which contained her ethic) and casting about for alternatives to it. I had to do both simultaneously, because the more I attempted to apprentice myself to my mother, and the more I learned about her through this effort, the more I saw that her world-view would ultimately exclude me. So M and her big loose enthusiasms became significant to me; she lodged in the back of my mind and stayed. When I think of the future she imagined for me—and suffer the attendant shock of realizing that for me any such future is past—the picture that accompanies my thoughts is a Polynesian landscape, a stylized palm tree against a mauve and black sky.

II. THE PRINCETON PARTY

A faculty wife remnant seems to have survived into my own generation as well, but this group hardly recognizes itself as such. I would not have acknowledged myself as one of their number if my husband and daughter and I had not spent his sabbatical year seven years ago at the Institute for Advanced Study in Princeton.

There the "members" lived with their families in a housing complex on the grounds of the institution. The wives, or spouses, as the administration took pains always to call us, were mostly a self-selected group, or at least the Americans among us were. These were women who had chosen to accompany their husbands on leave. Absent were the professionals, the lawyers, business women, doctors, tenure-track academics. Present were the potters, the painters, the jewelry-makers, the academic "part-timers," the writers. Also present were some particularly enterprising and devoted mothers of small children. Kangas, in other words, were everywhere. My daughter, then five, tore around the grounds with her cohort of faculty brats, safe and free and watched over as she would never be again. For a year, she lived my childhood.

The Institute, where Einstein and Von Neumann once worked, was a weird place, full of cultural contradictions. The receptions we attended in the vine-covered Administration building were high-toned, chilly affairs. White-coated waiters circulated with flutes of champagne and nest-baskets of devilled quail eggs. Life in the housing units was another, humbler story: too poor to use the communal laundromat, the peasant mothers of young Chinese physicists stumped out of the units every morning to string hand-washed towels and sheets from tree to tree across the grounds.

The Institute was a reservation for faculty wives. We gathered daily at the school bus stop, a multicultural group wearing our coats over our pajamas, herding our children and breathing steam, shuffling in place to keep warm. We loaded the children onto the bus and then dispersed into our days of solitary unpaid busyness, our grocery shopping, house cleaning, reading, translating, flute playing, novel writing. We gathered again at three when the bus returned.

I had found myself so isolated in my daughter's early years that at first the daily bus stop ritual seemed a reassuring emblem of community. I felt the novelty of knowing that I was among my own kind. But soon I began to understand that it would be difficult to make friends among the wives. I looked at them more carefully and I saw all the stigmata of shyness. This generation of Kangas had been affected by some curious attenuation. Except for a few loud, hale, natural-leader types—and only a month or two were required to reveal these as even more deeply insecure than the rest of us—we were a self-doubting, introspective group, abashed and reproachful, accustomed to solitude. We wore our graying hair in long ponytails; we favored wraparound skirts with commodious pockets and Birkenstocks with knee socks. Our noses were raw from the continuous cold our children brought home from school. Many of us had suspended the connections to the world we had established back home—the part-time job in the library, the graduate program, the circle of supportive friends—and we resented the loss. I did some internal thrashing around that year, anxious that I was being left out of something and yet baffled about what that could be, eager both to identify myself with this group and to distance myself from it. I also began, haltingly, to work on a novel, the first really serious and sustained literary project I had ever attempted. I think I picked up something confirming in the air, just enough to get me started.

Early in the fall semester some of the Institute fellows and their spouses were invited to a Sunday brunch at the home of a Princeton professor, a gathering of academics, mostly philosophers with an interest in politics and the social sciences. In spite of the well-meaning efforts of our hosts, themselves both philosophers, to put everyone at ease, this was an intimidating occasion. Guests arranged themselves through the book-lined spaces of that house in the mysteriously non-random and meaningful way that guests always do. The pattern here was established early, and it was striking. One room reserved itself for the wives, who huddled together in a semi-circle, softly discussing vaccination reactions and orthodontia. Two of them were nursing babies.

In an adjoining room there was loud lively talk, punc-

tuated by the laugh of sudden, delighted insight that philosophers seem particularly prone to. Perhaps a third of these dispu-
tatious intellectuals were female, but they seemed a different
species than the wives in the other room; they were upright,
mobile, angular, assertive, expressive. They were, I was thinking
from my place among the Female Women in the other room,
the Female Men.

To move from one of these rooms to the other was to feel
a change in emotional weather so extreme that a kind of physical
barrier seemed to erect itself. I noticed a few of the male academics hovering at the doorway, sending two-fingered waves
and guilty smiles to their wives. But somehow they seemed to
balk at the prospect of actually entering the room. This scene
was too primitively female for comfort, and I suspect the sight
of breast-feeding made these men shy.

The only person who travelled freely between the two
zones was our hostess, a woman far too gracious not to make an
effort. She stood over us and offered anecdotes about her
daughter's infancy, but these stories soon began to sputter in the
face of our assembled passivity. (I think we were exaggerating
the bovine act out of hostility.) She had been careful to acquaint
herself with our interests, and several times she leaned into the
Female Women's room in an effort to coax one or another of us
out. "Julia," she would call, "didn't you write your dissertation
on the social contract in a Nepalese village? Why don't you
come out here and tell us about it?" But I was the only one to
take the bait and follow her. "Emily," said my hostess, drawing
me into the ambit of a famous intellectual whose books I had
read and admired, "wrote a doctoral dissertation on Kafka."

"Master's thesis," I corrected. "Ah," said the famous intellectual, giving me a faint, bilious smile and turning back to his
eager interlocutors. I had no choice but to return to the welcoming circle of round-shouldered women, remarking to myself
on the wild irony of this situation. Of all places and times, I
thought, to be relegated to the prison of gender, the home of
two distinguished married academics in Princeton, New Jersey,
in 1989 seemed the least likely.

In one room, a scene of vigorous free intellectual exchange, apparently genderless. In the other, like atavistic phantoms, a group of females, babies and small children who might as well be huddled on an earthen floor in a thatched hut, poking at a fire with sticks. (Two or three of the small children being monitored by the Female Women at the Princeton party actually belonged, I should add, to Female Men.) But, of course, strictly speaking, the dividing line here was not gender, because women stood on either side of it. Nor was it education or aptitude. Most of the Female Women had advanced degrees; all were highly intelligent. Instead, it was something more like temperament. For whatever reasons, and if only temporarily, the Female Women lacked the assertiveness and ambition of the Female Men. Or perhaps, to put it more positively, they felt the nurturing imperative more strongly. And of course, the Female Women lacked one thing essential in order to be taken seriously these days at a faculty party—a university affiliation.

Maybe the odd nature of this gathering was a product of the artificial situation from which it sprang—guests were chosen from the roster of the Institute's members, academics spending a year among strangers and forming bonds on the basis of shared intellectual interests and accomplishments. So perhaps the wives, along for the year's ride, were unduly thrown back on one another and on the common denominator of baby and child talk. But this is not an adequate explanation; I've seen the same dilemma many times since, plausibly diluted, at various faculty functions.

Our hosts' dismay and embarrassment were obvious; it couldn't have been comfortable for them to preside over this apartheid-riven afternoon. What was happening? Why were the wives so sullenly resistant to the efforts of our hostess to integrate us into this gathering? I think we were unconsciously reaching back into our sixties arsenal of passive-resistance ploys, playing that trump card of modern ideology, the claim to authenticity. We had lost the respect we felt was our due; we had been marginalized, and so we arranged ourselves in a tableau which we knew would instantly evoke a shock of guilty recognition. We were far too liberated to plant ourselves at our husbands' sides to smile artificially until the ordeal of the party ended. We would revert instead to a more primitive, more compelling set of images. We would act the part of Woman—the burdened, the earthbound, the oppressed.

Which was ridiculous, of course. Whatever room we occupied we were all of us members of a class of people who take for granted unprecedented comfort and liberty. We had freely chosen our roles. Even so, the Female Women had reason to feel defensive and depressed. We had lost access to the protective environmental niche that an earlier generation of faculty wives had enjoyed. Gone was the set of understandings and expectations which established the idea that a wife and mother could enrich and decorate her family life by bringing to it the benefits of her education, festooning it with her art and learning. She lived outside the real-world economy, but inside a private economy which rewarded her efforts with validation and approval. Some of this reward came from her husband and children, but perhaps even more of it issued from the sisterhood of faculty wives. Without this reward, the latter day Faculty Wife's efforts come to seem pointless to her, cranky and anachronistic.

III. BAD WIVES

I recall no such separation at my parents' parties, which were frequent. There was an absolute gender divide along professional lines, of course, no females at all among the faculty members. The men talked shop and the wives talked babies, but only at the beginning. As the evening progressed and the guests became more lubricated the room integrated itself; groups of fours and fives, only a few of them single-sex, began to form, dissolve, re-form. When viewed directly from above, high up on the stair landing (children were expected to perform one turn with the hors d'oeuvres tray and then vanish), these human constellations looked like blossoms or starfish drawn in rough outline.

With experience I was able to recognize the stages of the party: after an awkward half-hour the manic yammer began to build, the conversational groups slowly contracting, then flaring outward in reaction to the punchline of the joke or the point of the anecdote. At this moment the party would feel to me like something single and organic, a breathing beast.

The noise would begin to modulate and steady until it had attained a raga-like drone. Then began a gradual migration toward the periphery of the room and a slow trickling into other parts of the house. The convivial roar was replaced by intelligible words and phrases, spoken softly and with a new earnestness. Now that the guests were seated I could see that they had arranged themselves in pairs and threesomes, and that many women were talking to men who were not their husbands and many men were talking to women who were not their wives. The hectic flirtation, the explosion of Dionysian energy and noise in the earlier stages of the party: all that had been in the service of this scattering and rearranging, and finally, this coming to rest. Conversations during this latter phase of the party had a relaxed intimacy, a quality I would later come to recognize as post-coital. During this magic interval—the hour of the coffee cups—men and women got to know one another as equals. Real talk went on, or so it seemed to me from my post on the landing.

The element of flirting is utterly absent at the academic gatherings of today. (Let me disarm the reader's suspicion that I draw this conclusion only because nobody is flirting with me. Believe me; nobody is flirting with anybody at these functions.) Children are often present; alcohol is far less central than it was in my parents' day. These parties—mostly pot luck suppers and Sunday open houses—usually begin with the establishment of zones: wives and small children gather on the couch, recapitulating in less dramatic form the pattern of the Female Women at the Princeton party. The older wives cluster in the kitchen, overseeing the food, while young faculty and graduate students congregate near the beer cooler; senior members of the department find nooks in which to lean together talking serious shop. Thus the party continues until it reaches its sober, sensibly early end. It is all very cozy and wholesome, but to my mind it is as much like a party as a shopping mall is like a town square.

Some devil gets into me on these occasions and makes me behave badly, or want to. I'm irritated by the sight of these men and women with their innocent eyes, their gentle and slightly fuddled manners, helping themselves moderately to drink and grazing among the raw vegetables. Where is their aggression, I ask myself. Where is their lust? I feel cheated of my childhood expectation that adult life would be charged with violent emotion, and all the more aggrieved because it happens to be true that I would be content to enjoy violent emotion vicariously, if only somebody would provide me that gratification.

They seem capable, these academics, of peevishness and spite, but none of the forthright, elemental energy that people on the outside have in abundance. Especially as we all grow older, they begin to seem marsupial to me. They have lived too long in an unevolved paradise; no wonder they were unprepared when conditions changed and a horde of young theory mongers, red in tooth and claw, dropped from the trees and ate or colonized them.

I don't mean to imply that what went on at my parents' parties was seamy, that it was anything like the suburban adultery clusters one encounters in Updike's early fiction. My parents' parties served to acknowledge and release sexual tension in a socially sanctioned way, and for the most part they were harmless. Only a few guests seemed unable to resist the temptation to ride the beast of the party out the door.

Among these the most memorable was J, the wife of a distinguished sociologist, the mother of a large brood of children and overseer of a big messy ambitious Kanga household full of musical instruments, books, baskets of rotting apples and unfolded laundry. She was a plump, busty woman with a slightly overblown Celtic prettiness. I disliked her, partly because my mother did, but also because I dreaded her temper. She had a terrifying way of moving from a fugue-like state of dreamy preoccupation to sudden quivering rage with no intermediate steps. I have a vivid memory of her small feet in scuffed flats, planted on the dusty floorboards of their music room. As I tilt the memory upward I can see her face, broad and rosy with anger as she berates me for dropping her son's violin.

J took pains to preserve appearances; she volunteered at the Women's Exchange and played the cello in a local quartet, but she was very promiscuous. I remember watching her from my top of the stairs vantage point at a party. She stood on tiptoe as she talked animatedly with a much taller man, one hand flattened with spread fingers against her breastbone in the classic flirting position, the other flung across her half-open mouth and flaming cheek in feigned amazement. Her high color—it frightened me to look into the oven of her face—her insinuating smirks and roguish smiles, how all this amazed and repelled me. Rumors circulated about her affairs, at least one of which was certainly true: she served as the mistress of a disreputable townie, a figure of fear to faculty children, a big rough man with picket teeth and a perpetual five o'clock shadow who once clambered drunkenly onto a float at a football rally to imitate a woman wriggling into her girdle. Eventually J's marriage broke up. Later she married a wealthy widower within a month of his wife's death; the two could often be seen downtown, J clutching her frail husband's arm tightly and steering him from store to store. My mother and her friends clenched their teeth and rolled their eyes at the mention of her name.

J was one of the cautionary tales of my childhood, but she was also a kind of inspiration. I didn't like to think about, nor did I know enough to imagine, the couplings of J. and the disreputable townie. (Today I can picture them spilling out of a parked car on a rural road late at night. I can hear her coy shriek and his laughing growl as he pursues her through the long grass of a field and brings her down with a thump.) But she gave me a sense for the parameters of adult passion; even as I recoiled at her gaminess I marvelled at the power of what burned in her. "She thinks with her glands," I overheard my mother say, and I wondered how she had mastered that trick and if one day I might be able to do it too.

I believe that what J did in her life would be impossible for a similarly situated woman today. She lived out a specifically female destiny, one fated to end in low comedy or in tragedy, or in some mixture of the two. Such a destiny is no longer available to a woman of J's socioeconomic class. While a woman might be just as compulsively unfaithful as J, society is no longer configured so as to register her actions, to mirror her back to herself as anything but unhappy. And nobody has time or energy to go in for promiscuity as a calling. My own daughter has no such bad examples to watch and wonder at. It would be hard to imagine the mothers of her friends in the role of courtesan or harlot. They are lean and healthy and tense; they wear beepers on their belts and carry daily planners in their bags. My daughter gets her notions more efficiently than I got mine; she watches MTV, where Salt 'n' Pepa do squats and point at their vulvas.

One often hears the African folk-saying that it takes a village to raise a child. True enough, but it also takes a village to produce a first-class adulteress.

IV. FEMINA LUDENS

At least for a while, our small town college society provided J just the combination of reluctant tolerance and steady, mild disapprobation that she required.

It was not so kind to R, a painter who looked like a dancer past her prime. She dressed in leotards and calf-length skirts. Her face was as pale as Anais Nin's, her hair a bleached, broomshaped helmet. She drank heavily even by the standard of that place and those days, when two stiff drinks before dinner and wine with it were a daily ritual. I can summon up a clear image of R drinking publicly—in front of people and at somebody's house—straight out of a bottle of gin. But that picture may come from the vault of apocrypha that occupies half my memory.

R was married to a historian, a tall man whose wry insouciance was undercut by weariness. She seemed constantly in a rage—I remember making way for her on the sidewalk as she

Guy Davenport

On Reading

To my Aunt Mae—Mary Elizabeth Davenport Morrow (1881–1964), whose diary when I saw it after her death turned out to be a list of places, with dates, she and Uncle Buzzie (Julius Allen Morrow, 1885–1970) had visited over the years, never driving over thirty miles an hour, places like Toccoa Falls, Georgia, and Antreville, South Carolina, as well as random sentences athwart the page, two of which face down indifference, "My father was a horse doctor, but not a common horse doctor" and "Nobody has ever loved me as much as I have loved them"—and a Mrs. Cora Shiflett, a neighbor on East Franklin Street, Anderson, South Carolina, I owe my love of reading.

Mrs. Shiflett, one of that extensive clan of the name, all retaining to this day the crofter mentality of the Scots Lowlands from which they come, a mixture of rapacity and despair (Faulkner called them Snopes), had rented a house across the street from us formerly occupied, as long as I could remember, by another widow, Mrs. Spoone ("with an *e*"), she and her son, whom we never saw, as he was doing ten years "in the penitencher." But before Mrs. Shiflett's son, "as good a boy to his mother as ever was," fell into some snare of the law, he had been a great reader. And one fateful day Mrs. Shiflett, who wore a bonnet and apron to authenticate her respectability as a good countrywoman, brought with her, on one of her many visits to "set a spell" with my mother, a volume of the Tarzan series, one in which Tarzan saves himself from perishing of thirst in the Sahara by braining a vulture and drinking its blood. She lent it to me. "Hit were one of the books Clyde loved in particular."

I do not have an ordered memory, but I know that this work of Edgar Rice Burroughs was the first book I read. I was thought to be retarded as a child, and all the evidence indicates that I was. I have no memory of the first grade, to which I was not admitted until I was seven, except that of peeing my pants and having to be sent home whenever I was spoken to by our hapless teacher. I have even forgotten her appearance and her name, and I call her hapless because there was a classmate, now a psychiatrist, who fainted when he was called on, and another who stiffened into petit mal. I managed to control my bladder by the third grade, but the fainter and the sufferer from fits, both classmates of mine through the ninth grade, when I quit school, kept teachers edgy until graduation.

No teacher in grammar or high school ever so much as hinted that reading was a normal activity, and I had to accept, as my family did, that it was part of my affliction as a retarded person. The winter afternoon on which I discovered that I could follow Tarzan and Simba and some evil Arab slave traders was the first in a series of by now fifty years of sessions in chairs with books. I read very slowly, and do not read a great deal as I would much rather spend my leisure painting and drawing, or writing, and I do not have all that much leisure. And as a teacher of literature I tend to read the same books over and over, year after year, to have them fresh in my mind for lectures.

From *Tarzan,* which I did not read efficiently (and Burroughs's vocabulary runs to the exotic), I moved on to available books. My father had a small library of a hundred or so, from which I tried a *Collected Writings of Victor Hugo,* mysteriously inscribed in my father's hand, "G.M. Davenport, Apr. 24, 1934, Havana, Cuba," where I am positive my father never set foot.

Under this inscription, he (or somebody) drew a cube, in ink that bled through to appear on the other surface of the page, on Victor Hugo's forehead in a frontispiece engraving. But Hugo is not Edgar Rice Burroughs, and I could make nothing of him.

Aunt Mae had inherited, with pride, the small library of my uncle Eugene, a soldier in World War I, buried in France a decade before my birth. This contained a complete Robert Louis Stevenson and James Fenimore Cooper, both of whom proved to be over my head. But there was a picture book of Pompeii and Herculaneum, which opened a door of a different sort, giving me my first wondering gaze into history and art. Aunt Mae was herself addicted to the novels of Zane Grey, whom I lumped in with Victor Hugo as a writer unable to get on with what he had to say, as bad at dawdling as Cooper.

And then I made the disovery that what I liked in reading was to learn things I didn't know. Aunt Mae's next-door neighbor, Mrs. McNinch, belonged to the Book-of-the-Month Club, which in 1938—I was eleven—sent its subscribers Antonina Vallentin's *Leonardo da Vinci.* Mrs. McNinch, a woman of fervent piety and a Presbyterian, had chosen this book because of *The Last Supper.* She lent it to me. I had not known until the wholly magic hours I spent reading it, all of a wet spring, that such a man as Leonardo was possible, and I was hearing of the Renaissance for the first time. I read this difficult book in a way I can no longer imagine. I pretended, I think, that I was following the plot and the historical digressions. I have not reread this book and yet I can in lectures cite details of Leonardo's career from it. Or think I can. I have read some forty studies of Leonardo since, and many books about his epoch, and may be fooling myself as to which source I'm remembering. But I can still see all the illustrations, the codex pages in sepia, the paintings in color.

When I returned the biography of Leonardo, the generous Mrs. McNinch lent me Carl Van Doren's *Benjamin Franklin,* also published in 1938 and a Book-of-the-Month Club selection. This was harder going, with phrases like "minister plenipotentiary," which I would mutter secretly to myself. It is a truism that reading educates. What it does most powerfully is introduce the world outside us, negating the obstructions of time and place. When, much later, I ran across the word *opsimathy* in Walter Pater, I could appreciate the tragic implications of late learning. All experience is synergetic: Bucky Fuller should have written, and probably did, about the phenomenon of Synergetic Surprise. We cannot guess what potential lies in wait for the imagination through momentum alone. The earlier Leonardo and Franklin enter one's mind, the greater the possibility of their bonding and interacting with ongoing experience and information.

My childhood was far from bookish. I spent a lot of it hunting and fishing, searching Georgia and South Carolina fields for arrowheads, longing to work on the Blue Ridge Railroad, playing softball in the street, building tree houses. The hunting was done with my Uncle Broadus Dewey on Saturdays with a bird dog named Joe. Joe was gun-shy and had conniption fits with pitiful howls when we took a shot at game. Many lives were spared, of squirrels and partridges and rabbits, to spare Joe's nerves. I myself never managed to shoot anything. What I liked was the outing and the comradeship and pretending to have Leonardo's eyes in looking at plants, rocks, the landscape. Back from hunting, I would try to imitate a page of the notebooks. On manila construction paper from Woolworth's I would draw in brown ink leaves in clusters, and rocks, and insects, hoping that the page resembled one by Leonardo.

When the first American paperbacks came along, they, too, opened other worlds: Sherlock Holmes and other detective fiction, leading me to read people in the Holmesian manner at the barbershop and on the street.

I now have ample evidence for tracing synergies in reading. A few summers ago I spent a beautiful day in Auvers-sur-Oise, standing by the graves of Vincent and Theo. The wheat field is still unmistakably there, across the road from where they are buried against the cemetery wall, the Protestant place; and Gachet's house and garden. This day began with Irving Stone's trashy and irresponsible biography and the hilariously vulgar film based on it, but one must begin somewhere. Opsimathy differs from early learning in that there are no taproots, no years of crossbreeding, no naturalization in a climate.

After I had taught myself to read, without reading friends or family, I kept at it, more or less unaware of what hunger I was feeding. I can remember when I read any book, as the act of reading adheres to the room, the chair, the season. Doughty's *Arabia Deserta* I read under the hundred-year-old fig tree in our backyard in South Carolina, a summer vacation from teaching at Washington University, having lucked onto the two volumes (minus the map that ought to have been in a pocket in vol. II) at a St. Louis rummage sale. (The missing map was given to me fifteen years later by Issam Safady, the Jordanian scholar.)

I read most of Willa Cather and Mann's Joseph tetralogy in the post library at Fort Bragg. The ordnance repair shop was on one side, the stockade on the other, and I was "keeping up my education" on orders from the adjutant general of the XVIIIth Airborne Corps, who kindly gave me Wednesday afternoons off specifically to read.

Proust I began among the spring blossoms of the Sarah P. Duke gardens in Durham, North Carolina, and finished forty years later by my fireplace in Lexington, Kentucky, convalescing from a very difficult operation to remove an embedded kidney stone. These settings are not merely sentimental; they are real interrelations. The moment of reading is integral to the process. My knowledge of Griaule's *Le renard pâle* is interwoven with my reading a large part of it in the Greenville, South Carolina, Trailways bus station. Yeats's *A Vision* belongs to the Hôtel Monsieur-le-Prince, once on the street of that name, as does *Nightwood* and *Black Spring. The Seven Pillars,* an Oxford room; *Fanny Hill,* the Haverford cricket field. And not all readings are nostalgic: the conditions under which I made my way through the *Iliad* in Greek were the violence and paralyzing misery of a disintegrating marriage, for which abrasion, nevertheless, the meaning of the poem was the more tragic. There are texts I can never willingly return to because of the misery adhering to them.

Students often tell me that an author was ruined for them by a high-school English class; we all know what they mean. Shakespeare was almost closed to me by the world's dullest teacher, and there are many writers whom I would probably enjoy reading except that they were recommended to me by suspect enthusiasts. I wish I knew how to rectify these aversions. I tell bright students, in conference, how I had to find certain authors on my own who were ruined for me by bad teachers or inept critics. Scott, Kipling, Wells will do to illustrate that only an idiot will take a critic's word without seeing for oneself. I think I learned quite early that the judgments of my teachers were probably a report of their ignorance. In truth, my education was a systematic misleading. Ruskin was dismissed as a dull, preacherly old fart who wrote purple prose. In a decent society the teacher who led me to believe this would be tried, found guilty, and hanged by the thumbs while being pelted with old eggs and cabbage stalks. I heard in a class at Duke that Joyce's *Ulysses* was a tedious account of the death of Molly Bloom. An Oxford don assured me that Edmund Wilson is an astute critic. Around what barriers did I have to force my way to get to Pound, to Joyce, to William Carlos Williams?

All of this points to our having a society that reads badly and communicates execrably about what we read. The idea persists that writing is an activity of thoughtful, idealistic, moral people called authors and that they are committed to protecting certain values vital to a well-ordered society. Books mold character, enforce patriotism, and provide a healthy way to pass the leisurely hour. To this assumption there has been added in our day the image of the author as a celebrity, someone worth hearing at a reading or lecture even if you have no intention of parting with a dime for one of the author's books.

There is little room in this popular concept of writing for the apprehension and appreciation of style. I had all along, I would like to think, been responding to style in my earliest attempts to read. I knew that the books I failed to enjoy—Scott's *The Black Dwarf* was the worst of these—were texts that remained foggy and indeterminate, like a moving picture experienced through bad eyesight and defective hearing. Style is radically cultural both linguistically and psychologically. I couldn't read Scott, Stevenson, and Cooper because I had not developed the imaginative agility needed to close the distance between me and the style of their texts. I could read, with excitement and a kind of enchantment, the biographies I encountered so early of Leonardo and Franklin not only because my curiosity about them was great, but because these biographies were in a contemporary, if academic, English.

My discovery of style came about through various humble books. Hendrik Van Loon's whimsical history of the world (a Pocket Book from Woolworth's) alerted me to the fact that tone makes all the difference. It was this book that began to make something of an aesthete of me, for I progressed to Van Loon's biography of Rembrandt (conflating the rich experience of the Leonardo biography with the pleasure of reading for style), a book I kept reading for the pleasure of the prose, despite my ignorance of his historical setting. In it, however, I saw the name Spinoza, which led me to dear old Will Durant, who led me to Spinoza's texts, and all fellow readers who have ever taken a book along to a humble restaurant will understand my saying that life has few enjoyments as stoical and pure as reading Spinoza's *Ethics,* evening after evening, in a strange city—St. Louis, before I made friends there. The restaurant was Greek, cozy, comfortable, and for the neighborhood. The food was cheap, tasty, and filling.

Over white beans with chopped onions, veal cutlet with a savory dressing, and eventually a fruit cobbler and coffee, I read the *De Ethica* in its Everyman edition, Draftech pen at the ready to underline passages I might want to refind easily later. Soul and mind were being fed together. I have not eaten alone in a restaurant in many years, but I see others doing it and envy them.

At some time, as a freshman in college I would guess, my pleasure in style came together with the inevitable duty of having to read for content. I became increasingly annoyed with inept styles, like James Michener's, or styles that did violence to the language (and thus knew nothing of sociology until I could read it in French), with the turkey gobble of politicians and the rev. clergy. I began to search out writers whose style, as I was learning to see, was an indication that what they had to say was worth knowing. This was by no means an efficient or intellectually respectable procedure. I found Eric Gill's writing (all of which has evaporated from my mind), Spengler (all retained), Faulkner (then unknown to my English profs), Joyce (whose name I found in Thomas Wolfe), Dostoyevsky.

A memory: I was desperately poor as an undergraduate at Duke, did not belong to a fraternity, and except for a few like-minded friends (Dan Patterson, who was to become the great student of Shaker music; Bob Loomis, the Random House editor; Clarence Brown, the translator and biographer of Osip Mandelstam) was romantically and self-indulgently lonely. I was already learning the philosophical simpleness that would get me through life, and I remember a Saturday when I was the only person in the library. I took out Faulkner's *Absalom, Absalom!* (buff paper, good typography) and went back to my room. I felt, somehow, with everybody else out partying (Dan Patterson was practicing the piano in the basement of Duke chapel), Faulkner deserved my best. I showered, washed my hair, put on fresh clothes, and with one of Bob Loomis's wooden-tipped cigars, for the wickedness of it, made myself comfortable and opened the Faulkner to hear Miss Rosa Coldfield telling Quentin Compson about Thomas Sutpen.

So it went with my education. God knows what I learned from classes; very little. I read Santayana instead of my philosophy text (the style of which sucked), I read *Finnegans Wake* instead of doing botany (in which I made an F, and sweet Professor Anderson, that great name in photosynthesis, wrote on the postcard that conveyed the F, "You have a neat and attractive handwriting"). Instead of paying attention to psychology I made a wide study of Klee and Goya.

On a grander scale I got the same kind of education at Oxford and Harvard, where I read on my own while satisfying course requirements. I can therefore report that the nine years

of elementary schooling, four of undergraduate, and eight of
graduate study were technically games of futility. If, now, I had
at my disposal as a teacher only what I learned from the formalities of education, I could not possibly be a university professor. I
wouldn't know anything. I am at least still trying. I've kept most
of my textbooks and still read them (and am getting pretty good
at botany).

Wendell Berry, that thoughtful man, once remarked that
teachers are like a farmer dropping an acorn into the ground.
Some years will pass before the oak comes to maturity. We give
grades, and lecture, and do the best we can. But we cannot see
what we have done for many years to come. In setting out to
write about the pleasure of reading, I find that I have equated
my private, venturesome reading with my education, such as it
is. There's much to be learned from this. All useful knowledge is
perhaps subversive, innocently and ignorantly so at first. I assumed, with the wisdom of children, that it was best not to
mention to my fourth- and fifth-grade teachers, Miss Taylor
(who made us all take a Pledge of Lifelong Abstinence from
Alcohol) and Miss Divver, that I had read Antonina Vallentin's
Leonardo and Van Doren's *Franklin,* and wanted very much, if I
could find them, to read *Frankenstein* and *Dracula.*

I also read in those grammar-school years the nine volumes of Alexander Dumas's *Celebrated Crimes,* a dozen or so
volumes of E. Phillips Oppenheim, and the three-volume *Century Dictionary* (I have always accepted dictionaries and encyclopedias as good reading matter).

Last year I met a young man in his twenties who is illiterate; there are more illiterates in Kentucky than anywhere else,
with the possible exception of the Philippines and Haiti. The
horror of his predicament struck me first of all because it prevents his getting a job, and secondly because of the blindness it
imposes on his imagination. I also realized more fully than ever
before what a text is and how it can only be realized in the
imagination, how mere words, used over and over for other
purposes and in other contexts, can be so ordered by, say, Jules
Verne, as to be deciphered as a narrative of intricate texture and

splendid color, of precise meanings and values. At the time of
the illiterate's importuning visits (I was trying to help him find a
job) I was reading Verne's *Les enfants du capitaine Grant,* a
geography book cunningly disguised as an adventure story, for
French children, a hefty two-volume work. I had never before
felt how lucky and privileged I am, not so much for being literate, a state of grace that might in different circumstances be
squandered on tax forms or law books, but for being able, regularly, to get out of myself completely, to be somewhere else,
among other minds, and return (by laying my book aside) renewed and refreshed.

For the real use of imaginative reading is precisely to sus-
pend one's mind in the workings of another sensibility, quite
literally to give oneself over to Henry James or Conrad or
Ausonius, to Yuri Olyesha, Bashō, and Plutarch.

The mind is a self-consuming organ and preys on itself. It
is an organ for taking the outside in. A wasp has a very simple
ganglion of nerves for a brain, a receptor of color, smell, and
distances. It probably doesn't think at all, and if it could write,
all it would have to say would concern the delicious smell of
female wasps and fermenting pears, hexagonalities in various
material (wood fiber, paper) in the architecture of nests, with
maybe some remarks on azimuths (for the young). Angels, to
move to the other pole of being, write history and indictments
only, and if Satan has written his memoirs they would read like
Frank Harris, and who would want to read them?

Music is as close as we will get to angelic discourse. Literature comes next, with a greater measure than music can claim of
the fully human. I am on slippery ground here, as the two arts
can share natures. *Don Giovanni* and the *Mass in B Minor* are
both music and literature; all of what we now call poetry was for
many centuries song. Even if we had all of Sappho's texts, we
would still be without the tunes to which they were sung—like
having only the libretto of *The Magic Flute.*

Shakespeare's sonnets and the *Duino Elegies* are a kind of
music in themselves.

By "fully human" I mean *The Miller's Tale* and Don *Qui-*

xote, Surtees and *Humphry Clinker,* Rabelais and Queneau. The fully human is suspect in our society; Kentucky high schools keep banning *As I Lay Dying.* We do not read enough to have seen that literature itself is not interested in the transcendental role society has assumed for it. The pleasure of reading has turned out not to be what our culture calls pleasure at all. The most imperceptive psychologist or even evangelist can understand that television idiotizes and blinds while reading makes for intelligence and perception.

Why? How? I wish I knew. I also wish I knew why millions of bright American children turn overnight into teenage nerds. The substitution of the automobile for the natural body, which our culture has effected in the most evil perversion of humanity since chivalry, is one cause; narcosis by drugs and Dionysian music is another. I cannot say that an indifference to literature is another cause; it isn't. It's a symptom, and one of our trivializing culture's great losses. We can evince any number of undeniable beliefs—an informed society cannot be enslaved by ideologies and fanaticism, a cooperative pluralistic society must necessarily be conversant with the human record in books of all kinds, and so on—but we will always return to the private and inviolable act of reading as our culture's way of developing an individual.

Aunt Mae didn't read the books she inherited from Uncle Eugene, slain in France fighting for my and your right to read what we want to. She read *Cosmopolitan* and *Collier's* and "the *Grit.*" And Zane Grey. She knew, however, that books are important, to be kept right-side up on a shelf in the living room near her plaster-of-Paris life-size statue of Rin Tin Tin.

The world is a labyrinth in which we keep traversing familiar crossroads we had thought were miles away, but to which we are doomed to backtrack. Every book I have read is in a Borgesian series that began with the orange, black, and mimosa-green clothbound *Tarzan* brought to me as a kindly gift by Mrs. Shiflett in her apron and bonnet. And the name Shiflett, I know because of books, is the one Faulkner transmuted to Snopes. And Aunt Mae, whose father was a horse doctor but not a common horse doctor, looked down her nose at the Shifletts of this world as common white trash (she was an accomplished snob, Aunt Mae). A few years ago, exploring the Cimitière des Chiens et Chats in Paris, I came upon the grave of Rin Tin Tin, Grande Vedette du Cinema, and felt the ghost of Aunt Mae, who had always intended "to visit the old country," very much with me, for I'm old enough to know that all things are a matter of roots and branches, of spiritual seeds and spiritual growth, and that I would not have been in Paris at all, not, anyway, as a scholar buying books and tracking down historical sites and going to museums with educated eyes rather than eyes blank with ignorance, if, in the accident of things, Aunt Mae and Mrs. Shiflett had not taken the responsibility of being custodians of the modest libraries of a brother and a son, so that I could teach myself to read.

Gilles Deleuze

Bartleby, or The Formula

"Bartleby" is neither a metaphor for the writer nor the symbol of anything whatsoever. It is a violently comical text, and the comical is always literal. It is like the novellas of Kleist, Dostoyevsky, Kafka, or Beckett, with which it forms a subterranean and prestigious lineage. It means only what it says, literally. And what it says and repeats is *I would prefer not to*. This is the formula of its glory, which every loving reader repeats in turn. A gaunt and pallid man has uttered the formula that drives everyone crazy. But in what does the literality of the formula consist?

We immediately notice a certain mannerism, a certain solemnity: *prefer* is rarely employed in this sense, and neither Bartleby's boss, the attorney, nor his clerks normally use it ("queer word, I never use it myself"). The usual formula would instead be *I had rather not*. But the strangeness of the formula goes beyond the word itself. Certainly it is grammatically correct, syntactically correct, but its abrupt termination, NOT TO, which leaves what it rejects undetermined, confers upon it the character of a radical, a kind of limit-function. Its repetition and its insistence render it all the more unusual, entirely so. Murmured in a soft, flat, and patient voice, it attains to the irremissible, by forming an inarticulate block, a single breath. In all these respects, it has the same force, the same role as an *agrammatical* formula.

Linguists have rigorously analyzed what is called "agrammaticality." A number of very intense examples can be found in the work of the American poet e. e. cummings—for instance, "he danced his did," as if one said in French *il dansa son mit* ("he danced his began") instead of *il se mit à danser* ("he began to dance"). Nicolas Ruwet explains that this presupposes a series of ordinary grammatical variables, which would have an agrammatical formula as their limit: *he danced his did* would be a limit of the normal expressions *he did his dance, he danced his dance, he danced what he did* . . . [1] This would no longer be a portmanteau word, like those found in Lewis Carroll, but a "portmanteau-construction," a breath-construction, a limit or tensor. Perhaps it would be better to take an example from the French, in a practical situation: someone who wants to hang something on a wall and holds a certain number of nails in his hand exclaims, J'EN AI UN DE PAS ASSEZ ("I have one not enough"). This is an agrammatical formula that stands as the limit of a series of correct expressions: *J'en ai de trop, Je n'en ai pas assez, Il m'en manque un* . . . ("I have too many," "I don't have enough," "I am one short" . . .). Would not Bartleby's formula be of this type, at once a stereotypy of Bartleby's and a highly poetic expression of Melville's, the limit of a series such as "I would prefer this. I would prefer not to do that. That is not what I would prefer . . ."? Despite its quite normal construction, it has an anomalous ring to it.

I WOULD PREFER NOT TO. The formula has several variants. Sometimes it abandons the conditional and becomes more curt: I PREFER NOT TO. Sometimes, as in its final occurrences, it seems to lose its mystery by being completed by an infinitive, and coupled with *to:* "I prefer to give no answer," "I would prefer not to be a little reasonable," "I would prefer not to take a clerkship," "I would prefer to be doing something else" . . . But even in these cases we sense the muted presence of the strange form that continues to haunt Bartleby's language. He himself adds, "but I am not a particular case," "there is nothing particular about me," *I am not particular,* in order to indicate that whatever else might be suggested to him would be yet another particularity falling under the ban of the great indeterminate formula, I PREFER NOT TO, which subsists once and for all and in all cases.

The formula occurs in ten principal circumstances, and in each case it may appear several times, whether it is repeated verbatim or with minor variations. Bartleby is a copyist in the attorney's office; he copies ceaselessly, "silently, palely, mechanically." The first instance takes place when the attorney tells him to proofread and collate the two clerks' copies: I WOULD PREFER NOT TO. The second, when the attorney tells Bartleby to come and reread his own copies. The third, when the attorney invites Bartleby to reread with him personally, tête à tête. The fourth, when the attorney wants to send him on an errand. The fifth, when he asks him to go into the next room. The sixth, when the attorney enters his study one Sunday afternoon and discovers that Bartleby has been sleeping there. The seventh, when the attorney satisfies himself by asking questions. The eighth, when Bartleby has stopped copying, has renounced all copying, and the attorney asks him to leave. The ninth, when the attorney makes a second attempt to get rid of him. The tenth, when Bartleby is forced out of the office, sits on the banister of the landing while the panic-stricken attorney proposes other, unexpected occupations to him (a clerkship in a dry goods store, bartender, bill collector, traveling companion to a young gentleman . . .). The formula bourgeons and proliferates. At each occurrence, there is a stupor surrounding Bartleby, as if one had heard the Unspeakable or the Unstoppable. And there is Bartleby's silence, as if he had said everything and exhausted language at the same time. With each instance, one has the impression that the madness is growing: not Bartleby's madness in "particular," but the madness around him, notably that of the attorney, who launches into strange propositions and even stranger behaviors.

Without a doubt, the formula is ravaging, devastating, and

leaves nothing standing in its wake. Its contagious character is immediately evident: Bartleby "ties the tongues" of others. The queer words, *I would prefer*, steal their way into the language of the clerks and of the attorney himself ("So you have got the word, too"). But this contamination is not the essential point; the essential point is its effect on Bartleby: from the moment he says I WOULD PREFER NOT TO (collate), he is no longer *able* to copy either. And yet he will never say that he prefers not to (copy): he has simply passed beyond this stage. And doubtless he does not realize this immediately, since he continues copying until after the sixth instance. But when he does notice it, it seems obvious, like the delayed reaction that was already implied in the first statement of the formula: "Do you not see the reason for yourself?" he says to the attorney. The effect of the formula-block is not only to impugn what Bartleby prefers not to do, but also to render what he was doing impossible, what he was supposed to prefer to continue doing.

It has been noted that the formula, I prefer not to, is neither an affirmation nor a negation. Bartleby "does not refuse, but neither does he accept, he advances and then withdraws into this advance, barely exposing himself in a nimble retreat from speech."[2] The attorney would be relieved if Bartleby did not want to, but Bartleby does not refuse, he simply rejects a nonpreferred (the proofreading, the errands . . .). And he does not accept either, he does not affirm a preference that would consist in continuing to copy, he simply posits its impossibility. In short, the formula that successively refuses every other act has already engulfed the act of copying, which it no longer even needs to refuse. The formula is devastating because it eliminates the preferable just as mercilessly as any nonpreferred. It not only abolishes the term it refers to, and that it rejects, but also abolishes the other term it seemed to preserve, and that becomes impossible. In fact, it renders them indistinct: it hollows out an ever expanding zone of indiscernibility or indetermination between some nonpreferred activities and a preferable activity. All particularity, all reference is abolished. The formula annihilates "copying," the only reference in relation to which something might or might not be preferred. I would prefer nothing rather than something: not a will to nothingness, but the growth of a nothingness of the will. Bartleby has won the right to survive, that is, to remain immobile and upright before a blind wall. Pure patient passivity, as Blanchot would say. Being as being, and nothing more. He is urged to say yes or no. But if he said no (to collating, running errands . . .), or if he said yes (to copying), he would quickly be defeated and judged useless, and would not survive. He can survive only by whirling in a suspense that keeps everyone at a distance. His means of survival is to prefer *not* to collate, but thereby also *not* to prefer copying. He had to refuse the former in order to render the latter impossible. The formula has two phases and continually recharges itself by passing again and again through the same states. This is why the attorney has the vertiginous impression, each time, that everything is starting over again from zero.

The formula at first seems like the bad translation of a foreign language. But once we understand it better, once we hear it more clearly, its splendor refutes this hypothesis. Perhaps it is the formula that carves out a kind of foreign language within language. It has been suggested that e. e. cummings's agrammaticalities can be considered as having issued from a dialect differing from Standard English, and whose rules of creation can be abstracted. The same goes for Bartleby: the rule would lie in this logic of negative preference, a negativism beyond all negation. But if it is true that the masterpieces of literature always form a kind of foreign language within the language in which they are written, what wind of madness, what psychotic breath thereby passes into language as a whole? Psychosis characteristically brings into play a *procedure* that treats an ordinary language, a standard language, in a manner that makes it "render" an original and unknown language, which would perhaps be a projection of God's language, and would carry off language as a whole. Procedures of this type appear in France in Roussel and Brisset, and in America in Wolfson. Is this not the schizophrenic vocation of American literature: to make the English language, by means of driftings, deviations, de-taxes or surtaxes (as opposed to the standard syntax), slip in this manner? To introduce a bit of psychosis into English neurosis? To invent a new universality? If need be, other languages will be summoned into English in order to make it echo this divine language of storm and thunder. Melville invents a foreign language that runs beneath English and carries it off: it is the OUTLANDISH or Deterritorialized, the language of the Whale. Whence the interest of studies of *Moby-Dick* that are based on Numbers and Letters, and their cryptic meaning, to set free at least a skeleton of the inhuman or superhuman originary language.[3] It is as if three operations were linked together: a certain treatment of language; the result of this treatment, which tends to constitute an original language within language; and the effect, which is to sweep up language in its entirety, sending it into flight, pushing it to its very limit in order to discover its Outside, silence or music. A great book is always the inverse of another book that could only be written in the soul, with silence and blood. This is the case not only with *Moby-Dick* but also with *Pierre*, in which Isabelle affects language with an incomprehensible murmur, a kind of *basso continuo* that carries the whole of language on the chords and tones of its guitar. And it is also the angelic or adamic Billy Budd, who suffers from a stuttering that denatures language but also gives rise to the musical and celestial Beyond of language as a whole. It is like the "persistent horrible twittering squeak" that muddles the resonance of words, while the sister is getting the violin ready to respond to Gregor.

Bartleby also has an angelic and Adamic nature, but his case seems different because he has no general Procedure, such as stuttering, with which to treat language. He makes do with a seemingly normal, brief Formula, at best a localized tick that crops up in certain circumstances. And yet the result and the effect are the same: to carve out a kind of foreign language within language, to make the whole confront silence, make it topple into silence. *Bartleby* announces the long silence, broken only by the music of poems, into which Melville will enter and from which, except for *Billy Budd*, he will never emerge.[4] Bartleby himself had no other escape than to remain silent and withdraw behind his partition every time he uttered the formula, all the way up until his final silence in prison. After the formula there is nothing left to say: it functions as a procedure, overcoming its appearance of particularity.

The attorney himself concocts a theory explaining how Bartleby's formula ravages language as a whole. All language, he suggests, has references or assumptions. These are not exactly what language designates, but what permit it to designate. A word always presupposes other words that can replace it, complete it, or form alternatives with it: it is on this condition that language is distributed in such a way as to designate things, states of things and actions, according to a set of objective, explicit conventions. But perhaps there are also other implicit and subjective conventions, other types of reference or presupposition. In speaking, I do not simply indicate things and actions; I also commit acts that assure a relation with the interlocutor, in keeping with our respective situations: I command, I interrogate, I promise, I ask, I emit "speech acts." Speech acts are self-referential (I command by saying "I order you . . ."), while constative propositions refer to other things and other words. It is this double system of references that Bartleby ravages.

The formula I PREFER NOT TO excludes all alternatives, and devours what it claims to conserve no less than it distances itself from everything else. It implies that Bartleby stop copying, that is, that he stop reproducing words; it hollows out a zone of indetermination that renders words indistinguishable, that creates a vacuum within language *[langage]*. But it also stymies the speech acts that a boss uses to command, that a kind friend uses to ask questions or a man of faith to make promises. If Bartleby had refused, he could still be seen as a rebel or insurrectionary, and as such would still have a social role. But the formula stymies all speech acts, and at the same time, it makes Bartleby a pure outsider *[exclu]* to whom no social position can be attributed. This is what the attorney glimpses with dread: all his hopes of bringing Bartleby back to reason are dashed because they rest on a *logic of presuppositions* according to which an employer "expects" to be obeyed, or a kind friend listened to, whereas Bartleby has invented a new logic, *a logic of preference,* which is enough to undermine the presuppositions of language as a whole. As Mathieu Lindon shows, the formula "disconnects" words and things, words and actions, but also speech acts and words—it severs language from all reference, in accordance with Bartleby's absolute vocation, *to be a man without references,* someone who appears suddenly and then disappears, without reference to himself or anything else.[5] This is why, despite its conventional appearance, the formula functions as a veritable agrammaticality.

Bartleby is the Bachelor, about whom Kafka said, "He has only as much ground as his two feet take up, only as much of a hold as his two hands encompass"—someone who falls asleep in the winter snow to freeze to death like a child, someone who does nothing but take walks, yet who could take them anywhere, without moving.[6] Bartleby is the man without references, without possessions, without properties, without qualities, without particularities: he is too smooth for anyone to be able to hang any particularity on him. Without past or future, he is instantaneous. I PREFER NOT TO is Bartleby's chemical or alchemical formula, but one can read inversely I AM NOT PARTICULAR as its indispensable complement. The entire nineteenth century will go through this search for the man without a name, regicide and parricide, the modern-day Ulysses ("I am No One"): the crushed and mechanized man of the great metropolises, but from which one expects, perhaps, the emergence of the Man of the Future or New World Man. And, in an identical messianism, we glimpse him, sometimes as a Proletarian, sometimes as an American. Musil's novel will also follow this quest, and will invent the new logic of which *The Man without Qualities* is both the thinker and the product.[7] And though the derivation of Musil from Melville seems certain to us, it should be sought not in "Bartleby," but rather in *Pierre; or, the Ambiguities.* The incestuous couple Ulrich-Agathe is like the return of the Pierre-Isabelle couple; in both cases, the silent sister, unknown or forgotten, is not a substitute for the mother, but on the contrary the abolition of sexual difference as particularity, in favor of an androgynous relationship in which both Pierre and Ulrich are or become woman. In Bartleby's case, might not his relation with the attorney be equally mysterious, and in turn mark the possibility of a becoming, of a new man? Will Bartleby be able to conquer the place where he takes his walks?

Perhaps Bartleby is a madman, a lunatic or a psychotic ("an innate and incurable disorder" of the soul). But how can we know, if we do not take into account the anomalies of the attorney, who continues to behave in the most bizarre ways? The attorney had just received an important professional promotion. One will recall that President Schreber unleashed his own delirium only after receiving a promotion, as if this gave him the audacity to take the risk. But what is the attorney going to risk? He already has two scriveners who, much like Kafka's assistants, are inverted doubles of each other, the one normal in the morning and drunk in the afternoon, the other in a perpetual state of indigestion in the morning but almost normal in the afternoon. Since he needs an extra scrivener, he hires Bartleby after a brief conversation *without any references* because his pallid aspect seemed to indicate a constancy that could compensate for the irregularities of the two others. But on the first day he places Bartleby in a strange arrangement: Bartleby is to sit in the attorney's own office, next to some folding doors separating it from the clerk's office, between a window that faces the side of a neighboring building and a high screen, green as a prairie, as if it were important that Bartleby be able to hear, but without being seen. Whether this was a sudden inspiration on the attorney's part or an agreement reached during the short conversation, we will never know. But the fact is that, caught in this arrangement, the invisible Bartleby does an extraordinary amount of "mechanical" work. But when the attorney tries to make him leave his retreat, Bartleby emits his formula, and at this first occurrence, as with those that follow, the attorney finds himself disarmed, bewildered, stunned, thunderstruck, without response or reply. Bartleby stops copying altogether and remains on the premises, a fixture. We know to what extremes the attorney is forced to go in order to rid himself of Bartleby: he returns home, decides to relocate his office, then takes off for several days and hides out, avoiding the new tenant's complaints. What a strange flight, with the wandering attorney living in his rockaway . . . From the initial arrangement to this irrepressible, Cain-like flight, everything is bizarre, and the attorney behaves like a madman. Murder fantasies and declarations of love for Bartleby alternate in his soul. What happened? Is it a case of shared madness, here again, another relationship between doubles, a nearly acknowledged homosexual relation ("yes, Bartleby . . . I never feel so private as when I know you are here . . . I penetrate to the predestinated purpose of my life . . .")?[8]

One might imagine that hiring Bartleby was a kind of pact, as if the attorney, following his promotion, had decided to make this person, without objective references, a man of confidence [*un homme de confiance*] who would owe everything to him. He wants to make him *his* man. The pact consists of the following: Bartleby will sit near his master and copy, listening to him but without being seen, like a night bird who cannot stand to be looked at. So there is no doubt that once the attorney wants to draw (without even doing it on purpose) Bartleby from behind his screen to correct the copies with the others, he breaks the pact. This is why Bartleby, once he "prefers not to" correct, is already unable to copy. Bartleby will expose himself to view even more than he is asked to, planted in the middle of the office, but he will no longer do any copying. The attorney has an obscure feeling about it, since he assumes that if Bartleby refuses to copy, it is because his vision is impaired. And in effect, exposed to view, Bartleby for his part no longer sees, no longer looks. He has acquired what was, in a certain fashion, already innate in him: the legendary infirmity, one-eyed and one-armed, which makes him an autochthon, someone who is born to and stays in a particular place, while the attorney necessarily fills the function of the traitor condemned to flight. Whenever the attorney invokes philanthropy, charity, or friendship, his protestations are shot through with an obscure guilt. In fact, it is the attorney who broke the arrangement he himself had organized, and from the debris Bartleby pulls a trait of expression, I PREFER NOT TO, which will proliferate around him and contaminate the others, sending the attorney fleeing. But it will also send language itself into flight, it will open up a zone of indetermination or indiscernibility in which neither words nor characters can be distinguished—the fleeing attorney and the immobile, petrified Bartleby. The attorney starts to vagabond while Bartleby remains tranquil, but it is precisely because he remains tranquil and immobile that Bartleby is treated like a vagabond.

Is there a relation of identification between the attorney and Bartleby? But what is this relation? In what direction does it move? Most often, an identification seems to bring into play three elements, which are able to interchange or permutate: a form, image, or representation, a portrait, a model; a subject (or at least a virtual subject); and the subject's efforts to assume a form, to appropriate the image, to adapt itself to this image and the image to itself. It is a complex operation that passes through all of the adventures of resemblance, and that always risks falling into neurosis or turning into narcissism. A "mimetic rivalry," as it is sometimes called. It mobilizes a paternal function in general: an image of the father par excellence, and the subject is a son, even if the determinations are interchangeable. The bildungsroman [*roman de formation*], or one could just as easily say the reference novel [*roman de reference*], provides numerous examples.

Certainly, many of Melville's novels begin with images or portraits, and seem to tell the story of an upbringing under a paternal function: *Redburn*, for instance. *Pierre; or, The Ambiguities* begins with an image of the father, with a statue and a painting. Even *Moby-Dick* begins by amassing information at the beginning in order to give the whale a form and sketch out its image, right down to the dark painting hanging in the inn. "Bartleby" is no exception to the rule. The two clerks are like paper images, symmetrical opposites, and the attorney fills the paternal function so well that one can hardly believe the story is taking place in New York. Everything starts off as in an English novel, in Dickens's London. But in each case, something strange happens, something that blurs the image, marks it with an essential uncertainty, keeps the form from "taking," but also undoes the subject, sets it adrift and abolishes any paternal function. It is only here that things begin to get interesting. The statue of the father gives way to his much more ambiguous portrait, and then to yet another portrait that could be of anybody or nobody. All referents are lost, and the formation [*formation*] of man gives way to a new, unknown element, to the mystery of a formless, nonhuman life, a *Squid.* Everything began *à l'anglaise* but continues *à l'américaine,* following an irresistible line of flight. Ahab can say with good reason that he is fleeing from everywhere. The paternal function is dropped in favor of even more obscure and ambiguous forces. The subject loses its texture in favor of an infinitely proliferating patchwork: the American patchwork becomes the law of Melville's oeuvre, devoid of a center, of an upside down or right side up. It is as if the traits of expression escaped form, like the abstract lines of an unknown writing, or the furrows that twist from Ahab's brow to that of the Whale, or the "horrible contortions" of the flapping lanyards that pass through the fixed rigging and can easily drag a sailor into the sea, a subject into death.[9] In *Pierre; or, The Ambiguities,* the disquieting smile of the unknown young man in the painting, which so resembles the father's, functions as a trait of expression that emancipates itself, and is just as capable of undoing resemblance as it is of making the subject vacillate. I PREFER NOT TO is also a trait of expression that contaminates everything, escaping linguistic form and stripping the father of his exemplary speech, just as it strips the son of his ability to reproduce or copy.

It is still a process of identification, but rather than following the adventures of the neurotic, it has now become psychotic. A little bit of schizophrenia escapes the neurosis of the Old World. We can bring together three distinctive characteristics. In the first place, the formless trait of expression is opposed to the image or to the expressed form. In the second place, there is no longer a subject that tries to conform to the image, and either succeeds or fails. Rather, a zone of indistinction, of indiscernibility, or of ambiguity seems to be established between two terms, as if they had reached the point immediately preceding their respective differentiation: not a similitude, but a slippage, an extreme proximity, an absolute contiguity; not a natural filiation, but an unnatural alliance. It is a "hyperborean," "arctic" zone. It is no longer a question of Mimesis, but of becoming. Ahab does not imitate the whale, he becomes Moby-Dick, he enters into the zone of proximity *[zone de voisinage]* where he can no longer be distinguished from Moby-Dick, and strikes himself in striking the whale. Moby-Dick is the "wall, shoved near" with which he merges. Redburn renounces the image of the father in favor of the ambiguous traits of the mysterious brother. Pierre does not imitate his father, but reaches the zone of proximity where he can no longer be distinguished from his half sister, Isabelle, and becomes woman. While neurosis flounders in the nets of maternal incest in order to identify more closely with the father, psychosis liberates incest with the sister as a becoming, a free identification of man and woman: in the same way Kleist emits atypical, almost animal traits of expression—stutterings, grindings, grimaces—that feed his passionate conversation with his sister. This is because, in the third place, psychosis pursues its dream of establishing a function of universal fraternity that no longer passes through the father, but is built on the ruins of the paternal function, a function that presupposes the dissolution of all images of the father, following an autonomous line of alliance or proximity that makes the woman a sister, and the other man, a brother, like the terrible "monkey-rope" uniting Ishmael and Queequeg as a married couple. These are the three characteristics of the American Dream, which together make up the new identification, the New World: the Trait, the Zone, and the Function.

We are in the process of melding together characters as different as Ahab and Bartleby. Yet does not everything instead set them in opposition to each other? Melvillian psychiatry constantly invokes two poles: *monomaniacs* and *hypochondriacs*, demons and angels, torturers and victims, the Swift and the Slow, the Thundering and the Petrified, the Unpunishable (beyond all punishment) and the Irresponsible (beyond all responsibility). What is Ahab doing when he lets loose his harpoons of fire and madness? He is breaking a pact. He is betraying the Whalers' Law, which says that any healthy whale encountered must be hunted, without choosing one over another. But Ahab, thrown into his indiscernible becoming, makes a choice—he pursues his identification with Moby-Dick, putting his crew in mortal danger. This is the monstrous preference that Lieutenant Starbuck bitterly objects to, to the point where he even dreams of killing the treacherous captain. Choosing is the Promethean sin *par excellence*.[10] This was the case with Kleist's Penthesilea, an Ahab-woman who, like her indiscernible double Achilles, had chosen her enemy, in defiance of the law of the Amazons forbidding the preference of one enemy over another. The priestess and the Amazons consider this a betrayal that madness sanctions in a cannibal identification. In his last novel, *Billy Budd,* Melville himself brings another monomaniacal demon into the picture with Claggart: the master-at-arms. We should have no illusions about Claggart's subordinate function: his is no more a case of psychological wickedness than Captain Ahab's. It is a case of metaphysical perversion that consists in choosing one's prey, preferring a chosen victim with a kind of love rather than observing the maritime law that requires him to apply the same discipline to everyone. This is what the narrator suggests when he recalls an ancient and mysterious theory, an exposé of which is found in Sade: secondary, sensible Nature is governed by the Law (or laws), while *innately depraved beings* participate in a terrible supersensible Primary Nature, original and oceanic, which, knowing no Law, pursues its own irrational aim through them. Nothingness, Nothingness.[11] Ahab will break through the wall, eve if there is nothing behind it, and will make nothingness the object of his will: "To me, the white whale is that wall, shoved near to me. Sometimes I think there's naught beyond. But 'tis enough."[12] Melville says that only the eye of a *prophet,* and not a psychologist, is capable of discerning or diagnosing such obscure beings as these creatures of the abyss, without being able to prevent their mad enterprise, the "mystery of iniquity" . . .

We are now in a position to classify Melville's great characters. At one pole, there are those monomaniacs or demons who, driven by the will to nothingness, make a monstrous choice: Ahab, Claggart, Babo . . . But at the other pole are those angels or saintly hypochondriacs, almost stupid, creatures of innocence and purity, stricken with a constitutive weakness but also with a strange beauty. Petrified by nature, they prefer . . . no will at all, a nothingness of the will rather than a will to nothingness (hypochondriacal "negativism"). They can only survive by becoming stone, by denying the will and sanctifying themselves in this suspension.[13] Such are Cereno, Billy Budd, and above all Bartleby. And although the two types are opposed in every way—the former innate traitors and the latter betrayed in their very essence; the former monstrous fathers who devour their children, the latter abandoned sons without fathers—they haunt one and the same world, forming alternations within it, just as Melville's writing, like Kleist's, alternates between stationary, fixed processes and mad-paced procedures: *style,* with its succession of catatonias and accelerations . . . This is because both poles, both types of characters, Ahab and Bartleby, *belong to this Primary Nature,* they inhabit it, they constitute it. Everything sets them in opposition, and yet they are perhaps the same creature—primary, original, stubborn, seized from both sides, marked merely with a "plus" or a "minus" sign: Ahab and Bartleby. Or in Kleist, the terrible Penthesilea and the sweet little Catherine, the first beyond conscience, the second before conscience: she who chooses and she who does not choose, she who howls like a she-wolf and she who would prefer-not-to speak.[14]

There exists, finally, a third type of character in Melville, the one on the side of the Law, the guardian of the divine and human laws of secondary nature: the prophet. Captain Delano lacks the prophet's eye, but Ishmael in *Moby-Dick,* Captain Vere in *Billy Budd,* and the attorney in *Bartleby* all have this power to "See": they are capable of grasping and understanding, as much as is possible, the beings of Primary Nature, the great monomaniacal demons or the saintly innocents, and sometimes both. Yet they themselves are not lacking in ambiguity, each in his own way. Though they are able to see into the Primary Nature that so fascinates them, they are nonetheless representatives of secondary nature and its laws. They bear the paternal image—they seem like good fathers, benevolent fathers (or at least protective big brothers, as Ishmael is toward Queequeg). But they cannot ward off the demons, because the latter are too quick for the law, too surprising. Nor can they save the innocent, the irresponsible: they immolate them in the name of the Law, they make the sacrifice of Abraham. Behind their paternal mask, they have a kind of double identification: with the innocent, toward whom they feel a genuine love, but also with the demon, since they break their pact with the innocent they love, each in his own manner. They betray, then, but in a different way than does Ahab or Claggart: the latter broke the law, whereas Vere or the attorney, in the name of the law, break an implicit and almost unavowable agreement (even Ishmael seems to turn away from his savage brother Queequeg). They continue to cherish the innocent they have condemned: Captain Vere will die muttering the name of Billy Budd, and the final words of the attorney's narrative will be, "Ah, Bartleby! Ah, humanity!" which does not indicate a connection, but rather an alternative in which he has had to choose the all-too-human law over Bartleby. Torn between the two Natures, with all their contradictions, these characters are extremely important, but do not have the stature of the two others. Rather, they are Witnesses, narrators, interpreters. There is a problem that escapes this third type of character, a very important problem that is settled between the other two.

The Confidence-Man (much as one says the Medicine-Man) is sprinkled with Melville's reflections on the novel. The first of these reflections consists in claiming the rights of a superior irrationalism (chapter 14). Why should the novelist believe he is obligated to explain the behavior of his characters, and to supply them with reasons, whereas life for its part never explains

indiscernibility in which it passes through all intensities in every direction, extending all the way to the homosexual relation between brothers, and passing through the incestuous relation between brother and sister. This is the most mysterious relation, the one in which Pierre and Isabelle are swept up, the one that draws Heathcliff and Catherine along in *Wuthering Heights*, each one becoming Ahab and Moby-Dick by turns: "Whatever our souls are made of, his and mine are the same. . . . My love for Heathcliff resembles the eternal rocks beneath—a source of little visible delight, but necessary. . . . I *am* Heathcliff—he's always always in my mind—not as a pleasure, any more than I am always a pleasure to myself—but as my own being . . ."[18]

How can this community be realized? How can the biggest problem be resolved? But is it not already resolved, by itself, precisely because it is not a personal problem, but a historical, geographic, or political one? It is not an individual or particular affair, but a collective one, the affair of a people, or rather, of all peoples. It is not an Oedipal phantasm but a political program. Melville's bachelor, Bartleby, like Kafka's, must "find the place where he can take his walks" . . . America.[19] The American is one who is freed from the English paternal function, the son of a crumbled father, the son of all nations. Even before their independence, Americans were thinking about the combination of States, the State-form most compatible with their vocation. But their vocation was not to reconstitute an "old State secret," a nation, a family, a heritage, or a father. It was above all to constitute a universe, a society of brothers, a federation of men and goods, a community of anarchist individuals, inspired by Jefferson, by Thoreau, by Melville. Such is the declaration in *Moby-Dick* (chapter 26): if man is the brother of his fellow man, if he is worthy of trust or "confidence," it is not because he belongs to a nation or because he is a proprietor or shareholder, but only insofar as he is Man, when he has lost those characteristics that constitute his "violence," his "idiocy," his "villainy," when he has no consciousness of himself apart from the proprieties of a "democratic dignity" that considers all particularities as so many ignominious stains that arouse anguish or pity.

America is the potential of the man without particularities, the Original Man. Already in *Redburn:*

> You can not spill a drop of American blood without spilling the blood of the whole world. Be he English-man, Frenchman, German, Dane, or Scot; the Euro-pean who scoffs at an American, calls his own brother *Raca,* and stands in danger of the judgment. We are not a narrow tribe of men, with a bigoted Hebrew na-tionality—whose blood has been debased in the at-tempt to enoble it, by maintaining an exclusive succes-sion among ourselves. . . . We are not a nation, so much as a world; for unless we may claim all the world for our sire, like Melchisedec, we are without father or mother. . . . We are the heirs of all time, and with all nations we divide our inheritance . . .[20]

The picture of the nineteenth-century proletarian looks like this: the advent of the communist man or the society of comrades, the future Soviet, being without property, family, or nation, has no other determination than that of being man, *Homo tantum.* But this is also the picture of the American, executed by other means, and the traits of the former often intermingle with or are superimposed over those of the latter. America sought to create a revolution whose strength would lie in a universal immigration, émigrés of the world, just as Bolshe-vik Russia would seek to make a revolution whose strength would lie in a universal proletarization, "Proletarians of the world" . . . the two forms of the class struggle. So that the messianism of the nineteenth century has two heads and is ex-pressed no less in American *pragmatism* than in the ultimately Russian form of socialism.

Pragmatism is misunderstood when it is seen as a sum-mary philosophical theory fabricated by Americans. On the other hand, we understand the novelty of American thought when we see pragmatism as an attempt to transform the world, to think a new world or new man insofar as they *create them-*

selves. Western philosophy was the skull, or the paternal Spirit that realized itself in the world as totality, and in a knowing subject as proprietor. Is it against Western philosophy that Melville directs his insult, "metaphysical villain"? A contemporary of American transcendentalism (Emerson, Thoreau), Melville is already sketching out the traits of the pragmatism that will be its continuation. It is first of all the affirmation of a world in *process,* an *archipelago.* Not even a puzzle, whose pieces when fitted together would constitute a whole, but rather a wall of loose, uncemented stones, where every element has a value in itself but also in relation to others: isolated and floating relations, islands and straits, immobile points and sinuous lines—for Truth always has "jagged edges." Not a skull but the vertebral column, a spinal cord; not a uniform piece of clothing but a Harlequin's coat, even white on white, an infinite patchwork with multiple joinings, like the jacket of Redburn, White Jacket or the Great Cosmopolitan: the American invention *par excellence,* for the Americans invented patchwork, just as the Swiss are said to have invented the cuckoo clock. But to reach this point, it was also necessary for the knowing subject, the sole proprietor, to give way to a community of explorers, the brothers of the archipelago, who replace knowledge with belief, or rather with "confidence"—not belief in another world, but confidence in this one, and in man as much as in God ("I am going to attempt the ascent of Ofo *with hope, not with faith. . . .* I will follow my own path . . .").

Pragmatism is this double principle of archipelago and hope.[21] And what must the community of men consist of in order for truth to be possible? *Truth* and *trust.*[22] Like Melville before it, pragmatism will fight ceaselessly on two fronts: against the particularities that pit man against man and nourish an irremediable mistrust; but also against the Universal or the Whole, the fusion of souls in the name of great love or charity. Yet, what remains of souls once they are no longer attached to particularities, what keeps them from melting into a whole? What remains is precisely their "originality," that is, a sound that each one *produces,* like a ritornello at the limit of language, but that it produces only when it takes to the open road (or to the open sea) with its body, when it leads its life without seeking salvation, when it embarks upon its incarnate voyage, without any particular aim, and then encounters other voyagers, whom it recognizes by their sound. This is how Lawrence described the new messianism, or the *democratic* contribution of American literature: against the European morality of salvation and charity, a morality of life in which the soul is fulfilled only by taking to the road, with no other aim, open to all contacts, never trying to save other souls, turning away from those that produce an overly authoritarian or groaning sound, forming even fleeting and unresolved chords and accords with its equals, with freedom as its sole accomplishment, always ready to free itself so as to complete itself.[23] According to Melville or Lawrence, brotherhood is a matter for original souls: perhaps it begins only with the death of the father or God, but it does not derive from this death, it is a whole other matter—"all the subtle sympathizings of the incalculable soul, from the bitterest hate to passionate love."

This requires a new perspective, an archipelago-perspectivism that conjugates the panoramic shot and the tracking shot, as in *The Encantadas*. It requires an acute perception, both visual and auditory, as *Benito Cereno* shows, and must replace the concept with the "percept," that is, with a perception in becoming. It requires a new community, whose members are capable of trust or "confidence," that is, of a belief in themselves, in the world, and in becoming. Bartleby the bachelor must embark upon his voyage and find his sister, with whom he will consume the ginger nut, the new host. Bartleby lives cloistered in the office and never goes out, but when the attorney suggests new occupations to him, he is not joking when he responds, "There is too much confinement . . ." And if he is prevented from making his voyage, then the only place left for him is prison, where he dies of "civil disobedience," as Thoreau says, "the only place where a free man can stay with honor."[24] William and Henry James are indeed brothers, and *Daisy Miller*, the new American maiden, asks for nothing more than a little confidence, and allows herself to die because even this meager request remains unfulfilled. And what was Bartleby asking for if not a little confidence from the attorney, who instead responds to him with charity and philanthropy—all the masks of the paternal function? The attorney's only excuse is that he draws back from the becoming into which Bartleby, through his lonely existence, threatens to drag him: *rumors* are already spreading . . . The hero of pragmatism is not the successful businessman, it is Bartleby, and it is Daisy Miller, it is Pierre and Isabelle, the brother and sister.

The dangers of a "society without fathers" have often been pointed out, but the only real danger is the return of the father.[25] In this respect, it is difficult to separate the failure of the two revolutions, the American and the Soviet, the pragmatic and the dialectical. Universal emigration was no more successful than universal proletarization. The Civil War already sounded the knell, as would the liquidation of the Soviets later on. The birth of a nation, the restoration of the nation-state—and the monstrous fathers come galloping back in, while the sons without fathers start dying off again. Paper images—this is the fate of the American as well as the Proletarian. But just as many Bolsheviks could hear the diabolical powers knocking at the door in 1917, the pragmatists, like Melville before them, could see the masquerade that the society of brothers would lead to. Long before Lawrence, Melville and Thoreau were diagnosing the American evil, the new cement that would rebuild the wall: paternal authority and filthy charity. Bartleby therefore lets himself die in prison. In the beginning, it was Benjamin Franklin, the hypocritical *lightning-rod Merchant,* who instituted the magnetic American prison. The city-ship reconstitutes the most oppressive law, and brotherhood exists among the topmen only when they remain immobile, high up on the masts *(White Jacket).* The great community of celibates is nothing more than a company of bons vivants, which certainly does not keep the rich bachelor from exploiting the poor and pallid workers, by reconstituting the two unreconciled figures of the monstrous father and the orphaned daughters *(The Paradise of Bachelors and the Tartarus of Maids).* The American confidence-man appears everywhere in Melville's work. What malignant power has turned the trust into a company as cruel as the abominable "universal nation" founded by the Dog-Man in *The Encantadas? The Confidence-Man,* in which Melville's critique of charity and philanthropy culminates, brings into play a series of devious characters who seem to emanate from a "great Cosmopolitan" in patchwork clothing, and who ask for no more than . . . a little human confidence, in order to pull off a multiple and rebounding confidence game.

Are these false brothers sent by a diabolical father to restore his power over *overly credulous* Americans? But the novel is so complex that one could just as easily say the opposite: this long procession *[théorie]* of con men would be a comic version of authentic brothers, such as *overly suspicious* Americans see them, or rather have already become incapable of seeing them. This cohort of characters, including the mysterious child at the end, is perhaps the society of Philanthropists who dissimulate their demonic project, but perhaps it is also the community of brothers that the Misanthropes are no longer able to recognize in passing. For even in the midst of its failure, the American Revolution continues to send out its fragments, always making something take flight on the horizon, even sending itself to the moon, always trying to break through the wall, to take up the experiment once again, to find a brotherhood in this enterprise, a sister in this becoming, a music in its stuttering language, a pure sound and unknown chords in language itself. What Kafka would say about "small nations" is what Melville had already said about the great American nation: it must become a patchwork of all small nations. What Kafka would say about minor literatures is what Melville had already said about the American literature of his time: because there are so few authors in America, and because its people are so indifferent, the writer is not in a position to succeed as a recognized master. Even in his failure, the writer remains all the more the bearer of a collective enunciation, which no longer forms part of literary history and preserves the rights of a people to come, or of a human becoming.[26]

A schizophrenic vocation: even in his catatonic or anorexic state, Bartleby is not the patient, but the doctor of a sick America, the *Medicine-Man,* the new Christ or the brother to us all.

1. Nicolas Ruwet, "Parallélismes et déviations en poésie," in *Langue, discours, société,* ed. Julia Kristeva and Nicholas Ruwet (Paris: Seuil, 1975), pp. 334–44 (on "portmanteau-constructions").

2. Philippe Jaworski, *Melville, le désert et l'empire* (Paris: Presses de l'Ecole Normale, 1986), p. 19.

3. See Viola Sachs, *La contre-Bible de Melville* (Paris: Mouton, 1975).

4. On Bartleby and Melville's silence, see Armand Farrachi, *La part du silence* (Paris: Barrault, 1984), pp. 40–45.

5. Mathieu Lindon, "Bartleby," *Delta 6* (May 1978): 22.

6. Kafka's great text almost reads like another version of "Bartleby." See Franz Kafka, *The Diaries of Franz Kafka: 1910–1913,* ed. Max Brod, trans. Joseph Kresh (New York: Schocken, 1948), p. 26.

7. Blanchot demonstrates that Musil's character is not only without qualities, but "without particularities," since he has no more substance than he does qualities. See *Le livre à venir* (Paris: Gallimard/Folio, 1963), pp. 202–3. This theme of the man without particularities, the modern-day Ulysses, arises early in the nineteenth century, and in France appears in the rather strange book of Ballanche, a friend of Chateaubriand; see Pierre Simon Ballanche, *Essais de palingénésie sociale,* notably "La ville des expiations" (1827), in *Oeuvres complètes* (Geneva: Slatkine Reprints, 1967).

8. Herman Melville, "Bartleby the Scrivener," in *Billy Budd, Sailor and Other Stories,* ed. Harold Beaver (London: Penguin Classics, 1967), p. 89.

9. Régis Durand, in his *Melville, signes et métaphores* (Paris: L'Age d'Homme, 1980), pp. 103–7, has pointed out the role played by loose lines aboard a whaler, as opposed to the formalized riggings. Both Durand's and Jaworski's books are among the most profound analyses of Melville to have appeared recently.

10. George Dumézil, preface to Georges Charachidzé, *Prométhée ou le Caucase: Essai de mythologie contrastive* (Paris: Flammarion 1986): "The Greek myth of Prometheus has remained, through the ages, an object of reflection and reference. The god who does not take part in his brothers' dynastic struggle against their cousin Zeus, but who, on personal grounds, defies and ridicules this same Zeus . . . this *anarchist,* affects and stirs up dark and sensitive zones in us."

11. On this conception of the two Natures in Sade (the theory of the pope in the *New Justine),* see Pierre Klossowski, *Sade My Neighbor,* trans. Alphonso Lingis (Evanston, Ill.: Northwestern University Press, 1991), pp. 99 ff.

12. Herman Melville, *Moby-Dick; or, the Whale,* chapter 36 (New York: Penguin Classics, 1992), p. 178.

13. See Schopenhauer's conception of sainthood as the act by which the Will denies itself in the suppression of all particularity. Pierre Leyris, in his second preface to the French translation of *Billy Budd* (Paris: Gallimard, 1980), recalls Melville's profound interest in Schopenhauer. Nietzsche saw Parsifal as a type of Schopenhauerian saint, a kind of Bartleby. But after Nietzsche, man still preferred being a demon to being a saint: "man would rather will *nothingness* than *not* will." Friedrich Nietzsche, *On the Genealogy of Morals,* trans. Walter Kaufmann and R. J. Hollingdale (New York: Random House, 1967), third essay, § 28, p. 163.

14. See Heinrich Kleist's letter to H. J. von Collin, December 1808, in *An Abyss Deep Enough: The Letters of Heinrich Von Kleist,* ed. Philip B. Miller (New York:

Dutton, 1982). Catherine Heilbronn had her own formula, close to that of Bartleby's: "I don't know" or simply "Don't know."

15. The comparison between Musil and Melville would pertain to the following four points: the critique of reason ("Principle of insufficient reason"), the denunciation of psychology ("the great hole we call the soul"), the new logic ("the other state"), and the hyperborean Zone (the "Possible").

16. See Francis Bacon and David Sylvester, *The Brutality of Fact: Interviews with Francis Bacon* (New York: Thames and Hudson, 1975), p. 22. And Melville said: "For the same reason that there is but one planet to one orbit, so can there be but one such original character to one work or invention. Two would conflict to chaos." Herman Melville, *The Confidence-Man*, ed. Stephen Matterson (London: Penguin Classics, 1990), p. 282.

17. See R. Durand, p. 153. Mayoux writes: "On the personal plane, the question of the father is momentarily postponed, if not settled. . . . But it is not only a question of the father. We are all orphans. Now is the age of fraternity." Jean-Jacques Mayoux, *Melville*, trans. John Ashbery (New York: Grove, 1960), p. 109, translation modified.

18. Emily Brontë, *Wuthering Heights* (London: Penguin, 1985), p. 122.

19. Kafka, *Diaries 1910–1913*, p. 28.

20. Herman Melville, *Redburn: His Maiden Voyage* (Evanston and Chicago: Northwestern University Press and Newberry Library, 1969), p. 169.

21. Jaworski has analyzed this world-as-archipelago or this patchwork experiment. These themes are to be found throughout Pragmatism, and notably among William James's most beautiful pages: the world as "shot point blank with a pistol." This is inseparable from the search for a new human community. In *Pierre; or, The Ambiguities*, Plotinus Plinlimmon's mysterious tract already seems like the manifestation of an absolute pragmatism. On the history of pragmatism in general, philosophical and political, see Gérard Deledalle, *La philosophie américaine* (Paris: L'Age d'Homme, 1983): Royce is particularly important, with his "absolute pragmatism" and his "great community of Interpretation" that unites individuals. There are many Melvillian echoes in Royce's work. His strange trio of the Aventurer, the Beneficiary, and the Insurer seems in certain ways to derive from Melville's trio of the Monomaniac, the Hypochondriac, and the Prophet, or even to refer to characters in *The Confidence-Man*, who would already prefigure the trio's comic version.

22. [In English in the original.—Trans.]

23. D. H. Lawrence, "Whitman," in *Studies in Classic American Literature* (New York: Viking, 1953). This book also includes two famous studies on Melville. Lawrence criticizes both Melville and Whitman for having succumbed to the very things they denounced; nonetheless, he says, it was American literature that, thanks to them, marked out the path.

24. [See Henry David Thoreau, *Walden and Civil Disobedience*, ed. Owen Thomas (New York: Norton, 1966), p. 233: "Under a government which imprisons any unjustly, the true place for a just man is also a prison."—Trans.]

25. See Alexander Mitscherlich's *Society without the Father: A Contribution to Social Psychology*, trans. Eric Musbacher (New York: J. Aronson, 1974), which is written from a psychoanalytic point of view that remains indifferent to the movements of History and invokes the benefits of the paternal English Constitution.

26. See Melville's text on American literature, "Hawthorne and His Mosses," in *The Portable Melville*, ed. Jay Leyda (New York: Viking, 1952), pp. 411–14, which should be compared with Kafka's text on "the literature of small peoples," in *The Diaries of Franz Kafka: 1910–1913*, entry for December 25, 1911, pp. 210 ff.

Lucy Grealy

My God

My God, My God, why hast Thou forsaken me?
—Mark 15:34, Matthew 27:46

Father, forgive them: they know not what they do.
—Luke 23:34

It is finished.
—John 19:30

My early religious education, to the age of six, consisted of memorizing all the words to the rock-opera "Jesus Christ Superstar." Actually, I did more than memorize them, I acted out the whole album, my own private version of the London musical, which opened earlier than the American. Combining my passion for this album with my crush on Mr. Ed, the talking horse. I had one of those innocent crushes that couldn't distinguish between loving Mr. Ed from wanting to *be* Mr. Ed. I would re-create the entire drama of Jesus and Judas and the twelve apostles as a talking horse. All this took place on a large yellow Chinese carpet which lay in front of the stereo in the living room. Each part of the carpet signified a character, and I would canter on my hands and knees from corner to corner to mouth each part as it came up. My knees carpet burning into a vivid red, I performed the entire drama single-handedly.

For the big chorus parts, I would mount my Hippty-hop, a

sort of big red rubber ball on which you could sit and propel yourself by holding onto a half-circle handle and bouncing. I'd race around the room, imagining that I was riding in complicated formation, banners flapping, as the apostles wondered what was happening, as the beggars and lepers overtook Jesus, as the crowd jeered, in harmony, for His crucifixion. The only drawback to the choruses was that my bouncing about often made the needle skip on the record, but it was also necessary, as it gave my knees a short rest. It wasn't the performance that made me love the album; that had to do with my courtship of the strong, safe, gleamingly visceral world of Mr. Ed. The music itself had an uncanny hold on me; the sways and turns of the emotional narrative entranced me, even, and maybe especially, when I didn't understand them. The Pharisees were my favorites because their voices were so exotically varied, plus they all seemed so confused and put upon, which, even at six, was a state I identified with. I had to hold my ears during the scene in which Jesus was whipped by the forty-nine lashes, not because I felt bad for him, but because the music itself seemed so dreadful.

Not surprisingly, for the rest of my childhood, I held a rather liberal take on the New Testament. Jesus obviously possessed quite a number of very human failings, and though I knew from other sources, such as early morning Sunday television, that he was a very kind person, he seemed fairly preoccupied a lot of the time in the gospel according to Andrew Lloyd Webber. I liked Judas far better, and felt very sorry when he killed himself: in truth, he seemed like the only one with any deep feelings at all, and I thought he'd been unjustly set up. He also had a much better singing voice. This was all I knew, and even this I kept to myself. Religion, in my family, was regarded as a highly specialized form of stupidity.

A few years later, when I was about ten and very ill, I began receiving letters of "hope and encouragement" from people I'd never met before, strangers who'd heard about a disfiguring affliction I had, and wrote in the hope of cheering me up.

Each and every one of these letters eventually got around to God. Had I accepted Him as my savior? How could these poor people ever guess the ridicule their letters received. My cynical older brothers, whose nasty humor I confused with worldliness, loved to read the letters out loud in the kitchen. Most of the letters were written in a rounded, overly even hand that I learned to recognize more than a decade later, when I began teaching, as the generic handwriting of a dull education. My brothers, nine and thirteen years older than me, had been educated in Ireland, and their teachers had all been priests. I don't think I had ever actually met a priest, not face to face, and these letters caused my brothers to thicken and coarsen their accents, imitating specific priests they'd both known. "Have you accepted Jesus Christ as your savior, young girl?" they'd ask me in their strange voices, adding odd and specific physical tics—eyes that roamed leftward, hands that trembled—and this would push them over the edge into tearful hysteria. Left out of the joke, I could only pause and feel jealous, learning by osmosis that anyone who believed such things as these letters hinted at was a certifiable fool.

Still, there was a part of me that longed to believe. If I believed, then perhaps I would be happy. My life at the time, due to my illness and the insanity endemic to my family, was outlined with every conceivable type of emotional, physical, social and psychic pain. Luckily, my interior life was up for the job, and the world I inhabited, though by this time less outwardly silly than pretending I was a talking horse playing out the New Testament, coursed like a fast stream over solidly built fantasies. I barely knew who I was, only who I pretended to be: a pony express rider, a space alien, an unrecognized genius, all of us flailing around in the white water of a desperation to escape.

Some of the letters also contained pamphlets. I would sit at the kitchen table, the cats rubbing around my legs, and read stories of saintly people who were able to bear any hardship, whether it was illness, solitude, poverty or the scorn of others, with a grace that actually shone from them in the illustrations—

shards of light emanating from the believer's head, depending upon the illustrator's skill, like either soft mists or awkward bolts. Everyone's eyes were blue. What affected me most was their unwavering calm, and I would look up from these pamphlets at my mother, sitting at the other end of the kitchen table, smoking furiously, making piles of different bills and lists and papers, her kinetic anger trembling with its own life in her hands. My mother's anger at everyone and everything possessed her like a daemon, making her life, as she herself often said, a living hell. She was probably aware, at times, what effect it had on ours, but most of the time she was too busy dealing with the tragedies that haunted our family or too busy stalking her own luminous sadness, to ever sit down and speak with these daemons.

Often, the pamphlets quoted verses from the Bible. These, too, were almost always about forgiveness and love, peace, and eternal joy. This was about as close as I got to actually reading the Bible. I did try reading it at one point, after finding a King James version downstairs in the basement. Starting with Genesis I decided to try, as one of the pamphlets suggested, reading a page a day for a year. I got to the first string of "begat"s and that ended that project. Meanwhile, what I had read seemed a peculiar story. Why would God pick on the snake like that? And why were women made in what seemed like an afterthought? And why did everyone for ever and ever have to suffer because of someone else's mistake?, a mistake which, to me, didn't really seem so terrible after all. Though I'd heard that many people believed all of this was something that truly happened, surely those people would have to be discounted as idiots. All I had to do was stand outside on the front lawn, listening to the complex screams of neighborhood children and to the vast songs of the birds, to just simply *know* it couldn't have happened in such a way. But then, why *did* so many people believe this? And how did Jesus fit into this? From what I could understand about him, he seemed a decent sort of fellow, so why did they kill him? And why (because I'd just been reading about it in history class) did people do something as horrible as the crusades in his name? And back in Northern Ireland, all that mess, why did that have to happen?

And yet I still longed desperately to believe. How could I cross that line? Did God exist? I conducted experiments in my room. Sitting Indian style on my carpet, I'd not so much ask as announce, "God, if you exist, prove it to me." Sometimes I'd qualify this, suggesting he (and He was always a he) do something like perhaps change the color of the carpet, or maybe make the family dog, who'd recently died, appear panting and wagging in front of me. I wanted the resounding silence following my questions to be the answer, the proof that I didn't have to waste my time wondering about such things anymore. Yet I also wanted so badly all that peace, all that joy and love.

At night I would lie in bed and pretend I was a saint. Often, I was simply an egomaniac, but that didn't matter. In my fantasy life, I learned what it felt like to have infinite patience and wisdom. I healed the sick, especially the grotesquely sick, and helped the poor, especially the poor no one else noticed, and especially the ones who lived in terror of despots. I read books about the holocaust and imagined how graceful I would have been there, that I withstood oppression with such nobility that the Nazis were forced to stop in their tracks. In Vietnam and Cambodia and amid the famines of Africa, I was there too, helping the lost and injured and sad. In my real life, I hated myself for being petty and shallow, because, try as I might, I could only manage my transmutation into benign understanding for moments at a time. Acts of charity—these I only seemed to manage with animals, and even with them, whom I loved so much, I was often experimentally cruel. And the humans immediately around me; they had griefs far subtler than abject poverty and leprosy, sorrows far too near and familiar, and all I could do was flee.

Vincent Van Gogh, in his letters to his brother Theo, outlined a life filled with the tangible. Vincent loved to look, to touch, to smell and taste the world about him. Most of all, he loved to look, and then *feel,* with his hands grasping the charcoal or brush, what he had just seen. His hands roamed all over his mind, trying to decipher the different grains of thought and emotion, the thin line between the actual and the imagined, between light and the things he saw with light. Though he never lived to hear of either Wave or Particle theories of light, Vincent understood that one doesn't just simply "see" a chair or table, but rather that one's eyes are actually caressed by the light that bounces off the object. [Color, while being the most visible thing we can know about a tree, is also created by that part of light that the tree has cast off. The tree absorbs all other light waves of color, welcomes them as part of itself: the green we see is the negative, the reflected reality it wants no part of. Where its definition of itself ends, our definition of it is just beginning.]

Vincent often mentioned to his brother what he called a longing for the old, old story. The first time I read this, as a freshman in college, I had no idea he was referring to the story of Jesus. But I'd only just taken up writing poetry, and something about the sadness of his longing, pricked at me. At that time, I was just discovering the world of writing, and it was the religion I'd been searching for all my life. That even such a short phrase as written by Vincent could elicit such ineffable feelings in me seemed miraculous. I'd spent most of my childhood using the small tactile details of the world as a way of escaping the world: how easy to separate myself from the shame and misery of certain moments by suddenly appreciating the texture of the carpet a doctor paced on, or the dew-like drops forming on the glass of water in front of my angry mother, its reflected rim a hoop of light quivering on the table.

Writing offered a way to take these small observations and transform them into a way of entering the world, a way of using language as the slow tear in the fabric I'd been wrapping myself up in. My own particular tool was language, but I loved art of all kinds, particularly visual art. The concept of time seemed at the heart of all these arts. Art, to me, was anything which brought you into the present moment, the nameless now that keeps dying and being reborn over and over and over. That the present moment should be so nameless, so inexpressible, I believed was the fundamental truth of art, and I defined beauty as the thing left over from the effort of trying to name it. The painter Robert Henri said it best in a quote that, during the height of my artistic evangelism, I learned by heart: *There are moments in our lives, there are moments in a day, when we seem to see beyond the usual. Such are the moments of our greatest happiness. Such are the moments of our greatest wisdom. If one but could recall his vision by some sort of sign. It was in this hope that the arts were invented. Signpost on the way to what may be. Signposts toward greater knowledge.*

My senior year in college I decided to take a course titled "The Bible as Literature." I took it because of the literature part of the title. In my endless quest for metaphors, I thought it might help my writing. The first assignment, naturally enough, was to read Genesis. I admit I only skimmed the begats. By this time I knew enough about anthropology, ancient myths, and other world religions to recognize Genesis as a good story. For a few years previous I'd been dabbling with Eastern Religion, with a little Western Philosophy thrown in as well. More and more, I came to see that, just as with art, the essence of the religious moment lay within the "now" moment, and that the heinous cliches of the world were born in the belief that you could capture this moment. Once you judged, once you decided, you were closed off, locked into misinterpretations of the past and misapprehensions of the future. The more I looked at it, the more religion looked like art.

As we read more of the Old Testament, I was seized by a great crisis. The closer I read, the more shocked I was by my own previous ignorance of what was going on in the Bible. I guess I'd always thought it was all about love and joy and peace. The violence and anger of the Old Testament terrified me, but the real terror lay in my having to acknowledge that the culture I lived in was based, in large part, upon this violent saga, a story as unfair as it was unforthcoming. That so many generations upon generations of people, that people living today, took this work to be the literal truth, deeply disturbed me. How could one be happy with such tautology, to simply be "told" the meaning of everything, never allowed to question it? And the entire drama of the story was based on God's will—all those humans forced into their roles—for it was God who hardened peoples hearts, God who closed their eyes against the truth, God who selected only a chosen few, leaving the rest to annihilation, or worse. What could the purpose of life be if it was already laid out in such monotonous script?

Early in the Christian era, Philo of Alexandria changed the course of history by being one of the first philosophers to undertake and, most important, to write about, an allegorical exegesis of the Hebrew Scripture.

Up until the time of Philo, the text of the Scripture was a kind of property, controlled by the religious officials. The text itself was mysterious to those who could not read, and faith was contained in the act of believing in the stories. It was a very physical, very visceral kind of belief, one that contended that the path to salvation lay within your ability to follow ritual and to control your body. Philo, a Jew, however, read the bible stories as allegorical. He wrote at length about the possibility that spirit and matter were separated, and that belief was an act of the mind, not simply of the body. You could perform rituals till the very end, but none of that mattered if you didn't believe with your head and heart, if you didn't actually think.

Philo inserted a new dimension into the whole concept of belief. "Truth," as he saw it, didn't exist in the stories themselves, in the words on the page, nor in the black and white world of absolute faith, but in the process of using the wit and judgment and intellect given to us by God in interpreting these words. In a sense, Philo was the first deconstructionist. Meaning, for Philo, and unlike for many of his contemporaries, occurred not on set planes but only during the shift between these planes. Later, of course, those different planes were all too firmly established, and rather than think for yourself, you could only move between meanings rigidly defined by the church. Philo himself, freely interpreting with only his instinct and edu-

cation to guide him, would have been seen as a heretic during
any number of inquisitions, despite the fact that it was his phi-
losophies that set the groundwork for them. Surely he could
never have forseen that once people were able to move past
literal methods of judging what was to become the Bible, that
they would then cast their abstract *ideas* about the Bible in do-
or-die terms, become willing to torture and kill those who did
not accept their ideas of what the Bible *meant*.

Not surprisingly, the information that impressed me most
in the Old Testament had been the use of time. If the Garden of
Eden was timeless, then linear history began with the Fall. The
Old Testament set up a very particular story, charted an inexora-
ble course. Within this history, which was one type of linear
time, or narrative,there was a second story with an even more
refined sense of linear time, or narrative, and this was the story
of the Covenant. On the simplest level, the Covenant was a deal
made between God and the Jews. At the beginning of this deal,
it was promised that once the narrative ran its course, once the
string of prophecies came true, God would end History and
bring his people to the promised land. This end was, paradoxically, to be a return to the beginning state, to a timeless, or
eternal, paradise. As I understood it, this made time in the bible
cyclical as well as linear.

By sheer luck, I was reading Gabriel Garcia Marquez's
One Hundred Years of Solitude at the same time I was reading
the New Testament. If my history of religion-bashing prevented
me from a full marveling at the narrative and artistic genius
behind the story of the Bible, I was at least free to marvel at
how Marquez intermeshed cyclical with linear time, showing
through images of magic realism (images which would be defined as miraculous in the bible) how we could always be in the
"now," but that also the string of nows moved inevitably forward. Death, after all, was the one now moment which brought
the inner and the outer life together: even if you've denied
every now moment in your life, you are still moving forward
towards that final inevitable moment. Marquez did this again
and again with images: a bedroom untouched by time even as

the house fell into decrepitude around it, the blind Ursula able to act as if she saw simply by knowing routines (time) so well. This same Ursula, the matriarch of the family, could also symbolically lift herself out of time, lift herself out of habits others were caught in, and find objects such as wedding rings others thought irrevocably lost. Marquez exemplified the paradox of cyclical and linear time with Ursula. The Bible did it with Jesus.

As a poet, I was struck by the sheer genius of Jesus as a narrative device, Jesus as the ultimate paradox. No wonder, I thought, this story has survived with such force, no wonder it has compelled so many. Again, it was the use of time that grabbed me. Of course, there were Jesus' sermons and parables themselves, which were beautiful and attractive for their gentle strength and wisdom, but I could find any number of similar stories and sayings anywhere else I chose to look. It was the way Jesus died that tied it all together, which brought poetic force to his teachings. In particular, it was the things Jesus said on the cross as he died, which, once I turned my whole life's experience toward interpreting these words, astounded me. In Luke, when Jesus says "Father, forgive them, they know not what they do," a way to approach this utterance is to look at what he does not say. He doesn't say, "Father, forgive them because soon they'll understand what they've done and they'll be sorry." This type of reasoning for forgiveness depends upon the passage of time: in a future moment, people will be forced to re-live the past and have their present moment forever sullied by that past. He doesn't say, "Father, forgive them because they are too stupid to understand what's going on and need to be pitied." To say this would be to say that humans are incapable of awareness because of a lack or deficit; rather, they know not what they do because they are trapped in the present moment and so can't understand the historical significance of their actions. And He doesn't say, "Father, forgive them, because they'll be judged later anyway." This would imply a purely apocalyptic sense of time: living a string of now moments isolated from each other by stupidity, as opposed to a string of now moments linked together by awareness. If you believe your life's meaning and value will be decided in the future, independent of what you do or suffer now, then there is no possibility of having your present life acquire meaning through being aware of that future, for that decision, unlinked to the now, could only be haphazard and incomprehensible.

What Jesus does say is "Father, forgive them, for they know now what they do." This implies that while the present moment may be incomprehensible, there is still the possibility of forgiveness, which would instill meaning and order not just to that single moment of future forgiveness, but would also instill meaning into all past and present moments, even those moments that were lived in doubt and chaos.

This last type of living in time is crucial to the concepts of Forgiveness and Redemption, so significant to Christianity. If the Father represents the eternal, then his ability to forgive action created by linear time is the ultimate fusion of cyclical and linear time. When Jesus says, in John, "It is Finished," I don't think he means just his life or his crusade. It is the end of the Old Testament sense of History: the prophecy has come to pass and the violent cause-and-effect type of history embodied in the Old Testament is over: a new sense of time is now in place, a sense of time being both eternally present and eternally changing. All these incredibly complex ideas, embedded in a few sentences. This terrified me.

Yet, obviously the old sense of history, of violent and unjust cause and effect, wasn't over with the crucifixion. If anything, the church itself became responsible for a great deal more violence. But those things *could* be changed, I believed, at least on the personal level, by acting with compassion and unconditional love. History itself would remain in place, as violent as ever, but small transcendent acts of personal dignity and grace could be performed regardless. In the face of chaos, one had to act as if order and meaning were possible, despite the fact that one could never be absolutely sure: the tangible miracle of the carpet changing color or the resurrected dog were not going to be the guidelines of success. Rather, I too had to use a much more abstract, internal gauge of spiritual success, recognizing all the while the possibility that I might simply be fooling myself. I recognized this process as exactly the same pattern of attempting to capture something in words or on a canvas, knowing all along that one will ultimately fail to produce an objective, final, and fully satisfying definition of beauty. I knew the moments in art where I was convinced I had produced something beautiful were not only the moments in which I was most likely wrong, but that the whole notion of being "convinced" was itself the seat of the problem. If paintings and poems were the signposts in art that reminded you again and again of your needs and beliefs rather than letting you get sucked into the abyss of your failures, then the words and deeds of Jesus could work the same way.

When Jesus was on the cross, depending on which gospel you're reading, he says several different things. One of them is a question. My God, my God, why hast thou forsaken me? Except, he doesn't even really ask that—in the two gospels it's present in, it's presented first in another language; *Eloi, Eloi, lama sabachthani,* Eloi coming from the Aramaic or, *Eli, Eli, lama sabachthani,* Eli coming from the Hebrew. The "original" is offered so we readers can fathom why those near him misunderstand and think he's calling for Elijah. There is more written on this one verse in gospels than perhaps on any other. "Is Jesus quoting the twenty-second Psalm?" the writing asks. "Is it instructive: is He questioning God so that we can see that it's acceptable to have moments of doubt?" It's when I read people writing about the Bible that I feel the most alien from religion; and also when I feel the most sorry for us all. Many interpreters have gone to great pains to prove that Jesus' question is answered: after all, it's followed in one gospel with "Father, into Thy hand I commend my spirit." Surely, that statement right there shows he was answered, doesn't it? And yet, in truth, Jesus' last living sound is neither question nor comment, but a cry, a loud cry (John 15:37). Even this "cry" has been under intense scrutiny: some writers going so far as to change it to "voice," and declaring it wasn't a wail, as any one else being crucified might let out, but actually a cry of victory. As if it would be too much to know that Jesus last words were wordless, a cry of deep sorrow and pain. The need to know, the need to have it all be all right, to all make sense.

What hasn't been written on very much is the fact that such a crucial moment in Christianity centers on translation. Other than the use of *Shibboleth* in the Old Testament, these last words of Jesus are the only moment of translation in the Bible, the only moment when alien words are included as part of the whole meaning. I view this as being about how sometimes, we can't understand each other, and need someone to intercede for us. That the final truth doesn't exist in one parcel of words or the other, but in both, and more importantly, in the space between the words, in that brief moment after you read the foreign words, yet before they are explained.

Even after discovering the Bible, I didn't want to Believe, not with a capital B. I didn't want to turn into the type of person I'd regarded as stupid my entire life. But there it was again: was I just being trapped by my own history; my own inability to let go of the past? It was as if I were sitting back on my childhood carpet, the smell of tomato sauce coming from the kitchen, the sounds of scraping pots, as I tried to appeal myself into a position of belief. Wasn't I supposed to just take the plunge now, that proverbial leap? Was it even a matter of will at all? I spent days lying on my bed in my college dorm, staring out the window at the gutter hanging down from the roof in the foreground, the top of an oak tree in the middle ground where large flocks of noisy starlings congregated each dusk, and the sky beyond.

I was taking chemistry at the time, and in lab each small group was handed little vials of an unknown substance. Our task was to determine what it was. In order to do this, we went through a series of tests, tests that were really questions: What is its density? What is its melting point? Will it oxidate? Some of the questions were useful to ask, some were not. If you had a mineral, asking its boiling point was meaningless, but stumbling upon the question of its fracture angle unlocked everything. Once we found the correct set of questions to ask, we gradually uncovered the chemical structure, and were eventually able to supply our professor with the substance's correct name. He, of course, knew all along what it was. The substance was itself the answer: our job was to find the right questions.

Toward the end of writing my memoir *The Autobiography of a Face*, in 197–, I realized I was becoming disgustingly, though perhaps not surprisingly, self-involved. Bitter and jealous, I stalked my own list of personal grievances. In particular, I was jealous of a woman who had cervical cancer: I thought she got to have all the "benefits" of a hard experience, but didn't have to suffer any permanent visible scars. She was beautiful and had just fallen in love with a friend of mine. I felt ugly and had just broken up from a traumatic affair. Able to see I was turning into something I didn't want to be, I kept trying to "get a new outlook." Eventually, after realizing there was no way to think my way out of this depressing state, I decided on real-world action. I called up a Hospice and volunteered to help dying patients write their own memoirs. It was an act of pure ego: I thought I would finally be able to view myself as that kind, loving person I so always wanted to be. As it turned out, most of the patients were too debilitated either to want or to be able to write, or even dictate, their stories. Most of the time I spent volunteering was spent sitting or standing next to a bed, offering what the hospice calls "a ministry of presence." I held onto their hands, I stroked their foreheads. Sometimes, I rubbed their feet, which is difficult, because it is true: the body dies in increments. The feet often go first, and what I had to take in my hands was often scaly and flaccid. I always thought of Christ washing the feet of his apostles. For me, it was pure symbol. For them, it was kindness, perhaps some small relief.

After several weeks on the inpatient ward, I noticed a curious thing. Many of the nurses, aides and other volunteers were in the habit of bringing men they were interested in into the hospice to meet patients of whom they were particularly fond. Ostensibly this was so the boyfriend could see part of his girlfriend's life, but as soon as he left there'd be a great conspiratorial rush to the patient's bedside. "So what do you think of him?" In the past, the dying have always been assigned great mystical powers of truth-saying, and in the way my new lovelorn co-workers hung on the patient's slow, painful words, words sometimes metered out a breathless syllable at a time, the same belief lived on. They would lean over the patients, in a ward always over-heated and over-lit, asking their questions with the belief that there is a final bottom to a person, that we can hit and distinguish a person fully if only we throw the penny down the well enough, and that it is only the dying who are unencumbered enough to tell us how.

Frank was a patient in the hospice who had been dying for two years, though he had been told dozens of times that only months were left. Everyone on the ward had a chance to get to know him quite well. Near the end he was on four grams of morphine a day; four *milligrams* is more than most people could take. He was like a man underwater, all his responses slowed almost to a halt. Often, he would fall asleep in mid-conversation, even mid-gesture, freezing in place, and you had to wait for him to wake back up. My friend Phoebe, his nurse, brought him blue Irises one day, and also her boyfriend. Frank held the unopened Irises one at a time and flicked at them with his forefinger and thumb, ever so slowly, to make them open. It was a trick his mother had taught him, and she had insisted they must be flicked twice. They opened, coming to life one at a time, so slowly, so very slowly, yet quicker than it took Frank to finish his second flick.

After the boyfriend was sent out for coffee, Phoebe leaned over Frank's bed. I was holding onto his feet, hot from being under the blanket I'd just pulled back off them. "Frank, what do you think?" Slowly, he told her, "I don't want to give you bad news." "What Frank, tell me, you didn't like him?" Frank held his arm up to look at his watch, and then actually fell asleep in that position, his arm held up in front of his face, his body wrapped up in a blue cotton blanket. Phoebe didn't see that he'd fallen asleep. "Frank, you can tell me, is it bad?" Then she realized and started to laugh. She looked up at me and said, "Frank is always turning my dialogues into monologues." Then the boyfriend walked back in. He seemed a decent enough person, carrying a streaked brown cardboard carrier with three particularly bright Styrofoam cups. It had been raining all day and water dripped off the coat he hung on the door. He didn't say anything. The three of us sat there, waiting for Frank, waiting for him to wake back up and turn Phoebe's monologue back into a dialogue, waiting for him there with his Irises, holding our unnaturally white cups of coffee.

David Lazar

Further Father: Remembering John Waterman

A paradox: when I try to think of the most generic name imaginable, I think past John Smith (a tiny graduate student I served with somewhere in the disarmed forces of academia), Tom Brown (whose schooldays intrude on the common names of my schooldays: Schwartzes and Petrocellis), and John Doe (a name I've always found both silly and elegant, whose etymology I've wondered about with the idle curiosity that does not send one on etymological crusades) to John Waterman, a name I find singularly bland, but which nominally resonated throughout my childhood through my teenage years. John Waterman was my father.

Sort of. John Waterman was my father's pseudonym, pragmatically crafty alter ego, his all-purpose floating other who served us well through his many guises, positions, familiarities, and resources.

Last month, back to New York for a visit, I was making reservations at a midtown restaurant for my father and step-mother, brother and sister-in-law and myself. My father hovered nearby: "Make it in the name of John Waterman," he said, with a genial smirk. I did so. Old scams die hard.

My father's name is Leo Lazar, a name I've never grown tired of, as though, the swift syllabic balance, the semantic suggestion of lion and leper, embodied the Runyonesque vitality, operatic temper, bad-joke spilling, egocentric generosity of this man I've known for forty years. My brother and I had a joke, in adolescence, that still tells. In the midst of our greatest dread at our father's anger (which we had seen reduce grown women to sobs, grown men to inward-pulling dark unresponsiveness bordering on despair) we would refer to him secretly as Leola Czar. Leo La Czar might have done the trick—we were, after all, descended from turn of the century refugees from Nicholas II, on my mother's side—except for the fact that the preservation of my father's first name failed to convey the metamorphic quality he achieved in rage. Leola, though feminine sounding, captured the Arabian Nights strangeness of the dervish who would spew out invective when provoked. And it didn't take much. But, fantasies aside, my father has always been *Leo Lazar*, that quick alliterative combination with the pleasurable effect of a left hook; it rises and falls on its vowels, and then it's over. My friends take pleasure in saying the name, and if I alternate between references to my father and to Leo in this essay, it is because I think of him both as my kindred source of all sources, and as a slightly avuncular *character* who is sometimes quite escapable, quick with a riposte, loud-spoken, eager to retell a joke (I prefer the strangeness of the ones with a Yiddish punchline, since it puts the joke a bit out of reach and into a cultural realm I feel affection for, albeit distance from).

It's perhaps difficult for some to imagine the cultural difference between first-generation parents raised in the depression, and second generation teenagers raised in the sixties. My father's parents had escaped pogroms in Austria and Rumania to come to New York at the turn of the century. My grandfather was a small silent man who spent fifty years working his way from waiter to busboy, mostly at New York's then-host of "dairy" restaurants, beat kosher family places that have all-but vanished. Ratner's, on Delancey Street, hangs on still, but every visit there, performed at four or five year intervals, frequently as a cultural service to my usually non-Jewish girlfriend of the time, confirms that any given trip back may be the last. It languishes in a half-hearty way. My father was a smart kid, by all accounts. Quick-witted, astute, academically inclined simply by quickness of mind, rather than extreme diligence. He whizzed through school. Can any word, I wonder, be further from the Yiddish my father grew up with than *whizzed?* "Is there anything further, father," Zeppo Marx asks Groucho in *Horsefeathers,* in which Groucho plays the college president, Zeppo his collegiate athlete son. Groucho's retort: "That can't be right. Isn't it anything fa(r)ther further?"

My father graduated high school at fifteen—in the graduation photos he looks like a twelve-year-old greenhorn. Right off the boat and into the cap and gown. Strange, for a Jewish immigrant family, what happened next. My father was awarded a scholarship to Cornell University. He intended, he tells me, to study animal husbandry, which boggles my mind considering that my only experience of my father and animals consists of him railing for fifteen years at the cow-shaped fox terrier that soiled and befouled our shag carpets with impunity, and the memory of a family bursting out laughing at the Miami Monkey Jungle, circa 1962, when a large ape ceremoniously looked my father in the eye and slowly turned, spread her cheeks, and offered a rosy view of its world.

My father offered to get a job in the wake of his own father's depressing (I believe it would last forty or fifty years) depression, and the "family," meaning his mother, unexpectedly accepted. A note here (Mr. Waterman, hold the phone, I haven't forgotten you): my father's family was an uncertain matriarchy. My grandmother, Minnie, whom I remember unfondly as shrill, obese, given to operatic sighs preceding opera-length monologues on her proximity to departed relatives (she would join them thirty years later) seemed to have the last word in the family. My father speaks of her younger generosity, holding a large extended family together, providing for them with difficulty while my grandfather, Benny, brought home the pitiful tips left by other pitifully marginal men. Perhaps. He also apparently had a bit of a gambling problem, hard as it is for me to imagine that man with the visage of Elmer Fudd and the personality of Road Runner—beep beep, sit in the chair and light another stogie—doing anything that smacks of obsession. Considering this information, though, I have been treated on several occasions to one of the strangest lines I've ever heard in the context of family historiographies; when I've asked my father about his family's financial situation, he has frequently told me that his mother felt that his father "pissed all his money away on cigars." Am I missing something? A pittance on poker, and a fortune on cheap sweets? How much can one man smoke? The line that got Groucho taken off the air, said to a female guest who said that she had seven children and that her husband operated a screwing machine: "Look, lady, I like my cigar, but even I take it out sometimes." I have images of a Jewish Elmer Fudd in dreamland, tattered pajamas, a beaten-up mattress, sounds of the street picking up the metal taste of a tenement iron fire escape on a hot Orchard Street night, a thin plume of smoke escaping from the lit cigar, puffing alternating with snoring. It's possible that in my father's mind, what his mother told him as avoidance or euphemism for gambling, cigars, took on a parallel explanatory function, cigars and gambling. I mean, after all, he probably smoked while he dealt or tossed. Or perhaps I just hold onto the phrase for the unlikely combination of "pissed" and "cigars," which would seem to cancel one another out. In any case, my father skipped college, went to work at a travel agency, and then a ribbon company for the next eight years until Pearl Harbor. They treated him well in the ribbon business. He cut the mustard. Will there be anything further, father? You bet your life.

Where was I? The affinity of this question to where am I. I was making dinner reservations in the name of John Waterman. My father had a John Waterman phone in his office, and when my brother and I worked for my father's travel agency, mostly answering phones or running errands, we were under strict orders to answer this phone only, "John Waterman's office. Can I help you." John Waterman was protean. Sometimes he was

bosomed normal school types who, at the age of fifty-five or so, had managed to cultivate an air of boredom that would do justice to the shallow existentialist of your choice. Once, in an attempt to impress her, I told her that I had been reading Bernard Malamud's novels. "Yes, yes," she replied abstractly, "he writes very nice children's books." I resisted correcting her for two reasons: 1) I was not the correcting type. I was the make a note of that type, equal parts polite and introverted, and 2) What would it have mattered? She obviously didn't care, so I couldn't very well tell her what she already both knew and didn't know. She knew she was wasting our time and hers, so why should she have cared about Bernard Malamud?

We all had to memorize and recite several speeches for this class. There was no clear pedagogical explanation for this; it was simply what we did. And, indeed, I'm grateful, since I remember everything I recited. My first toe-ing of the recitation line was near-traumatic; worse, it was baffling. I had chosen the classic soliloquy from Macbeth: "Tomorrow and tomorrow and tomorrow . . ." I spoke the first line, and at every *and* the entire class spontaneously burst out into a mocking exaggeration of my pronounciation. *Eeeund,* they kept repeating. I had no idea of what was going on for a moment or two, until I realized that they were mocking my accent. This is a very strange memory for me to consider, since no matter how strong my accent may have been, it's difficult to believe that theirs was not equally strong, or even more, shall we say, pronounced. Was it, I wonder, a moment of recognition, even self-consciously, that managed to escape their understanding? They kidded me about it for days, and I could see the look of anticipation when my next turn came—I had chosen Puck's last speech this time. But by this time the *a's* had softened with my own self-consciousness, beginning a process that would accelerate when I went to college.

I went to an expensive somewhat experimental college in New England. All right, I went to Bennington. I've always had an excuse to be a bit queasy about that. First it was the years of response beginning, "I thought that was a girls' school," one of those idiotic responses akin to "I thought you were dead." What was I supposed to say, "Yes, it is, but I look great in drag"? After that, thanks to a *Time* article, my inquisitors would angle their heads and smirk out, "Isn't that the most expensive school in the country?" It was for a time, and I went there thanks to my father's generosity and John Waterman's many successful enterprises. My father flatly told me that I could go to any school I chose, a gesture completely endearing and more than understandable from one who didn't get to go at all. These days, my embarrassment about Bennington is more direct: I hate the manipulative faculty-bashing moves of its current administration. If a school exists on a kind of fraternity with its graduates, I disown it.

But I was never completely owned by it. I was one of the outsiders there: ethnic, uncool, studious, and still with a wash of Brooklyn in the accent. But I made it my business to get rid of it. I took voice lessons from a man who had an almost cult-like following; he was a longtime faculty member who had had a stroke and communicated in whispers. Singing lessons were like vespers. One had to concentrate, and there was, for many, a kind of sacred aura about studying singing and voice from a man who could not perform the former, and could barely produce the latter. He kept missing my diaphragm in individual lessons, straying so low that the odds of a mere mistaken brush of the hand seemed impossible. Twice I bellowed "No" at him, the way one would upbraid an unruly dog or a straying child. This ended my singing career, which was marked with a fine vibrato only when I was nervous enough to produce it unnaturally.

But, privately, I kept refining my accent, moderating my vowels, softening my consonants. A friend at the time said I sounded like an English don. That must have been my progression from Brooklyn don. Corleone to Cambridge, made easy.

But this wasn't a dark obsession, the need to rid myself of background and blend it. It was more specific than that, clearly, since my greatest joy at Bennington was dinner with Roy Weinberg. We had about the same demographic profile, other than the fact that he had moved to Manhattan from the Bronx as an adolescent. We would meet in what I called the Pariah dining room, one of the smaller halls, off to the side. The bluebloods didn't venture there. But even the ragtag lot who did were sometimes quieted and disquieted by the conversations Roy and I had: boisterous, improvisatory, and full of the Lower East Side. We would talk as two old clothing merchants, invoke the doggerel of Mott Street, praising our far backgrounds by mockingly invoking it. We would have felt, on a rather profound level, that "Tell me what street/Compares with Mott Street/In July" had an irony that was entirely gentle.

"So, how's business?"

"Metza, metza. It comes, it goes."

"You got new suits?"

"I got new suits. What else I'm gonna get if not new suits?"

"It's a question, all right? Not necessary to put on a shigun."

That kind of thing. We howled. We liked seeing unsophisticatedly devoted to our backgrounds. But we both also developed rather flat elocutionary styles, slower, flatter, dappled with irony, as opposed to bursting with the sarcasm we had grown up with. Both of our ways paid by fathers who had made good: made good money. We could be of our background, or, in the larger world, unplaceable. If Leo had ruses that brought in the bucks and got us the tough tickets, then I had my own ruse: I could assimilate perfectly, when I wanted to. My culture was something I invoked when comfortable. Otherwise, I became other wise. I was so savvy that the only possible way to exist seemed to me to be enigmatic, persona-empowered. I enjoyed the guessing games about where I was from when I met someone. I suppose I thought I was winning something.

At times, there clearly seemed to be some pleasure on Leo's part at the success of *his* ruses; a small smile would creep across his face-as-Waterman, a smile that seemed to indicate the satisfaction of the scam—the practical joke with a material payoff. I could and can understand this. As a matter of fact, I have, ironically, never trusted anyone who was incapable of "putting one over," as though the inability to be obviously untrustworthy at least some of the time bespeaks a moral weakness, or thinness of character. But how much deeper and in what other directions did my father's satisfaction go? This is speculation on my part, but I wonder about the mantle of the *other* he was donning, what that felt like. Living Jewish in New York can be very comfortable and hermetic, true, but my father had certainly had his experiences *out there;* he had been in the service in Oklahoma and India when, despite the host of war movies with the bespectacled egg-headed and more or less accepted Jewish serviceman as a standard type, he must have encountered veritable worlds of otherness unprotected by the surrounding cushion of familiarity he had had, and would have in New York. Was there a frisson of transgression in being a temporary goy?

My father told me a story recently that I had never heard. He was in the service waiting for assignment overseas. I believe it was a couple of months in Tennessee, circa 1942. He started dating a young local woman named Virginia, the name itself a far cry from Lower Broadway, and an incriptive redoubling of his journey south of Mason and Dixon. His description of the affair is rather generic—she was "a very nice girl and we were in love." And he considered marriage. To my astonishment, Leo told me that he asked *his* parents for permission. And they declined. "I didn't really want to, but I broke it off. She was a shiksa and my parents couldn't accept it, and I just couldn't go against their wishes."

I was stunned by this story. My father is a formidable man: headstrong, wily, and before the mellowing of his later years, following my mother's untimely death, full of rage. Rage is a word that should not be used for merely excessive anger; it denotes a state far enough beyond anger as to constitute a separate state, a qualitative rather than merely quantitative difference. And my father held full citizenship. In the offices of Comet Travel, several times a week, a preternatural quiet would settle on the dusty desks when my father's telephone explosions would suck all the oxygen out of the room. Screaming epithets into the phone-ear of some airline functionary—frequently prefaced by "Never in my life . . ."—Leo as Leo would reduce the target of his rage to single cellular status. Sometimes these would be followed with mild apologies to the supervisors who had performed whatever service it was my father was, shall we say, requesting, usually, however, accompanied by a disclaimer that indicated the outburst would not have been necessary if he or she had known what to do: serve. I would get very queasy during these episodes, having been the target myself any number of times. My father, these days, likes to tell the story of when I was implored by my mother, that sweet Jewish intercessor, to go in and apologize to my father before bed for whatever infraction was performed or perceived. I did so, reluctantly, hang-dog. My father launched into a rather vituperative lecture on my worthlessness. My endgame response, sullen but somewhat brave considering what I was up against, was: "I just wanted to say I'm sorry." My father tells this story with a very mild and implicit self-mockery. I am far from unsympathetic; having achieved a free and funny, a speak-your-mind and kibitzing kinship with my near-dotage Dad, I grow weary and bored at the idea of stashing and rehashing wounds as a lugubrious form of postponed adolescent entertainment. I keep them, for literary purposes, to my essays. I don't need to work much out with a smart survivor of an old man who has, all things considered, been rather good to me. Nevertheless, or is it be that as it may, I did experience a withering, what sometimes felt apocalyptic dressing down with a disturbing frequency in my childhood and adolescence.

Remember, I got over it. But it took awhile to understand, forget, transcend, whatever it was I did. There was the time, for example, when Leo, in a rage upstairs, was screaming to my mother's witness-ears that he didn't love my brother and me, and probably never had. My brother Scott and I were hunched silently on the stairs, eavesdropping, if such a thing is possible at dangerous decibel levels. We never discussed this moment. Once, I believe in my early twenties, in the throes of primary therapizing, I mentioned this moment to my father and received a resounding lack of confirmation. To say such things was clearly an impossibility. I have come to accept that not only is the debated history of paternal excess a seminal childhood experience, but that, past a certain age, confirmation can be a cold comfort. My bones are getting old and need less to settle on hard-won familial-historical accuracies. But yet, I will tell you I felt rather small and orphaned at that moment. True rage is radical: it can diminish or destroy. I'm more concerned at this moment, though, with the need that fed the urge to diminish, rather than the diminishee.

So my father, a grown man, yielded again to the narrow interests of his parents. The equanimity with which he speaks of this is striking. Of course, considering the happiness of his married life with my mother, I suppose this fragment of the past could be consigned to the happy accident category. (And lest this characterization seem incongruous in the wake of my previous paragraph, let me say this: our family's problems, such as they were, always did an end run around my father and mother's relationship. At the darkest moments of my unhappiness, or my sense of injustice at my father's temporary insanities or my mother's defense of them—"Go apologize" was close to a mantra—I marvelled at the equanimity the two of them maintained.) In these versions one can pay homage to old obstacles and injustices that paved the way to moments, scenarios, lives that would not have otherwise been lived. This has always struck me as Panglossian, the blessing of past troubles. For despite the apparent optimism of the outlook is the belief that things couldn't have been better. I mean, the man who falls and breaks his leg and misses the airplane crash today could have changed his flight, saved his leg, and won the lottery, too. I'm leery about giving fate the hail fellow when I just know he's thinking *Not so fast—If you only knew.* I'm reminded of the man in Primo Levi's *Survival in Auschwitz,* davenning in thanks for having been spared from a selection. Levi's devastating remark, "If I were God I would spit in his face," strikes me as a terribly sane view of the world. Behind every *thank God it wasn't me* is a *thank God it was them,* which is, shall we say, uncharitable.

Let me clarify: I really do admire an optimistic view of the past, if that isn't oxymoronic. I just like to see a healthy dose of irony thrown in. But my father is from a less ironic generation. Despite its wonderfully melodramatic dark side, even *The Best Years of Our Lives* ends affirmatively. I mean, we won the war, and most people got houses and sent their kids to college. I really don't mean to be sardonic about this—the older I get the more I am full of awe and admiration for my parents' generation. I'm not invoking a false-Fifties consciousness; I'm just tired of my own generation's narcissism when compared to the generation that allowed them to skulk and sulk around with it. And if I have trouble at times understanding my father's lack of bitterness at his parents' foibles and follies, perhaps it is because in the slight peering of my relationship with my father, I feel a bit paternal toward him at times, a bit protective, even about what I consider old wrongs.

I seem to keep losing John Waterman in this essay. But I want to return to him, to his protean and pragmatic shadow life by the telephone. Why *did* Leo choose such a wonderfully generic gentile name in the creation of this *Other* Everyman? He says he doesn't remember, picked it out of a hat (does anyone still wear a hat? as the Sondheim song ruefully asks). But that doesn't hold Waterman for me. For one thing, this nom de telephone had to be a non-Jew, even if these reasons were derived subconsciously. A non-Jewish name would be flexible, useful for both the Jewish and non-Jewish worlds. It would have authority in both. Borough Jews of my father's age were remarkably uninformed about the Christian world, despite the exposure of the war. This was partly willful—a desire not to be contaminated, not to assimilate the culture of Christian America more than was necessary, other than the unavoidable and naturalized but mostly understated presence of it in the media. It was a way of saying *We expect your world to be the world of TV and the movies, more or less, but we're going to try to make believe that Christmas doesn't exist, especially since you simply refuse to acknowledge that Jesus was a nice Jewish boy who went a little soft in the head because of his dubious parentage.* To know more than that, though, I think was to put oneself in danger of being seduced. There was also some pique involved. After all, *They* know absolutely nothing about us . . . This sentiment is so strong that it spilled over—over the years, when I brought a non-Jewish woman home, my father would sometimes act as though she were slightly slow. He would painstakingly instruct on how to cut a bagel, or ask if she had ever had pastrami, or begin mini-paeans to the Jews with something like *The Jews are a very ancient people*. For decorum's sake, I would correct Leo gently, saying something mild and sensitive like, "Jesus Christ, she didn't just step out of the Spaceship Trinity, having come from the planet Shiksa!"

The moxie in the charade was that to be Protestant Mr. Waterman only required certainty, and my father's decades of hard work, a kind of single-minded devotion to what used to be called *building a life*, equipped him bountifully with this. Of course, the point is that he was right. In all the years of charades, all the outlandish anouncements of position—Waterman as vice president of Nabisco, Waterman as Doris Day's brother, Waterman as England's vice counsel to the UN—there never was a slip; the ruse always sailed clear, never foundering on the dubious questions of the rusee. In this my father engaged two bits of fundamental psychology: most workers were too disaffected to care enough to question a status higher than theirs, even if they dared to, which usually they did not; and the knowledge that certainty is convincing. Marlon Brando may have found Lee Strasberg in the early fifties, but he might as well have studied with Leo Lazar. You don't become the character, but it works.

Of course Waterman felt nothing, and I think Leo felt that most people are easily fooled. There must have been some satisfaction in this, some recompense about his own undeveloped education. At 77, my father has lost none of his mental agility, although I sometimes talk to him and sense the wall, the wall of more subtle understandings that an education, or the company of those outside his world might have led him toward a ways. He has a healthy and balanced vision of the world, a philosophical streak. It is mixed with fixed ideas and bits of information that are frequently partial, a little too dependent on questionable received information. But Leo knows that I at least will challenge him—he gets a kick out of the way I get riled up when he presents me with what I consider both dubious arguments and statistics in favor of capital punishment. I get a kick out of it too, after I've cooled down. These usually begin in the car from the airport, somewhere right after *how was the flight*. Once a few years ago, in the midst of one of these engaging automotive welcomes, I interrupted my father to ask what John Waterman thought of whatever political imbroglio we were entertaining. He said, "Didn't I tell you, Waterman's dead."

"Did you go to the funeral," I inquired?

"In a manner of speaking." Touché.

Sometimes I think of John Waterman as the gentile George Kaplan. George Kaplan was a cog in Hitchcock's maguffin, in *North by Northwest*. You may remember it is George Kaplan's name that is being announced by a waiter when Cary Grant waves to get his attention. The cold warrior thugs watching from the doorway think Grant is responding to the Kaplan call. Throughout much of the rest of the film, Grant first tries to deny, then plays the role of Kaplan, a very secret agent, so secret in fact that he doesn't even exist. He's a decoy, a name checked into hotels so the good guys (Us, or in Cold War terms, U.S.) can check on the bad guys (Them). But I've always wondered why Ernest Lehmann, the scriptwriter, chose a Jewish name for the decoy. Perhaps he figured that most moviegoers wouldn't recognize it as such, and placed it there as a wink to the Jews in the house. But I've sometimes thought of Kaplan as the missing Jew of the fifties, the Jew who didn't die in the camps, or live to tell, who didn't serve and return to Saturday services, but was assimilated away into an empty room, who became the organization man, who became, in one reading, John Waterman, who had been Morris Levine, or Heshy Abramowitz. My father stayed very much a Jew, but needed a chaser of Waterman, an invisible factotum. Perhaps John Waterman helped Leo Lazar stay Leo Lazar, in a sense. John Waterman married the girl down South, and the Orchard Street kids who made it to Cornell bought houses in the Hamptons. We lived in Brooklyn and always had the best seats in the house, whether the house was the Eugene O'Neill Theater, Carnegie Hall, or Madison Square Garden.

I had a classmate in elementary school, P.S. 216 in Brooklyn, whose name was James Johnson. He was a Jewish kid, but nonobserving, which was a peculiar phenomenon back then. All the Jewish kids I grew up with went to Hebrew school after regular school for years (not that we learned much of anything there) in gradual preparation for our Bar Mitzvahs. But not James Johnson. And what kind of a name was that? I could piece together the shortened names—Bloom from Bloomberg, Fink from Finkelstein (that was a trade up), Lazar from Lazarowitz—but not this one. And James? You might as well smear mayo on your corned beef. My father explained that James Johnson Sr. (another anomaly, since Jews don't name offspring after the living, and therefore the custom of Jrs. and Srs. doesn't exist) worked for a large company that didn't hire many Jews and that this was his way of trying to make it. I was fascinated, and a little disgusted. The idea of having to fake your way to the top felt so instinctively demeaning that I couldn't understand why anyone would want to make it that way.

Understand, in the neighborhoods of Brooklyn, there was no dreamy fantasizing about wanting to be a normal blue-eyed Protestant kid from a wholesome midwestern family. In my neighborhood—Ocean Parkway, between Flatbush and Brighton Beach, sometimes called Gravesend, you could be Italian Catholic or Eastern European Jewish, period. When a Protestant kid showed up in school, once in a blue moon, having moved to Brooklyn from somewhere out there where the buffalo roam, we thought he was freaky. We liked our pizza and spumoni, our chicken soup and chopped liver, and had no desire to trade it in. James Johnson, whose family did, was considered a bit freaky, too, especially because there didn't even seem to be any payoff for the tradeoff—he was no materially better off than we were, was in fact in the bottom to middle level, since he was apartment bound, and many of us were rowhoused.

John Waterman was a Protestant genie locked in a black phone. No combination of exchanges, neither Murray Hill, nor Gramercy, Dewey, or Esplanade with any combination of numbers trailing would set him free. And even though his phone had an aura of danger around it (what would happen, I sometimes wondered, if I screwed up, answered the Waterman phone with *Comet Travel,* or *Leo Lazar's office?* Would it bring the Feds in, some square and threatening G-men come to arrest my father for impersonating a Protestant, which I imagined to be a felony?) it was mostly a magical object of fun. My father certainly had the knack of doing the voices of other regions and nationalities, and I picked it up. There's a thrill in impersonation that I still get a kick out of. Though I've progressed a bit beyond Sir Walter Raleigh in a can, I do enjoy leaving enigmatic phone messages for friends in voices impossible to identify. I don't get tickets to the game for this, but one takes one's amusement where one finds it.

I feel that I've skirted around my subject a bit, taken the long route via anecdote and digression *(You heard me baby, meet me on the corner of Anecdote and Digression. Ever heard of Bushwick?).* Where are we left, you and I, having circled around the story of a phone and a name? Maybe we're left with the question of entree, of using what the culture gives us by the back door when the front door seems unavailable, a large NO SOLICITATION sign.

My father has told this story many times: he was a staff sergeant, was stationed in Calcutta, having dinner at the mess. Leo used to wax lyrical, disgusted about the torments of Army food. About spam: he left his plate half-full (half empty?) and a passing lieutenant ordered him to *clean it.* He refused, was reported, performed the requisite KP, and never advanced further in rank. *Anything further father?*

There are things we refuse, turn down, turn away from—bigger houses out of the ethnic soup of Brooklyn, for example, or women in Tennessee with yellow hair, who almost seem to shine with a shiksa brightness, or the grail of a diploma of higher learning. And there are things we end-run around, for compensation, for a sense of efficacy, for love of family and opportunity.

In 1972, I went to see Groucho Marx at Carnegie Hall. It was one of the hottest tickets ever in New York, a legendary swan song: just Groucho up on stage, with young Marvin Hamlisch providing accompaniment at the piano. There were stories, jokes, bits of songs: *Lydia the Tattooed Lady, It's Better to Go to Toronto, Than Live in a Place You Don't Vant to* . . . I got there early, went with my best friend. I can't remember ever being more excited about a performance. My brother and I knew virtually every Marx Brothers routine by heart. We'd riff off them for hours: This is so simple a four-year-old child could understand it. Somebody run and get me a four-year-old child. Or, to Margaret Dumont: Meet me tonight under the moon. You wear a tie so I'll know it's you. Or the speakeasy scene from *Horsefeathers:* Chico: I give you three guesses. It's the name of a fish. Groucho: Is it Mary? Chico: That's a no fish. Groucho: Oh, yeah, she drinks like one. My friend and I cruised around Carnegie Hall, talked to Dick Cavett for awhile, hoisted him up on stage at one point. The crowd started drifting in. In a burst of chutzpah, I went over to Mayor Lindsay, who was seated with his wife, and asked if he was going to drop out of the presidential race so that he wouldn't hurt McGovern's chances. In gentlemanly fashion, he said he hadn't decided yet, but was glad to see a young man so engaged with politics. I snagged autographs from some of my favorites (including Lindsay!): Jules Feiffer, Paul Simon and Art Garfunkel, Woody Allen, and just to round out the list Chuck McCann, the sometime character actor and children's show host famous for his manic readings, in costume, of Little Orphan Annie. It was a heady night, the crowd packed with celebrities.

I sat in the fourth row center, waiting for the next wave of wisecracks from the pantheon, the Ur-wit, Minnie's boy become a legend. John Waterman got me the tickets, in a move I vaguely remember as especially daring. Maybe he was deputy director of United Jewish Appeal, or perhaps the grand duke of Fredonia. In any case, I remain grateful.

Rediscovery

J. B. Jackson

Ghosts at the Door

The house stands by itself, lost somewhere in the enormous plain. Next to it is a windmill, to the rear a scattering of barns and shelters and sheds. In every direction, range and empty field reach to a horizon unbroken by a hill or the roof of another dwelling or even a tree. The wind blows incessantly; it raises a spiral of dust in the corral. The sun beats down on the house day after day. Straight as a die the road stretches out of sight between a perspective of fence and light poles. The only sound is the clangor of the windmill, the only movement the wind brushing over the grass and wheat, and the afternoon thunderheads boiling up in the western sky.

But in front of the house on the side facing the road there is a small patch of ground surrounded by a fence and a hedge. Here grow a dozen or more small trees—Chinese elms, much whipped and tattered by the prevailing gale. Under them is a short expanse of bright-green lawn.

Trees, lawn, hedge, and flowers—these things, together with much care and a great expenditure of precious water, all go to make up what we call the front yard. Not only here on the western farmstead but on every one of a million farms from

California to Maine. All front yards in America are much the same, as if they had been copied from one another, or from a remote prototype.

They are so much part of what is called the American scene that you are not likely to wonder why they exist. Particularly when you see them in the East and Midwest; there they merge into the woodland landscape and into the tidy main street of a village as if they all belonged together. But when you travel west you begin to mark the contrast between the yard and its surroundings. It occurs to you that the yard is sometimes a very artificial thing, the product of much work and thought and care. Whoever tends them so well out here on the lonely flats (you say to yourself) must think them very important.

And so they are. Front yards are a national institution— essential to every home, like a Bible somewhere in the house. It is not their size which makes them so. They are usually so small that from a vertical or horizontal distance of more than a mile they can hardly be seen. Nor are they always remarkable for what they contain. No, but they are pleasant oases of freshness and moving shade in the heat of the monotonous plain. They are cool in the summer and in the winter their hedges and trees do much to break the violence of the weather. The way they moderate the climate justifies their existence.

They serve a social purpose, too. By common consent, the appearance of a front yard, its neatness and luxuriance, is an index of the taste and enterprise of the family who owns it. Weeds and dead limbs are a disgrace, and the man who rakes and waters and clips after work is usually held to be a good citizen.

So this infinitesimal patch of land, only a few hundred square feet, meets two very useful ends: it provides a place for outdoor enjoyment, and it indicates social standing. But in reality, does it always do those things?

Many front yards, and by no means the least attractive, flourish on western ranches and homesteads many miles from neighbors. They waste their sweetness on the desert air. As for any front yard being used for recreation, this seems to be a sort of national myth. Perhaps on Sunday afternoons when friends come out from town to pay a visit, chairs are tentatively placed on the fresh-cut grass. For the rest of the week the yard is out of bounds, just as the now obsolete front parlor always used to be. The family is content to sit on the porch when it wants fresh air. It admires the smooth lawn from a distance.

The true reason why every American house has to have a front yard is probably very simple: it exists to satisfy a love of beauty. Not every beauty, but beauty of a special, familiar kind; one that every American can recognize and enjoy, and even after a fashion recreate for himself.

The front yard, then, is an attempt to reproduce next to the house a certain familiar or traditional setting. In essence, the front yard is a landscape in miniature. It is not a garden; its value is by no means purely esthetic. It is an enclosed space which contains a garden among other things. The patch of grass and Chinese elms and privet stands for something far larger and richer and more beautiful. It is a much reduced version, as if seen through the wrong end of a pair of fieldglasses, of a spacious countryside of woods and hedgerows and meadow.

Such was the countryside of our remote forebears; such was the original, the protolandscape which we continue to remember and cherish, even though for each generation the image becomes fainter and harder to recall.

Loyalty to a traditional idea of how the world should look is something which we do not always take into account when analyzing ourselves or others. Yet it is no more improbable than loyalty to traditional social or economic ideas or to traditional ideas in art. The very fact that we are almost completely unaware of our loyalty to a protolandscape allows us to express that loyalty with freedom. We have not yet been made ashamed of being old-fashioned. But what precisely is that landscape which our memory keeps alive and which an atavistic instinct tries to recreate?

It is not exclusively American. It is not New England or colonial Virginia or Ohio. It is nothing based on pictures and vacation trips to the East. It is northwestern Europe. Whatever the ethnic origin of the individual American, however long his family may have lived in this country, we are all descendants, spiritually speaking, of the peoples of Great Britain and Ireland, of the Low Countries, and to a lesser extent of northern France and western Germany. It was from those countries that the colonists transferred the pattern of living which is still the accepted pattern of living in North America. It may not remain so much longer, but that is something else again. We are all of us exiles from a landscape of streams and hills and forests. We come from a climate of cold dark winters, a few weeks of exuberant spring, and abundant snow and rain. Our inherited literary and popular culture both reflect that far-off environment, and until recently our economy and society reflected it too.

For almost a thousand years after the collapse of the Roman Empire, the history of Europe was the history of a slow and persistent deforestation. When the classical civilization began to die, Europe ceased to be one unit and became two. The region around the Mediterranean preserved a good deal of the Roman heritage; for the most part its population did not greatly change and the land remained under cultivation. But for several reasons the entire northwestern portion of the empire—Great Britain, the Low Countries, northern France, and western Germany— began to revert to wilderness. Roads, towns, cities, and farms were gradually abandoned, fell into ruin, and in time were hidden by brush and forest. The peoples whom we call the barbarians, who later moved in from the East, had thus to reclaim the land all over again. They were obliged to take back from the forest by main force whatever land they needed for farms and pastures and villages. They were pioneers no less tough than those who settled our own West. Their numbers were so few and their means so primitive that every lengthy war and every epidemic saw much newly cleared land revert to undergrowth once more. It was not until a century ago that the last wastelands on the Continent were put under cultivation. The whole undertaking was an extraordinary phase of European history, one which we know very little about. How well it succeeded is shown by the fact that Holland, now a land of gardens, originally meant "Land of Forests."

Could this incessant warfare with the forest fail to have an effect on the men who engaged in it? Does it not help to explain an attitude toward nature quite unlike that of the peoples farther south? The constant struggle against cold and solitude and darkness, the omnipresent threat of the wilderness and the animals that lived in it, in time produced a conviction that there was no existing on equal terms with nature. Nature had to be subdued, and in order to subdue her, men had to study her and know her strength. We have inherited this philosophy, it sometimes seems, in its entirety: this determination to know every one of nature's secrets and to establish complete mastery over her; to love in order to possess and eventually destroy. It is not a point of view which has worked very well here in the West. If we had thought more in terms of cooperation with a reluctant and sensitive environment, as the Mediterranean people still do, and less in terms of "harnessing" and "taming," we would have not made such a shambles of the southwestern landscape.

That aggressive attitude is, however, only part of what the earliest farmers in northern Europe bequeathed us. Since they created the human landscape themselves and under great difficulties, they had a deep affection for it. They looked upon the combination of farmland and meadow and forest as the direct expression of their way of life. It was a harsh and primitive landscape, just as by all accounts it was a harsh and primitive way of life, but it was not lacking in a sentiment for the surrounding world, nor in an element of poetry. The perpetual challenge of the forest stirred the imagination as did no other feature in the environment. It was the forest where the outlaw went to hide, it was there that adventurous men went to make a new farm and a new and freer life. It teemed with wolves, boars, bears, and wild oxen. It contained in its depths the abandoned clearings and crumbling ruins of an earlier civilization. It was a place of terror to the farmer and at the same time a place of refuge. He was obliged to enter it for wood and game and in search of pasture. For hundreds of years the forest determined the spread of population and represented the largest source of raw materials; it was an outlet for every energy. Its dangers as well as its wealth became part of the daily existence of every man and woman.

When at last it was removed from the landscape, our whole culture began to change and even to disintegrate. A Frenchman has recently written a book to prove that the decline in popular beliefs and traditions (and in popular attitudes toward art and work and society) in his country was the direct outcome of the destruction a century ago of the last areas of untouched woodland. If he is correct, how many of those traditions can be left among us who have denuded half a continent in less than six generations? The urge to cut down trees is stronger than ever. The slightest excuse is enough for us to strip an entire countryside. And yet—there is the front yard with its tenderly cared for Chinese elms, the picnic ground in the shadow of the pines, and a mass of poems and pictures and songs about trees. A Mediterranean would find this sentimentality hard to understand.

The old ambivalence persists. But the reverence for the forest is no longer universal. Our household economy is largely free from dependence on the resources of the nearby forest, and any feeling for the forest itself is a survival from childhood associations. Until the last generation, it might have been said that much of every American (and northern European) childhood was passed in the landscape of traditional forest legends. Time had transformed the reality of the wilderness into myth. The forest outlaw became Robin Hood. The vine-grown ruins became the castle of Sleeping Beauty. The frightened farmer, armed with an axe for cutting firewood, was the hero of Little Red Riding Hood and the father of Hansel and Gretel. In a sense, our youngest years were a reenactment of the formative period of our culture, and the magic of the forest was never entirely forgotten in adult life. Magic, of course, is part of every childhood; yet if a generation grew up on the magic of Superman and Mickey Mouse and Space Cadet instead, if it lived in the empty and inanimate landscape which provides a background for those figures, how long would it continue to feel the charms of the forest? How long would the Chinese elms be watered and cared for?

After the forest came the pasture, and the pasture in time became the lawn. When a Canadian today cuts down trees in order to start a farm, he says he is "making land." He might with equal accuracy say that he is "making lawn," for the two words have the same origin and once had the same meaning. Our lawns are merely the civilized descendants of the medieval pastures cleared among the trees. In the New Forest in England, a "lawn" is still an open space in the woods where cattle are fed.

So the lawn has a very prosaic background, and if lawns seem to be typically northern European—the English secretly believe that there are no true lawns outside of Great Britain—that is simply because the farmers in northern Europe raised more cattle than did the farmers near the Mediterranean, and had to provide more feed.

As cattle and sheep raising increased in importance, the new land wrested from the forest became more and more essential to the farmer: he set the highest value on it. But to recognize the economic worth of a piece of land is one thing; to find beauty in it is quite another. Wheat fields and turnip patches were vital to the European peasant, yet he never, as it were, domesticated them. The lawn was different. It was not only part and parcel of a pastoral economy, it was also part of the farmer's leisure. It was the place for sociability and play; and that is why it was and still is looked upon with affection.

The common grazing land of every village is actually what we mean when we speak of the village common, and it was on the common that most of our favorite group pastimes came into being. Maypole and Morris dances never got a foothold in northern America, and for that we can thank the Puritans. But baseball, like cricket in England, originated on the green. Before cricket the national sport was archery, likewise a product of the common. Rugby, and its American variation, football, are both products of the same pastoral landscape, and golf is the product of the very special pastoral landscape of lowland Scotland. Would it not be possible to establish a bond between national sports and the type of terrain where they developed? Lawn bowling is favored in Holland and near the Mediterranean—both regions of gardens and garden paths. A Continental hunt is still a forest hunt; the English or Irish hunt needs a landscape of open fields and hedgerows. Among the many ways in which men exploit the environment and establish an emotional bond with it, we should not forget sports and games. And the absence among certain peoples of games inspired by the environment is probably no less significant.

In the course of time, the private dwelling took over the lawn. With the exclusion of the general public, a new set of pastimes was devised: croquet, lawn tennis, badminton, and the lawn party. But all of these games and gatherings, whether taking place on the common or on someone's enclosed lawn, were by way of being schools where certain standards of conduct and even certain standards of dress were formed. And in an indefinable way the lawn is still the background for conventionally correct behavior. The poor sport walks off the field; the poor citizen neglects his lawn.

Just as the early forest determined our poetry and legend, that original pasture land, redeemed from the forest for the delectation of cows and sheep, has indirectly determined many of our social attitudes. Both are essential elements of the proto-landscape. But in America the lawn is more than essential; it is the very heart and soul of the entire front yard. We may say what we like about the futility of these areas of bright green grass; we may lament the waste of labor and water they represent here in the semi-arid West. Yet to condemn them or justify them on utilitarian or esthetic grounds is to miss the point entirely. The lawn, with its vague but nonetheless real social connotations, is precisely that landscape element which every American values most. Unconsciously, he identifies it with every group event in his life: childhood games, commencement and graduation with white flannels or cap and gown, wedding receptions, "having company," the high school drill field and the big game of the season. Even the cemetery is now landscaped as a lawn to provide an appropriate background for the ultimate social event. How can a citizen be loyal to that tradition without creating and taking care of a lawn of his own? Whoever supposes that Americans are not willing to sacrifice time and money in order to keep a heritage alive regardless of its practical value had better count the number of sweating and panting men and women and children pushing lawnmowers on a summer's day. It is quite possible that the lawn will go out of fashion. But if it does, it will not be because the toiling masses behind the lawnmower have rebelled. It will be because a younger generation has fewer convivial associations with it; has found other places for group functions and other places to play: the gymnasium, the school grounds, the swimming pool, or the ski run. It will be because the feeling of being hedged in by conventional standards of behavior has become objectionable.

To hedge in, to fence in; the language seems to shift in meaning and emphasis almost while we use it. Until not long ago, neither of those words meant "to keep in"; they meant "to keep out." A fence was a de-fence against trespassers and wild animals. The hedge was a coveted symbol of independence and privacy. Coveted, because it was not every farmer who could have one around his land.

Like the lawn and the tree, the hedge is something inherited from an ancient agricultural system and an ancient way of life. The farming of the Middle Ages is usually called the open-field system. Briefly, it was based on community ownership (or community control) of all the land—ownership by a noble amounted to the same thing—with fields apportioned to the individual under certain strict conditions. Among them were rules as to when the land was to lie fallow, what day it was to be plowed, and when the village cattle were to be allowed to graze on it. Much modified by social and economical revolutions, the open-field system still prevails over much of northern Europe. Fences and hedges, as indications of property lines, naturally had no place in such a scheme.

In the course of generations, a more individualistic order came into being, and when for several good reasons it
was no longer desirable to have the cattle roaming at will
over the countryside, the first thing to appear, the first
change in the landscape, was the hedge. With that hedge to
protect his land against intruders of every kind, the individual
peasant or farmer began for the first time to come into his
own, and to feel identified with a particular piece of land. He
did not necessarily own it; more often than not he was a tenant. But at least he could operate it as he saw fit, and he
could keep out strangers.

Each field and each farm was defined by this impenetrable
barrier. It served to provide firewood, now that the forests were
gone, shelter for the livestock, and a nesting place for small
game. Most important of all, the hedge or fence served as a
visible sign that the land was owned by one particular man and
not by a group or community. In America we are so accustomed
to the fence that we cannot realize how eloquent a symbol it is
in other parts of the world. The Communist governments of
Europe do realize it, and when they collectivize the farms, they
first of all destroy the hedgerows—even when the fields are not
to be altered in size.

The free men who first colonized North America were
careful to bring the hedge and fence with them, not only to
exclude the animals of the forest but to indicate the farmers'
independent status. Hedges and fences used to be much more
common in the United States than they are now. One traveler in
revolutionary New England enumerated five different kinds,
ranging from stone walls to rows of upended tree stumps. In
Pennsylvania at the same period, fields were often bordered
with privet. As new farms were settled in the Midwest, every
field as a matter of course had its stone wall or hedge of privet
or hawthorn, or permanent wooden fence. And along these
walls and fences a small wilderness of brush and vine and trees
soon grew, so that every field had its border of shade and movement, and its own wildlife refuge. The practice, however inspired, did much to make the older parts of the nation varied

and beautiful, and we have come to identify fences and hedges with the American rural landscape at its most charming.

As a matter of fact, the hedge and wooden fence started to go out of style a good hundred years ago. Mechanized farming, which started then, found the old fields much too small. A threshing machine pulled by several teams of horses had trouble negotiating a ten-acre field, and much good land was wasted in the corners. So the solution was to throw two or more fields together. Then agricultural experts warned the farmers that the hedge and fence rows, in addition to occupying too much land, harbored noxious animals and birds and insects. When a farm was being frequently reorganized, first for one commercial crop then another, depending on the market, permanent fences were a nuisance. Finally, Joseph Glidden invented barbed wire, and at that the last hedgerows began to fall in earnest.

There were thus good practical reasons for ridding the farm of the fences. But there was another reason too: a change in taste. The more sophisticated landscape architects in the midcentury strongly advised homeowners to do away with every fence if possible. A book on suburban gardening, published in 1870, flatly stated: "that kind of fence is best which is least seen, and best seen through." Hedges were viewed with no greater favor. "The practice of hedging one's ground so that the passer-by cannot enjoy its beauty, is one of the barbarisms of old gardening, as absurd and unchristian in our day as the walled courts and barred windows of a Spanish cloister."

Pronouncements of this sort had their effect. Describing the early resistance to the antifence crusade during the last century, a writer on agricultural matters explained it thus: "Persons had come to feel that a fence is as much a part of any place as a walk or a wall is. It had come to be associated with the idea of home. The removal of stock was not sufficient reason for the removal of the fence. At best such a reason was only negative. The positive reason came in the development of what is really the art-idea in the outward character of the home . . . with the feeling that the breadth of setting for the house can be increased by extending the lawn to the actual highway."

Utilitarian considerations led the farmer to suppress the fences between his fields; esthetic considerations led the town and city dwellers to increase the size of their lawns. Neither consideration had any influence on those who had homesteaded the land, lived on it, and therefore clung to the traditional concept of the privacy and individualism of the home. The front yard, however, had already become old-fashioned and countrified fifty years ago; the hedge and picket fence, now thought of as merely quaint, were judged to be in the worst taste. Today, in spite of their antiquarian appeal, they are held in such disrepute that the modern architect and the modern landscapist have no use for either of them; and they are not allowed in any housing development financed by the FHA.

Why? Because they disturb the uniformity of a street vista; because they introduce a dangerous note of individualistic non-conformity; because, in brief, they still have something of their old meaning as symbols of self-sufficiency and independence. No qualities in twentieth-century America are more suspect than these.

It is not social pressure which has made the enclosed front yard obsolescent, or even the ukase of some housing authority, egged on by bright young city planners. We ourselves have passed the verdict. The desire to identify ourselves with the place where we live is no longer strong.

It grows weaker every year. One out of a hundred Americans lives in a trailer; one out of every three American farmers lives in a rented house. Too many changes have occurred for the old relationship between man and the human landscape to persist with any vigor. A few decades ago the farmer's greatest pride was his woodlot, his own private forest and the forest of his children. Electricity and piped-in or bottled gas have eliminated the need for a supply of fuel, and the groves of trees, often fragments of the virgin forest, are now being cut down and the stumps bulldozed away. The small fields have disappeared, the medium-sized fields have disappeared; new procedures in feeding and fattening have caused meadows to be planted to corn, range to be planted to wheat; tractors make huge designs where cattle once grazed. A strand of charged wire, a few inches off the ground, takes the place of the fence, and can be moved to another location by one man in one day. The owner of a modern mechanized farm, and even of a scientific ranch, need no longer be on hand at all hours of the day and night. He can and often does commute to work from a nearby town. His children go to school and spend their leisure there, and the remote and inconvenient house on the farm is allowed to die.

All this means simply one thing: a new human landscape is beginning to emerge in America. It is even now being created by the same combination of forces that created the old one: economic necessity, technological evolution, a change in social outlook and in our outlook on nature. Like the landscape of the present, this new one will in time produce its own symbols and its own beauty. The six-lane highway, the aerial perspective, the clean and spacious countryside of great distances and no detail will in a matter of centuries be invested with magic and myth.

That landscape, however, is not yet here. In the early dawn where we are, we can perhaps discern its rough outlines, but we cannot have any real feeling for it. We cannot possibly love the new, and we have ceased to love the old. The only fraction of the earth for which an American can still feel the traditional kinship is that patch of trees and grass and hedge he calls his yard. Each one is a peak of a sinking world, and all of them grow smaller and fewer as the sea rises around them.

But even the poorest of them, even those which are meager and lonely and without grace, have the power to remind us of a rich common heritage. Each is a part of us, evidence of a vision of the world we have all shared.*

---

* "Ghost at the Door," *Landscape* I, no. 2 (Autumn 1951): 3–9.

Luc Sante

Lingua Franca

In order to write of my childhood I have to translate. It is as if I were writing about someone else. As a boy, I lived in French; now, I live in English. The words don't fit, because languages are not equivalent to one another. If I say, 'I am a boy; I am lying in my bed; I am sitting in my room; I am lonely and afraid,' attributing these thoughts to my eight-year-old self, I am being literally correct but emotionally untrue. Even if I submit the thoughts to indirect citation and the past tense I am engaging in a sort of falsehood. I am playing ventriloquist, and that eight-year-old, now made of wood and with a hinged jaw, is sitting on my knee, mouthing the phrases I am fashioning for him. It's not that the boy couldn't understand those phrases. It is that in order to do so, he would have to translate, and that would mean engaging an electrical circuit in his brain, bypassing his heart.

If the boy thought the phrase, 'I am a boy', he would picture Dick or Zeke from the school books, or maybe his friends Mike or Joe. The word 'boy' could not refer to him; he is *un garçon*. You may think this is trivial, that *garçon* simply means 'boy', but that is missing the point. Similarly, *maman* and *papa* are people; 'mother' and 'father' are notions. *La nuit* is dark and filled with fear, while 'the night' is a pretty picture of a starry field. The boy lives in *une maison* with a house on either side. His *coeur* is where his feelings dwell, and his heart is a blood-pumping muscle. For that matter, his name is Luc, pronounced *lük;* everybody around, though, calls him 'Luke', which is an alias, a mask.

He regards the English language with a curiosity bordering on the entomological. Watching the *Amerloques* moving around in their tongue is like seeing lines of ants parading through tunnels, bearing sections of leaves. He finds it funny, often enough. In school, for instance, when nutrition is discussed, the elements of a meal are called 'servings', a word that always conjures up images of footmen in claw-hammer coats bearing covered dishes. Since he knows that his classmates, however prosperous their parents might be, aren't likely to have servants, he substitutes the familiar advertising icon of Mother entering the room with a trussed turkey on a platter, which is no less alien or ridiculous. He gathers that this scene has some material basis in the lives of Americans, although it appears to him contrived beyond belief. American life, like the English language, is fascinating and hopelessly phoney.

His vantage point is convenient, like a hunter's blind. He has some struggles with the new language—it will be years, for example, before his tongue and teeth can approximate the 'th' sound, and in the meantime he will have to tolerate laughter every time he pronounces 'third' as 'turd'—but at the same time he is protected. No one will ever break his heart with English words, he thinks. It is at home that he is naked. If the world outside the door is a vast and apparently arbitrary game, inside lies the familiar, which can easily bruise or cut him. No, his parents aren't monsters, nothing like that, although they may not appreciate their own power. Anyway, he has raised and nurtured enough monsters by himself to inflict pain without need of assistance. The French language is a part of his body and his soul, and it has a latent capacity for violence. No wonder he has trouble navigating between the languages at first: they are absurdly different, doors to separate and unequal universes. Books might allege they are the same kind of item, like a pig and a goat, but that is absurd on the face of it. One is tissue and the other is plastic. One is a wound and the other is a prosthesis.

Of course, the French language would not be so intimate, wrenching, and potentially dangerous to him if he had remained in a French-speaking world. There he would be bombarded by French of all temperatures, flavours, connotations. His friends, his enemies, his teachers, his neighbours, the newspaper, the radio, the billboards, people on the street, pop songs, movies, assembly instructions, lists of ingredients, shouting drunks, mumbling lunatics, indifferent officials, all would transmit in French. Pretty girls would speak French. He would pick up slang, poesy, academese, boiler-plate, specialized jargon, cant, nonsense. He would not only hear French everywhere but absorb it unconsciously all the time. He would learn the kind of things no dictionary will tell you: for example that apparent synonyms are in reality miles apart, each with its own calluses of association. By and by, *je* would become more than his private self, would find itself shoulder to shoulder with the *je* of a million others. There would be traffic and commerce between inner life and outer world. A great many things would go without saying, be taken for granted. It would seem as though language had arisen from the ground, had always been and would always be.

Instead French festers. It is kept in darkness and fed meagrely by the spoonful. It isn't purposely neglected, of course; there is nothing intentionally punitive about the way it is sequestered and undernourished. On the contrary: it is cherished, cosseted, rewarded for just being, like an animal in a zoo. But like that animal it can only enjoy a semblance of its natural existence. Its memory of the native habitat grows sparser all the time, and its attempts at normality become play-acting, become parody, become rote. Its growth has been stunted, and it correspondingly retains many infantile characteristics. Even as the boy grows gradually tougher and more worldly in English, he carries around a French internal life whose clock has stopped. He is unnaturally fragile, exaggeratedly sensitive in his French core. Not surprisingly, he resents this, wants to expunge it, destroy it, pour salt on its traces to prevent regeneration.

What does this say about the boy's view of his family circumstances? That is a complicated matter. French is his soul, and it is also a prison, and the same terms could be applied to his family. At home he is alone with his parents; no one else exists. It is stifling and comforting in equal measure. Out in the world he is entirely alone. He is terrified but he is free. Or potentially free, anyway; he's too young to know. But one of the things that sustains him in the world is the knowledge of his French innards. He can feel superior about it (his peers don't possess anything equivalent, and they'll never have any idea what it feels like) but it is simultaneously a source of shame. At home he may be alone with his parents, but while they have an awesome power over his infant core, his growing English self is something they don't know and can't touch. You can take all these propositions as mathematical equations. Work them out, forwards or backwards, and you will always arrive at the same reduction, the same answer: he is alone.

My attempt to put any sort of words in the boy's mouth is doomed. He doesn't yet have a language. He has two tongues: one is all quivering, unmediated, primal sensation, and the other is detached, deliberate, artificial. To give a full accounting he would have to split himself in two. But I don't know whether I might not have to do the same myself, here and now. To speak of my family, for example, I can hardly employ English without omitting an emotional essence that remains locked in French, although I can't use French, either, unless I am willing to sacrifice my critical intelligence. Could I, employing English, truly penetrate my parents' decision to emigrate? I was born in Verviers, in south-eastern Belgium, birthplace of everyone bearing my last name for at least 800 years. The city was dominated by its textile industry for nearly a millennium, but that industry began to die in the 1950s, and my father was out of a job, and no others were to be had. The notice of bankruptcy of my father's employer was posted in French; the agonized conversations between my parents were conducted in French; the war bride and her brother, my father's childhood friends, invited my parents to consider joining them in New Jersey, phrasing their inducements in French. I now understand such grave adult matters, but I understand them in English. A chasm yawns between languages, between my childhood and my present age. But there is an advantage hidden in this predicament: French is an archaeological site of emotions, a pipeline to my infant self. It preserves the very rawest, deepest, least guarded feelings.

If I stub my toe, I may profanely exclaim, in English, 'Jesus!' But in agony, such as when I am passing a kidney stone, I might cry, *'Petit Jésus!'* with all the reverence of nursery religion. Others have told me that when I babble in feverish delirium or talk in my sleep, I do so in French. Preserved, too, in French, is a world of lost pleasures and familial comforts. If someone says, in English, 'Let's go visit Mr and Mrs X,' the concept is neutral, my reaction is determined by what I think of Mr and Mrs X. On the other hand, if the suggestion is broached in French, *'Allons dire bonjour',* the phrasing affects me more powerfully than the specifics. *'Dire bonjour'* calls up a train of associations: for some reason I see my great-uncle Jules Stelmes, dead more than thirty years, with his fedora and his enormous white moustache and his soft dark eyes. I smell coffee and the raisin bread called *cramique,* hear the muffled bong of a parlour clock and the repetitive commonplaces of chit-chat in the drawling accent of the Ardennes, people rolling their Rs and leaning hard on their initial Hs. I feel a rush-caned chair under me, see white curtains and a starched tablecloth, can almost tap my feet on the cold ceramic tiles, maybe the *trompe l'oeil* pattern that covered the entire floor surface of my great-uncle Albert Remacle's farmhouse in Viville. I am sated, sleepy, bored out of my mind.

The triggers that operate this mechanism are the simplest, humblest expressions. They are things that might be said to a child or said often within a child's hearing. There are common comestibles: *une tasse de café, une tartine, du chocolat.* There are interjections and verbal place-markers: *sais-tu, figure-toi, je t'assure, mon Dieu*. And, naturally, there are terms of endearment. In my family, the use of someone's first name was nearly always an indication of anger or a prelude to bad news. My parents addressed me as *fifi, chou* (cabbage), *lapin* (rabbit), *vî tchèt* (meaning 'old cat' in Walloon, the native patois of southern Belgium), *petit coeur*. If I'd done something mischievous, my father would laugh and call me *cûrêye* (Walloon for 'carcass' or 'spavined horse'—like saying, 'you're rotten'); if I'd made myself especially comfortable, such as by taking up most of the couch, he'd shake his head and grin and call me *macrale* (Walloon for 'witch'). I regularly got called *tièsse èl aîr* (head in the clouds; Walloon). If my mother was teasing me in mock anger, she'd call me a *petit chenapan* (little scamp); if it was my father, he'd be likely to say *'t'es ô tièssetou'* ('you're a stubborn one', in Walloon). My father's real anger was rare and grave; my mother's boiled over quickly even if it faded just as fast. She might call me a *vaurien* (good-for-nothing) or a *sale gosse* (dirty kid), an *èstèné* (an idiot, literally 'bewildered'; Walloon) or a *singlé* (a simpleton) or a *nolu* (a nullity; Walloon). If I'd really stung her, though, she'd yell *chameau!* (camel), and I liked that, because she was acknowledging I had some kind of power. There are worse words, which still have the capacity to make me cringe: *cochon* (pig), *crapuleux* (vile, vicious), *crotté* (filthy), *mâssî* (ditto; Walloon). Those words are woven through the fabric of my early adolescence.

A few years ago, early in the morning, I was waiting to cross a street in Liège. I wasn't quite awake yet, and was lost in thought, so that when I heard someone shout *'Fais attention! Regarde!'* I immediately stiffened. All of a sudden I was back at the age of eight or nine, being reproved by my parents. As it happened, there was a small boy standing next to me, holding a tray of empty coffee cups which he was returning to the café opposite; his father, manning a flea-market booth behind us, had observed the kid putting a toe into the street unmindful of oncoming traffic. It can easily happen to me, when faced with some officious fracophone creep, shopkeeper or librarian or customs agent, that I lose thirty years and two feet off my height. If

I haven't briefed myself beforehand, I crumple. This can happen even though I've kept my French alive internally through reading, as well as occasional conversations with friends. But even in such circumstances I can find myself tripped up, suddenly sprawled. I can be reading something truly scabrous, something by Georges Bataille, say, turning the pages as an imperturbable adult, and then a turn of phrase will shock me, not some description of outlandish vice but rather a perfectly innocent locution lying in the midst of the smut. It will throw everything else into a new relief. Suddenly it is as if one of my aunts had looked up from her coffee and started spewing obscenities.

Since I live almost entirely in English now, I can regard French with some of the same detachment and sense of the ridiculous with which I once regarded my adopted tongue. If I walk into an American discount store and the loudspeaker starts braying 'Attention shoppers!' I will consign the noise to the realm of static, switch off its ability to reach me except as an irritant. On the other hand, if I am in a Belgian supermarket and the loudspeaker begins its recital, nearly always in a polished female murmur rather than the American male bark: 'Monsieur, madame, nous vous conseillons . . .' I am bemused, imagining the rapport between the voice and its sleek, well-dressed target, someone so exquisitely put together that he or she can purchase low-fat frozen entrées with a withering superiority, as if picking out a *grand cru classé*. I am never the 'you' of American advertising because I consciously slam the door, but in French I am never given the opportunity to spurn the come-on. I am excluded at the gate. Naturally there is a class factor involved—in French I revert to proletarian status as easily as to childhood—but the exclusion is also due to my status as a counterfeit Belgian, an American pretender.

I can cross the border between English and French, although I can't straddle it. Years ago, when I worked behind the cash register in a store, I resented the demands of the customers and sometimes went out of my way to be rude to them, to put them in their place. After work, though, I might go to some other shop, and there, trying to find out whether the shirt came in a larger size or a darker colour, would find myself resenting the arrogance and apathy of the clerks. I had jumped from one side of the fence to the other. I could no more simultaneously occupy the mentality of clerk and client than I could bat a ball to myself in the outfield. Each claim effaced the other. It was useless to try and apportion blame; customers and clerks were both rude and both justified, were in fact interchangeable. This insight is perhaps the closest I've ever got to understanding the psychology that lies behind nationalism. The situation is a bit like one of the famous optical illusions, in which the silhouettes of two facing profiles form the outline of a vase. You can see the vase, and then you can see the profiles, but you can't see both images at once.

Belgium is an ill-fitting suit of a country. Stitched together from odds and ends, it represents a purely strategic decision on the part of the larger powers to create a nation state. It unnaturally couples two language groups (actually three language groups if you include the relatively untroubled German-speaking minority—no more than 70,000 souls in any case), and both have ambiguous ongoing relationships with the majority stockholders of their languages, i.e., the Dutch and the French. The Flemish and the Dutch in recent years have been forming cultural and trade partnerships, and apparently enjoying themselves at it. Their mutual history is somewhat more vexed, with the Dutch regarding the Flemings with a certain benign hauteur, and the Flemish viewing the Dutch as worldly, as apostates, as lacking in seriousness, not to mention virtue. But they read each other's literatures, and just as the Flemings have adopted the grammar and usage of their cousins, so the Dutch appreciate the particular flavour of Flemish expressions, and have helped themselves to dashes of the idiom. Between the Walloons and the French the situation is less comfortable. Essentially, the French feel superior and the Walloons oblige them by feeling embarrassed. There has long been a Francophile segment of the Walloon population, and, as the national tension has risen, so has the noise emitted by a certain minority that favours the detachment of Wallonia from Belgium and its adherence to France. The French have shown no corresponding interest in acquiring five impoverished and déclassé eastern provinces.

The language reflects this French superiority and Belgian embarrassment. Popular manuals for the identification and eradication of *belgicismes* have been published since at least the eighteenth century. Today *Le Soir,* out of Brussels, has a weekly feature that reiterates the same cautions. When speaking of buttered bread say *beurrée,* not *tartine;* and so forth. That example might serve to demonstrate that the wish to eliminate native expressions has nothing to do with grammatical rigour or the rectification of ambiguities, but is merely the expression of a classbound shame. Visitors always note that Belgians say *septante* for seventy and *nonante* for ninety, whereas the French say *soixante-dix* and *quatre-vingt-dix* respectively. I have no idea why Belgians do not also say *octante* for eighty, the three simpler expressions have been used by French-speaking proletarians of both lands for centuries; the arithmetical puzzles are owed entirely to class pretension. A more recent example of this tendency is what happened across the country to the name of the establishments that make and sell fried potatoes. For untold decades and throughout my childhood they were known as *fritures,* until at some point in the 1970s a humourless functionary decreed the name incorrect, since *friture* is the word for the fat in which the potatoes are fried. Now only establishments older than twenty-five or so years can continue to name themselves that way; the more recent shops must be called *friteries.*

The French, particularly through the agency of their Academy, have long policed their language in such petty ways. Neologisms and loanwords are forbidden, shifts in grammar and usage swiftly curtailed. French was once a major force in the world, among other things the international language of diplomacy. Those who wonder why it has ceded so much of its power to English need look no further than this wish to preserve a seventeenth-century cadaver. Belgians who submit their language to French rules concede twice over. But the submission is by now traditional; after all Walloons have done a fairly effective job of killing off their own tongue.

Walloon is usually identified as a dialect of French, whereas it derived on its own from the Latin of the Roman legions, and is just as old as the patois of Ile de France, which became the official language. The eleventh edition of the *Encyclopaedia Britannica* in fact identifies it as the northernmost Romance language. I once asked a linguist-translator: What is the line separating a language from a dialect? He replied that the situation could be summed up in a phrase: History is written by the victors. The dialect of Ile de France was the patois of the French kings; it subjugated Walloon as well as Provençal, Norman, Lorrain, Gascon, Picard, Occitan, and so on, and reduced them from languages to dialects. The effect of linguistic imperialism is well described by the great Verviétois philologist Jules Feller (1859–1940) in his *Notes de Philologie wallonne* (1912):

> Political necessity, material interest, constraint, and the moral superiority of the conqueror and his language can create within a single century the troubling phenomenon of a tongue being entirely forgotten by its nation. The first generation does its best to gabble the idiom of the foreign invaders. The second generation, if it be to its advantage, already knows the new language better than the old. The third generation for all practical purposes knows and employs only the new.

Feller uses this model to describe the impact of Latin on the Celto-Germanic population of Gallia Belgica, but it applies just as well to the effect of French upon Walloon over the last century (and, incidentally, it is likewise true of the linguistic process that accompanies immigration). Feller goes on to characterize French as 'a brilliant soldier of fortune in the army of Romance dialects who has become a general', while Walloon is 'a little corps of soldiers, consigned to the fringe of the battalion, who have never gotten the chance to distinguish themselves'.

Walloon might yet have had a chance to develop in the nineteenth century, had the Belgian educational establishment seized the opportunity afforded by the country's independence to teach Walloon in schools. Instead the opposite occurred: steps were taken to suppress the language, and teachers took it as their mission to 'cure' pupils of their native tongue. But Walloon did have its golden age. It was brief, lasting from the mid-1880s until just before the First World War. That period saw an efflorescence of Walloon literature, plays and poems primarily, and the founding of many theatres and periodicals. The New York Public Library possesses a surprisingly large collection of literary works in Walloon, quite possibly the largest outside Belgium, and its holdings are statistically representative of the output. Out of nearly a thousand plays in the collection, only twenty-six were published before 1880 and only twenty-one of them after the First World War. The reasons for this decline remain a mystery; it was not occasioned by the war itself. Literary production occurred at different paces in different cities, but Liège, Verviers, Namur and Charleroi led the pack. At its peak, Walloon literature was like a massive exhalation of breath long held in. It approached—as in the comte de Lautréamont's exhortation—poetry made by all.

Walloon was the household tongue of all the relatives of my grandparents' generation. Their parents in turn might have spoken nothing else; that no one bothered to establish rules for the writing of Walloon until Jules Feller did so at the very beginning of this century, just in time for its decline in currency, partly accounts for the fact that nearly everyone in the family tree before my grandparents' era was illiterate. When I hear Walloon spoken, which is not often, I hear the table talk of countless generations of workers and farmers and their wives; not that I particularly wish to subscribe to notions of collective ethnic memory, but the sound of the language conveys the mentality of its speakers so vividly that it is dense with imprints, like

fossils. Hearing old men greet each other—'*Bôdjou,
Françwès*'—can move me nearly to tears. It is the keenest tangible manifestation of what I've lost, even if it is now pretty much
lost to everyone. In my childhood it was already a ghost, if a
lively one. My mother's parents ceded to the tenor of their
times; they spoke Walloon between themselves but did not
teach it to their children and discouraged their bringing bits of it
home. My father, on the other hand, grew up in a Walloon-
speaking household in a city with a rich Walloon tradition.

Walloon today is the province of the elderly, at least those
of the working class or in rural communities, along with a few
younger diehards and hobbyists in the cities. Most people regard it with a certain embarrassment, like the memory of a
bastard grandsire who ate with his hands. The young, who are
media-fixated and thus Parisianized or Americanized, couldn't
care less. To me, growing up, it was both familiar and strange.
Sometimes my parents reached for an English phrase and came
up with a Walloon one instead—the confusion was understandable given the Germanic strain running among Walloon's Latin
roots. (An often-told story in my family related how Lucy Dos-
quet, when her GI suitor arrived looking like a slob, angrily
ordered him in Walloon, '*Louke-tu el mireu!*' He understood
perfectly, and studied his reflection.) Sometimes my parents
said things to each other in Walloon they didn't want me to
understand—pertaining to Christmas presents, maybe. I was
never taught Walloon, but I had a fair-sized vocabulary anyway
(there were concepts I could only express in Walloon; growing
pains, for example, were always *crèhioûles*), and I simply absorbed its structure from hearing bits of it from my parents and
from hearing my grandparents and great-aunts and great-uncles
speak it. I can read it with ease; other applications don't present
themselves. Like the lives of my ancestors, Walloon appears
humble and yet mighty, elemental and at the same time complex, remote but a part of my fibre. I use what I have of it only
internally. It is that sad paradox, a silent tongue.

One of the great stalwarts of Verviétois Walloon in this
century was Jean Wisimus (1868–1953) who managed to com-

bine the tasks of textile dealer, newspaper columnist, lexicographer (he compiled the only dictionary of the Verviers tongue that exists), historian, author (of *Dès Rôses èt dès Spènes*—Roses and Thorns—a volume of rather affecting reminiscences of the old Verviers), and founder and long-time president of Lu Vî Tchène (The Old Oak), the last major Walloon organization in the city. His first book, however, published in 1921, was *L'Anglais langue auxiliaire internationale* (English, the international second language). Its publication may have been delayed by the war; in any case he begins by addressing concerns that have a distinctly pre-1914 air about them. Universal languages were all the rage then. Dr Zamenhof's Esperanto, Monsignor Schleyer's Volapük, Sudre's Solresol, Dyer's Lingualumina, Bauer's Spelin, Dornoy's Balta, Marchand's Dilpok, the Marquis de Beaufort's Ido—all were supposed to bring about international harmony by tearing down the tower of Babel and making the crooked ways straight, and all of them smell like the sort of decorous, idealistic Edwardian science fiction that was about to be buried in the trenches of Verdun. Wisimus has no patience at all with such nonsense. 'An artificial language is like canned food; it's a product without flavour or aroma.' By contrast there is English, which has the simplest and most analytical grammar, and furthermore has already invaded every domain ('you visit the *world's fair,* buy a *ticket,* go to the *bar,* watch out for *pickpockets* . . . see the *cakewalk,* the *looping-the-loop, cow-boys* from the *far-west* . . .'). Although some people will always grumble about its errant spelling, its destiny is clear, and anyway, '*Un beau désordre est un effet de l'art*' (a beautiful mess is an artistic effect: Boileau). English, he predicts, will become a worldwide medium of convenience, like the telephone and the telegraph. Unless, that is, Japan conquers the planet . . .

Somehow, like some sort of Jules Vernian astronaut, I wound up making the journey from Wisimus's Verviers into the very heart of the linguistic future. For my first communion I was presented with a dictionary whose jacket copy promised it to be 'as up to date as Telstar!' Two years later I decided I wanted to be a writer, and having made that decision never thought of

writing in any language but English. It was at hand, it was all
new, it was not the language of my parents, it *was* the language
of Robert Louis Stevenson and Ray Bradbury and the Beatles, it
contained a ready-made incentive to competition, and besides,
Mrs Gibbs in the fourth grade at St Teresa's School in Summit
told me I had talent, and that clinched it. Gradually, I success-
fully passed myself off as another being. I was thirteen or fourteen the last time anyone complimented me on my charming
accent. English became my rod and my staff, my tool and my
weapon, at length my means of making a living. My mask
merged with my skin. My internal monologue ever so gradually
shifted from French into English; I even began to talk to cats
and dogs (who understand all languages) in English. My most
intimate conversations came to be conducted in English. Today,
when someone addresses me as 'Luke' I respond without a second thought; when I hear '*lük*' I jump as if I've gotten an electric shock. Even though I know better, I feel as if someone had
just looked down into my naked soul.

I still speak French with my parents, of course, although
French is perhaps a misleading word there, since over the years
we've developed a family dialect, a Franglais that is a lot like
Spanglish: '*Nous sommes allés chez les séniores citizeunnes,*' my
mother will tell me, describing a visit to the local old-folks club,
'*et nous avons mangé du cornebif et du cabbage.*' I am almost
physically unable to talk to my parents in English, even when
they are using the language out of politeness because there is an
English speaker present. Talking to my parents in English would
be like exchanging nonsensical pleasantries studded with code
words, as though we were surrounded by the Gestapo and anxious to give nothing away. Or maybe it would be as if I had
invited my parents to a wild party I was throwing for my friends.

I suppose I am never completely present in any given
moment, since different aspects of myself are contained in different rooms of language, and a complicated apparatus of
airlocks prevents the doors from being flung open all at once.
Still, there are subterranean correspondences between the linguistic domains that keep them from stagnating. The classical

order of French, the Latin-Germanic high-low dialectic of English, and the onomatopoeic peasant lucidity of Walloon work on one another critically; they help enhance precision and reduce cant. They are all operative, potentially. Given desire and purpose, I could make my home in any of them. I don't have a house, only this succession of rented rooms. That sometimes makes me feel as though I have no language at all, but it also gives me the advantage of mobility. I can leave, anytime, and not be found.

Gerald Early

The Frailty of Human Friendship

But I have called you friends; for all things that I have heard of my Father I have made known unto you.
—John 15:15

I

When I die, I do not think I will find myself saying, as one famous person did, that if I could do it all over again, I would have had more friends. I would like to think that when I die, there will be a fair number of people who will identify themselves as my friends. We all need a level of reassurance that while we certainly die alone, we won't die lonely.

This is not to say that I have a great number of friends. Indeed, I would have to say that I have no close friends at all. The obvious reason for this is that I don't have the time to cultivate or nurture friendships as I should. Reading and writing are solitary endeavors, and I devote myself to them with a monastic energy. I am sure that I am attracted to these pursuits because they make an active social life difficult. There is a great responsibility in having good friends, a great deal of keeping up your end. The reciprocity of friendship is both its great pleasure and its great burden. And, after all, what are the rewards of friendship compared to the effort of maintaining it?

Yet I do not think my loner impulse, my shyness, is a result of disappointment in friendships past but rather an inclination I inherited from my mother. At least my wife likes to tell me that. My mother is very much a loner, had very few friends when I was growing up, and indeed warned me and my sisters against too much dependence on friendship, as if the implicit paradox of friendship is inevitable betrayal, through your own agency or the other person's. I thought my mother a wise and principled, if somewhat narrow, woman and trusted her word. I felt embarrassed by friendship as a sign that I was not sufficiently self-reliant. My mother taught me to think of excessive or even normal preoccupation with friendship as a sign of weakness or a sign that one did not have enough to do with one's time.

Friendship might become a kind of imposition. Even today I find it difficult to accept tokens of generosity from friends, thinking myself an opportunist. In the end, my over-intellectualized, over-moralized analysis of the epistemology of friendship boils down to one issue: why does this person like me? Am I unworthy of his or her regard or much too superior to it? This is a decidedly "clinical" combination of diffidence, low self-esteem, ass-backward humility, a craving to please, anger, and unmitigated, nearly serene arrogance. I think my mother also exhibits these qualities, but I do not have her strength of character or limitation of experience. I want everyone to think I am nice and being nice is a form of interpersonal paralysis. It is hard to know, from that vantage point, exactly what kind of person you are presenting to someone to be friends with.

While I would not characterize any of my relationships as close friendships or even friendships at all, at least not as I understood and experienced friendship as a child, there are many people I am deeply fond of. But I do not share their lives. I would not think of asking a favor of them, although I know most of them would help me if they could. And I would like to think that I would do anything for them, but something pulls me up short. I have the strange sense of having let down the people who know me, of having disappointed them in some vague way. Doubtless, I bear some secret guilt and think myself unworthy of having friends, just a large circle of acquaintances and associates.

friendships. Friendship in a marriage (often, a married couple become each other's best friend and it is surely advisable in the case of most marriages) precludes, though not forecloses, the force of other friendships because marriage demands a great deal of work that the couple must do together or singly but in support of one another. One never depends on any friend as much as one depends on a spouse, not simply for great support but also for the most mundane things.

Ida must grouse at times about the irony that I am, for better or for worse, her new girlfriend. I now get dragged along (and have been dragged along for years) when she shops for shoes, for makeup, for clothes. I beg to be relieved of this, feel that I am not good at it. Indeed, she even tells me that I am no good at it. I make a lousy girlfriend but she drags me along, not because she could not find a woman to take (and she sometimes does, to my great thankfulness) but because there is a certain pleasure in having a steadfast but slightly inadequate friend, a non-competitive friend, a friend who is unquestionably happy when his friend is happy. There is something very pleasing to Ida about my clumsy masculinity, my seeming indifference to her appearance, my ignorance; I am, in some way, an ideal companion because I can, in effect, be taught. As Ida has always felt herself to be deeply influenced by me in some areas, here is her chance to teach the teacher and about no better subject than herself, alas. There is always, I think, a great deal of pedagogy in any friendship worth anything.

Ida puzzles over the enigma of friendship itself, what the need for it signifies, why the memory of friendship lost is more powerful and more vivid than the friendship itself. She really can't recall a single thing she and Delores Shedd ever did. Her interest in this friendship, why it has stayed with her, says something deep and perhaps deeply elusive about her childhood. Perhaps it expresses a certain skepticism about friendship itself and the mystery of how people come together and how they fall apart. How much can friendship obey the will to maintain itself? What married person would not think about this, that marriage

Now the memory of childhood is also something of a problem. Like Wordsworth, I have this sort of "Tintern Abbey" sense of friendship as a child being the ideal of intimacy, of secret sharing, of measured yet carefree reciprocity. Friendships at that stage of life are so intense, so deeply personal, and one's love seems so boundless. One does not weary of a friend in childhood just as one does not weary of a lover in the first, fresh months of a relationship. It is all pure discovery of yourself and another! There was no overarching homophobic fear of same-sex friendship. (I remember, when I was seven, feeling so good about being with my best male friend of the moment, Calvin, that I innocently but feelingly kissed him full on the lips.) There was no heterosexual goading in cross-gender relations. (I could, as a boy, play with girls for hours and not see them in any sort of sexual way, never want to kiss them or hold them; later, when I understood other ways of knowing girls, these older days seemed such a relaxation and relief.)

In Sunday School I memorized what Jesus said in the Book of John: "Greater love hath no man than this, that a man lay down his life for his friends." Self-sacrifice became embedded in my concept of friendship, and I thought that I would be willing to die for my childhood friends, imagining this in a setting of war where men specifically seemed to have such opportunity. Women had plenty of opportunities, I thought as a boy: they were mothers, after all, and mothers always suffered, even wanted to suffer for the sake of others. (The war movies of my boyhood reiterated this theme—the self-sacrifice of friends— perhaps as a cultural message to socialize men. Somehow, in my childish mind, it seemed that what got one a Congressional Medal of Honor and a burial in Arlington National Cemetery also got one into heaven. Friendship, heroism, and Christianity fused in a delightful and absurdly profound way!)

Yet when considered soberly, this cannot possibly be true of childhood friendship. Childhood and school are often theaters of cruelty and conformity. Friends betray you on the flimsiest grounds; reject you because you did not or would not fit into a certain group; shun those with physical oddities. I saw kids savagely beat other kids. I saw kids victimized by mob psychology, terrorized by psychotic kids, cheated by junior confidence men. There is no innocence in childhood, only less mature depravities. I have never hated as deeply or as often as an adult as I did as a child, and most of my hatred was directed not toward adults but toward other children. (And when I think back on the children I hated as a child, I wish to hate them still!) It is amazing how true friendship survives such a social cauldron, and it is more amazing when one recalls how few true friends one had as a child.

Naturally race made matters even more trying. It was difficult for me to negotiate being friends with both black and white children who were decided enemies of each other. It was tiresome to hear from working-class, ethnic white kids that I was "different" from other black kids, although I am sure, in some ways, I learned to cultivate this difference to my advantage. On the other hand, I was, ironically, considered a privileged kid by my black working-class friends (I knew no middle-class kids, either black or white, until I reached high school.) Yet, in every single instance, my family was economically worse off than any of theirs. I also knew that the black kids secretly admired the fact that I sounded "like a white kid," that I had friendships among the enemy because I took the friendships so casually and because they never precluded my having friendships among the blacks. Yet I felt a deep stress about friendship as a child that I hope I will never have to re-experience. My best friend in eighth grade was a Puerto Rican kid named Gilbert Perez. We used to walk home from school singing Beatles tunes that were currently in the Top Ten. I knew that I could not do this with my black friends. I felt a kind of dishonesty in all of this, but I could not tell with whom I was actually being dishonest. There was no sublimity in childhood friendships.

II

My wife, Ida, likes to evoke the idea of friendship through her remembrance of a childhood friend, Delores Shedd, and their

falling-out one day over God knows what. In the world of childhood friendships, fallings-out were common, sudden, vehement, and inexplicable. In a search perhaps for continuity, in an imaginative conjuration meant to join the ideal of friendship and the fickleness of childhood, Ida has brought up Delores Shedd at regular intervals over the last twenty years. Her yearning for the lost romance of childhood is mixed with bewilderment before the mystery of why the people who populate our childhood often disappear without a trace from our adult life. She brings up Delores Shedd either to talk about what a wonderful friendship they had (at age twelve or so) and how she has never had another like it, or to wonder what Delores Shedd is doing today, would they recognize each other, would they have anything to say to each other. "I wish I had a best friend," she sometimes says (by which she means a best girlfriend of the sort, say, played by Valerie Harper in *The Mary Tyler Moore Show*, a wisecracking, hip, youthful, good-hearted, and generous version of a Jewish mother—one supposes, in this case, a Jewish sister). "I haven't had one since I married you."

Somehow I am blamed for this. My loner, antisocial personality, my lack of interest in making friends has affected, or better put, infected her, much as Mark Twain's apostasy poisoned poor Livy Langdon's bourgeois Presbyterianism and left her bereft of spiritual solace on her deathbed. Husbands, I think, are always rather to blame for taking away their wives' innocence. Every woman likes to imagine that the man she marries (for those who are interested in men) has something of the scoundrel, the maladjusted adolescent, or the boyish boor about him. Women love being somewhat exasperated by their husband's lack of social graces as long as the lack is not terribly serious and the patient amenable to a sufficient bit of cure. Is it not wives who plan the social agendas of most marriages, who organize outings and dinner parties, who mail Christmas cards, who make sure all social debts are paid?

But I think Ida is preoccupied, in her recall of Delores Shedd, in her hope and longing for the long-lost sister-friend, with how friendship between spouses precludes other types of

itself, despite the power of the sanction of church and state, is largely a mysterious and precarious affair, sometimes as fickle as a childhood friendship? Spouses are fine but the eternal rock of our salvation, the best of all our hopeful friends, must be not our childhood friends but our own children.

III

When I was a bit younger than now, that is, a young adult, if anyone had asked why I had children or why I wanted children, I would have said because I want friends when I am an old man. I want to shape perfect companions who will understand their old man's quirks, sense of failure, crankiness, basketful of sins and hypocrisies and not reproach me for them. Rather this companionship would be based on their appreciation of my cleverness, wit, intelligence, refined taste, endearing eccentricities, and the like. What I sought in my children was the idealized friendships of childhood brought about through the power of adulthood, of parenthood. I wished not only to be loved unconditionally but to be liked unreservedly.

Hearing this, the other parents would laugh at my naiveté, laugh at the egregious, Frankensteinlike assumption that I could mold two beings in a certain way. Perhaps the laughter was to cover the embarrassment of recognizing one's own yearning or the fear that parenting is a deeper expression of perversity and depravity than we might be willing to admit. A wag would say, "Well, why don't you have more than two children if you believe that? That way, in your old age you can be surrounded by a tribe of grateful friends." I would say to myself that I was not such a fool as to think that I could have success in the many and that my luck would work, if at all, with only a few. Better to concentrate on a couple than spread yourself thin with a boatload. God had a good reason not to try the Eden experiment with, say, a dozen or two dozen, at the outset. That only would have delayed the eating of the tree of knowledge by conference meetings, strategizing, training sessions, leadership quests, choosing up sides, betrayals, the creation of a religion or two, perhaps a minor war, but no different end result. I thought my chances, as God thought his, as good with two as with a dozen.

Others would laugh at the assumption that I would even like my children after a certain age and would care if they liked me. Parents of older children would simply say, "I used to think that too when my children were young. I didn't know about something called the teenage years." They would giggle self-consciously at this truism but the upshot was fair warning from older to younger parents: in the end, don't count on your children. I could only think to myself in response, "Then, for Chrissakes, who else am I to count on? I expect them to be at least the equivalent of Job's friends when he was on his bed of suffering. I expect at least witnesses to the suffering that will be my lot should I live long enough to cash in that check. They owe me that much." "You don't owe me anything," my mother would always say when I was younger. "Children don't owe their parents anything. They didn't ask to be born." When my mother last said this to me, I was visiting her in Philadelphia, and my children, two daughters, were just starting school. I turned to her and grinned, "Yes, that's true. But they didn't ask not to be, either. Let us assume theirs is the consent of the silent."

But I do not think about the Book of Job as mere casual association. As the most profound and extended meditation on friendship in all the literature that I have read, Job seems to get to the heart of the matter. Nowhere in the Bible is the word "friends" used more. In the midst of his afflictions, Job is visited by three friends who try to comfort him by saying that he must, in some way, deserve his trials. One of his friends, Zophar the Naamathite replies: "Should not the multitude of words be answered? and should a man full of talk be justified? Should thy lies make men hold their peace? and when thou mockest, shall no man make thee ashamed? for thou hast said, My doctrine is pure, and I am clean in thine eyes. But oh that God would speak and open his lips against thee; And that he would show thee the secrets of wisdom, that they are double to that which is! Know therefore that God exacteth of thee less than thine iniquity deserveth."

Job answers his friends: "How long will ye vex my soul, and break me in pieces with words? These ten times have ye reproached me: ye are not ashamed that ye make yourselves strange to me. And be it indeed that I have erred, mine error remaineth with myself. If indeed ye will magnify yourselves against me, and plead against me my reproach: Know now that God hath overthrown me, and hath compassed me with his net. Behold, I cry out of wrong, but I am not heard: I cry aloud, but there is no judgment." Job's friends offer him no solace. They refuse to see his side. In the end, God, in his odd justification before Job, to whom he apostrophizes his inscrutable, unreachable, unknowable Godhood while acknowledging his need of the human subjects he created in order for his act of apostrophizing to have meaning, rebukes the friends, who must make a burnt offering to Job as tribute.

Perhaps thinking my children might serve me as Job's friends served him is not asking too much after all. For the Book of Job shows the frailty of human friendship. The comfort it provides is limited, meager, and often timid. But it is the best we can expect: for our friends to show up in our affliction, to feel themselves fortunate that they are not thus afflicted, and to blame us for our afflictions, but for them to wish to bear witness, to strengthen us with a sense of community, to succor us with their bumbling solicitations, to vouchsafe our humanity through the ironical mercy of its imperfection.

A religious-minded girl at Fisk University tells the story of how she tried to get her alcoholic mother to a treatment center, walking her down the street one night, a shamed, burdened girl stumbling along with a drunken, wretched woman. And the daughter says: "Mother, you have betrayed yourself and God. You have made your bed in the darkness and turn from the almighty power of God." And the mother says: "What say you, silly girl? I suffer my affliction in the full light of God, in full view of all his tender mercies." No, let my children bear the office of my friends when the time comes, so that I might say to them as a full confession to all my friends of this life: O, what I might have done for you, had I not been so selfish! And they can say, for all my friends: O, what we might have done for you, had you thought yourself worthy of even this little!

Murray Kempton

Once Ain't for Always

An Explanation of My Title: Historical scholarship, that rag-bag of myth, holds that once in 1927, while recording at the Columbia Studios, Bessie Smith had run through all her prepared material and then found herself with enough time left for another song and no way to use it except by making up the lyrics as she went along.

The result was "Lost Your Head Blues" and one of Bessie's supposed improvisations was:

> Once ain't for always
> And two ain't but twice.

The beauty of the lines was inexplicable and so was their meaning. Exegeses of Bessie's work have always tended to err in the direction of the coarse; and we pursued the mystery of the import of these words for the longest while among esoterica of sexual reference far beyond our own puny experience.

But we never solved their puzzle; and it teased me into late middle age until suddenly I understood. Bessie had meant to speak not about some unfamiliar variety of sexual congress but about a human condition that, if it is not universal, has inescapably been my own.

To say that once ain't for always is to remind us that to have done what we ought to have done is no assurance that we will do it the next time we ought and that to have left undone what we ought to have done is no condemnation to the leaving of all future oughts undone.

"Lost Your Head Blues" has since resided in me as the revelatory text for a life history that has been a continual process of confronting and suppressing one bad part of my character and then finding and struggling to suppress quite another bad part on and on and probably unto the last breath.

Now it has occurred to me that I may not be alone in this condition and that it might, as Clarendon put it, be not unuseful to the curiosity if not the conscience of mankind to attempt a memoir each of whose chapters would record some new discovery and transient overcoming of another deformed aspect of my nature. That is what I will try to do if the Lord has the kindness to allow me time to complete my recitals of successive combats with devils who once surprised with their newness and are now old and apparently old, gone, and replaced. Only His hand can finally spare me from unexpected encounters with some next one.

I came back from the war with nothing scarred about my person except a cartridge clip shot from my fatigue trouser pocket north of Bataan in February of 1945.

In the years before its disappearance I would occasionally happen upon it in a bureau drawer and be reminded less of how close life's wounds scrape than how unaware they take us when they do.

We had been whiling an afternoon away in a firefight where we had, as amateurs do, been wasting our stocks of ammunition, and a squad of Japanese stragglers had been, as professionals must, disciplinedly conserving theirs. Now and then we would subside from our clamors, and one of them would fire a single round to set us off again and advance the

hour when we would have used up our stores and be forced
to let them be.

Somewhere in the midst of these futilities, I felt a light
slap, smelled smoke at my haunch, and looked down to see the
.45 caliber cartridges ascending and scattering from my side
pocket. If you make the most of the noise long enough, you
settle into the delusion that there is no one in the room except
yourselves.

And so I at once took it for granted that someone in our
troop had shot too close from my rear and yelled out to
straighten the line. A Philippine scout as raw as we and fatally
more anxious to please stood up to obey my unfranchised command, was shot under the eye, and fell among his brains.

The work of the day went profitlessly on for another hour
before his comrade scouts picked up the body and carried it for
deposit upon the bamboo porch where his mother was standing.
He had died the soldier's death in a war scarcely half a kilometer from the ground where he had learned to walk. I told the
mother and brothers and sisters around her that he had been
brave. All he had been, of course, was dumbly respectful of a
thoughtless, hasty, and unauthorized order. I also said how sorry
we all were, which commonplace and guilt-unconscious nicety
could hardly, since I had no Tagalog, have reached her there
among the mute and immutable sorrows of the East.

Back at our outpost, I looked at my violated cartridge clip.
Its lips had been parted so neatly as to give free play to its
spring. The top cartridge must have exploded, which would explain the clap and the smoke. The shot had then come from the
front and would near to a certainty have passed by unnoticed if
it hadn't struck this piece of metal jutting out too far behind my
own flesh to have served it for shielding.

We spoke of the dead scout that evening with too much
more sentimentality than sentiment, and then so far forgot him
as not even to wonder about the funeral where we might have
formed a useless but not unfeeling guard of honor. He had died
to make no difference between his freedom from harsh but
seldom-seen conquerors and his deference to callous liberators

it had been his misfortune to understand too little and to trust too much.

We would soon forget everything about him except the startling ruddiness of the heap of his brains. Young men are careless people and never so much a danger to themselves and others as when most of what they are seeking is relief from boredom.

For what else but boredom could have brought me to such engagements uncompelled by the will and irrelevant to the desires of my commanders and driven to them by that least bearable of boredoms, the one that turns life to lead for those who feel denied every function of use and value?

I had come to the South Pacific doubly deprived of purpose because my military speciality and my assigned duty had already withered into obsolescence. My training had been as a radio operator assumedly equipped to send and receive International Morse Code at a speed of twenty-five words a minute. My wrist was stiffer and my fist infirmer than this rating attested; and these disabilities might have troublesomely betrayed themselves if the continuous wave transmissions of dots and dashes had not been outmoded by voice radio awhile back.

Since the Signal Corps had so small a residual need for my superseded skills, it could not be blamed for shuffling me off to its even-worse-superseded ground-observer service. There had existed an age when the air spotter had been a valued instrument for early warning of a hostile flight's approach and had occasionally earned himself a modest portion of legend. But the development of radar had long since pushed him nearer and nearer to wherever the observation balloon had gone before him.

Even so radar had its blind spots; and ground-observer teams went on being deployed to points of isolation on the unlikely chance that some Japanese plane might fly between mountains and hedgehog over peaks and so conceal itself from the radar's beam that only human eyes could detect it. It was so hard to take pride in having no excuse for being except as insurance against all-but-inconceivable circumstances that I took to self-identification as "Forward Observer attached to the Air Force," a desperate essay at being mistaken for those artillery-men who had something real to do and did it under conditions that could stand a man's hairs on end. Everyone else with a title to dignities larger than our own went on speaking of us as "groundhogs."

It did not take long, for the burden of being survivor and relic not just of one but of two of the auxiliary arts of warfare so weighed me down with my uselessness that I took to bobbing up whenever two or three were to be gathered together for adventures lurid as anticipation and pallid as experience.

For awhile at Lae in New Guinea, I took to patrolling with an Australian Sixth Division squad fleshed out by veterans of the European Theater. Two or three among them had been harried from Greece through Crete and at last turned fiercely to bay in North Africa. Then, having followed and endured the gloomy Anzac destiny of profiting the Empire's interests more abundantly than their own, they had been recalled to face up to the Japanese advance upon their own home continent.

They had walked from Port Moresby over the Kakota Trail and down toward Buna, formed themselves as though on parade, and, singing "Waltzing Matilda," marched straight forward until the Japanese opened up from the embankments that would be as close to Australia as they would ever thereafter go. Whatever the case, such was the legend, told, as always with the Aussies, by others than themselves. The reality was sufficiently superb, for in that week, the Australian Sixth and the American 23rd had won the Battle of Buna and decided the New Guinea campaign two years before I threw my feather's weight into the balance.

My Aussies knew that their business was done, that they were indisposed to further goes, and had settled into nights of reminiscence and days of desultory patrols, whose unoffending objective was to remind the enemy's leftovers that they were beaten and would be senseless to act otherwise. There are more fruitful ways to pursue the illusions of adventure than with companions who have already nobly undergone the destruction of most of their own. And so we spent our days scouring for nothing; and I can barely recall sensing, let alone confronting, a foe armed and dangerous.

My comrades could have taught me all manner of craft; and I have no doubt that they would have handsomely done so if some laboratory exercise had been forced upon them. As it was I picked up only two lessons. One was never to set forth for marsh or crag without first shining your shoes. The other was what I came to think of as the "Lick."

I noticed early on that each of the squad's elders had the habit of touching some part of his body—usually the crotch or abdomen—before entering some spot of brush where insecurities might hide. Later on, when I had strayed into patrols less secure against hazard, I caught myself now and then sweeping my hand across my forehead just above the eyebrow and could fairly hear the interior voice whispering that, if I were not hit there, I would be hit nowhere. And then I understood the tic for what it was, the talismanic gesture that restores the delusions of invulnerability and is the faint suggestion of recoil that defines the countenance of the him or the her who has known the supreme crisis.

I have recognized its look on the face of a woman just after her first child has been born and as surely I have marked it upon the drunken soldier with his forged leave pass and have noted his distinction from the arresting MP half again as tall and with his traded-for or extorted paratrooper boots crowing on his feet. From then on I understood that what had conveyed me to these wanderings had not merely been boredom but an almost possessed desire to earn that look and some lodgement with those who had been there.

To have departed ashamed of myself from as many places as I had before and would again had bound me as with iron to the need to leave this one at least without cause for apology. We always must of course, and so too would I soon and three times over, once for cowardice, once for the coarsest breach of the decencies of warfare, and a third time that would have been worse than either if I had not been summoned back from its almost overmastering temptations just in time.

And so, from dreams of being more than I could ever be, I went on volunteering for anything that was not kitchen police and, for what now seems to have been an eternity, I was cheated in each and all.

The B-17 crews gave me leave to ride a few times on their bomb runs to Wewak, whose official status as last bastion of the Japanese air arm in Australian New Guinea was already dissolving into an abstraction. I would sit at the .50 caliber machine gun station in the belly turret with naught to challenge and little to enchant me except the vistas of the coral seas.

I further played my spectatorial part in five or so assault landings upon beaches so obscure that most of them slip by without mention in the shorter histories of the war and even I cannot say for sure how many they were.

Upon discharge I was issued five campaign ribbons, three of them with the arrow that signified—and in my case oversuggested—repetitive encounters with hostile beachheads. One such arrow certified my service under conditions of combat in the Admiralty Islands, which I had never seen. But then the army is never so generous as with compliments that cost it nothing; and my papers credited me with ten D-Day landings, four of them over and done with while I was yet stateside.

But then, if I had indeed played these four fictional roles, it is hard to imagine them as much different from the routine our commanders would never vary and our enemies could never interrupt. We would tune our radios to a Japanese frequency that as usual told us precisely where we were going and as always promised to redden the seas with our blood when we got there. We would bed down as well as we might against bulkheads neither tropic air nor moonlight could soften until we made our half-slumbering way down the rope to the landing craft.

Military convention had fixed our appointment for two

hours after the infantry's first wave. The wait was a spectacle whose gauds never ceased to delight, with the great cruisers—we never rated a battleship—grumbling behind us and the little destroyers firing the streams of their rockets into vacant beaches. Then, as though to announce the break of day, the B-17s would let loose their bombs for majestic descent in orderly stacks into trackless forests while the infantry fanned out no farther than it needed to establish room for an airstrip, a communications system, supply tents, a hospital, space for the Salvation Army's doughnut wagons, and like necessaries for this way station to the next leapfrog in General MacArthur's vision.

We would debark to the anticlimax of flailing our shovels and tools against the coral and contriving foxhole enough to shelter us for a night's sleep before being told, as we quite often wouldn't be, what we were then supposed to do.

No image from these undifferentiated excursions has kept so vivid an impress in my memory as one from a half-lit morning off Sansopar when I was sitting in my stall in the landing craft and reading *Victory*. I had arrived at the passage where Axel Heyst, beset by peril on presumably civilized premises, remembers "with regret the gloom and the dead stillness of the forests at the back of the Geelvink Bay, perhaps the wildest, the unsafest, the most deadly spot on earth from which the sea can be seen."

I looked up and there before me spread the forests at the back of the Geelvink Bay, wild and gloomy and still as the tomb to be sure yet all else but unsafe for me in my armor-surrounded immunity. No other moment in New Guinea drew me so close to an epiphany; and yet, having been received as it were on loan from Conrad, it was not enough my own to realize fulfillments more complete than those quasi epiphanies accessible to any tourist with his guidebook.

And so it was as tourists still that we debarked upon the Luzon beaches off the Lingayen Gulf in January of 1945. We arrived, however, heartened by prospects of employments less empty than had been our lot. The air force had at last taken account of the inanition of its ground-observer teams and thought to change their duty to voice radio guidance for the fighter bombers in their works of close support for the infantry. We would transmit the grid coordinates of enemy positions to pilots who could then match them with their own flight maps and avoid mistaken inflictions upon our own troops.

These chores were sufficiently simple to accord with the generally low estimate of our competence; but they offered our first promise of actual service as far as, if no farther forward than, a battalion headquarters. We had even been indulged with a dress rehearsal directing P-51 sorties around the road to Bagulo and escaping serious damage to our credit.

But our sentence to limbo was not yet commuted; and we docilely resumed the ground observer's otiose existence and went down the road toward Mazilla and stopped at Aglao to mount guard against the improbable apparition of a hostile plane that had eluded the radar's notice and might take the advancing infantry unaware.

We were welcomed as liberators by the first authentic civilians to speak to us in the past thirteen months, established our outpost in their barrio's most impressive hutch, and began keeping our object-unrewarded watch around the clock.

One early evening—our third in office—one of our new neighbors came on the run to report that he had sighted a full Japanese company half a kilometer away and grouping for an attack on Aglao.

There were four of us Yanks and at least fifteen Philippine scouts, the makings of a respectable garrison: We nonetheless panicked like so many tourists, stammered our excessive alarms in a message to the rear echelon, shot up our radio, snatched our codebook, and scuttled a full kilometer down the hill followed pell-mell by scouts overdependent on the leadership of Americans who could display no more inspiring symbol of leadership than the spectacle of their heels in flight.

We spent a haunted night in the brush until the sun was high enough to embolden us to sneak back to Aglao. We found her peaceable as ever and all our stores pillaged to the last

K-ration can and all but the last thread. We had been well and thoroughly set up. The only enemy in the neighborhood had been the cunning hidden somewhere beneath the fair face of our welcomers.

We had earned ourselves a court-martial and would, I suppose, have gotten one if persons of substance had mistaken anything we did for stuff that mattered for good or ill. The rear echelon sent up a new radio and a fresh stock of rations and spared itself the bother of reproaches. We had been relieved of every inconvenience except the ignominy whose weight bore down upon each and all of us ever present and never spoken of.

Our looters had overlooked one of my shirts; and, since to ask supply for a reissue of clothing would have been to call further attention to my shame, I had to make do with that shirt and the one I had worn on that night of worst disgrace. And so the discovery of the little I would ever know about war was carried through with two shirts, one pair of fatigue trousers, and the last pair of socks that I would wash and let dry every night while I stood my watch barefoot.

If the war had ended that night, I doubt that I could thereafter have found stomach to mention my part in affairs that, after continually denying me all opportunity for tactile experience, had finally deprived me of all dignity. But life sometimes blesses us with reprieves; and, having encumbered myself with dishonor fleeing a fantasy of the Japanese, I would find a kind of redemption running away from the fact of them.

A squad from the 38th Division set up in Aglao the week after our debasement; and we joined its daily patrols in company with the scouts. Our searches brought us into five or so skirmishes, bloodied only twice on our side and, so far as I can judge, only once on theirs.

The Japanese had lost their corner of the war and were much too shrewd at cover and concealment for us to catch them unless boredom impelled them to stand and fight. I have often wondered why they cared. Perhaps it was the itch to instruct.

They were the only authentic, because the most fully completed, soldiers with whom I would in my dealings ever reach intimacy; and no apprentice could ever want for better teachers or reasonably expect to stay alive with ones less meagerly equipped with armament.

They closed school on us one afternoon in March just after we hit upon a straggler scrounging in a *comote* patch. Our leadman shot him and he stumbled and presumably fell in a grove. We were too cautious to follow since one of him argued more of them; and we moved up to a hill overlooking a rice paddy and stretched ourselves prone in the skirmisher line.

And then just down and to our left we saw a Japanese soldier carrying on his back the comrade we had left wounded, and all down the line we opened up on him. There were at least twenty meters between him and any cover at all; and he walked them like a farmer at his plow with all that metal hurling death around without ever straining beyond the solemn and deliberate majesty of his stride. My war was not overabundant with specimens of bravery in its purest essence; but this one will do for a good many.

He kept walking and we kept firing enough to leave him dead ten times over and we never hit him once. Some guardian angel had saved us from the ultimate infamy of killing a soldier carrying a wounded man off the field. I am no witness to the end of this one's trek, because we noticed two others setting up one of those rickety-ticky Japanese machine guns across the way and turned our weapons toward them. And then the ambush was sprung.

It was work of the highest art. They had used the interval of our malevolent distraction to emplace snipers in the trees behind and they were firing at us from the rear with reports so close and loud as to make me think that they were using my shoulder for a gun rest. The machine gun commenced to tap like a woodpecker; and we took our departure with sufficient discipline to pick a route for the rout as near as we could keep to the foliage at the rice paddy's border.

I was next to last in the line of retreat with the Browning

Automatic rifleman behind me; and I ran while that silly machine gun putt-putted behind me and the two carbines fairly burst my eardrums from overhead and the little shots were splitting apart when they hit the grass around me, until I at last fell gasping behind a tuft of cane stalks.

It was only fifty yards to absolute safety; and I was familiar enough with the woodpecker to know that its gunners could only fire five times before having to stop and push the drum back in order to start again. The full limit of demand upon me was to stay low, count five putts, and then get up and run ten or so yards toward total security. The gunners dealt their ration from what sounded like an increasingly comfortable distance; and then just as I was picking myself up for another dash, the BAR man called out that he had been hit.

The last minute or so had been consumed with desperate efforts to seem invisible to everyone behind me; and I dedicated the next ten seconds to seeming deaf as well. I lay there fixed in denial that I had heard this voice in its distress. I was in that moment as quit of the war as if the copy of my discharge papers had lain for a century in Washington's files. My vow to go home with no grounds for apology had already been twice violated; and I should surely had done it a third time if the BAR man had not cried out against that awful silence, "Oh, don't go away and leave me."

No words other than those particular seven could have brought him my help or me some shoring-up of my honor in its ruins. But these served for the miracle of taking me back to where seconds before I would not have gone for God or man; and, when I went to see what might be done for him, I covered the distance erect and uncaring what the enemy might see in the numbed conviction that my life was now forfeit anyway.

His wound was in the right thigh and none too bad a one; but he was too damaged to walk and too large for me to carry. I fiddled with fingers scarcely more practical than sticks to mount his BAR and contrive some impression that he was yet fit for combat, wished him a peaceful wait, and, without time to waste with deals of concealment, I ran across what no longer resounded as the field of one-sided fire and down the trail to find bearers stronger than myself.

I found my comrades in a commendable condition of calm, and explained why we would have to return. They prepared to follow me without a flicker of dubiety; and before we went, I handed my Thompson machine gun to a scout and took his carbine instead. The Thompson had been my talisman; to watch the arc of .45 caliber bullets exiting its muzzle was to feel safe and shielded from all man's malice. The carbine had no such claim on reason or superstition; but neither was of consequence by then and even weaponry wasn't, because I knew to a dead certainty that here was the hour of my last breath. The carbine's point was that it was lighter than the Thompson; a twig would have been better still.

We made our way through the heaviest of silences upward to where his mates gathered up the BAR man while I stood with my rifle pointed across that lately dreadful field in a counterfeit of the protective cover I had lost the will to provide. I had simply become a target. The enemy across the way let us be; the twenty minutes that had begun with our coarse denial of all gallantry toward one of them was ending with their free and easy tender of chivalry toward one of us.

A while afterward I came upon those pages where Antoine de St. Exupéry recalls his flight on reconnaissance to Arras to observe and report on the deployments of the French in a place from which the Germans had already driven them. He had come down for a closer look at the lines and, as he descended alone, naked and surrounded by the puffs from the antiaircraft guns, he became suddenly aware that war is the acceptance of death.

So I had lived once in that state of acceptance in that unforgettable paddy near Aglao and it would never happen again. I took to wondering how many occasions before the fatal last are allowed a soldier for feeling all his sensations distilled into those of the target that can no longer act for itself but only wait for death to dispose as it chooses. Once in hospital—for jungle rot—I put the question to Sergeant Herman Boetcher, a great soldier indeed; and he answered that he well knew the sense of the accepted death because he had undergone it five times. A few weeks after he came out of hospital, I read that he had been killed. So the limit for acceptances of death is perhaps six.

By sunset back in Aglao we were surprised by how much light we could make of the afternoon. There is a curious spiritual uplift in being done to so delicious a turn. The BAR man had been hurt just enough for a chance to go home and none of the rest of us was the worse for the day. We laughed more delightedly still when word came that the Japanese were walking guard formation in their renewed pride not a hundred yards away. And so they were, or anyway one of them imperturbably was, more than a hundred yards off but well within .30 caliber range.

I am embarrassed to confess that I did not render him the salute that was his due.

There could not have been more than six of them and there were never fewer than twenty of us; and our advantage in metallic weight was far crueler than in numbers. I myself carried more killing power on my shoulder than all of them could summon up with their .25 caliber single-shot carbines.

We had been taken by surprise but we had not entirely lost our heads; and it would be by no means unreasonable to inquire why, instead of withdrawing in order, we did not respond as patrols are expected to and simply turn our weapons on these overmatched enemies and transform their ambush into their terminal disaster. I have once or twice asked myself the same question. Respect for our betters perhaps; and in any case rather more than just as well.

They had made out of us the stuff of what must have been the last clear Japanese victory in the Pacific, and they deserved the satisfactions of a pride that had outlasted what may or not once have been their arrogance.

I recovered my Thompson and some of my aplomb; and we returned to our patrols the next day and for a week or so and, outside of an indecisive brush or so, never intimately engaged them. It was now near the end of March and we had been more than two months in Aglao. The normal span of our languid duties was D-Day plus 19. Our very existence had been forgotten; and, for two or three days, we went so far as to close down communications with net control and take off like the addicts we had become to join our old fellow travelers from the 38th on patrols around the Wewak Dam.

At last we were recalled to headquarters. I came down out of the hills as one who, while in no sense a tiger, had feasted and been near feasted upon by tigers and would never be the poor thing he had been before. I told myself with entire assurance that I had for all time to come dammed and copper-lined the turbulent bank-caving river of my life and that I would never again flinch or flee from anything and that, most especially, I would never go away and leave anyone. It had been true: once ain't for always.

But it is a truth with two faces. One of them looks back and is a consolation. The other looks forward and is a warning. We had been back in the rear area for no more than a week when the sound of the guns awoke me in the night and I came out of the tent to see the little white tracers that identified what had to be the last airworthy Japanese Betty in the whole of Luzon. If I had really been what I thought I had become, I would have gazed serenely at her futile gallantry and tried to conceive whence she had come and to where she could possibly return. Instead I surrendered to my old thought-conquered self and scuttled in aimless terror from tree to tree. Once indeed ain't for always.

I knew then that timidity and, yes, cowardice would be the permanent tenants of my interior and that I could never hope to trust my courage and would have to settle for preserving my dignity, a virtue whose keeping depends upon constant care to protect it from takings by surprise. It would be some years more before I discovered the equal worthlessness of my assurance that I would never again go away and leave anyone.

André Aciman

The Capital of Memory

Alexandria, 1996

To those who asked, I said I went back to touch and breathe again the past, to walk in shoes I hadn't worn in years. This, after all, was what everyone said when they returned from Alexandria—the walk down memory lane, the visit to the old house, the knocking at doors history had sealed off but might pry open again. The visit to the old temple, the visit to uncle so-and-so's home, the old school, the old haunts, the smell of the dirty wooden banister on days you rushed and almost glided downstairs on your way to a movie. And then, of course, the tears, the final reckoning, the big themes: the return of the native, the romance of the past, the redemption of time. All of it followed by predictable letdowns: The streets are always much narrower than before, buildings grow small with time, everything's in tatters, the city is dirty, shabby, in ruins. There are no Europeans left, and the Jews are all gone. Alexandria is Egyptian now.

As I step onto the narrow balcony of my room at the Hotel Cecil and try to take in the endless string of evening lights speckling the eastern bay, I am thinking of Lawrence Durrell and of what he might have felt standing in this very same hotel more than fifty years ago, surveying a magical, beguiling city—

the "capital of memory," as he called it, with its "five races, five languages. . . . and more than five sexes."

That city no longer exists; perhaps it never did. Nor does the Alexandria I knew: the mock-reliquary of bygone splendor and colonial opulence where my grandmother could still walk with an umbrella on sunny days and not realize she looked quite ridiculous, the way everyone in my family must have looked quite ridiculous, being the last European Jews in a city where anti-Western nationalism and anti-Semitism had managed to reduce the Jewish population from at least fifty thousand to twenty-five hundred by 1960 and put us at the very tail end of those whom history shrugs aside when it changes its mind.

The Alexandria I knew, that part-Victorian, half-decayed, vestigial nerve center of the British Empire, exists in memory alone, the way Carthage and Rome and Constantinople exist as vanished cities only—a city where the dominant languages were English and French but where everyone spoke in a medley of many more, because the principal languages were really Greek and Italian, and in my immediate world Ladino (the Spanish of the Jews who fled the Inquisition in the sixteenth century), with broken Arabic holding everything more or less together. The arrogance of the retired banker, the crafty know-it-all airs of the small shopkeeper, the ways of Greeks and of Jews, all of these were not necessarily compatible, but everyone knew who everyone else was, and on Sundays—at the theater, in restaurants, at the beach, or in clubs—chances were you sat next to each other and had a good chat. My grandmother knew Greek well enough to correct native Greeks, she knew every prayer in Latin, and her written French, when she was vexed, would have made the Duke of St-Simon quite nervous.

This is the Alexandria I live with every day, the one I've taken with me, written about, and ultimately superimposed on other cities, the way other cities were originally sketched over the Alexandrian landscape when European builders came, in the middle of the nineteenth century, and fashioned a new city modeled after those they already loved. It was this Alexandria I came looking for—knowing I'd never find it. That did not bother me. For I had come not to recover memories, nor even to recognize those I'd disfigured, nor to toy with the thought that I'd ever live here again; I had come to bury the whole thing, to get it out of my system, to forget, to hate even, the way we learn to hate those who wouldn't have us.

I am, it finally occurs to me, doing the most typical thing a Jew could do. I've come back to Egypt the way only Jews yearn to go back to places they couldn't wait to flee, only to be reminded of the one thing they've always known: that they were outsiders, exiles. Jews. The Jewish rite of passage, as Passover never tells us, is also the passage back to Egypt, not just away from it.

Until the mid 1950s, Jews had done extremely well in Egypt. They had risen to prominence and dominated almost every profession, and they were among the major financiers who brokered Egypt's passage from a European to a national economy, serving as important conduits for foreign investors. Jews managed a significant share of Egypt's stock exchange and owned some of the biggest banks and almost all of the department stores; the country boasted the greatest number of Jewish multimillionaires in the Middle East. Jews, though very few in number, even held seats in the Egyptian parliament.

These were, for the most part, observant Jews, but in a cosmopolitan city like Alexandria, where overzealous piety was derided and where friendship was almost never based on creed, many of these Jews were quite relaxed when it came to religion, particularly since most of them, educated in Catholic schools, tended to know more about the religions of others than about their own. Seders, I remember, were rushed affairs; no one wanted to inflict Passover on Christians who happened to be visiting and were induced to stay for dinner.

Following the Israelis' 1948 defeat of the Arabs, anti-Semitism rose sharply in Egypt, and there were some deadly incidents in the wake of the war. Matters became worse after 1956, when Israel joined forces with France and England in a tripartite attack on Egypt after Nasser nationalized the Suez Canal.

British and French residents of Alexandria were summarily expelled from Egypt, as were many Jews; everyone had their assets, businesses, and properties seized by the state. Aunts and
uncles, friends, grandparents, some of whom hadn't been expelled, read the writing on the wall and left within a few years of
the 1956 war, abandoning everything they owned. Most settled
in Europe, others in America.

Some, like us, simply waited, the way Jews did elsewhere
when it was already too late to wait for miracles. We saw the city
change and each year watched European shop names come
down and be replaced by Egyptian ones, the way we would hear
of streets being renamed, until—as is the case now—I didn't
know a single one.

The only street whose name hasn't changed is the water-
front road known as the Corniche, *al-Corniche,* a thick bottle-
neck mass of tottering loud vehicles emitting overpowering gas
fumes.

I try to rest both arms on the balustrade outside my hotel
room, as I'd envisioned doing on receiving the glossy brochure
with the Cecil's picture. But the small, Moorish/Venetian-style
balcony is entirely taken over by a giant compressor unit; it's
impossible to maneuver around it. Bird droppings litter the
floor.

Two men are speaking in Arabic downstairs. One is telling the other about his very bad foot and of the pain at night.
The other says it might go away. They don't know how surreal ordinary talk can seem to someone who's been away for
thirty years.

On the main square facing the hotel stands the ungainly
statue of the Egyptian patriot Sa'ad Zaghlul, one leg forward in
the manner of old Egyptian statues, except that this one wears a
fez. I used to pass by here every morning on my way to school.

Beyond Sa'ad Zaghlul is a villa housing the Italian consul-
ate, and farther yet is the city's main tramway station and to its
right the Cinema Strand, all unchanged, though worn by age. To
my right is Délices, one of the city's best pastry shops. It hasn't

moved either. Nothing, I think, is unfamiliar enough. I haven't forgotten enough.

Across the bay sits the fortress of Qayt-bay, its ill-lit, brooding halo guarding the Eastern Harbor. The fortress is said to occupy the site of the ancient Pharos lighthouse, one of the Seven Wonders of the Ancient World. Some say that the fort was built with stones taken from the old lighthouse itself. A French archaeological company has been commissioned to dig here. The area is cordoned off and considered top secret.

Not far from the dig lies the Western Harbor, which the ancients used to call the Harbor of Safe Return, Portus Eunostus, from the Ancient Greek *eu,* meaning good, safe, and *nostos,* meaning return. *Nostalgia* means the ache to return, to come home; *nostophobia,* the fear of returning; *nostomania,* the obsession with going back; *nostography,* writing about return.

So this is Alexandria, I think, before shutting the window, feeling very much like Freud when, in his early forties, he had finally achieved his lifelong dream of visiting Athens and, standing on the Acropolis, felt strangely disappointed, calling his numbness *derealization.*

I look at my watch. It is one in the afternoon New York time. I pick up the telephone to call America. After a short wait, I hear my father's voice. In the background, I make out a chorus of children, mine probably—or is it the clamor of a school recess down his block?

"How is it?" he asks. I describe the view from my window.

"Yes, but how is it?" he presses. What he means is: Has it changed and am I moved?

I can't find the right words.

"It's still the same," I reply. "It's Egypt," I finally say, all else failing.

Each year the city sees many ex-Alexandrians return and wander along its streets. Like revenants and time travelers, some come back from the future, from decades and continents away, A.D. people barging in on B.C. affairs, true anachronoids drifting about the city with no real purpose but to savor a past that, even before coming, they know they'll neither recapture nor put behind them, but whose spell continues to lure them on these errands in time.

The Portuguese have a word: *retornados*, descendants of Portuguese settlers who return to their homeland in Europe centuries after colonizing Africa—except that we are African-born Europeans who return to Africa as tourists, not knowing why we come, or why we need to come again, or why this city that feels like home and which we can almost touch at every bend of the street can be as foreign as those places we've never seen before but studied in borrowed travel books.

The first thing I want to do tonight is roam the streets by myself. The downtown shops are still open, and people are literally spilling out into the streets, an endless procession of cars going up the Rue Missallah (Obelisk), renamed Rue Saffeyah Zaghlul after the patriot's wife. The same stores stand in exactly the same spots, the same pharmacies, bookstores, restaurants; and everywhere that unbroken chain of shoe stores and third-tier haberdasheries with wares dangling over the sidewalks, and always that muted spill of lights which reminds me of Cavafy's nights and Baudelaire's Paris. I manage to recognize the Gothic-Venetian window sashes of an old restaurant. When I walk into Flückiger's, the pastry shop, and tell the cashier that I am just looking around, she smiles and says, as she must have told hundreds like me, *"Ah, vous êtes de nos temps,"* as if time could ever belong to anyone. Do I want to buy cakes? I shake my head. "They're still the same. We're still Flückiger," she adds. I nod. One would have thought that I shopped there every day and had stopped now on my way from work, only to change my mind at the last minute. The idea of eating cake to summon my past seems too uncanny and ridiculous. I smile to myself and walk out through the beaded curtain. It too hasn't changed.

Nor have the buildings. They are far more beautiful than I remember, the architecture a mix of turn-of-the-century French and floral Italian. But they are also grimier, some of them so rundown it's impossible to tell how long they've got. It's no different with cars here. Many are rickety thirty-plus patched-up jobs, part rust, part tin, part foil; soldered and painted over with the sort of Egyptian ingenuity that knows how to preserve the old and squeeze residual life out of objects which should have perished long ago but whose replacement will neither come from abroad nor be manufactured locally. These are not really cars, but, rather, elaborate collages of prostheses.

I turn right and walk into a murky street that used to be called Rue Fuad. Next to the Amir Cinema looms a strange, large structure I have never seen before. It is the newly dug up Roman amphitheater I've been reading about. I ignore it completely and turn left, where I spot Durrell's pastry shop, and walk down a narrow street, where I find the Cinema Royale and, right across from it, the old Mohammed Ali known as the Sayyed Darwish Theater, the pride of Alexandria's theater elite.

And then it hits me. The Mohammed Ali is my last stop tonight; I now have nowhere else to turn but the Hotel Cecil. To my complete amazement, I have revisited most of my haunts in Alexandria in the space of about eight minutes!

Once on crowded streets again, I walk the way I have come, along the edge of the sidewalk, my eyes avoiding everyone else's, my gait hurried and determined, everything about me trying to discourage contact with a city that is, after all, the only one I think I love. Like characters in Homer, I want to be wrapped in a cloud and remain invisible, not realizing that, like all revenants, I am perhaps already a ghost, a specter.

The next morning, I head out on another exploratory walk. But fifteen minutes later I have already reached Chatby, the very place I was meaning to see last. This is where most of the cemeteries are located. Pehaps I should pay a visit to my grandfather's tomb now.

I try to find the Jewish cemetery, but I am unable to. Instead, I head in a different direction and decide to visit my great-grandmother's house. As soon as I near her neighborhood, I find myself almost thrust into the old marketplace. It too hasn't changed since my childhood. The pushcarts and open shops are still in place, as is the unforgettable stench of fish and meat, and always the screaming and the masses of people thronging between stacks of food and crates of live chickens.

I could go upstairs, I think, once I reach the building on Rue Thèbes, but people are watching me fiddle with my camera, and someone actually pops his head out of the window and stares. I decide to leave. Then, having walked to the next block, I change my mind and come back again, trying to let the building come into view gradually, so as to hold that magical moment when remembrance becomes recovery. I am resolved not to be intimidated this time and make my way straight into the main doorway.

A woman appears with a child in her arms; she is the caretaker's wife: the caretaker died a few years ago; she is the caretaker now. A man also shows up. He lives on the street floor, he says in English, and has lived there since the early fifties. I tell him I too lived here once, at number 15. He thinks for a moment, then says he doesn't remember who lives there now. I tell the caretaker that I want to knock at apartment 15. She smiles and looks at me with suspicion. She is thinking. "Sit Vivi," she says. Mme. Vivi. I am almost on the verge of shaking. Vivi was my great-aunt. "They left," she says. Of course they left, I want to shout, we all left thirty years ago! "May I knock at the door?" I ask. "You may," she replies, with the same smile, "but no one is there." When will they be back? She looks at me with a blank stare. No one has occupied the apartment since.

I know that if I push the matter and tip her well, I might persuade her to show me the apartment. But the thought of a dark apartment where no one's been for three decades frightens me. Who knows what I'd find creeping about the floor, or crawling on the walls. It's all well and good for a German to go digging for the ghost of Troy or sifting through Helen's jewels. But no Trojan ever went back to Troy.

When I point to the elevator and ask her whether *this* still works, she laughs. *This* had died long ago. And she adds, with inimitable Egyptian humor, "Allah yerhamu." May God have mercy on its soul.

I step into the main courtyard and look up to our old

service entrance: I can almost hear our cook screaming at the maid, my mother screaming at the cook, and our poor maid's heartrending yelp each time the tumor on her liver pressed against her spine. I am trying to decide whether I should insist and ask to be taken upstairs, or perhaps she could show me another apartment in the same line. I see a cat playing in the foyer; next to it is a dead mouse. The caretaker does not notice it. Even the man from the first floor doesn't seem to notice, doesn't care.

I know I'll regret not insisting, and also that this is typical of my perfunctory, weak-willed attempts at adventure. But I am tired of these ruins, and the smell of the old wood panels in the foyer is overpowering. Besides, this is how I always travel: not to experience anything at the time of my tour, but to plot the itinerary of a possible return trip. This, it occurs to me, is also how I live.

Outside, I spot an old woman with a shopping basket; she looks European. I ask her whether she speaks French. She says she does. She is Greek. I am almost ready to tell her about my entire life, everything about my grandparents, my mother, our apartment that was never lived in since the day we left so many years ago, and all these ruins scattered everywhere, but I break in midsentence, hail a cab, and ask to be taken to the museum— by way of the Corniche, because I want to see the water.

The Corniche always breaks the spell of monotonous city life, the first and last thing one remembers here. It is what I think of whenever I sight a beckoning patch of blue at the end of a cross street elsewhere in the world. The sky is clear and the sea is stunning, and my cabdriver, who speaks English, tells me how much he loves the city.

The Graeco-Roman Museum was where I would come to be alone on Sunday mornings in 1965, my last year in Alexandria.

I pay the fee and, as usual, rush through the corridors and the quiet garden, where a group of Hungarian tourists are eating potato chips. The Tanagra statuettes, the busts of Jupiter and Alexander, the reclining statue of a dying Cleopatra, all these I pass in haste. There is only one thing I want to see, a Fayyum portrait of a mummified young Christian. I linger in the old, musty room. The painting is exquisite indeed, more so than I remember. But I am astonished that this bearded man looks so young. There was a time when he was older than I. Now I could almost be his father. Otherwise, nothing has changed: I'm standing here, and he's lying there, and it's all as if nothing has happened between one Sunday and the next.

I want to buy his picture in the museum shop. There are no postcards of Fayyum portraits. I want to buy E. M. Forster's guide to the city, but they haven't had it in a long time. I ask whether they have any of the Durrell books. They haven't carried those in a long time either. There is, in fact, really very little to buy. And very little else to see. I have seen everything I wanted to see in Alexandria. I could easily leave now.

An entire childhood revisited in a flash. I am a terrible *nostographer*. Instead of experiencing returns, I rush through them like a tourist on a one-day bus tour. Tomorrow I must try to find the cemetery again.

Turb'al yahud, Alexandria's Jewish cemetery, is located at the opposite end of the Armenian cemetery and lies only a few steps away from the Greek Orthodox. Farther down the quiet, dusty, tree-lined road is the Catholic cemetery. Magdi, a native Alexandrian who is employed by the American school I attended as a child, swears that Turb'al Yahud must be somewhere close by but can't remember where. "I come here only once a year for my mother," he explains, pointing to the Coptic cemetery not far along the same road.

Magdi double-parks and says he will ask directions from the warden of the Armenian cemetery. We have been driving around for more than two hours in search of my parents' old summer beachside home, but here too without luck. Either it's been razed or lies buried in a chaos of concrete highrises and avenues built on what used to be vast stretches of desert sand.

Soon Magdi comes out looking perplexed. There are, as it turns out, not one but two Jewish cemeteries in the area.

"Which one has a gate on the left?" I say, remembering my very early childhood visits to my grandfather's grave four decades ago. "That's the problem," says Magdi, drawing on his cigarette. "Both have gates to the right."

I am dismayed. I can situate the grave only in relation to the left gate. We decide to try the nearest cemetery.

Magdi starts the car, waits awhile, then immediately speeds ahead, leaving a cloud of dust behind us. In a matter of minutes, we have parked on a sidewalk and ambled up to a metal gate that looks locked. Magdi does not knock; he pounds. I hear a bark, and after a series of squeaks, a man in his early fifties appears at the door. I try to explain in broken Arabic the reason for my visit, but Magdi interrupts and takes over, saying I have come to see my grandfather's grave. The warden is at a loss. Do I know where the grave is, he asks? I say no. Do I know the name then?

I say a name, but it means nothing to him. I try to explain about the door to the left, but my words are getting all jumbled together. All I seem to remember is a pebbled alleyway that started at the left gate and crossed the breadth of the cemetery.

The warden has a three-year-old son wearing a very faded red sweatshirt bearing the initials CCCP—not unusual in a place where ancient relics come in handy. Their dog, fleeced from the neck down, has a large bleeding ulcer on his back.

"Oh, that door," the warden responds when I point to another, much smaller gate at the opposite end of the cemetery. "It's locked, it's never been used." Indeed, the gate at the end of the alleyway looks welded in place. I am almost too nervous to hope. But I pick my way to the end of the path and, having reached the left gate, climb over a wild bush whose dried leaves stick to my trousers, turning with a sense of certainty that I am trying to distrust, fearing the worst.

"Is this it?" asks Magdi.

I am reluctant to answer, still doubting that this could be the spot, or this the marble slab, which feels as warm and smooth to the touch as I knew it would each time I rehearsed this moment over the years. Even the name looks dubious.

"Yes," I say, pointing to the letters, which I realize he can't read.

The warden knows I am pleased. His son trails behind him. A fly is crawling around his nose. Both of them, as well as the warden's wife, are barefoot. Bedouin style.

I take out my camera. Everyone is staring at me, including the warden's ten-year-old daughter, who has come to see for herself. It turns out that no Jew ever visits here. "No one?" I ask. *"Walla wahid,"* answers the daughter emphatically. Not one.

There are, it occurs to me, far more dead Jews in this city than there will ever again be living ones. This reminds me of what I saw in a box at the main temple earlier this morning: more skullcaps than Jews to wear them in all of Egypt.

The warden asks whether I would like to wash the tombstone. I know Magdi has to go back to work; he is a bus driver and school ends soon. I shake my head.

"Why?" asks the warden. *"Lazem."* You must.

I have lived my entire life outside rituals. Now I am being asked to observe one that seems so overplayed and so foreign to me that I almost want to laugh, especially since I feel I'm about to perform it for them, not for me. Even Magdi sides with the warden. *"Lazem,"* he echoes.

I am thinking of another ritual, dating back to those days when my father and I would come on quiet early morning visits to the cemetery. It was a simple ritual. We would stand before my grandfather's grave and talk; then my father would say he wished to be alone awhile, and, when he was finished, hoist me up and help me kiss the marble. One day, without reason, I refused to kiss the stone. He didn't insist, but I knew he was hurt.

I pay the warden's family no heed and continue to take pictures, not because I really want to, but because in looking through the viewfinder and pretending to take forever to focus,

I can forget the commotion around me, stand still, stop time, stare into the distance, and think of my childhood, and of being here, and of my grandfather, whom I hardly knew and scarcely remember and seldom think of.

I am almost on the point of forgetting those present when in totters the warden lugging a huge tin drum filled with water. He hoists it on a shoulder and then splashes the dried slab, flooding the whole area, wetting my clothes, Magdi's, and the little boy's feet, allowing the stone to glisten for the first time in who knows how many decades. With eager palms, we all go about the motions of wiping the slab clean. I like the ritual. Magdi helps out silently, but I want it to be my job. I don't want it to end. I am even pleased that my clothes are wet and dirty.

I still can't believe I was able to find my grandfather's grave so quickly. Memories are supposed to distort, to lie. I am at once comforted and bewildered.

In the distance I can hear the tireless drone of Alexandrian traffic, and farther off the loud clank of metal wheels along the tramway lines—not obtrusive sounds, for they emphasize the silence more—and I am reminded of how far Grandfather is from all this: from all these engines; from the twentieth century; from history; from exile, exodus, and now return; from the nights we spent huddled together in the living room, knowing the end had come; from our years in cities he had never visited, let alone thought some of us might one day call home. Time for him had stopped in the early fifties on this dry, quiet, secluded patch of dust that could turn into desert in no time.

I look around and recognize famous Jewish names on tombstones and mausoleums. They too, like my grandfather, were lucky not to have seen the end. But they also paid a price: No one ever comes here. The opulent mausoleums, built in Victorian Barococo, were meant to house unborn generations that have since grown up elsewhere and don't know the first thing about Egypt.

"Are you happy now?" I want to ask my grandfather, rubbing the stone some more, remembering a tradition practiced among Muslims of tapping one's finger ever so gently on a tombstone to tell the dead that their loved ones are present, that they miss them and think of them. I want to speak to him, to say something, if only in a whisper. But I am too embarrassed. Perhaps this is why people say prayers instead. But I don't know prayers. All I know is that I cannot take him with me—but I don't want to leave him here. What is he doing here anyway? In a hundred years, no one will even know my grandfather had lived or died, here or elsewhere. It's the difference between death and extinction.

I pretend to want to take another picture and ask Magdi, the warden, and his family to pose in front of one of the palm trees, hoping they will stay there after the picture and leave me alone awhile. I can feel my throat tighten, and I want to hide the tears welling up inside me, and I am, once again, glad to cover my eyes with the viewfinder. The warden's daughter comes closer. She wants a picture by herself. I smile and say something about her pretty eyes. I give her father a good tip.

Everyone thinks it's been a good visit. Perhaps all cemetery visits are.

On my last evening in Alexandria, I and a group of young teachers from the American school have gathered at a pizzeria to celebrate someone's birthday. We've parked on a narrow alleyway, halfway on the sidewalk, exactly where my father would park his car. Everyone at the party orders pizza, salad, and beer. It occurs to me that we might easily be in Princeton or New Haven.

By eleven the party breaks up. Before getting into the car, we take a stroll toward the Church of St. Saba. The streets are very dark, and after spending time in the American bar, I am suddenly confronted with the uncanny thought that we are, after all, very much in Egypt still. Maybe it's the alcohol, but I don't know whether I'm back in Egypt or have never left, or whether this is all a very cruel prank and we're simply stranded in some old neighborhood in lower Manhattan. This, I realize, is what happens when one finally comes home: One hardly notices, and it doesn't feel odd at all.

Later that night, as I'm looking out from my balcony, I think of the young man from Fayyum, and of the young man I used to be, and of myself now, and of the person I might have been had I stayed here thirty years ago. I think of the strange life I'd have led, of the wife I would have, and of my other children. Where would I be living? I suppose in my great-grandmother's apartment—it would have fallen to me. And I think of this imaginary self who never strayed or did the things I probably regret having done but would have done anyway and don't wish to disown: a self who never left Egypt or ever lost ground and who, on nights such as these, still dreams of the world abroad and of faraway America, the way I, over the years, have longed for life right here whenever I find I don't fit anywhere else.

I wonder if this other self would understand about him and me, and being here and now and on the other bank as well—the other life, the one that we never live and conjure up when the one we have is not the one we want.

This, at least, has never changed, I think, my mind drifting to my father years ago, when we would stop the car and walk along the Corniche at night, thinking of the worst that surely lay ahead, each trying to give up this city and the life that came with it in the way he knew how. This is what I was doing now as well, thinking of the years ahead when I would look back to this very evening and remember how, standing on the cluttered balcony at the Cecil, I had hoped finally to let go of this city, knowing all the while that the longing would start again soon enough, that one never washes away anything, and that this marooned and spectral city, which is no longer home for me and which Durrell once called "a shabby little seaport built upon a sand reef," would eventually find newer, ever more beguiling ways to remind me that here is where my mind always turns, that here, to quote this century's most famous Alexandrian poet, Constantine Cavafy, I'll always end up, even if I never come back:

> For you won't find a new country,
> won't find a new shore,

The city will always pursue you,
And no ship will ever take you away . . .
         from yourself.

And then I remembered. With all the confusion in the cemetery that afternoon, I had forgotten to ask Magdi to show me Cavafy's home. Worse yet, I had forgotten to kiss my grandfather's grave. Next year, perhaps.

Robert McLiam Wilson

Sticks and Stones: The Irish Identity

I am five foot eleven. I weigh around 170 pounds. I have brown hair, green eyes, and no real distinguishing marks. I'm heterosexual, atheist, liberal, and white. I don't shave as often as I should and I have pale, Irish skin. I smoke and I always wear a suit. I drive a small black car and I don't drink much alcohol. I prefer cats to dogs.

I don't know what that makes me, but I suspect that it makes me what I am.

When I was seventeen, I decided that I wanted to be Jewish. Like most Roman Catholics, I had only the vaguest notion of what this might entail. I stopped being good at sports and frequented the only kosher butcher in the city. (How he blushed for me, the poor man). I could never understand why no one took me seriously. I could never understand why I should not simply decide such questions for myself. Why was I such a goy? Who had decided that this should be so?

Like that of most citizens of Belfast, my identity is the subject of some local dispute. Some say I'm British, some say I'm Irish, some even say that there's no way I'm five foot eleven and that I'm five ten at best. In many ways I'm not permitted to contribute to this debate. If the controversy is ever satisfactorily concluded, I will be whatever the majority of people tell me I am.

As a quotidian absolute, nationality is almost meaningless. For an Italian living in Italy, Italianness is patently not much of a distinction. What really gives nationality its chiaroscuro, its flavor, is a little dash of hatred and fear. Nobody really knows or cares what they are until they meet what they don't want to be. Then it's time for the flags and guns to come out.

So when the airport cops ask me what I am, how do I explain that I live in the northeastern segment of an island sliced like a cheap pizza and with as many titles as a bar full of yuppie cocktails—Ireland, Northern Ireland, Britain, Eire, Ulster, etc. How do I explain how little that would tell them?

I suppose I could tell them that I live in a place where people have killed and died in an interminable fight over the names they should call themselves and each other. (In Belfast, sticks and stones may break your bones but names will blow you to pieces on a regular basis.) I could tell them about the self-defeating eugenic templates of racial purity by which no human being still living on the island can be properly deemed Irish. That the English and the Scottish have been here a long time and that we're all smudged by now—café au lait, mulattoes, half-breeds, spicks, wops, and dagos. I could tell them that I don't really understand the question.

Irishness is unique amongst the self-conscious nationalisms. A self-conscious Frenchman bores everyone. A self-conscious American is a nightmare. And a self-conscious Englishman makes you want to lie down in a darkened room. But a self-conscious Irishman is a friend to the world and the world listens attentively. The reviews are always good. There's a global appetite for Irishness that is almost without parallel.

Nationalistic self-obsession is corrupt, corrosive, and bogus enough without this extra angle. When well-received, this fake concoction of myth and bullshit is reflected in the mirror of imprecise good will and sentimental foolishness. This in itself produces further distortions which are then seamlessly incorporated into the "genuine" article. Over the years I've watched the fundamental concepts of what it is to be Irish being altered by common-currency American errors. Here in the "old country," when we hear that New Yorkers are marching in green-kilted bagpipe bands (an entirely Scottish phenomenon) on St. Patrick's Day, we immediately look around for somewhere to buy green kilts and bagpipes. Our racial authenticity is an extremely negotiable commodity.

Yet I've always believed that such Americans have it just about right. Their ideas of Irishness are as fake as a hooker's tit, but then so are ours.

To understand all things Irish, you must understand something fundamental. Everyone knows that Ireland is the land of myth. And myth is a beautiful and resonant word. It sounds so profound, so spiritual. There is something visceral in it. Our mythmaking is vital to the self-imposed standardized norms of nationality that are current here at home. Catholics are Irish, so Irish, and Protestants are British, poor things. The common assumption that the Irish language, Irish music, and Irish history are pure Catholic monoliths, and the oft-suppressed expression of the indigenous culture, ignores the truth that the Irish linguistic, musical, and cultural revivals were the product of nineteenth-century Protestant historicism. Everything we say is myth. The lies are old and dusty. The waters are muddy and the truth long gone.

Even our understanding of our own history—you know the kind of thing, perfidious Albion, eight hundred years of oppression, etc.—teems with bullshit. King William of Orange waged war in seventeenth-century Ireland and is still a Catholic-baiting Protestant icon who causes trouble here. No one remembers that he was blessed by the Pope. Wolfe Tone is a much-loved historical rebel leader who sailed with a French army to liberate Catholic Ireland. No one mentions that he was defeated by a Catholic militia. The President of Ireland called on a German minister to express his official condolences after Hitler's suicide at the end of World War II. Nobody wrote any songs about that.

In some ways, the Irish tendency for romancing can be seen as harmless, almost charming. It is, after all, what produces our leprechauns, our fairy rings, all our beguiling fakery. But it also produces people who will murder for lies they only half-believe and certainly never understand—for the Irish have always armed their ideas. We don't have any white lies here anymore. We only have the deadly barbaric type.

Given the wildest differences in latitude and climate, it is remarkable how countries can remind you of one another. In cold March Manhattan, the air is as thick, dark, and injurious as any Berlin winter. In Paris, the rain falls and stains the pale stone with the same dispiriting grace you find in Cambridge on most days of the year. London can look and feel like everywhere.

If true of the places, how much truer of the people. *Quod erat demonstrandum* and then some.

We are a pretty poor species. Even the most gifted of us, the wisest and most studious of us, are weak-minded. We toss aside our Pushkin and read Judith Krantz. We watch goofy TV shows and asinine movies. We can't help liking big noises, colored lights, and pictures of naked people.

Our beliefs are often fantastic alloys of fear, self-interest, prejudice, and ignorance. As Tolstoy gloriously demonstrates, our finest moments of heroism, selflessness, and grandeur are usually founded on the meanest egotisms and vanities. Our notion of the sublime is laughable. In acts of worship, many of us pay homage to some form of invisible man who mimics us in the pettiest detail. Apart from our uncharacteristic capacity for love (a mistake, a design flaw), we're a shambles.

It is the things we say that most prove what monkeys we still are. We are driven to generalize, to sweep on through, to prognosticate, to diagnose. Typically male, we say, typically female. That's the problem with rich people, we opine. The poor were ever so. Gentlemen prefer blondes. Fuck right off, I can't help thinking.

Our most outrageous banalities are reserved for questions of race and nationality. This is how the French behave, we say. How do we know? Have we met them all? Have we asked any of them? Millions of people are summoned and dismissed in a few moments of robust fatuousness.

I'm five foot eleven. I weigh around 170 pounds. I have brown hair, green eyes, and so on. Irish or British is very far down on my list—somewhere below my favorite color. Nonetheless, I must concede that nationality is tenacious. People have real stamina when it comes to this business. I must further concede that Irishness is a great arena for disquisitions on national identity. Because the Irish conflict is internecine (it has nothing to do with the English anymore), definitions of Irishness have particular charm. Nationalities primarily define themselves by what they're not. The Swiss are not German, the Scottish are not English, and the Canadians are definitely not American. But the Irish make internal distinctions as well. Some of the Irish aren't properly Irish. Some of the Irish aren't even vaguely Irish. In pursuit of the mantle of absolute Irishness, brother kills brother and sisters look on and applaud.

A few years ago I had an apartment on a leafy South Belfast street called Adelaide Park. A police station was being rebuilt across the street from my building (the original had been flattened by a bomb a few years before). It was a controversial building site, naturally. Apart from their well-known attacks on the policemen, soldiers, prison officers, and almost everyone else, the IRA liked to target construction workers who helped build police stations. Thus, the site was guarded round the clock by the police. For nearly six months there were always a couple of cops standing in my driveway, all peaked caps, submachine guns, and high anxiety. This was okay in the spring. It was fine in the summer, and manageable in the fall. But as winter set in, the position of these guys became more and more unpleasant. It was windy and cold, and it rained for months. As night fell, I would look out my apartment window and watch the damp rozzers. It was obviously not a good gig.

For weeks I debated whether or not I should take them cups of coffee. It was more complicated than it might sound. Policemen and soldiers here are very unlikely to accept such things from the public now. Twenty-five years of ground glass, rat poison, and Drano in friendly cups of tea discouraged them from accepting such largesse. Not long before, a woman had handed some soldiers a bomb in a biscuit tin in a charming incident near Derry. Additionally, of course, there might have been swathes of people willing to do me grief for being nice to the police.

Policemen are usually Protestant and I myself am customarily Catholic. They couldn't have known that I was a Catholic, but they would have been suspicious. (In this country, the big haters can't really tell each other apart. How we envy those who hate black or white people—that obvious difference, that demonstrable objection.)

It was a small thing, a minor transaction, an unimportant detail. The weeks passed, the wind blew, and the rain rained. I didn't hand out any coffee.

—July 1997

Hilary Masters

In Montaigne's Tower

It is, as he writes, exactly sixteen "pages" across the thick paving stones of the circular floor. Two large windows are set into the curve of the stone wall, opposite from where his writing table was, to look out on the garden below and the landscape that falls away from this high butte on which the chateau was built. Greek and Latin inscriptions use the ceiling timbers of the room as a commonplace of collected wisdoms, but, of course, the book shelves that Montaigne had carpenters fit into the stone radius of the outside wall are long gone and the beloved, well-thumbed volumes they kept put into a national archive.

It is Wednesday, the first of May; a sunny, cool morning that can almost be savored on the palate like the crisp, fruity Entre Deux Mers from the vineyards nearby. The city of Bordeaux, of which Montaigne was mayor in the 1580's, lies about fifty kilometers to the west. The château's caretaker is my casual guide, and he has continued to describe Montaigne's regimen in a manner that indulges my hobbled French. *Voici*—he walks to a far diameter of the room—is *le trou sanitaire* that the Master had masons open in the medieval wall; an innovative bit of 16th century plumbing so that the calls of nature would only briefly interrupt the composition of an essay. On the opposite side of the chamber, another vent connects this tower study via an air shaft to the family chapel three floors below. Montaigne could remain scribbling at his desk and yet still hear the daily masses celebrated there.

My guide's right arm sweeps up and around in a wide windmill motion as he delivers what seems to be an often made but no less worn observation. His Gascon expression is only slightly lifted. Yes, *je vois,* I nod; I get the idea: spiritual inspiration rises from below on one side to infuse the genius at his desk, and then the waste of this exchange is disposed through the opening opposite. He offers the procedure as a kind of basic model of creativity. *Aussi, c'est pratique!*

This pilgrimage made to my master's snug retreat has also been a journey to satiate, once and for all, my appetite for France. Some of us may remember *les pommes frites* of the late 1940's. Plump slabs of potato sauteed in olive oil and shallots, sprinkled with parsley, that accompanied a *biftec* that was often *plus cheval que boeuf.* This cut of *frites* has all but disappeared, replaced by anonymously extruded perfections, deep fried and common to restaurants and road stands across the Republic. But, yesterday, I stopped for lunch at a Rouliers on the outskirts of Nicole on N 113 to eat with truck drivers. Roast pork had been the *plat du jour,* and the tender slices of meat were accompanied by hand-cut chunks of potato sauteed crispy brown around the edges, redolent of garlic and sprinkled with chopped, fresh tarragon. Prefabricated spuds have yet to come to that part of the Lot-Garonne.

But I digress, for it is not only the food and wine that has mapped this ramble up from Provence and along the Garonne River. I have come to that time in my life when a return visit to a favorite place on earth will probably be my last view of it, my last taste of it. For instance, all the idling meanders I have made up and down the Meuse Valley, along the old battle lines of that horrible slaughter that defined my century, have bred a melancholy passion for those fields of grain that indolently stretch out in the brilliant summer sun of Lorraine, beneath the dark green shoulders of the Argonne. The grieving recitative between piano and oboe in the second movement of Ravel's Concerto in G can musically reproduce this scenery for me. Awful carnage occurred there and its horrors, muted by time, season my understanding of human idealism gone astray, remind me of how greed and stupidity can pollute the best intentions of men and women.

And here's another idea, surely preposterous in its vanity, that in these places—this Dordogne Valley for instance where at certain turns of the road I encounter an earlier self—I might leave something of myself behind. Maybe years from now in some of these villages the guise of my figure turning a corner will be confused by a resident with another. So, once again to digress, I seem to be talking now about memory, that two-way mirror we all carry of the past and before which we adjust our histories to fit the present. I don't recall that Montaigne ever specifically writes about memory, not even in any of his digressions, and this is curious for a man who so immersed himself in the bound volumes of antiquity. Perhaps his time was so consumed by the present, by its current events—the Reformation with all its attendant barbarisms to cite just one—that the 16th century "now generation" found no space in their reflections for past events, for memory. His father, Pierre, was born only a couple of years after Columbus had discovered the New World, and that astounding happening was still making front page news in Montaigne's day, stimulating him to write one of his better known essays, "Of Cannibals."

So it is these memories of France, this glut of its past, that has partly driven me here to give homage to Montaigne, while satisfying once and for all this craving that almost amounts to a strange jealousy. It is no wonder that Montaigne and his contemporaries—like Shakespeare and Cervantes, or Copernicus and Galileo—were so brilliantly glib: they had brand new material to write about! To fly to the dead orb of the moon and return is an amazing feat but only that. On the other hand, to return with stories of an alter world populated with people much like us, who are going about their odd religions, raising zinnias, and putting the Julian calendar into stone steps—now, that's the stuff of supermarket tabloids! Some inspiration! It is like the past catching up with the present to make an entirely different here and now. These days, it seems we mostly write of what might have been and our significant characters are all has-beens.

"I am overwhelmed by the past," Wright Morris will say to me. I am now on another pilgrimage, this one to California, and he has just met me at the door of his apartment in a retirement facility. The comic, complex intelligence that has so enriched our literature, and the understanding of our literature in his essays, is losing sight of its own perimeter to become almost as seamless as the inner wanderings and wonderings of his characters in such novels as *Field of Vision, Ceremony at Lone Tree, Works of Love* or *Love Among the Cannibals*—to cite only some favorites from a huge bibliography. The astute focus on things, on moments that "tell all," effortlessly hones the conversation, but the *all* these things are supposed to tell has mysteriously eluded identification, fallen through the witty schema. A dry Nebraskan humor still edges the droll appraisal in the blue eyes; it is the look of a prairie town barber who knows all about Pascal and Henry James, but isn't so sure his customers should hear about it. Just yet. "You see what is happening here," he will tell me with an uncanny objectivity. "This isn't what I expected."

It is as if time, that he had used so skillfully to arbiter his characters' inner lives, has lost the hands of its clock, though the mechanism continues to function. Past and present are all one, real and unreal undivided. "I knew who you were, Hilary, when I came to the door, but which Hilary you were out of the pasts we shared, I did not know."

Last night I stayed in a small family hotel in the village of Branne. Montaigne's tower is open to the public for only a few hours once a week, on Wednesdays, and I have arrived on Tuesday, the last day of April. At the *hôtel de ville* in Castillon-de-la Bataille, I was given directions to St-Michel-de-Montaigne, the tiny feudal hamlet established to serve the needs and security of the manor family. My Michelin tells me that Castillon received its distinctive title from a battle fought here in 1453 in which the English lost their control over this part of the Aquitaine, an early demonstration of the real being separated from the unreal which the British are still having problems learning today. But I digress.

My hotel is situated on the banks of the Dordogne River and at one corner of the village's covered market. In fact, when I open the window shutters in my room, I look directly out on the river, which is fairly wide and fast-flowing at this point. Here, also, a modern steel truss bridge spans the crossing, probably a replacement of a stone bridge destroyed during one of the century's battles over the ownership of this territory. Almost due north from my window, at a distance of about eight kilometers, are the heights of St-Emilion, and I promise myself something from that *domaine* at dinner.

And it is a Chateau de l'Arrosse of the grand cru, rich in merlot, that *Mme. la Proprietaire* decants for me in the hotel's plain dining room. About ten tables are placed correctly upon a gleaming wood floor, each with a small vase of blossoms, a kind of small lily, set precisely in the middle of the white paper table covers. Windows overlook the roof of an adjoining building and toward a slice of the river beyond. Two couples are already into their first courses as I taste the wine. They are of about the same advanced age, but one couple seem to be local citizens having a night out at the town's hotel. I had seen them earlier in the establishment's bar, having their apéritif, and they had been included in the family-like gossip, the give-and-take of the place. The second couple, seated near me and travelers like myself, speak a peculiar language that turns out to be Flemish.

"You speak French very well," the man says to me in a heavy English. I had only ordered the 80 franc menu from the timid young woman someone apparently has pushed out of the kitchen to take our orders. So this compliment on my language skills puts me on guard. Am I being conned? I lightly tap the shape of my billfold within my jacket's breast pocket. But then, I

put them together with the large Mercedes that is parked next
to my little Peugeot in the market square. In addition, the authority of the man's polished baldness suggests respectability.
They are, in fact, art dealers returning to Belgium from a business trip in Spain.

My duck is crisp and tasty and served with a pureed me-
dallion of something that could be turnip and its musty root
flavor plays off well against the sweet pungency of the fowl.
Mme. Proprietaire has brought her young son, a boy of about
three or four, into the dining room to greet the guests. The
child, guided by his mother, makes a solemn tour of our three
tables, offering his hand with a large-eyed frankness. I met his
father in the lounge before dinner, just as the man returned
from his daytime job. He had put his lunch pail down next to
the bar sink, rolled up his sleeves, and took up the gossip and
the servicing of the locals as his wife left to attend to kitchen
matters. The art dealers have been trying to engage me in conversation, mostly their complaints on the state of contemporary
painting. They say that all worthwhile work has already been
collected. My mind is elsewhere, and has no place for their
dilemma.

Montaigne's tower was closed today, but I had been able
to visit the ancient, small church of St-Michel in the writer's
village. A local resident had shown me the crypt behind the altar
where the writer's heart had been buried. Whether at his behest
or by his widow's sympathetic direction, I do not know, but his
heart was placed alongside the remains of his father in September of 1592. The rest of him was entombed in a cathedral in
Bordeaux only to be moved about in the next several centuries
in a ludicrous pawn game run by prefects, archbishops, and
academicians. But his heart remains next to his father in his
home village.

We know something about that relationship. A robust *sei-
gneur* of the Renaissance, the elder Montaigne trained servants
to wake his baby son to the strains of harp and flute. Moreover,
all the help who served the young child spoke only Latin to him,

and he to them; he heard no French until his fifth or sixth year. Pierre Montaigne, something of an early environmentalist, introduced his son to animal husbandry and a respect for all animals, for the miracles of plant life and the cultivation of the vineyard and granary. The arts of war were not neglected, and his father showed him the handling of weapons and armor, for the young noble would need this expertise if he was to serve his king and protect his estate. In this last curriculum, horsemanship was the important course of instruction, and under his father's tutelage, the two of them often riding side-by-side into Bordeaux, Montaigne learned a life-long appreciation for horses, a pleasure in the power and movement of a good horse under him even when enduring the awful agony of kidney stones that attacked him late in life. He writes that the inspiration for many of his essays came to him on the back of a horse, contrary to the theory to be suggested by my guide at the tower. "We can't afford to take the horse out of his essays," Emerson was to write centuries later.

I read of this companionship, so intimate and resolute even in death, with a mixture of wonder and envy. My own father, separated from me in life as well as death, lies in the small village of Petersburg in central Illinois—his "heart's home," he called it. No part of me will ever join him in that rural graveyard for our destinies have put us on divergent paths; yet, he did pass on to me some important lessons. Not in horsemanship, for sure. No Latin and less Greek, but an affection for the ideas and literature born in those languages. A love of music, though I have not his heavy taste for such composers as Brahms and Dvořák. My skepticism of certain human endeavors and pretenses—such as altruism—is a reflection of his thinking. But books, keeping a library. There's the connection.

To my wife's agitation, books are piled on our tables, spill in heaps from stuffed shelves, lie about the floor and on chairs like spoiled pets. I have a miser's greed for books, and I pick them up at random to read a passage or follow an argument, inhabit a poem. I carry them from room to room, portable transitions of thought, of the past into the present, only to put them down in a maddening disorder. Guests sometimes ask, "Have you read all these books?" My answer must be, no. But they are there for me to read, or re-read, some day. If I am to have wealth it is in my books and when I regard their spines pressed together on the bookshelves, observe the casual sculptures they make on a table, my spirit becomes cozily furnished.

My father's love of books can be measured by the depth of his anguish caused by the loss of his library in the course of his first marriage's divorce. In all of our meetings, my visits to him in New York City, the loss of that library invariably entered his conversation. By then, of course, he had collected other volumes of Homer, Goethe, Keats & Company, but these were reproductions, so to speak, and did not carry the imprint of that first handling, the scent of that first enthusiasm. Over the years, he would write the son of that marriage, pleading with him to find some way to return the books of his library to him, but my half-brother always claimed vague difficulties; he could do nothing. After my father's death, the son revealed he had had the library all along. He even listed its contents in an angry memoir, but what happened to those books after his death is a mystery.

So, in this modest dining room of this small hotel in Branne, I have been taking account of these quite different relationships between fathers and sons; one so ardently physical, using Aristotle's empirical methods to learn of the world, and the other distant, cooly intellectual and seeking wordliness in books. It must be evident that I have nearly consumed the St. Emilion, for, together with the silky surfeit of a *crème brulée*, my senses have become transported, reality addled, and sentimentality ascends. I yearn to fit myself beneath that bony cheek in Illinois.

"All the Rembrandts in the Hermitage are fake," the art dealer says. The Belgian couple finish their coffee and leave.

This morning, their big, gray Mercedes has gone when I throw my bag into the Peugeot and drive across the Dordogne to retrace the 20 kilometers east toward St-Michel-de-Montaigne. The tower, and its companion at the opposite end of a stone rampart, are all that is left of the chateau that Montaigne knew. The main building was destroyed by fire and re-built along the same lines in 1885. However, the portal is the same one Montaigne had used, and the family chapel on the ground floor of the tower was unharmed. A mural on the wall behind the small altar shows St. Michel subduing a dragon within the lion paws of the family crest. A trompe l'œil fresco around the walls attempts to suggest a larger diameter for this cell.

The second floor contains a bedroom where Montaigne often spent the night, too weary from creating this new form of literature to cross the courtyard to the family chambers. Even what we call the genre was his invention from the French verb *essayer*—to try, to test. Then, the top floor, this large circular garret with a much smaller alcove with fireplace. Winter quarters for the essayist. On one wall of this room, he had painted the declaration of his retirement on his thirty-eighth birthday; "long weary of the servitude of the court and public employments, while still entire . . . to the bosom of the learned Virgins." That is, the Muses. The tower is thereby consecrated to "his freedom, tranquility and leisure."

Following my guide up the narrow corkscrew stairs to this top floor, it's amused me to fit my feet into the same worn hollows of the stone treads that Montaigne must have trod; the apprentice's footfalls literally following in the master's steps. But the attic where genius labored is a barren place. The textures of the thousand books, by his count, that once lined the room and which may have softened its hard ambiance, are missing and the place looks like a prison, a dungeon with windows. At the age of thirty-eight, Montaigne voluntarily exiled himself from family and friends; put himself in this stone tower to serve the Muses, the cruelest and most demanding of wardens. Sometimes either Henry III or Henry of Navarre would call him out for shuttle diplomacy between their warring thrones, or a turn at the Bordeaux mayoralty would be forced upon him, but this is where he spent most of his remaining 21 years. It's tempting to think that all those books gave him the freedom to travel through these walls, through space and time, but I've never been entirely convinced of the idea that the act of creation, of choice, grants freedom. Moreover, if freedom is to be gained, it is usually at the expense of others.

Yet, in this bastille, the human mind was liberated to discover itself, and this amazing mind put together the means for that discovery. "What do I know?" he penned one morning at his desk and the question stimulated 103 essays in answer. The domain of human sensibility was enlarged as Columbus's elementary navigation had enlarged the external world.

". . . but I am no longer so sanguine, being less certain than I once was as to what it is to be human," wrote Wright Morris in an essay on photography, "The Camera Eye." And it is curious that this major American novelist, so inventive of character in his pages, focused on only one human figure as a photographer—the famous back of "Uncle Harry" entering a barn doorway. His photographs picture the things and objects people have used; combs and chairs and implements as well as the rooms and barber shops and dining rooms they have passed through; just left maybe. These subjects of his photographs are sympathetic companions to his fiction. Tangible possessions are transformed by Morris's wordless camera into emblems of the men and women who may have owned them, whereas the actual people could only be "captured" on the high speed emulsion of his language. Words on paper made the real picture.

Perhaps what we mistakenly call reality is only the subject that has held still long enough to be photographed. The energies and multi-layered qualities of human ambition are never at rest and move too fast for ordinary film. They can only be "taken" by the novelist, the poet, or the playwright. Recent attempts to transfer to movies the wordy musings on the human condition by Wharton, James, and Conrad have resulted in earnest, entertaining failures. And we must accept the filmmakers' defense that movies are a different medium. They are. They are only composed of pictures, but are they as real as they should be? Really real?

Perhaps Montaigne's claim that he was the only subject of his essays was made once too often to believe its humility; however, looking into himself, he captured an authentic picture of his world and its citizens. Mulling through the volumes that once lined these walls, he recovered his world's past in order to reproduce its present. I stand in this cool, stone cell where these translations took place and still feel their heat. I think of the albums of photographs that supposedly represent our time. Go to your local used magazine store and flip through the piles of old *Life* magazines, see *Life* going to the party that was this XX century. But they won't give you the whole picture. Only the camera of the mind can produce images adequate to the authors of the time.

"Look at that," Wright Morris will say to me in California. On the floor beside his easy chair is a large, coffee-table-format book of photographs; the planet earth taken from space, from the moon. The cover shows a blue disc scarfed in wispy egg whites of clouds, and not a sign of life. "It doesn't look like anything," he will say.

Edward W. Said

Così Fan Tutte at the Limits

C*osì fan tutte* was the first opera I saw when I came to the United States as a schoolboy in the early 1950s. The 1951 Metropolitan Opera production was directed by renowned theater figure Alfred Lunt, and, as I recall, much celebrated as a brilliant yet faithful English-language rendition of an elegant opera that boasted an excellent cast—John Brownlee as Don Alfonso, Eleanor Steber and Blanche Thebom as the two sisters, Richard Tucker and Frank Guarrera as the young men, Patrice Munsel as Despina—and a fastidiously executed conception as an eighteenth-century court comedy. I remember a lot of curtseying, many lace hankies, elaborate wigs, and acres of beauty spots, much chuckling and all-round good fun, all of which seemed to go well with the very polished, indeed even superb singing by the ensemble. So powerful was the impression made on me by this *Così fan tutte* that most of the many subsequent performances of the work that I saw or listened to seemed simply variations on that quintessentially classical production. When I saw the 1958 Salzburg production with Karl Böhm conducting and Elisabeth Schwarzkopf, Christa Ludwig, Rolando Panerai,

Luigi Alva, and Graziella Sciutti in the cast, I took it to be an elaboration of the Metropolitan realization.

Although I am neither a professional musicologist nor a Mozart scholar, it has seemed to me that most, if not all, interpretations of the opera stress the aspects that Lunt picked up on: the work's effervescent, rollicking, courtly fun, the apparent triviality of its plot and its characters, who verge on silliness, and the astonishing beauty of its music. Although I have never been completely convinced that that particular mode was the right one for this superb yet elusive and somewhat mysterious opera, I have also resigned myself to performances that are firmly grooved within it.

The only real departure from the pattern was, of course, Peter Sellars's production, staged along with the two other Mozart-Da Ponte collaborations at the now defunct PepsiCo Summerfare in Purchase, New York, in the late 1980s. The great virtue of those productions was that Sellars managed to sweep away all of the eighteenth-century clichés. As Mozart had written the operas while the ancient régime was crumbling, Sellars argued, they should be set by contemporary directors at a similar moment in our own time—with the crumbling of the American empire alluded to by characters and settings, as well as by class deformations and personal histories that bore the marks of a society in crisis. Thus Sellars's version of *La Nozze di Figaro* takes place in the overblown luxury of Trump Tower, *Don Giovanni* on a poorly lit street in Spanish Harlem where dealers and junkies transact their business, *Così fan tutte* in Despina's Diner, where a group of Vietnam veterans and their girlfriends hang out, play tricky games, and get frighteningly embroiled in feelings and self-discoveries for which they are unprepared and with which they are largely incapable of dealing.

To the best of my knowledge, no one but Sellars has attempted such a full-scale revisionist interpretation of the three Da Ponte operas, which remain in the repertory as essentially courtly, classical, eighteenth-century operas. Even Salzburg's recent Patrice Chéreau production of *Don Giovanni*—despite its striking savagery and relentlessly obsessive pace—functions within what we take to be Mozart's strictly conventional theatrical idiom. What makes Sellars's productions of the three operas so powerful is that they put the viewer directly in touch with what is most eccentric and opaque about Mozart: the obsessive patterning in the operas, patterning that finally has little to do with showing that crime doesn't pay or that the faithlessness inherent in all human beings must be overcome before true union can occur. Mozart's characters in *Don Giovanni* and *Così fan tutte* can indeed be interpreted not just as individuals with definable biographies and characteristics but as figures driven by forces outside themselves which they make no serious effort to comprehend. These operas, in fact, are much more about power and manipulation than most opera directors acknowledge; in them, individuality is reduced to a momentary identity in the impersonal rush of things. There is little room therefore for providence, or for the heroics of charismatic personalities, although Don Giovanni himself cuts a defiant and dashing figure within a very limited scope.

In comparison with the operas of Beethoven, Verdi, or even Rossini, the world that Mozart depicts is amoral and Lucretian, a world in which power has its own logic, undomesticated either by conditions of piety or verisimilitude. As much as he seems to have looked down on Mozart's lack of seriousness, Wagner shares a similar worldview, I think, and that is one of the reasons that his characters in *The Ring, Tristan und Isolde,* and *Parsifal* spend as much time as they do going over, renarrating, and recomprehending the remorseless chain of actions in which they are imprisoned and from which there can be no significant escape. What is it that keeps Don Giovanni irrecusably bound to his licentiousness or *Così's* Don Alfonso and Despina to their schemes and fixings? Little in the operas themselves provides an immediate answer.

Indeed, I think Mozart has tried to embody an abstract force that drives people by means of agents (in *Così fan tutte*) or sheer sexual energy (in *Don Giovanni*), without the reflective consent of their mind or will. As many commentators have noted, the plot of *Così fan tutte* has antecedents in various "test" plays and operas and, as scholar Charles Rosen says, it resembles the "demonstration" plays written by Marivaux among others. "They demonstrate—prove by acting out—psychological ideas and 'laws' that everyone accepted," Rosen adds, "and they are almost scientific in the way they show precisely how these laws work in practice." He goes on to speak of *Così fan tutte* as "a closed system," an interesting if insufficiently examined notion, which does in fact apply.

The intrigue in *Così fan tutte* is the result of a bet between Alfonso and his young friends Ferrando and Guglielmo that is inspired neither by a sense of moral purpose nor by ideological passion. Ferrando is in love with Dorabella, Guglielmo with Fiordiligi; Alfonso bets that the women will be unfaithful. A subterfuge is then enacted: the two men will pretend that they have been called off to war. Then they will come back in disguise and woo the girls. As Albanian (i.e. Oriental) men, the two attempt to seduce each other's fiancées: Guglielmo quickly succeeds with Dorabella. Ferrando needs more time, but he too is successful with Fiordiligi, who is clearly the more serious of the two sisters. Alfonso is helped in the plot by Despina, a cynical maid who assists in her mistresses' downfall, although she does not know of the bet between the men. Finally the plot is exposed, the women are furious, but return to their lovers even though Mozart does not specify whether the pairs will remain as they were at the outset.

We can learn much about *Così fan tutte* in the late-eighteenth-century cultural setting by looking at Beethoven's reactions to the Da Ponte operas, which he, as Mozart's younger contemporary and an Enlightenment enthusiast, seems always to have regarded with a certain amount of discomfort. Like many critics of Mozart's operas, Beethoven is—so far as I have been able to discover—curiously silent about *Così fan tutte*. To generations of Mozart admirers, including Beethoven, the opera does not seem to offer the kind of metaphysical or social or cultural significance found readily by Kierkegaard and other luminaries in *Don Giovanni, Die Zauberflöte,* and *Figaro.* Therefore, there seems to be very little to say about it. Significantly enough, Beethoven seems to have thought *Die Zauberflöte* the greatest of Mozart's works (mainly because it was a German work), and he has been quoted in several instances as expressing his dislike of *Don Giovanni* and *Figaro;* they were too trivial, too Italian, too scandalous for a serious composer. Once, however, he expressed pleasure at *Don Giovanni's* success, although he was also said not to have wanted to attend Mozart's operas because they might make him forfeit his own originality.

These are the contradictory feelings of a composer who found Mozart's work as a whole unsettling and even disconcerting. Competitiveness is clearly a factor, but there is something else. It is Mozart's uncertain moral center, the absence in *Così fan tutte* of a specific humanistic message of the kind about which *Die Zauberflöte* is so laboriously explicit. What is still more significant about Beethoven's reactions to Mozart is that *Fidelio* Beethoven's only opera, written fifteen years after *Così fan tutte,* can be interpreted as a direct and, in my opinion, somewhat desperate, response to the earlier opera. Take one small but certainly telling example: *Fidelio's* heroine Leonore appears, at the beginning of the opera, disguised as a young man, *"Fidelio,"* who comes to work as an assistant at the prison, where her husband, Florestan, is being held as a political prisoner by the tyrannical governor of Seville, Don Pizarro. In this guise, Leonore engages the amorous attentions of the jailer's daughter Marzelline. You could say that Beethoven has picked up the part of *Così's* plot in which the disguised lovers return to Naples and proceed to advance on the wrong women. However, no sooner does the intrigue start up than Beethoven puts a stop to it, revealing to the audience that young Fidelio is really the ever faithful and constant Leonore, come to the prison in order to assert her fidelity and conjugal love to her imprisoned husband.

Still, Leonore's central aria, *"Komm Hoffnung,"* is full of echoes of Fiordiligi's *"Per pietà, ben mio"* in Act Two of *Così,* which she sings as a last, forlorn plea to herself to remain constant and to drive away the dishonor she feels might be over-

coming her as she suffers (and perhaps slightly enjoys) the impress of Ferrando's importuning: *"Svenerà quest'empia voglia,
L'ardir mio, la mia costanza, Perderà la rimembranza, Che
vergogna e orror me fà."* ("I'll rid myself of this terrible desire
with my devotion and love. I'll blot out the memory that causes
me shame and horror.") Memory is something to be banished,
the memory she is ashamed of: her trifling with her real, but
absent, lover Guglielmo. Yet memory is also what she must hold
onto, the guarantee of her loyalty to her lover—for if she for-
gets, she loses the ability to judge her present, timidly flirtatious
behavior for the shameful wavering it really is. Mozart gives her
a noble, horn-accompanied figure for this avowal, a melody that
is echoed in key (E major) and instrumentation (also horns) in
Leonore's great appeal to hope, *"lass den letzen Stern des
Müden nicht erbleichen"* ("let this last star for the weary not be
extinguished"). But although, like Fiordiligi, Leonore has a secret, hers is an honorable one; and she does not doubt love and
hope, she depends on them. There is no wavering, no doubting
or timidity in Leonore, and her powerful aria, with its battery of
horns proclaiming her determination and resolve, seems almost
like a reproach to Fiordiligi's rather more delicate and troubled
musings.

Doubtless, in *Fidelio,* Beethoven wrestled with various issues that were important to him, fully independently of *Così,*
but I think we have to grant that something about Mozart's
operatic world in his mature and greatest works (with the exception of *Die Zauberflöte)* kept bothering Beethoven. One aspect,
of course, is their sunny, comic, and southern setting, which
amplifies and makes more difficult to accept their underlying
critique and implied rejection of the middle-class virtue that
meant so much to Beethoven. Even *Don Giovanni,* the one Da
Ponte opera whose twentieth-century reinterpretations have
turned it into a "Northern" psychodrama of neurotic drives and
transgressive passions, is essentially more unsettlingly powerful
when enacted as a comedy of heedlessness and enjoyable insouciance. The style of famous twentieth-century Italian Dons like
Ezio Pinza, Tito Gobbi, and Cesare Siepi prevailed until the

1970s, but their characterizations have given way to those of Thomas Allen, James Morris, Ferruccio Furlanetto, and Samuel Ramey, who represent the Don as a dark figure heavily influenced by his readings in Kierkegaard and Freud. *Così fan tutte* is even more aggressively "Southern," in that all of its Neapolitan characters are depicted as being shifty, pleasure-centered, and, with the exception of a brief moment here and there, selfish and relatively free of guilt, even though what they do is, by *Fidelio's* standards, patently reprehensible.

Thus the earnest and deeply serious atmosphere of *Fidelio* can be seen as a reproach to *Così*, which, for all its irony and beauty, is grippingly without any kind of gravity at all. When the two pseudo-Oriental suitors are repulsed by Fiordiligi and Dorabella at the end of Act One, they drag the sisters into a broadly comic, false-suicide scene; what transpires is based on the ironic disparity between the women's earnest concern for the men, and the two suitors' amused playacting. Genuine emotion is thus undercut by the ridiculous. In Act Two, where the disguises and playacting advance quite significantly into the emotions of the four main characters, Mozart extends the joke even further. The result is that the four do fall in love again, though with the wrong partners, and this undermines something very dear to Beethoven: constancy of identity. Whereas Beethoven's Leonore takes on the mask of the boy Fidelio, her disguise is designed to get her closer to, not further away from, her real identity as faithful wife. Indeed, all the characters in *Fidelio* are rigorously circumscribed in their unvarying essence: Pizarro as unyielding villain, Florestan as champion of good, and so forth. This is at the opposite pole from *Così*, where disguises, and the wavering and wandering they foster, are the norm, and constancy and stability mocked as impossible.

Still *Così fan tutte* is an opera whose strange lightheartedness hides, or at least makes light of, an inner system that is quite severe and amoral in its workings. I do not at all want to say that the work must not be enjoyed as the brilliant romp that in many ways it is. The critic's role, however, is to try to lay bare what it is that Mozart and Da Ponte were intimating through their merry tale of deceit and displaced love. I shall therefore try to elucidate the way in which *Così fan tutte* is, at its concealed limits, a very different work than its rollicking exterior and sublime music suggest.

We now know that Mozart composed the ensembles of *Così* before he took on the arias or even the overture. This sequence corresponds to the opera's concentration on relationships between characters rather than on brilliant individuals as encountered in earlier operas such as *Figaro* or *Don Giovanni*. Of the three Da Ponte operas, *Così fan tutte* is not only the last and, in my opinion, the most complex and eccentric, but also the most internally well organized, the most full of echoes and references, and the most difficult to unlock—precisely because it goes further toward the limits of acceptable, ordinary experiences of love, life, and ideas than either of its two predecessors. The reasons for this, and indeed for *Così's* opacity and even resistance to the kind of interpretive analysis that *Figaro* and *Don Giovanni* generally permit, are partly to be found in Mozart's life in 1789 and 1790, while he was at work on *Così*. But they are also to be found in the way Mozart and Da Ponte created the work together, without a well-known play or legendary figure to provide them with framework and directions. *Così* is the result of a collaboration, and its dynamics, the symmetrical structure of its plot, and the echoic quality of so much of its music are internal factors of its composition, not imposed on it by an outside source.

Many of the numbers of Act One, for example, are written to emphasize how the characters think, act, and sing in pairs; their lines generally imitate one another and recollect lines sung earlier. Mozart seems to want us to feel that we are inside a closed system in which melody, imitation, and parody are very difficult to separate from one another. This is superbly in evidence in the First Act sextet, which enacts a sort of mini-play in which Alfonso draws Despina, then the two disguised men, then the two women into his plot, while commenting on the action. The whole number is a dizzying maze of advance and expostulation, statement, echo, and inversion that rivals anything Mozart ever wrote for elegance, invention, and complexity. It simply sweeps aside the last trace of stability and gravity that we have so far been able to hold onto.

To come to terms with *Così* is first of all to be reminded that, when it premiered in Vienna on January 26, 1790, it was a contemporary opera, not a classic, as it has become today. Mozart began to work on it in the first part of 1789, at a time when he had just passed through a period of great difficulty. Critic Andrew Steptoe points out that, after he had completed *Don Giovanni* in 1787, "Mozart's personal health and financial security deteriorated." Not only did a German tour he undertook fail, but he seems to have passed through "a loss in creative confidence," composing very few works and leaving an unusual number of fragments and unfinished pieces. We do not really know why he took up work on *Così fan tutte,* although Steptoe volunteers (correctly, I think) that the piece "was therefore located at a pivotal moment, and must have been seized upon by the composer both as an artistic challenge and a golden opportunity to recoup financially." The score that he finally did produce bears the marks, I believe, of other aspects of his life in 1789. One is his wife Constanze's absence for a rest cure in Baden while he worked on the opera. While there, she "displayed improprieties" that prompted a letter from Mozart which cast him as the constant one and his wife as the flighty, embarrassing partner who needed to be reminded of her position and domestic status:

> Dear little wife! I want to talk to you quite frankly. You have no reason whatever to be unhappy. You have a husband who loves you and does all he possibly can for you. . . . I am glad indeed when you have some fun—of course I am—but I do wish that you would not sometimes make yourself so cheap. In my opinion you are far too free and easy with N.N. . . . Now please remember that N.N. is not half so familiar with other women, whom they perhaps know

more intimately, as they are with you. Why, N.N. who is usually a well-conducted fellow and particularly respectful to women, must have been misled by your behavior into writing the most disgusting and most impertinent sottises which he put into his letter. A woman must always make herself respected, or else people will begin to talk about her. My love! Forgive me for being so frank, but my peace of mind demands it as well as our mutual happiness. Remember that you yourself once admitted to me that you were inclined to comply too easily. You know the consequences of that. Remember too the promises you gave to me. Oh, God, do try, my love!

How important Mozart's own almost Archimedean sense of stability and control was in dealing with Constanze is remarked by Steptoe, who argues that because Mozart did not believe in "blind romantic love" he went on to "satirize it mercilessly (most notably in *Così fan tutte)."* Yet the letters from the *Così* period tell a more complicated story. In one, Mozart tells Constanze how excited he is at the prospect of seeing her, and then adds, "If people could see into my heart, I should almost feel ashamed." We might then expect him to say something about seething passions and sensual thoughts. Instead he continues: "To me, everything is cold—cold as ice," and notes that "everything seems so empty." In a subsequent letter, Mozart speaks again of "feeling—a kind of emptiness, which hurts me dreadfully—a kind of longing, which is never satisfied, which never ceases, and which persists, nay rather increases daily." In Mozart's correspondence there are other letters of this sort that characterize his special combination of unstilled energy (expressed in the sense of ever increasing emptiness and unsatisfied longing) and cold control: these seem to me to have a particular relevance for the position of *Così fan tutte* in his life and oeuvre.

*   *   *

Just as the themes of memory and forgetting are imperative to *Così*'s plot, the opera itself looks back to earlier works
and is full of "thematic reminiscences," as Andrew Steptoe calls
them. In addition, at one point in Act One (Dorabella's accompanied recitative *"Ah, scostati"),* the orchestra suddenly plays
the rapid scale passages associated with the Commendatore in
Don Giovanni. Mozart's use of counterpoint in the opera gives
the music added substance, so that in the E-flat Canon in the
Second Act's finale one experiences not only a remarkable sense
of rigor, but also a special ironic expressiveness well beyond the
words and the situation. For, as the lovers have finally worked
their way around to the new reversed pairing, three of them sing
polyphonically of submerging all thought and memory in the
wine they are about to drink, while only one, Guglielmo, remains disaffected—he had had greater faith in Fiordiligi's
power to resist Ferrando, but he has been disproved—and he
stands outside the canon; he wishes that the women *("queste
volpi senza onor")* would drink poison and end the whole thing.
It is as if Mozart wanted the counterpoint to mirror the lovers'
embarrassment in a closed polyphonic system, and also to show
how even though they think of themselves as shedding all ties
and memories, the music, by its circularity and echoic form,
reveals them to be bound to each other in a new and logically
consequent embrace.

Such a moment is only to be found in *Così fan tutte:* it
depicts human desire and satisfaction in musical terms as essentially a matter of compositional control that directs feeling and
appetite into a logical circuit allowing no escape and very little
elevation. But the whole opera—plot, characters, situation, ensembles, and arias—tends toward such a cluster because it is
derived from the movement of two intimate couples, two men
and two women, plus two "outside" characters, coming together
in various ways, and then pulling apart, then coming together
again, with several changes along the way. The symmetries and
repetitions are almost cloying, but they are the substance of the
opera. We know very little about these figures; no traces of a
former life adhere to them (unlike *Figaro* and *Don Giovanni,*

both of which are steeped in earlier episodes, entanglements, intrigues); their identities exist in order to be tested and exercised as lovers, and once they have gone through one full turn and become the opposite of what they were, the opera ends. The overture, with its busy, clattering, round-like themes, catches the spirit of this movement quite perfectly. Remember that Mozart wrote it after he had finished most of the main body of the opera, that is, after the schematic character of what he was elaborating had impressed itself on his mind. Only one figure, Don Alfonso, stands apart from all of this: his is the only activity that begins before the opera opens, and it continues uninterruptedly to the very end. Who is he really? He certainly belongs to a line of senior authority figures that extends through Mozart's life and works. Remember the Commendatore in *Giovanni,* or Sarastro in *Die Zauberflöte,* or even Bartolo and Almaviva in *Figaro.* Yet Alfonso's role is different from the others in that he seeks to prove not the underlying moral fiber but the inconstancy and unfaithfulness of women—and he succeeds. In the final ensemble, when he is denounced by the women as the man who misled them and staged their fall, Alfonso responds without a trace of regret: what he has done, he says, is to have *undeceived* the lovers, and this, he adds, puts them more under his command. *"V'ingannai, ma fu l'inganno Disinganno ai vostri amanti, Che più saggi omai saranno, Che faran quel chi'io vorrò"* ("I deceived you, but my deception was to undeceive your lovers. From now on they'll both be wiser, and they'll do just as I say"). "Join hands," he says, "so that all four of you can laugh, as I have laughed and will laugh again." It is interesting and not entirely a coincidence that what he sings contains striking anticipations of *Die Zauberflöte,* an opera that Mozart perhaps wrote as a more morally acceptable version of the plot used in *Così fan tutte.* Whereas constancy doesn't win out in *Così,* in *Die Zauberflöte* it does.

Like Sarastro, Don Alfonso is a manager and controller of behavior—although, unlike Sarastro, he acts with neither solemnity nor high moral purpose. Most accounts of *Così* scarcely pay attention to him, and yet in the unguardedly amoral world of the opera he is not only a crucial or pivotal figure but a fascinating one as well. His many references to himself—as actor, teacher, scholar, plotter, courtier—do not directly allude to the one thing he seems above all others to be—that is, a mature libertine, someone who has had much worldly sexual experience and now wishes to direct, control, and manipulate the experiences of others. In this he resembles a schoolmaster, military strategist, and philosopher: he has seen much in the world and is more than able to stage another drama of the sort he has presumably lived through himself. He knows in advance what conclusion he will come to, so the action of the opera furnishes him with few surprises, least of all about the behavior of women. Plowing the sea, sowing on sand, trying to ensnare the wind in a net: these impossibilities (to which he refers) define the limits of Alfonso's reality, and they accentuate the element of radical instability in which, as a teacher of lovers and a practiced lover himself, he lives. But this does not apparently prevent him from enjoying both the experience of loving and the opportunity to prove his ideas more than once.

I do not want to suggest that Don Alfonso is anything other than a comic figure. But I do want to argue that he stands very close to a number of cultural and psychological actualities that were very important to Mozart, as well as to other relatively advanced thinkers and artists of the time. Consider first the unmistakable progression in Mozart's operatic invention from Figaro, to Don Giovanni, to Don Alfonso. Each in his own way is unconventional and iconoclastic, although only Don Alfonso is neither punished, like Don Giovanni, nor in effect domesticated, as Figaro is. The discovery that the stabilities of marriage and the social norms habitually governing human life are inapplicable because life itself is elusive and inconstant has placed Don Alfonso in a new, more turbulent and troubling realm, one in which experience repeats the same disillusioning patterns without relief. What he devises for the two pairs of lovers is a game in which human identity is shown to be as protean, unsta-

ble, undifferentiated as anything in the actual world. Not surprisingly, then, one of the main motifs in *Così fan tutte* is the
elimination of memory in favor of the present. The structure of
the plot, with its play-within-a-play abstractions, enforces that:
Alfonso sets up a test that separates the lovers from their past
and their loyalties. Then the men assume new identities, entering into their roles as much as the women, taking seriously their
charge as lovers, and, in the process, prove what Alfonso knew
all along. Yet Guglielmo is not so easily resigned to Fiordiligi's
apparent fickleness and therefore remains for a time outside
Alfonso's circle of happy and deceived lovers; despite his bitterness, however, he eventually rallies round to Alfonso's thesis,
given full articulation in the opera now for the first time. This is
a late moment in the opera. Alfonso has been biding his time
before putting things as flatly, in as unadorned and reductive a
manner as this. It is as if he, and Mozart, needed Act One to set
up the demonstration and Act Two to let it spin itself out, before
he could come forward with this conclusion, which is also the
musical root, finally revealed, of the opera.

In this respect, Don Alfonso represents the standpoint not
only of a jaded, illusionless man of the world, but also of an
indefatigable practitioner and teacher of his views, a figure who
needs subjects and space for his demonstrations, even though
he knows in advance that the pleasures he sets up are far from
new. Alfonso resembles an understated version of his near contemporary the Marquis de Sade, a libertine who, as Foucault
describes him memorably:

> is he who, while yielding to all the fantasies of desire
> and to each of its furies, can, but also must, illumine
> their slightest movement with a lucid and deliberately
> elucidated representation. There is a strict order gov-
> erning the life of the libertine: every representation
> must be immediately endowed with life in the living
> body of desire, every desire must be expressed in the
> pure light of representative discourse. Hence the rigid
> sequence of "scenes" . . . and, within the scenes, the

meticulous balance between the conjugation of bodies
and the concentration of reasons.°

We recall that in the first number, when Alfonso speaks,
he calls himself *"ex cathedro,"* a man with gray hair and long
experience: we are to assume, I think, that having yielded to
desire in the past he is now ready to illuminate his ideas "with a
lucid and deliberately elucidated representation." The plot of
Così is a rigid sequence of scenes, all of them manipulated by
Alfonso and Despina, his equally cynical helper, in which sexual
desire is, as Foucault suggests, profligacy subjected to the order
of representation—that is, the enacted tale of lovers being
schooled in an illusionless, yet exciting love. When the game is
revealed to Fiordiligi and Dorabella, they accept the truth of
what they have experienced and, in a conclusion that has troubled interpreters and directors with its coy ambiguity, they sing
of reason and mirth without any specific indication at all from
Mozart that the two women and two men will return to their
original lovers.

Such a conclusion opens up a troubling vista of numerous
further substitutions, with no ties, no identity, no idea of stability or constancy left undisturbed. Foucault speaks of this cultural moment as one in which language retains the capacity to
name, but can only do so in a "ceremony reduced to the utmost
precision," and "extends it to infinity": the lovers will go on
finding other partners, since the rhetoric of love and the representation of desire have lost their anchors in a fundamentally
unchanging order of Being.

Responsible for this is Don Alfonso, a parodic Virgil leading young, inexperienced men and women into a world stripped
of standards, norms, certainties. He speaks the language of wisdom and sagacity, allied to an admittedly small-scaled and limited vision of his power and control. There are plenty of classical
references in the libretto: none of them refers to the Christian
or Masonic deities that Mozart seems to have venerated else-

° *The Order of Things,* pp. 209–10.

where (he became a Mason in 1784). Don Alfonso's natural world is in part Rousseau's, stripped of sanctimonious piety, volatile with fancy and caprice, made rigorous with the need to experience desire without palliatives or conclusion. Even more significantly for Mozart, Don Alfonso is only the second authority figure to appear in his operas after the death of Mozart's father, Leopold, in 1787; given some urgency by Leopold's death, the terrifying Commendatore in *Don Giovanni* embodies the stern, judgmental aspect of Leopold's relationship with his son—an aspect that is not at all present in Alfonso, who is not easily provoked, gives every appearance of wanting to play the game with his young friends, and seems completely untroubled by the pervasive faithlessness his "scenes" uncover.

Alfonso, I believe, is an irreverent and later portrait of the senior patron, someone quite audaciously presented not as a moral instructor but as an amorous virtuoso, a libertine or retired rake whose influence is exerted through hoaxes, disguises, charades, and finally a philosophy of inconstancy as norm. Because he is an older man, Alfonso intimates a sense of mortality that is very far from the concerns of the young lovers. A famous letter written by Mozart to his father in the final period of the latter's life, on April 4, 1787, expresses a mood of illusionless fatalism: "As death," he says, "is the true goal of our existence I have formed during the first few years such close relations with this best and truest friend of mankind, that his image is not only no longer terrifying to me, but is indeed very soothing and consoling! . . . Death is the key that unlocks the door to our true happiness. I never lie down at night without reflecting that— young as I am—I may not live to see another day." In the opera, death is rendered less intimidating and formidable than it is for most people. This is not the usual, conventionally Christian sentiment, however, but a naturalist one: death as something familiar and even dear, a door to other experiences. Yet its prospect also induces a sense of fatalism and lateness—that is, the feeling that one is late in life and the end is near.

So the father figure has become the friend and cheerful, tyrannical mentor, a person to be obeyed who is somehow neither paternalistic nor minatory. And this status is confirmed in Mozart's style, in which posturing characters are displayed in such a way as to permit Alfonso to enter into a game with them, not as hectoring senior presence nor as admonishing pedagogue, but as an actor in the common entertainment. Alfonso predicts the conclusion or end of the comedy but here, according to musicologist Donald Mitchell,

> we stumble . . . on the most uncomfortable aspect of the opera's factuality. What we yearn for is the possibility of a fairy-tale reconciliation. But Mozart was far too truthful an artist to disguise the fact that a healing forgiveness is impossible where all the parties [Alfonso included] are not only equally "guilty" but share to the full the knowledge of each other's guilt. In *Così*, the best that can be done is to present as brave a front as one may to the fact of life [and, I could add, of death]. The coda that succeeds the *dénouement* does exactly that and no more.°

The conclusion of *Così* is really twofold: this is the way things are because that is what *they* do—*Così fan tutte*—and, second, they will be like that, one situation, one substitution, succeeding another, until, it is implied, the process is stopped by death. All are the same, *Così fan tutte*, in the meantime. As Fiordiligi says, *"e potra la morte sola far che cangi affetto il cor"* ("only death can affect the heart"). Death takes the place of Christian reconciliation and redemption, the key to our true, if unknown and indescribable, hope of rest and stability, soothing and consoling without providing anything more than a theoretical intimation of final repose. But like nearly every serious subject with which the opera flirts, death is kept at bay, indeed is mostly left out of *Così fan tutte*.

Within its carefully circumscribed limits, *Così fan tutte* allows itself only a number of gestures toward what stands just

---

° *Cradles of the New*, p. 132.

beyond it, or to vary the metaphor a bit, through what stands just inside it. Mozart never ventured so close to the potentially terrifying view he and Da Ponte seem to have uncovered of a universe shorn of any redemptive or palliative scheme, whose one law is motion and instability expressed as the power of libertinage and manipulation, and whose only conclusion is the terminal repose provided by death. That so astonishingly satisfying a musical score should be joined to so heedless and insignificant a tale is what *Così fan tutte* accomplishes with such a unique virtuosity. But I think we should not believe that the candid fun of the work does any more than hold its ominous vision in abeyance—that is, for as long as *Così fan tutte*'s limits are not permitted to invade the stage.

Edward Hoagland

Wild Things

I was lucky as a child. I not only had books in the house that allowed me to conceive of myself as Mowgli, Dr Dolittle, Little Black Sambo and other people whose lives were intertwined with those of animals, I also knew a whole spectrum of animals myself. Living in the country, I could read *The Wind in the Willows* and encounter live toads and moles as well as wood-chucks and muskrats. And in 1951, at the age of eighteen, I got a job working with real tigers, elephants, monkeys and panthers in the menagerie of the Ringling Brothers and Barnum & Bailey Circus, crossing America from Connecticut to Nebraska for fourteen dollars a week, all I wanted to eat at the cookhouse and half of a triple-decker bunk on the first of the three trains (seventy cars) that carried the show to the next town on its nightly hops. We didn't realize then the rarity of what we were doing: that in 1956 the big circus would close, and that tigers would become desperately endangered—their ground-up vitality used as a potion for human fertility (which the world hardly needs).

We would arrive in each town about four-thirty in the morning, which meant that we were on duty, in a casual fashion, for sixteen hours a day, interspersed with naps or swims, if the circus lot lay alongside a river, or playing with the animals. There were twenty-four Indian elephants, led by Ruth, Babe, Jewel, Modoc and other matriarchs, plus some ninety horses. Being allergic to hay, I didn't take care of them. Instead I was assigned to an old chimp and a baby orang-utan, a black rhinoceros, a pygmy hippo and a gnu, a mandrill, several mangabey monkeys, the two giraffes and a tapir. But I yearned to commune with the big cats, and eventually was apprenticed to 'Chief', the Mohawk Indian who had charge of them. The next summer, when I came back, I found he had been clawed in Madison Square Garden, had married his nurse from the hospital and stayed in New York. So I had them to myself till I went back to school.

Lions are straightforward, sociable animals, easy breeders and blessed with a humdrum, sand-coloured coat that people have not wanted to strip from them and wear on their backs. Also they're lucky enough not to share a continent with the crazy Chinese, inventing mystic applications for their pulverized bones. I had a pair of lions, a maned male and a splendid female, who patiently managed to share the cramped cage, five feet by five, that Ringling Brothers provided for them. That companionship, with their bodies overlapping, seemed to calm them so much you hardly felt sorry for them, compared to our solitary, pacing tigers. I used to sleep under the lions' cage at night, if we stayed over in a large city, both because of the protection that their paws, hanging out between the bars, afforded me from wandering muggers, and for the midnight music of their roars—glorious-sounding guttural strings that they exchanged with the circus's other lions, performing in the centre ring under the whip of Oscar Konyot (a man so highly strung he sometimes had to stand and whip one of the side poles after his act, in order to decompress).

Tigers are more moody and less predictable. Unlike lions, they don't form gangs, or prides, and can't be herded in the ring by somebody who knows their group dynamics and can turn the leaders and stampede them. They're more willowy and individually explosive and must be dealt with singly, persuaded subtly, in a sort of time-fuse confrontation. You can apply affection, but it's more a matter of slow seduction, one-on-one in the training sequence, than just becoming pals with a bunch of fractious, energetic, snarling lions. I was only a cageboy, not a trainer—a dreamer, not a player—but I regarded my tigers as God's cymbals when they roared and God's paintbrush when they didn't, and though of course I thought their captivity was a kind of travesty, the idea that wild tigers might not even outlive my own lifespan wouldn't have occurred to me.

There was a store in downtown Manhattan I used to visit, near where the banana boats came in, that sold pythons, tiger cubs, pangolins, parrots, ocelots, leopards—what couldn't you buy? For all the looting of the earth's wild places, there seemed to be no end to such trophies. I remember how little fuss was made when I went backstage at the circus during a performance in Boston, and two little baby tigers had just died in the cage with their mother. The bosses were sorry about it (as about the cagehand who was lying on the cement floor in a pile of straw with high-fever pneumonia), but there was no sense of a significant financial or gene-pool loss. On the books, I notice from the circus's archives from the early 1950s, adult tigers were carried at a valuation of only about $1,100 apiece; a polar bear, $1,200; a sun bear, $200. Chimpanzees were about $600; orang-utans about $2,000; and 'Toto', the star-attraction gorilla, $9,800. Giraffes were worth $2,200; cheetahs $1,000.

Most of our cages were old army ammunition wagons from the Second World War, eleven feet long and partitioned so that, for instance, the two lions were housed with an enormous yolk-yellow, black-striped male Bengal tiger who must have weighed a quarter of a ton. In the tiny space allotted to him, he ignored the two lions on the other side of the dividing screen and seemed the very picture of dignified placidity. The lions didn't ask for trouble, but, sprawling over each other's legs in their claustrophobic cage, were plainly prepared to shred anybody who reached inside. They bristled and snarled, their handsome lips contorting into gigantic peach pits, if you had to disturb them while cleaning their cage with the long iron rod that pulled the dung out. But the tiger just lay on exhibit, stuffed unjustly into his narrow cage, with an extraordinary tranquility that was much more seductive than the bluff normalcy of the two lions. In his peacefulness he was cryptic, like a hostage king. You felt sorry for him, yet respectful.

Occasionally, some neophyte, one of the new workhands who had joined the circus because they were hungry (gulping that first meal down), would show off for the townie girls after the afternoon show. After prodding old Joe, the ruddy-maned lion, to roar, he might move the few feet on to silent, watchful Rajah, Joe's still bigger counterpart in the adjacent cage, and instead of tormenting him, might tentatively begin to pet that beautiful black-and-yellow coat through the bars, which were spaced wide enough to get even your elbow through. And—about once a year—when that young man, half-soused, did so, while the girls oohed and aahed, Rajah would wait till his hand moved up past his ribs to his magnificent shoulder, then whirl in a flash and grab and crunch it, pull the arm all the way in, rip it out of its socket and claw it off. The stump would be sewn up, and he'd get a free night in the hospital, then be put on a Greyhound bus for wherever his home was, still howling in agony at every jounce.

We used to scratch the rhino's itchy cheeks and the jaguar's risky flank, the cheetah's reluctant scalp, the hippo's willing tongue and the four leopards' luxurious coats. It was complicated fun. Bobby, the rhino, for example, wouldn't have deliberately hurt somebody, but he didn't know his own strength when playful, or particularly care, and might inadvertently have crushed an arm against the bars in lurching about. For him, as for Chester, the large hippo (Betty Lou, the pygmy hippo, was rather unfriendly), who gaped his huge maw so that you could stick your hand in and scratch his tongue and the walls of his mouth, it was a natural procedure, akin to how the tick birds along the Nile would have searched both their bodies for parasites. The cheetah, by contrast, growled softly if touched—didn't like it, but probably wouldn't bite—whereas the jaguar objected with a mild rumble, and undoubtedly would have if he could have done so without bestirring himself. He was a frank, solitary animal, like the tigers but less complex than them, and a night-roarer like the lions, but less bold and various in how he emitted his messages, maybe because he had no other jaguars to answer him. He was penned in a cage three-and-a-half feet wide, alongside the cheetah's similar, pathetic space (the fastest animal on earth!) and a Siberian tiger confined in the third compartment of the wagon, who appeared to have gone mad, he was such a coiled spring of rage. The two giraffes, Edith and Boston, leaned down and licked the salt on my sweaty cheeks every hot day; but the Siberian would have minced me, as he tirelessly made plain.

I believed at this point in my life that no man was complete without a parrot on his shoulder, or at least a boa constrictor looped partly over him like a friend's arm. So when I say that tigers were my first love, I mean simply sexually. I was a bad stutterer, still a virgin, could scarcely talk to other people, and felt at home in the circus partly because aberrancies were no big deal there. I would not have masturbated a pet dog or cat because it would have seemed like an imposition, a perversity. But we had two great big orange female tigers compartmented in the two halves of an eleven-foot ordnance wagon, who regularly, when they were in heat, presented their vulvas to me to be rubbed. So, standing at chest-level with the floor of the cage, I used to reach in and gingerly do it. Chief had shown me how. There was also an ex-con who, like so many other hoboes, materialized one day in Ohio and worked a little while before vanishing in Indiana. The idea that caged creatures needed some solace came naturally to him. He even rubbed the old chimp's penis; not the least bothered by what's now called 'homophobia'. I *was* bothered by that and also by the fact that the chimpanzee was infinitely stronger than me and very disgruntled—being, after all, an individual who had been raised closely with people to perform as a cute baby in the centre ring, and then abandoned to solitary confinement when he outgrew his childhood. Though he was lucky, in fact, not to have been sold for experimentation like the rest, he didn't know that, and I thought I fathomed his resentment clearly enough to steer clear of his hands and teeth, which you would be at the mercy of while masturbating him. But this fiftyish guy just out of jail went to the cage and talked to him sympathetically, when he happened to be working nearby, and then reached in and massaged him a bit, much as you might ease the nerves of a murderer and be in no danger, nor even ask for a cigarette in exchange afterwards.

The white-ruffed lady tigers, however, needed to come to the bars, swing around, squat down, and present their hind ends to be rubbed, which meant that, unlike the chimp, they weren't in a position to grab me—their mouths faced away. Then the one I was doing would stand (the other tigress in the meantime observing edgily), pace off and turn and come back and try to kill me, swiping downwards with one tremendous paw extended through the bars and a roar like the crack of a landslide that brought tears to my eyes. Knowing what was coming, I liked to step back far enough that her paw just missed me but the wind made my hair hop on my head, and her open mouth three feet away ended up in a deliciously subliminal snarl that she could ratchet up to motorcycle volume if she wished to. The other tigress might share her agitation and chime in, while Rajah wheeled and sprayed pee, scent-marking the ground outside his cage.

Yet this was not much more furor than when tigers mate naturally. Soon she would return and squat peaceably for me to put my fingers into her vagina again; then maybe roar, swipe at me and come to the water pan when I slid it under the bars. I'd talk to her in her own language by making a soft chuffing sound, blowing air over my lower lip, and she'd answer—as zoo tigers also would, in New York or wherever I went, as long as I kept in practice. The secret lies in relaxing the lips; it's the opposite of a trumpeter's embouchure.

Intimacy; and I believed that I had a sixth sense. At Mabel Stark's little zoo in California, I once climbed into a mountain lion's cage. She was another female in heat whom I had been petting through the bars. She bounded at me immediately, thrusting her paw straight into my face, keeping her claws withdrawn. I also used to chance my arm with one of our leopards. She was called 'Sweetheart', and was the most handsome leopard I have ever seen, with a splendid, white, breastly undercarriage and a rich, dazzling top coat, like camouflage for an empress. She loved caresses: with her you didn't have to move gingerly. You could simply donate your arms to her and push your face against the bars while she crouched over them, licking them like long hunks of meat with her thrillingly abrasive tongue, or else twitching her tail and purring like steady thunder as you scratched her stiff-napped, oriental-carpet back. Her two grown daughters milled and whirled over and about your arms and next to your face, as swift and electric as four-foot fish—the tails an extra length, lolloping up and down like puppets. The daughters purred also; and the yearling male, who was unrulier because he was beginning to shed the docility of kittenhood, would vault around and sometimes seize my hand in his teeth and pull it as far into the cage as it would reach— without breaking my skin, but pressing down threateningly if I resisted him. Then, when he had my arm under control, he would flip over on his back underneath it and in mock fashion 'disembowel' it, like a gazelle that he had caught by the throat, with all four paws bicycling upwards against the flesh. But just like that mountain lion in California, instead of destroying my arm, he kept his claws in.

In East Africa, as a tourist, you watch lions from the safety of a well-roofed Land-Rover, comprehending, nevertheless, as soon as a lioness stalks towards you, why early people invented spears. And you grieve for the thoughtful-looking, suffering elephants existing in shattered little herds, who have obviously witnessed so many other elephants being butchered for their ivory. Safaris are a well-oiled industry now, tooled for an ever-shrinking theatre of operations; but these days you have to reach into your mind's eye for the intimations of our origins that came quite easily in Africa even twenty years ago.

When I went to southern India in 1993—flying from Nairobi to Bombay and taking an overnight sleeper from there to Madras—I found that wildlife-viewing, like everything else, was very different. In this vast disorganized democracy, the remnant wilderness preserves were shrinking, strangling really, and the larger beleaguered animals knew it. The crush and kaleidoscope of people was unlike anything I was used to. But it did not involve mass anarchy and the collapse of tribal certainties, cruel politics and looming starvation. Democracy is invigorating.

Forty years had passed since I was a mute young man who could speak freely only to animals and had played with Ringling Brothers' elephants and tigers. Yet though I had become more interested in people, I was still typecast as a nature writer, and sent off to wild places to pursue old loves. In Bombay, Madras and the newly industrial city of Coimbatore, I was lingering and lagging to walk the raucous, mysterious streets, thereby disrupting the schedule of my local handlers, who wanted me out of town and up in the mountain scenery as soon as possible, where they hoped to make money from my visit. They were travel agents—Air India had given me a free plane ticket on the assumption that I would go up into the Nilgiri Hills and write about sambars and sloth bears, tigers and tahrs—and figured that if I publicized their eco tours, then lots of rich Americans might follow me, enabling them to accomplish what they each aspired to do, which, because they were young men, was either to pay for a marriage to a Brahmin or else fly to California and go hang-gliding in the Sierras.

I wasn't enthusiastic about the idea and said that I hoped they'd protect the area as best they could from what might happen if it became a profit centre. I was also a laggard because I loved Madras and walked or rickshawed in the streets all day and then explored the huge iridescent crescent beach in the moonlight (startled to find the unmarked graves of a few of the city's destitute underfoot at the dune line). Like Bombay, Madras was a far less berserk, vertiginous city than the African ones that I was familiar with. Religion and democracy were the glue. People believed in their gods and souls and had the hope of the ballot. They weren't going to crack me on the head just for a chance at my wallet. Indeed, a dead pauper in New York would fare much worse than an anonymous burial on that immortal great beach, with Ridley's sea turtles climbing out of the waves to lay their eggs next to you. I found a new hatchling scrimshawing the sand and helped it into the sea.

The train out of Madras I'd been supposed to be on derailed into a ravine. We went by its wreckage and stopped to pick up three passengers with broken arms. From Coimbatore we drove up into the Animalai Hills to a high old British logging camp called Top Slip—because the teak and rosewood had been slid downhill from there. It is now the Indira Gandhi Wildlife Sanctuary, though with the aid of elephants the hills are still being partially logged. The hushed, handsome, rising and plunging forest had a panoply of birds—golden orioles, scarlet minivets, racket-tailed drongos, pretty 'dollar birds', crow-pheasants, green barbels, blue-winged parakeets, blossom-headed parakeets, red-wattled lapwings, paradise flycatchers, whistling thrushes, golden-backed woodpeckers, mynah birds, green parrots, magpies, hoopoes, hornbills and nine-coloured pitta birds. We saw these, and also tahrs (an endangered wild goat) and sambars (a large dark form of deer), big bison and wild boars, a black-and-white porcupine, mongooses and civets, plentiful chital deer, red with white spots, and flamboyant-plumaged jungle fowl, langur monkeys, macaques and mouse-deer holes.

I was travelling with Salim, a university-educated Shi'ite Muslim from Madras. His father was a travel agent posted to Abu Dhabi; his mother was a Hindu; his early schooling Catholic. His first language had been English, because his father otherwise spoke Urdu. Our local guide, Sabrimathu, was about seventy years old, and what is called in India a 'tribal', meaning from one of the fragile indigenous tribes, in his case the Kadar. Despite a few protections the government gives them (analogous to those offered to American Indians), they tend to miss the British when you talk to them because the British praised and encouraged their tracking skills. Sabrimathu carried a little sack of tobacco leaves to chew and a bush knife; and like the British, I was delighted to listen to him communicate with another Kadar man on the opposite hillside, by means of langur barks, regarding the whereabouts of a dozen elephants we were following. We broke off hastily when the other man told us they had a baby with them.

Originally, Sabrimathu said, two peoples had inhabited these high woods. The Kadar carried spears and lived by gathering small creatures and forest plants, or scavenging from red dog (dhole) kills, if they could surround the pack and drive them off. With brands from a campfire as weapons and windfall shelters, they could coexist with the forest's tigers and also the bison (which are like the African buffalo). But there was no way to stand up to the elephants. They had to hide and run, hide again, and abandon any permanent settlement the elephants approached. The other tribe, the Kurumbas, used bows and arrows to hunt with, shooting birds out of the trees for food and skirmishing with Sabrimathu's group, whose language they didn't speak. They too fled the elephants when a playful herd or a rogue bull in 'must' rampaged through, but feared the teak loggers and British more, and so vanished north.

Sabrimathu's group numbers only a few hundred now, in ten or fifteen tiny communities of thatch huts, on this rugged borderland between the Cochin district of the state of Kerala and Tamil Nadu, where I'd come from. Sabrimathu himself had a confiding face, unkempt grey hair, a woodsman's elastic sense of time and a blurry sort of chuffing manner by which he tried to elide and conceal his feelings when supervisors and clerks condescended to him. Of course I, on the contrary, was all ears. He pointed up a forest stream to where the pythons bred, and later at a knot of crags under a cliff of the Perunkundru Hills, where a leopard mother retreated each year to bear her kits; and to a distant thicket of sidehill evergreens where a tiger generally did the same. Up on a bare saddle of scree, a bit of footpath was visible where he had met a tiger coming towards him—that situation where, he said, you 'just stand still and see whether your time has come'. It hadn't, though once a tiger

jumped at him in the underbrush when he was helping a forestry official track a man-eater. It missed. He was injured another time, when he surprised a bison on a narrow trail and it
charged and knocked him out and horned his arm; he showed
me the scars, healed by forest medicines.

The British had naturally encouraged the Kadar people to
become the mahouts here, capturing and training the local wild
elephants—which they tentatively did, overcoming their age-old
fears. I remember hearing, in northern Canada and Alaska, how
the New World Indians at first had been unsatisfactory guides
on grizzly-hunting expeditions because even though they might
be wizards at tracking grizzlies, for thousands of years equipped
with 'stone-age' weapons, their purpose in doing so was mainly
to avoid them. They were so fearful that newcomers—white
bully boys with fat-calibre rifles—still made fun of them. But
here, in this other kind of devouring, homogenizing democracy,
it was not the Raj or later visiting whites, but other Indians who
made difficulties. And about twenty years after Independence,
Sabrimathu's remnant tribe, so fragile anyway in the new India,
had been ousted from their livelihood as elephant-handlers by a
new people—cattle-herders, more adaptable and sophisticated,
who came up from the plains—at first two families, then more.
After apprenticing with the Kadar, they had finagled or bribed
or genuinely convinced the authorities that they would be better
at it.

We stopped at their camp, located beside a boisterous
small river, the Varagaliar, in a cut between hills in the deep
lovely woods, where they earn three times a labourer's wage for
working a dozen elephants. We arrived in the evening as the
usurpers were finishing washing the beasts, and they jeered at
poor Sabrimathu's chagrin as they showed us a five-year-old
they were training to blow on a harmonica, lift one of her feet
with her trunk and cover one eye with her ear. She lay down in
the swirling warm stream with only her trunk raised above the
current to breathe, while the foreman washed her tusks, lips and
eyelids. The others were not as tame, and, after being watered,
washed and fed, were chained for the night, though the wild

herd kept close tabs on them from nearby and sometimes came down in the night and mingled with them.

The several families of interlopers had small children, and it was idyllic, with the foaming creek and the rushing wind in the trees, miles from another human sound, yet protected from any wandering tiger by the throng of elephants, swaying on their rhythmic feet and swinging their idiosyncratic trunks to private tempos. I remembered feeling this safe in the circus, sleeping under the big cats' cages, knowing that any mugger who crept up on me would provoke a roar that would stop his heart.

Naturally I wanted to see a tiger, though there wasn't much chance of that. We drove to a few overlooks where they occasionally were sighted on a beach of the stream below, but didn't walk anywhere after dark. An old Kadar man with prostate problems had been seized in Sabrimathu's little hamlet the year before when he needed to pee in the middle of the night and left his hut. But the same villagers went out in the wood every day gathering teak seeds from the forest floor to sell, or honey and beeswax from the right clefts in cliffs and hollow trees, or sago, cardamon and ginger, or soapnuts for making shampoo, or guided the Forestry Service men on inspection tours, in order to obtain the rice which had become their new staff of life and didn't grow here. They also used to catch civets for the perfume industry, and guided tiger-rug hunters, but these latter ventures were now illegal and what poaching went on was done by gangs of in-and-out thugs with connections to outside smugglers, not by native tribal people. Sabrimathu reminded me of various aged Eskimos, American Indians and African subsistence hunters I've met over the years, who, like him, knew a thousand specifics no one will know at all when they are gone, though nobody they had any contact with seemed to care much now about what they knew. They too lived wind-scented, sunlit, star-soaked, spirit-shot lives. Humble on one level, proud on another, Sabrimathu was vulnerable to exploitation and insult partly just because he was so tactile and open to everything else. Like those millions of American Indians, he was rooted-in-place. He could be chopped like a tree or shot like a songbird.

Early on our last day at Top Slips, I woke Salim—my young travel-agent, biology-major, Muslim-Hindu-Christian escort—and told him I'd like to go on a bird walk. Amenable though sleepy, he drove me ten miles downhill through the woods to Thunnakadu Reservoir, which is a pretty lake that was created in 1967 and looks perhaps four miles long. The valley it drowned is also lovely, set between protected bands of forest highlands of the Cardamom Hills and flowing towards the Malabar coastline on the Arabian Sea. The road we travelled gets only one bus a day, and at the lake there was no settlement at all except half a dozen wooden cabins for the road crew. They were still asleep, so we simply walked across the top of the dam to the wild side of the lake, as the fragrant, misty blues of dawn were broken by the strong-slanting yellow sun. Cormorants and kingfishers were diving, and pond herons prowling the bank, and we saw a fishing eagle. There was a bamboo raft tied ashore, of the sort the Kadar use to go angling for arm-length larder fish that they can dry.

We walked and chatted on a footpath along the lake, while red-wattled lapwings, the 'policemen of the forest', kept noisy watch over our progress, along with several 'babblers', as Salim called them, the 'seven sisters' birds, because they always move in a group. A big Brahmini kite, white-headed but otherwise a beautiful orangy brown, was being hassled by a bunch of crows above the trees, much as birds of prey are in the United States. We saw a leopard's precise tracks, and then a largish tiger's sprawling pugs, and four bear faeces, berry-filled, in different stages of drying out, as if this path were a thoroughfare. Though Salim had never seen a leopard or tiger, he wanted to turn back. There was no disputing what we were looking at—the tiger and the bear could have been nothing else—yet we could have expected that these animals would come down to drink and forage a bit at night, before climbing the bluff behind the lake again.

Overhead, a troop of langur monkeys swinging in the branches began to whoop the alarm. It had been quiet except for the bird calls at dawn and sunrise and a few magpie and lapwing minatory cries. But entering this neck of the woods provoked a monkey cacophony, a real hollering that seemed part fearful bark or howl and part self-important fun—a rather gay razzing once they were accustomed to us and had done their primary job. We continued our stroll for another quarter-mile, occasioning lots of hubbub because each marginal youngster had to prove that he knew his duty too, not just the sentinels and the leaders.

But then there was an added note, deeper in pitch, exasperated and abrupt. The langurs' hullabaloo at first had masked it, or the fact that with our presence so much advertised, we had now felt free to gab in normal tones, and therefore didn't hear the gravelly, landslide-sounding rumble a little ahead of us.

We kept walking. Then we heard it again. Not only bigger lungs and a lower pitch: the temper of the roar was totally different, like a combat colonel interrupting a bunch of excited privates. Rajah had roared horrendously at me a few times when I hosed his cage or cleaned it with the long iron rod and bumped him inadvertently. And from a distance of forty years, those capsizing blasts reverberated again for me.

'That's not a monkey!' Salim and I said simultaneously. Then, in about the time that a double-take takes, 'Isn't that a tiger?' We each nodded and smiled—then, after three or four steps, stopped in our tracks. The lake was on our left, and the woods extended to the bluff, a few hundred feet high to the right, which was one reason why a nettled tiger might feel he had been hemmed in. That he had roared at us, instead of waiting silently in the undergrowth beside the trail to simply kill us, was a good sign. On the other hand, he could have withdrawn up the valley or a hundred yards to the side without our ever knowing about him. He or she was obviously not doing that. Was he lying on a kill? Or was she a lady with some halfgrown cubs? The roars, instead of ceasing when we turned around and started walking back towards the area of the dam, now redoubled in exasperation, as if the tiger, like the two caged females I'd masturbated in the circus, had flown into a sudden, unreasonable rage. Furthermore (from the volume and tone it sounded like a male), he was now paralleling us, maybe forty or fifty yards in—not visible, but roaring repeatedly, not letting us depart without a terrific chastening. He could have cut us off and mauled us, or driven us into the lake, but didn't; and eventually we met four Kadar men in dhotis who were collecting teak seeds and told them about him. Like us, they turned around immediately and fled at an inconspicuously quick scuttle.

The crew chief, when we got back to the road, said to Salim, 'Oh, you shouldn't have gone there. That side of the lake is where the tiger lives.' The estimate of the wildlife warden at headquarters was thirty-five tigers in these seven hundred square miles.

Being a fan of adages such as 'a stitch in time', 'an apple a day', 'turn about is fair play' or 'what goes around comes around', I was pleased by the symmetry of an old tiger cageboy like me being spared in India forty years later. I was glad, too, that it was still possible to experience a fright from a wilderness creature. In this Tamil Nadu region in 1993, one didn't hear talk yet of tigers being poached for the Chinese aphrodisiac market—only elephants for their tusks and sandalwood for its scented properties. But there are more than 900 million people in India, and only 2,000 tigers. And since Indira Gandhi had decided they ought to be protected, it was said that a number of generations of tigers had grown up that were less afraid of people, at the same time as the territory available for them to roam in was being constricted from every side. The point about tigers is that from our standpoint they are not predictable. They fly off the handle when pressured, and need more than just a specified number of miles to provide a food source or enough prey animals. They need space for their whims and passions and shifts of emotions. They weave more as they walk.

A few days later I was in a different part of southern India, in Hallimoyar, one of the villages along the Moyar river. This time, my guide was Murugan, a young man from the Irula tribe. The Irulas were the indigenous people here on the Moyar river—hunters and trackers, snake-catchers and soothsayers—and still have a few cohesive villages in the forest. My impression was that they were holding together marginally better than the Kadars, partly because they still had a function. Few people in modern India care whether the surviving Kadars, like Sabrimathu, could still track tigers. But the Irulas had until very recently caught cobras for snake charmers all over India—they were the *ur*-snake-charmers—and also as guard-figures for traditionalist temples in places where native cobras had all been killed. They caught crocodiles for the World Wildlife Fund's famous 'Crocodile Bank', near Madras, from which river breeding stock can be sent to other zoos or wildlife preserves, or anywhere crocodiles will be wanted down the road. Nevertheless, they, too, were hunkered down in hard-scrabble poverty.

Murugan was named after an ancient Tamil and Hindu god always seen with a trident. He was also known as 'Bear' because, five years before, he had been gripped and bitten by a bear—he has scars—which his father drove off by ripping a handful of thatch from the roof and setting it afire. He says his grandmother was so tough that she once killed a bear with her hands—it had attacked her on the footpath when she was coming home from the market. His father collected tamarind seeds in the forest, which was dangerous because the elephants collected them also. Other Irulas kept watch on platforms in the paddy fields for a dollar a night, throwing firecrackers or lighting piles of hay to fend off the wild pigs and elephants (three years ago, two of them had been stomped and killed). Murugan himself—wiry, cheerful and untidy like a man-of-the-woods— collected honey for a living every March, and had spotted nine bees' nests on the cliffs so far by a careful reconnaissance. The bees placed them as inaccessibly as they could, but he slipped on a bedsheet with eyeholes cut in, and worked at night, rappelling down the cliff from above, with a burning stick tied to his belt for extra protection and a big tin container to fill. Each of these nests provided him with about ten dollars' worth of honey and wax. And there were eleven Irulas, he said, who worked the ramparts of the cliffs and found more than two hundred nests, though the bears and the leopards diligently competed with them, sometimes almost alongside.

As many as forty British officers used to come to the Moyar river every year to hunt on horseback with tiger hounds, and four Irulas, including Murugan's grandfather, served as trackers, while their wives did the cooking. I asked whether Murugan had ever encountered a tiger himself. He said that, yes, four months ago, when he was doing one of his preliminary searches for honey up a tributary valley, he had seen a tiger with kittens that 'could leap sixty feet' that had killed a cow. She was crouching over it, sucking blood from its throat and, like a nervy cat, tapping the top of her head with the tuft on the end of her tail. No tiger had killed anybody recently, but five people had been killed by elephants in the past eight years (one man tusked to death in front of our rest house). But 'the elephant was the king of the jungle', he said, and shouldn't be shot, no matter what he did. During the latest frenzy of poaching, an elephant had been found in the forest, disabled and kneeling but still alive, with his trunk nailed to the ground with a sharpened crowbar and L-shaped cuts under his cheeks where his tusks had been cut out. That kind of thing, Murugan said, 'may be why they're mad'.

In India, ivory poaching has decimated only the males, because female elephants (unlike their African counterparts) do not have tusks. So what you have is herds of angry females who have witnessed a number of cruel, treacherous, lingering deaths of bulls they've known well. If chased by elephants, you run in a zigzag, hide and dash when discovered, hide again and dash if rediscovered, then turn suddenly, and turn again, because an elephant, though fast in a straight line, is less manoeuvrable than you are. It will stop and listen for you, raising its trunk to sniff the air, sometimes pawing one foot and spreading its ears like a cobra's hood. It can push down the sort of tree you might be able to climb, so you want to get up into the rocks or squeeze into a culvert under the road, if you can run that far. Though when my guide did that, a mile from here on a little jeep track, the elephant found where he was and knelt and reached as deeply as she could into the culvert with her trunk. Then she got up and stood over it and stamped her feet, trying to squash it in.

That night a leopard came into somebody's house through an unshuttered window and killed a goat, but was unable to pull it off its rope and get it back out the window, so merely crouched licking its blood at the throat. The owner of the goat, trying to save it, was so flustered that he tripped, fell and broke his arm. But his neighbours, rushing over, frightened the leopard out. This same troublesome female, with kittens to feed, had grabbed a small boy one evening a few weeks before and started to haul him away by his head. But he was heavy, and his father bravely gave chase, caught up, and rescued his son. The boy was all right now, though we saw the tooth marks.

We went on a stroll to catch some fish and look at crocodile drag-marks in the deep sand on a plump beach several miles below Hallimoyar. The river rustled by in corded currents under grandly proportioned trees. We built a driftwood fire for cooking, and napped when we weren't doing anything else. An elephant path crossed the river at this point, and we found hyena prints and dung with sambar hair in it. You could wade out in the silky water and sit on knobby rocks, or cradle yourself on the lowest branches of two or three of the trees that arced out over the river.

The water ran hip-deep near the bank, yet, though a cow was said to have been bitten on the nose upstream the day before, we trusted our guide's assurance that he knew the nature of crocodiles, and enjoyed the afternoon till sunset: whereupon we started walking back to Hallimoyar on the ox-wagon track. A brown-and-white Brahmini kite was being buzzed by a swift grey hawk. We'd seen a black buck run off in a hurry on our trip in, and expected to stumble upon other animals as dusk approached. A river temple stood along the trail, with a cobra living in a termite mound alongside that Murugan said he'd put there. I'd hoped to see the cobra, but we weren't inclined to linger, because we'd already dawdled too long at the beach. It was growing dark, and the twelve hours of night belonged to the animals.

Clouds hid the moon. Fortunately the path was composed of a whitish soil that we could fix our eyes on. But then I happened to glance up, and dimly noticed that we were about to collide with a baby elephant. How nice, I thought for just a second, a baby elephant. *A baby elephant!* Then, sure enough, the mother's shape loomed indistinctly in the gloom. Her shadowy trunk hardly moved, not yet swinging forwards and up; her tree-trunk legs looked the very pattern of patience. But as we alerted one another agitatedly in whispers, her great ears really did spread out above us like a cobra's hood. We could also make out other females at her shoulders—two, three, maybe four, waiting.

'We're trapped,' whispered our guide. 'Our luck has gone bad.'

The elephants were preparing to enter the road, so we didn't run backwards. Instead we ran upwards, up the side of a rocky ridge that fortuitously stood to our right. They could have charged uphill, but rocks are not to a pachyderm's liking. We scattered, but angled slantwise along the slope to a drop-off that seemed high enough that their trunks couldn't reach us if they followed and stood on their hind legs, trying. Looking down at the trail in a slice of moonlight, we saw more elephants in the dusk. Another group was arriving. We tried to count: thirty or forty were slowly shuffling towards the river. It was amazing, almost surreal in the dark. Fearfully, we lit a fire on a flat part of the rock—and heard a groan from some of the animals below, as though they were murmuring: *what are these crazies going to do, set the valley, too, on fire?*

After they had moved on, we yelled for a couple of hours before a gust of wind caught our voices properly and carried them to the nightwatchmen in Hallimoyar's paddy fields. Bravely, they set out to rescue us, though they didn't know who we were, and thought we might be bandits, smugglers, poachers or whatever. They said later they had been as scared of us as of the possibility that the elephants might still be on the road. The fire would have protected us for the rest of the night from cats, bears, bison, dholes or hyenas, but we were impatient, and glad of their generous spirit.

In the current happy excitement about whether we may soon discover signs of primitive life on Mars, there is a weird and tragic incongruity, because we are losing dozens of more complex but unexamined species every day right here on Earth and doing little about it. And it isn't just beetles. Creatures such as tigers and rhinos are also disappearing, creatures which from childhood have been part of the furniture of our minds. Indeed, they may have helped create our minds. When you see a tiger at the zoo you know innately that your ancestors did too. And even if children's authors have tended to create 'wild things' that are amalgams instead of simply using the real thing, these creations are surely blended from the same old veldt or jungle citizenry that shaped our imagination to begin with.

In Madras, my plane was delayed because up in New Delhi there were bomb scares at the airport. So, feeling in suspension, I persuaded a guy at the terminal to drive me up to the nearby hill where Doubting Thomas, according to some reports, was crucified. It seems natural that, in his regret, St Thomas would have been the Apostle who travelled furthest afterwards—clear to the Bay of Bengal, there to re-enact Christ's fate. I felt a link to him, because my parents used to call me 'Doubting Thomas' when I was young and rebellious and 'doubted' their Episcopalian liturgy.

On this cathedral hill, schoolchildren were planting trees while a gang of jackdaws disputed possession of the sky with some vultures and kites, and the smell of uric acid and rotting carbohydrates drifted up from Madras's five million people below. But I also saw an egret sitting on a cow's back and a blackbird on a buffalo. A drove of white ducks on the way to market, even a drove of pigs. Brahma, Vishnu and Shiva—creator, preserver and destroyer—had topped St Thomas's appeal in this part of the world. They ride, on a swan, an eagle and a bull, among the androgynous exuberance of sculpted figures from the animal kingdom scrambling like totems up the compact temple towers. These are metaphors, of course, but with a bit of glee or mischief thrown in, and the undergirding of real elephants, cobras and tigers only a day's walk away.

Yet one does not leave wild places hopefully nowadays. Amalgams indeed are what we'll have. Virtual wilderness. 'Albino king snakes' are already in the pet stores, and 'ligers' and 'tiglons' feature in dealers' catalogues (apparently, selling a cross evades the endangered-species laws). When I remember that Siberian tiger caged in eighteen square feet in the circus, or the black-maned movie lion confined in a piano box which I cared for in California in 1953, I can't romanticize how things were at mid-century. The cruelty was abominable, but was still enclosed in a world that seemed closer to being whole. The ultimate wild things are incidentally dangerous—white sharks, harpy eagles, polar bears—and unpredictable. Even the most gorgeous tiger is less athletic, more complicated than a leopard, say, which may sometimes seem like a single, lengthy muscle. But the tiger's spirit, when ferocious, feline and imperial, can parallel ours, though without the monkeying primate qualities that have given us our berserk streak. Tigers are less heartbreaking than the beleaguered elephant, because they are not social creatures, are reactive, not innovative. But they are an apex, a kind of hook the web of nature hangs from. To know them marked my life.

David Foster Wallace

Certainly the End of *Something* or Other, One Would Sort of Have to Think

"Of nothing but me . . . I sing, lacking another song."
—Updike, *Midpoint*, Canto I, 1969

Mailer, Updike, Roth—the Great Male Narcissists* who've dominated postwar realist fiction are now in their senescence, and it must seem to them no coincidence that the prospect of their own deaths appears backlit by the approaching millennium and on-line predictions of the death of the novel as we know it. When a solipsist dies, after all, everything goes with him. And no U.S. novelist has mapped the interior terrain of the solipsist better than John Updike, whose rise in the 60's and 70's established him as both chronicler and voice of probably the single most self-absorbed generation since Louis XIV. As were Freud's, Updike's big preoccupations have always been with death and sex (not necessarily in that order), and the fact that his books' mood has gotten more wintery in recent years is understandable—Mr. Updike has always written largely about himself, and since the surprisingly moving *Rabbit at Rest* he's been exploring, more and more overtly, the apocalyptic prospect of his own death.

Toward the End of Time concerns an incredibly erudite, articulate, successful, narcissistic, and sex-obsessed retired guy

---

* Hereafter, "G.M.N.'s"

who's keeping a one-year journal in which he explores the apoc-alyptic prospect of his own death. It is, of the total 25 Updike books I've read, far and away the worst, a novel so mind-bend-ingly clunky and self-indulgent that it's hard to believe the au-thor let it be published in this kind of shape.

I'm afraid the preceding sentence is this review's upshot, and most of the remainder here will consist simply of presenting evidence/justification for such a disrespectful assessment. First, though, if I may poke the critical head into the frame for just one moment, I'd like to offer assurances that your reviewer is not of these spleen-venting, spittle-spattering Updike-haters one often encounters among literary readers under 40. The fact is that I am probably classifiable as one of very few actual sub-40 Updike *fans.* Not as rabid a fan as, say, Nicholson Baker is, but I do think that *The Poorhouse Fair, Of the Farm* and *The Centaur* are all great books, maybe classics. And even since *Rabbit Is Rich*—as his characters seemed to become more and more re-pellent, and without any corresponding indication that the au-thor understood that they were repellent—I've continued to read Mr. Updike's novels and to admire the sheer gorgeousness of his descriptive prose.

Most of the literary readers I know personally are under 40, and a fair number are female, and none of them are big admirers of the postwar G.M.N.'s. But it's Updike in particular they seem to hate. And not merely his books for some reason— mention the poor man *himself* and you have to jump back:

"Just a penis with a thesaurus."

"Has the son of a bitch ever had one unpublished thought?"

"Makes misogyny seem literary the same way Rush makes fascism seem funny."

And trust me: these are actual quotations, and I've heard even worse ones, and they're all usually accompanied by the sort of facial expression where you can tell there's not going to be any profit in arguing or talking about the sheer aesthetic plea-sure of Updike's prose. None of the other famous phallocrats of Updike's generation—not Mailer, not Exley or Bukowski or even the Samuel Delany of *Hogg*—excites such violent dislike. There are, of course, some obvious explanations for part of this dislike—jealousy, iconoclasm, P.C. backlash, and the fact that many of our parents revere Updike and it's easy to revile what your parents revere. But I think the major reason why so many of my generation hate Updike and the other G.M.N.'s has to do with these writers' radical self-absorption, and with their uncritical celebration of this self-absorption both in themselves and in their characters.

Updike, for example, has for years been constructing protagonists who are basically all the same guy (see for example Rabbit Angstrom, Dick Maple, Piet Hanema, Henry Bech, Rev. Tom Marshfield, *Roger's Version*'s "Uncle Nunc") and who are all clearly stand-ins for the author himself. They always live in either Pennsylvania or New England, are unhappily married/divorced, are roughly Updike's age. Always either the narrator or the point-of-view character, they all have the author's astounding perceptual gifts; they all think and speak in the same effortlessly lush, synesthetic way Updike does. They are also always incorrigibly narcissistic, philandering, self-contemptuous, self-pitying . . . and deeply alone, alone the way only a solipsist can be alone. They never belong to any sort of larger unit or community or cause. Though usually family men, they never really love anybody—and, though always heterosexual to the point of satyriasis, they especially don't love women.° The very world around them, as beautifully as they see and describe it, seems to exist for them only insofar as it evokes impressions and associations and emotions inside the great Self.

I'm guessing that for the young educated adults of the 60's and 70's, for whom the ultimate horror was the hypocritical conformity and repression of their own parents' generation, Updike's erection of the libidinous self appeared refreshing and even heroic. But the young educated adults of the 90's—who

---

° (Unless, of course, you consider constructing long encomiums to a woman's "sacred several-lipped gateway" or saying things like "It is true, the sight of her plump lips obediently distended around my swollen member, her eyelids lowered demurely, afflicts me with a religious peace" to be the same as loving her.)

wife Gloria, and remembering the ex-wife who divorced him for adultery, and rhapsodizing about a young prostitute he moves into the house when Gloria's away on a trip. It's also got a lot of pages of Turnbull brooding about senescence, mortality, and the tragedy of the human condition, and even more pages of Turnbull talking about sex and the imperiousness of the sexual urge, and detailing how he lusts after assorted prostitutes and secretaries and neighbors and bridge partners and daughters-in-law and a little girl who's part of the group of young toughs he pays protection to, a 13-year-old whose breasts—"shallow taut cones tipped with honeysuckle-berry nipples"—Turnbull finally gets to fondle in the woods behind his house when his wife's not looking.

In case this sounds like a harsh summary, here's some hard statistical evidence of just how much a "departure" for Updike this novel really is:

Total # of pages about Sino-American war—causes, duration, casualties: 0.75

Total # of pages about deadly mutant metallobioforms: 1.5

Total # of pages about flora around Turnbull's home, plus fauna, weather, and how his ocean view looks in different seasons: 86

Total # of pages about Mexico's repossession of the U.S. Southwest: 0.1

Total # of pages about Ben Turnbull's penis and his various feelings about it: 7.5

Total # of pages about what life's like in Boston proper without municipal services or police, plus whether the war's missile exchanges have caused fallout or radiation sickness: 0.0

Total # of pages about prostitute's body, particular attention to sexual loci: 8.75

Total # of pages about golf: 15

Total # of pages of Ben Turnbull saying things like "I want women to be dirty" and "She was a choice cut of meat and I hoped she held out for a fair price" and "The sexual parts are fiends, sacrificing everything to that aching point of contact," and ". . . ferocious female nagging is the price men pay for our

were, of course, the children of all the impassioned i
and divorces Updike wrote about so beautifully, and v
watch all this brave new individualism and self-expre
sexual freedom deteriorate into the joyless and ano
indulgence of the Me Generation—today's sub-40's l
different horrors, prominent among which are anomie
lipsism and a peculiarly American loneliness: the pro
dying without once having loved something more than
Ben Turnbull, the narrator of Updike's latest novel, is
old and heading for just such a death, and he's shitlessly
Like so many of Updike's protagonists, though, Turnbul
to be scared of all the wrong things.

   Toward the End of Time is being marketed by th
lisher as an ambitious departure for Updike, his foray i
futuristic-dystopic tradition of Huxley and soft sci-fi. The
A.D. 2020, and time has not been kind. A Sino-American
war has killed millions and ended centralized government
know it. The dollar's gone; Massachusetts now uses scrip
for Bill Weld. No taxes: local toughs now get protection
to protect the upscale from other local toughs. AIDS has
cured, the Midwest is depopulated, and parts of Bosto
bombed out and (presumably?) irradiated. An abandoned
orbit space station hangs in the night sky like a junior m
There are tiny but rapacious "metallobioforms" that have
tated from toxic waste and go around eating electricity and
occasional human. Mexico has reappropriated the U.S. So
west and is threatening wholesale invasion even as thousand
young Americans are sneaking south across the Rio Grande
search of a better life. America, in short, is getting ready to

   The book's postmillennial elements are sometimes co
and they really would represent an interesting departure
Updike if they weren't all so sketchy and tangential, for the m
part worked as subordinate clauses into the narrator's endle
descriptions of every tree, plant, flower, and shrub around l
home. What 95 percent of *Toward the End of Time* actual
consists of is Turnbull describing the prenominate flora (ov
and over again as each season passes) and his brittle, castratin

much-lamented prerogatives, the power and the mobility and the penis": 36.5.

The novel's best parts are a half-dozen little set pieces where Turnbull imagines himself inhabiting different historical figures—a tomb-robber in ancient Egypt, Saint Mark, a guard at a Nazi death camp, etc. They're gems, and the reader wishes there were more of them. The problem is that they don't serve much of a function other than to remind us that Updike can write really great imaginative set pieces when he's in the mood. Their justification in the novel stems from the fact that the narrator is a science fan (the novel has minilectures on astrophysics and quantum mechanics, nicely written but evincing a roughly *Newsweek*-level comprehension). Turnbull is particularly keen on subatomic physics and something he calls the "Theory of Many Worlds"—which actually dates from 1957 and is a proposed solution to certain quantum paradoxes entailed by the principles of Indeterminacy and Complementarity, and which is unbelievably abstract and complicated . . . but which Turnbull seems to believe is roughly the same thing as the Theory of Past-Life Channeling, apparently thereby explaining the set pieces where Turnbull is somebody else. The whole quantum setup ends up being embarrassing in the special way something pretentious is embarrassing when it's also just plain wrong.

Better, and more convincingly futuristic, are the narrator's soliloquies on the blue-to-red shift and the eventual implosion of the known universe near the book's end, and these would be among the novel's highlights, too, if it weren't for the fact that Turnbull is interested in cosmic apocalypse all and only because it serves as a grand metaphor for his own personal death— likewise all the Housmanesque descriptions of the Beautiful But Achingly Transient flowers in his yard, and the optometrically significant "Year 2020," and the book's final, heavy description of "small pale moths [that] have mistakenly hatched" on a late-autumn day and now "flip and flutter a foot or two above the asphalt as if trapped in a narrow wedge of space-time beneath the obliterating imminence of winter."

The clunky bathos of this novel seems to have infected

even the prose, John Updike's great strength for almost forty years. *Toward the End of Time* has occasional flashes of beautiful writing—deer described as "tender-faced ruminants," leaves as "chewed to lace by Japanese beetles," a car's tight turn as a "slur" and its departure as a "dismissive acceleration down the driveway." But a horrific percentage of the book consists of stuff like "Why indeed do women weep? They weep, it seemed to my wandering mind, for the world itself, in its beauty and waste, its mingled cruelty and tenderness" and "How much of summer is over before it begins! Its beginning marks its end, as our birth entails our death" and "This development seems remote, however, among the many more urgent issues of survival on our blasted, depopulated planet." Not to mention whole reams of sentences with so many modifiers—"The insouciance and innocence of our independence twinkled like a kind of sweat from their bare and freckled or honey-colored or mahogany limbs"—or so much subordination—"As our species, having given itself a hard hit, staggers, the others, all but counted out, move in"—and such heavy alliteration—"The broad sea blares a blue I would not have believed obtainable"—that they seem less like John Updike than like somebody doing a cruel parody of John Updike.

Besides distracting us with worries about whether Updike might be injured or ill, the turgidity of the prose here also ups our dislike of the novel's narrator (it's hard to like a guy whose way of saying his wife doesn't like going to bed before him is "She hated it when I crept into bed and disturbed in her the fragile succession of steps whereby consciousness dissolves," or who refers to his grandchildren as ". . . this evidence that my pending oblivion had been hedged, that my seed had taken root"). And this dislike absolutely torpedoes *Toward the End of Time,* a novel whose Tragic Climax (in a late chapter called "The Deaths") is a prostate operation that leaves Turnbull impotent and extremely bummed. It is made very clear that the author expects us to sympathize with and even share Turnbull's grief at "the pathetic shrunken wreck the procedures [have] made of my beloved genitals." These demands on our compassion echo the major crisis of the book's first half, described in a flashback, where we are supposed to empathize not only with the rather textbookish existential dread that hits Turnbull at 30 as he's in his basement building a dollhouse for his daughter—"I would die, but also the little girl I was making this for would die . . . There was no God, each detail of the rusting, moldering cellar made clear, just Nature, which would consume my life as carelessly and relentlessly as it would a dung-beetle corpse in a compost pile"—but also with Turnbull's relief at discovering a remedy for this dread—"an affair, my first. Its colorful weave of carnal revelation and intoxicating risk and craven guilt eclipsed the devouring gray sensation of time."

Maybe the only thing the reader ends up really appreciating about Ben Turnbull is that he's such a broad caricature of an Updike protagonist that he helps us figure out what's been so unpleasant and frustrating about this gifted author's recent characters. It's not that Turnbull is stupid—he can quote Kierkegaard and Pascal on angst and allude to the death of Schubert and distinguish between a sinistrorse and a dextrorse *Polygonum* vine, etc. It's that he persists in the bizarre adolescent idea that getting to have sex with whomever one wants whenever one wants is a cure for ontological despair. And so, as far as I can figure out, does *Toward the End of Time*'s author— Updike makes it plain that he views the narrator's impotence as catastrophic, as the ultimate symbol of death itself, and he clearly wants us to mourn it as much as Turnbull does. I'm not especially offended by this attitude; I mostly just don't get it. Erect or flaccid, Ben Turnbull's unhappiness is obvious right from the book's first page. But it never once occurs to him that the reason he's so unhappy is that he's an asshole.

Rediscovery

Donald Barthelme

Worrying About Women

Worrying about women. Woman is an imaginary being, a fabulous animal kin to the manticore, the hippogriff, the ant-lion. Woman does not exist. What exists in the space "woman" would occupy, if she existed, is a concatenation of ideas about women. Throughout history men and women have attempted to zoo the animal. Imagine an immense net, woven of paintings, epigrams, laws, courtesies, lies, clothing, Polaroids, aggression, desire, and dreams. Imagine a net as big as a sea, stretching from the Advanced Palaeolithic to the present time. Imagine human beings standing along the circumference of the net, doing their best to support it—the mighty effort, the colossal straining. Yet the animal escapes. And a strange thing happens. The net becomes the animal.

The nonexistence of woman has occasioned a certain anxiety among women. Some feel that it is the result of a male conspiracy perhaps twenty million years old. Others contend, with Hegel, that there is in consciousness itself a fundamental hostility toward every other consciousness and that this adequately accounts for the scandal. All would probably agree that *looking* is crucial.

"The looking at a woman sometimes makes for lust," says Thomas Aquinas, in one of the great understatements of the thirteenth century. Philosophers of the gaze, that terrible regard which can illuminate or extinguish its object, are part of the net. Simone de Beauvoir, whose work on women is definitive, finds that a man's gaze is in all cases a loss of value for a woman. "The eye is a secret orator," says Burton, "the first bawd."

Women now demand a presuppositionless regard, one into which are wound no definitions of woman. The disembawdiment of the eye will not be easily achieved. The kind of mystification from which women wish to free themselves may be seen, for example, among enthusiasts of concavity/convexity. The traditional view, based on the morphology of the sexual organs, is that women "are" concave. Convexity, with its connotations of assertiveness, imperialism, domination, is said to be male. Woman, in this formulation, is a dish containing "the statically expectant ova" [Erik Erikson]. Theories proliferate from this slender base, insights accumulate, conclusions are drawn. Such thinking makes objects of us all.

Moods change. Men, exhausted by the accomplishments of reason, whose processes undergo further refinement even as its products are discovered to be often pernicious, realize that something is wrong. With reason suffering a partial discredit, with science increasingly suspect, there is a turning toward other ways of knowing, the nonrational, the "feminine," feeling-with. Women choose this moment to mobilize. If, as Oretga says, the core of the feminine mind is occupied by an irrational power [he intends this positively], the next hundred years are going to be wonderfully different from the last, in ways which no one has contemplated.

The question of Beauty disturbs the Movement, as beauty disturbs. Its very discussion, in the vocabulary of the revolution, is somehow inappropriate—like the startling appearance, in the 1572 edition of the Bishops' Bible, of a woodcut of Jupiter visiting Leda in his swansuit. When art enters the dialogue, the situation is further confused. Women in the gallery, literally on pedestals, or hanging on the walls, like skins, like trophies—

perfect objects at last. One does not know how to behave. The slightest perusement of the mesial groove is done guiltily. As in life.

Art, touching mysteries, tends to darken rather than illuminate them. Artists enrich and complicate (whatever else they may also be doing). In terms of sexual politics, this means adding to the mystification. But more than politics is involved. Women as a subject, a pretext, for art, become momentarily free. Art's refusal to explain itself translates into a refusal to explain women. They are, for a moment, surrounded by a blessed silence.

Margaret Talbot

Chicks and Chuckles

Poor glutted smirking us. We live in an age when pop culture is our history and history is our flea market. Kitsch never dies; it lacks the gravity to die; it just circles back, with a new price tag and a hopeful air. It turns out that no junk is junky enough to be consigned to the obsolescence for which it was intended—not fake fur or Formica, not Russ Meyer or Ed Wood, not Esquivel or Abba. We do not lament the passing of things that were meant to last; we lament the passing of things that were meant not to last. We refuse to be robbed of a past by a culture of transience. It is our lot, therefore, to be overrun, or to overrun ourselves, with the schlock not only of today, but of two, three, four decades past. Oblivion, it seems, is worse than vulgarity. And so we claim ephemera for posterity.

There are technological explanations for this phenomenon, and economic ones, too. The Internet, with its capacity for linking up thousands of otherwise furtive fans and collectors, for bringing everybody and everything in from the periphery to the center, for infinitely replicating shards and shards of trivia, has accelerated the redemption of kitsch. So has the CD, for which it seems that there never was a minor composer or a justly neglected performance or a girl group too obscure or a lounge act too goofy. Consider only the Capitol CD series with such self-consciously retro titles as "Bongo Land," "Ultra-Lounge" and "Bossanovaville," risibly awful music brought proudly and brilliantly back. The shorter the history, the more relentless the recycling. (It was American popular music that invented the concept of "instant gold.") Or consider Nick-at-Nite-type cable TV, with its endless appetite for content as familiar and as soothing as the wallpaper in our childhood bedrooms.

But behind these material facts is a sensibility, an attitude toward the past, and toward collecting, that might be described as ironic preservationism. Ironic preservationism differs from its straight counterpart—the world of genealogy and heritage movements and lovingly restored country houses—in that it resurrects objects not for their beauty or their craftsmanship or the lasting superiority of their forms or materials, but for the very inverse of these qualities: their cheesiness, their triviality, their banality, their disposability. It differs, too, from earlier preservationist movements in that the appeal of an object does not lie in the way that time has made it recondite. For the ironic preservationist, mystery holds no attraction. The more crudely legible an artifact, the better. An original poster for *Reefer Madness*, or *Faster, Pussycat, Kill, Kill*, is a great find partly because it is so undemanding of the mind or the sensibility, so unashamedly garish, so naked of pretension.

The ironic preservationist is ironic because he is preserving what was made to be forgotten. The danger for such a collector is that he begins to see the past as a congeries of gags, a grab bag of "novelty items" (a term of art, in the world of American kitsch, like the term "collectibles"), a freak show. He believes in regress, but he is not what you would call conservative; he is trying instead to recapture the impermanence of yesteryear. Of course, this is impossible, and so the precious artifacts are merely fetishized. In the tackiness of the B-movies and the third-rate torch songs of the '50s and '60s, he finds innocence. (Nobody in the '50s and '60s did.)

The ironic preservationist is not indifferent to history so much as addled by it. In part his attitude is a rejection of the discontinuities of consumer culture, the swift passing of the latest thing. By honoring all this negligible stuff, he asserts his mastery over the acceleration of the past. The "new and improved" are a joke to him. (He will enjoy them later.) The more fads and entertainments the culture produces, the more stubbornly he clings to those of earlier decades for stability. The usual explanation for historic preservation movements is that, in a throwaway society, people will hunger for something that lasts, for an object made with some care and to some kind of serious accepted aesthetic standard, and intended for some kind of posterity. But what if you determine to make the throwaway itself endure? To make it outlive the use-by date that capitalism stamps in ghostly ink on every pop cultural creation? Now that is a victory!

As the British historian Raphael Samuel writes, describing the more mainstream phenomenon of retro-chic, the idea is not to "deceive anyone into a hallucinatory sense of oneness with the past, but on the contrary [to cultivate]an air of ironic detachment and distance. Retrochic . . . involves not an obsession with past but an indifference to it: only when history has ceased to matter can it be treated as a sport." There is some truth to this argument, but it is a little unfair. The motives of the ironic preservationist are complicated. There is tenderness in his inanity. He wants access to a kind of purity: the purity of pure schlock. Like Frank O'Hara, he longs to be "at least as alive as the vulgar." He is often more sentimental than cool. Sometimes the ironic preservationist exalts the kitsch of the past—his Yma Sumac records, his velvet paintings, his pulp novels—because it is bizarre or amusing, sometimes because it reminds him, humbly, of something that's missing from the time in which he must live now. And so it is with the lubricious dreamworld of Bettie Page.

From 1950 to 1957, Bettie Page was America's underground pin-up queen, the secret crush of thousands of men who married young and wondered what they had missed. Her career as an erotic icon took her from moderately saucy beach blanket shots (the stuff of calendars hung discreetly in the garage) to mail-order stag films with sadomasochistic themes and titles such as *Captive Jungle Girl* (the stuff of congressional investigations). It took her from a time in porn history when nearly nude pictures of nearly pretty girls in static cheesecake poses were still scandalous enough to pack an erotic charge to a time in which psychosexual motifs such as fetishism and domination were increasingly mass-marketed and porn was supposed to tell a story (with a beginning, a middle and a climax).

She started out posing nude or in homemade bikinis, frolicking in the Long Island surf for the benefit of amateur "camera clubs"—hobbyists, shutterbugs and geeks who took pictures for their personal use and so were not bound by the obscenity laws that limited nudity in men's publications of the day. From there, she did cheerful photo spreads for magazines such as *Wink* and *Tattler* and *Eyeful; Dare* and *Bold* and *Peek; Art Photography* and *Modern Sunbathing*. And finally, in what Bettie Page's fans call her "Dark Angel" period, she did a noirish series of photos and silent film loops shot in New York by a genially sleazy stag photographer named Irving Klaw and his devoted sister Paula.

Bettie and the other Klaw models, all women, usually wore the distinctive, thickly armatured underwear of the '50s—appropriately called foundation garments—and high, high heels as black and glistening as wet asphalt. Sometimes they performed burlesque shimmies, sometimes they donned leather corsets and gloves and brandished whips and hairbrushes, sometimes they trussed one another up. As in all s & m, props played a vital role and were lavished with beady-eyed attention. The settings were always delightfully low-rent; the action slow, deliberate, exaggerated. Since no men appear in the films—to include men would have been to guarantee an obscenity conviction—these short films sometimes suggest a sort of lesbian theme park, an underground network of tacky motels where you could always find tough babes playing cards in their underwear, smoking cigarettes in their underwear, menacing one another with hairbrushes in their underwear, rolling around on shag rugs in their underwear.

In each of these guises, Bettie Page looked much the same. She always wore her dark hair long and loose, with pageboy bangs, which gave her a modern, intelligent look. In almost any decade, this particular hairstyle—straight hair and bangs, the bob or a variation on it—seems to grant its wearers a purchase on modernity. (Think of how contemporary Louise Brooks appears next to other stars of the 1920s.) Partly by virtue of its association with the flapper, the straight-hair-and-bangs style has long signified free-thinking, self-possession and a crisp, unromantic Bohemianism.

Bettie Page was nearly always well-toned and smooth-skinned, with a flattering all-over tan. But she had a body that was unusual among sex goddesses then and now in that it was lovely in a plausible way—neither as impossibly sinewy as a contemporary fashion model's nor as busty as Mansfield's or Monroe's. It was, above all, a body in which she always managed to look supremely at ease. She seemed as comfortable as a pre-adolescent girl, though with her full breasts, and the womanly pooch of her slightly convex tummy, she hardly looked the ga-mine.

We know all this about Bettie Page not only, or even primarily, because she was so fervently admired in her brief hey-day. Those first admirers tended to keep their obsession to themselves. We know it because she is so fervently admired today, the object of a cult that has done nothing to keep its secret to itself. Page is the subject of a two-hour documentary that aired on the cable network E! Entertainment Television last spring, and of a forthcoming HBO movie. On the web, you can find more than 100 sites dedicated to her. Her photographs from the '50s fetch good money at trade shows and at groovy little downtown shops and at Bettie Page theme nights hosted by clubs in Los Angeles, New York and Atlanta. Hip models have been photographed to look like her (they don't); hip designers claim to have been influenced by her. There is a fan club, The Bettie Scouts of America, based in Kansas City, Kansas, and a magazine, *The Bettie Pages,* published in New York by an unusually dedicated Bettie buff named Greg Theakston. And now there is a handsome, besotted tribute book, *Bettie Page: The Life of a Pin-Up Legend* by Karen Essex and James L. Swanson, a biography of a sort, which has an anecdote-laden text based on interviews with the 74-year-old Page.

So, you might reasonably ask, what is it about Bettie Page? Why does her image still capture the imagination, while legions of her cohorts in the nudie modeling trade could barely sell a publicity still to save their pasties?

Bettie's fans tend to answer that question with the naughty-but-nice paradox. For Karen Essex and James L. Swanson, Bettie Page "embodied the stereotypical wholesomeness of the Fifties and the hidden sexuality straining beneath the surface. . . . Her fresh-faced beauty was the perfect camouflage for what lurked beneath her veneer—the exotic, whip-snapping dark angel. In Bettie Page, forbidden longings were made safe by an ideal American girl." For Steve Sullivan, the author of a methodically researched history of the pin-up called *Va Va Voom!,* there's a "fascinating duality" in Bettie's photographs, "which run the gamut from sunny innocence to sinister darkness." Truth is, though, that's a gamut run rather often in pornography. The appeal of the sweet-faced girl with the bod for sin is as old as the oldest dirty postcard, and as common as guilt.

It is true that Bettie Page may have been especially gifted at conveying the naughty-but-nice fantasy. Hers was an era in which the expectation of female frigidity was still a widely accepted axiom of sexual lore. When it came to sex, explained an article in *Life* magazine in 1953, the female is "simply by virtue of her own physiology and through no coyness or stubbornness of her own, disinterested, unresponsive, and in fact sometimes downright frigid. . . . The average woman . . . can certainly take sex or leave it alone." She "considers the human body, if anything, rather repulsive." In such a context, the look of sweet sexual eagerness—neither too aloof nor too ravenous—that was Bettie Page's specialty must have gone a long way.

Still, it can't entirely explain her popularity, particularly today. To account for it, we have to go further afield—into the realm of nostalgia and the yearning for a vanished sense of the illicit, a sense of the illicit that was the other side of a sense of the innocent. We could do worse, though, than to start with her smile.

Bettie Page's smile—it looks more and more bemused, especially in some of the Klaw photographs—is crucial not only to the naughty-but-nice effect, but also to something more complex and lasting about her appeal. Above all else, perhaps, her pictures, and the expressions that she adopts in them, convey a sensation of joy in her work—her joy, not the viewer's. It is the joy of a talent finding an outlet, and it hardly matters that the talent is not for painting or policy analysis, but for exhibitionism. These are images of a woman who will not be ruined by sex, but made by it. In her nude photos, she holds her head up high. She wears her insouciance like a halo. If eroticism is the promise of pleasure, then these pictures are not, strictly speaking, erotic. For they promise nothing. They are not images of desire, they are images of happiness. And so what they demonstrate, in a way, is the unerotic character of happiness. If one tingles at the sight of them, it is almost with envy.

In fact, when it comes to certain clichés of nude modeling, Bettie Page is clearly inept. She never stares vacantly into the middle distance, dreamy and compliant. She can't really smolder, and she doesn't do sultry. When she acts the part of the dominatrix in the Klaw photographs, she narrows her eyes and knits her brow fiercely and mostly looks silly. When she plays the passive role, tied up by another Klaw model, her moue of distress is goggle-eyed, comically exaggerated; she might as well be a silent movie heroine lashed to a train track. She's game, she's diligent, but she never seems to inhabit a role or to let it consume her. She won't take it seriously. And no woman ever inflamed a man by giggling.

In *Bettie Page: The Life of a Pin-Up Legend*, Paula Klaw praises Bettie as a woman of many expressions who "could have been an actress." But the truth is that she always looks the same; and that is her particular grace. What lifts her photos above the blankness and the deadness of so much porn and pseudoporn is the stubborn, exuberant persistence of a self, the irreducible core of a personality shining through. Bettie is never inert; she is always Bettie; the girl can't help it. Often her pictures are curiously unarousing, as though the undeniable presence of a particular person in all these erotic set-ups (Bettie in pom-poms, Bettie in heels, Bettie in chains) could only undermine their purpose. The effect is of objectification without anonymity; objectification without abstraction. In this way, the aim of pornography—to let the viewer generalize from this body to other bodies, including his own—is unwittingly thwarted.

There is a wonderful photo in Essex and Swanson's book, a candid shot taken in Irving Klaw's "studio." Klaw is in the background, rumpled and overweight and grinning because he's just put his foot through a shabby prop staircase. Bettie is standing in front of him, wearing black-and-white lace lingerie and vivid coral-red lipstick. She has her head thrown back and she's cracking up—laughing, one imagines, at the whole enterprise of dirty pictures. And what's wonderful about the photo is that it's not really so different, in its mood of gentle mockery, from some of the posed photos taken in the same setting. It reminds you that in interviews Bettie Page always described her modeling as a kick. "I was happy cavorting around stark naked on the beach," she said. Or, of the Klaw photos, "The other models and I enjoyed doing these crazy things. The craziest thing I was asked to do was pose as a pony, wearing a leather outfit with a lead and everything. We just died laughing." Bettie Page represents something unusual: she's the sex joke who's in on the joke. Unlike the Judy Holliday type, the sexy ditz who isn't supposed to know that she is sexy, Bettie Page is fully aware of the comedy of desire. It was altogether appropriate that in October 1955 she adorned the cover of a magazine called *Chicks and Chuckles.*

Of course, remarks such as the ones I've just quoted might suggest that Bettie Page achieved her equanimity about her work at the price of a certain lack of imagination. To this day, she can't seem to fathom why anyone would have considered Klaw's work pornographic. By today's standards, it wasn't—it contained no nudity, no simulated sex acts. Still, her disingenuousness can make her sound a bit thick. About the Kefauver Commission, the congressional investigation that targeted Klaw in 1955, Page professes bafflement. "They thought Irving was doing pornography. I don't know where they got that idea," she told Essex and Swanson. "Irving was a very nice fellow, his models were never naked and there were never any men in the pictures." And her own role in the fetish photographs? "It was part of posing and posing was very natural to me." Besides, she says, "I was young and open to new experiences."

Anti-porn feminists, among others, might dismiss such attitudes as evidence of false consciousness, a numb refusal to acknowledge a career built on her own abjection. But Page's comments remind me of something else: the attitude of a whole generation of entertainers who came to Hollywood or New York from small towns in middle America, propelled by their good looks, prepared to work hard and generally modest in their expectations of success. There were hundreds, maybe thousands, of such B-movie actors in the '40s and '50s. They never studied the Method, never thought of what they did as art, never figured on living like Hollywood royalty. They called their work show biz, and felt forever grateful that it was a biz at all, that they could actually be paid for playacting. (They tended to be rather dim when it came to managing money.) There was about performers like that—and about Bettie Page and some of her peers in the middlebrow cheesecake line—a common but sublime sincerity, an ability to laugh at themselves but not ironically, a disposition workmanlike and quietly exultant. Call it the dignity of silly work.

*   *   *

It is this sincerity, incidentally, that makes Bettie Page an unfit subject for an academic field such as cultural studies, which has produced so many admiring tomes on the likes of Madonna, Mae West and Larry Flynt. Some of the discipline's leading practitioners are certainly drawn to porn and its above-ground analogues (Calvin Klein ads, Victoria's Secret catalogs, Spice Girls videos). There is Laura Kipnis, an associate professor in the Department of Radio-Television-Film at Northwestern University, who lionizes Flynt as a symbol of "Rabelaisian transgression" in her book *Bound and Gagged: Pornography and the Politics of Fantasy in America;* and there is Constance Penley, who teaches a class on dirty movies at U.C. Santa Barbara and has written an essay called "Crackers and Whackers: The White Trashing of Porn." For Kipnis and Penley and their ilk, self-described feminists who argue earnestly for the "transgressive" and "subversive" qualities of, say, *Hustler* magazine, an interest in salacious pictures must always be justified in (leftish) political terms. As Kipnis writes, in the introduction to *Bound and Gagged,* pornography poses "a number of philosophical questions . . . questions concerning the social compact and the price of repression . . . questions about how sexuality and gender roles are performed, about class, aesthetics, utopia, rebellion, power, desire, and commodification. . . . [Porn] speaks to its audience because it's thoroughly astute about who we are underneath the social veneer, astute about the costs of cultural conformity and the discontent at the core of routinized lives and normative sexuality." For all their assurances that they are really wild women, capable of slinging obscenities and laughing at gross-out jokes, there is something priggish about the work of these professors, and its insistence that there is far, far more to porn than getting off. They're like middle-class radicals swilling Pabst Blue Ribbon not because they like it, but because it's what the proles drink.

Anyway, Bettie Page is a little too sunny, a little too close to the philistine ideal of sex, for the cultural studies types. Unlike Mae West, she's not offering a vision of femininity so exaggerated that it verges on parody or transvestism. She's a more regular fantasy. Strictly speaking, she's not even a fantasy. Who in his right mind would try to seduce *her?* And what women tend to like about her—many of her fans are women—is her ease in her body, the sense that she conveys of having made sex her ally.

One reason that Bettie Page may have managed to look as blithe as she does in so many of her photographs is that when she posed she was often surrounded by women. And they weren't just models, but photographers, too. Indeed, one of the surprising aspects of the pin-up world in those days—surprising given what we think we know about sex roles in the 1950s and what we think we know about the "male" gaze—is the extent to which it was populated, even dominated, by women. Hardworking Paula Klaw not only trussed and tied the models on bondage shoots, she also took many of the pictures. There were female photographers in the camera clubs, who helped create what Bettie called "the homey atmosphere" on the shoots. And Bettie worked frequently with the pin-up photographer Bunny Yeager, who had herself been a model, and who considered her empathy with her subjects one of her greatest assets. (Yeager produced one of the few genuinely witty pictures of Bettie, and it's kind of a girl joke: Bettie posing stark naked, but with the accoutrements of lady-like femininity—elegant pocketbook, tearoom hat, pursed lips, finishing school posture.)

Ironically, if Bettie Page had seemed more estranged from her body, able to speak of it (or at least treat it) as though it were a commodity, she might be of greater interest to the cultural studies crowd. Jayne Mansfield, the creamhorn with the grand tetons, always knew exactly how much her endowment was worth. And in talking about it, she sometimes sounded a note of sophisticated alienation that cultural studies scholars might find sufficiently subversive. "I have a ridiculous body. My waist is practically invisible, and my bust is floundering around somewhere in the 40s," Mansfield once said. "And there's no point in discussing the rest. It's a wild body, and I'm just sick of it for being so unusual. . . . The only good thing about it is that

it's a commercial body. . . . It got me where I am." But Bettie
Page never had the pontoon-like breasts that, in the age before
plastic surgery created bazongas for the masses, seemed to grant
their owners the status of freakish high-priestesses in a mam-
mary cult. Pin-up stars such as June Wilkinson ("The Bosom")
or Meg Myles ("Miss Chest 1957") or Jayne Mansfield (whose
studio chair on the Warner Brothers' lot bore the figures 40–21–
35½ in lieu of her name) could not escape their breasts. They
were their breasts. The more moderately endowed Bettie had
the possibility—the luxury, you might say—of seeing her own
body whole.

The Bettie Page photographs, like all pin-ups, are incitements, but not only to sex. They are incitements also to nostalgia. I look at her pictures and I wonder what it was like to be a
young woman on one's own in the city, one of those single girls
who came to New York in the 1950s and early '60s hoping to
escape their allotted destinies as young wives, young mothers
and young suburbanites. In Essex and Swanson's book, there is
a scrapbook photo of Bettie and her sister Goldie as teenagers
that is like a prehistory, in miniature, of that migration. The year
is 1941, and Bettie and Goldie are in their backyard in Nashville, pretending to be Ziegfeld girls. Everything in the background of the picture—the smudgy clouds, the drooping telephone wires, the clapboard house, the overgrown garden—
seems to suggest Home. And everything in the girls' stance—
the way they've twitched up their floral wrappers to show off
their pretty legs, the expressions they've adopted, self-consciously sexy and wistful at the same time—suggests the yearning to leave Home. In a way, all the pictures that came later, all
the pin-ups of Bettie in torpedo bras, fishnet stockings, harem-
girl outfits, polka-dot bikinis or nothing at all, are the record of
what happened to that yearning, that electric hankering to be
someone new somewhere else.

Bettie Page's particular cohort of city girls was mostly
working class. They headed for New York or Chicago after the

war, hoping for a job in the expanding pink-collar sector—in some glamorous office tower with wedding cake trim, maybe. Scared girls, sexy girls, average girls; but a little bit braver. Girls with names like Gladys and Rita and Thelma. Girls who listened to Julie London and Peggy Lee records. Girls who lived in Brooklyn. Girls who went out with married men and took themselves to the Automat for Boston cream pie and black coffee. Girls with hennaed hair and pallid skin and bitten fingernails. Girls who wore tight skirts and cinch belts made of patent leather. Girls who might be played, in the movies, by Gloria Grahame or Jane Greer or Shelley Winters. Girls who left small towns where they could hardly breathe without causing a scandal. Girls with families that never knew just what to make of them. Girls who weren't really trying to carve out a new path to autonomy, just banking on a new rotation of guys to get loaded with on Saturday night, or a new view out the window. Girls who never gave a thought to their rights, except perhaps their right to fun.

A young woman's decision to transplant herself, alone, to the big city was a bold one in those days. She was defying generations of cautionary tales that told her the metropolis was a girl's undoing. The last great wave of female migration to the cities—the factory girls, the telegraph operators and the "typewriters" of the 1880s and '90s—had produced a vast storehouse of anxious reportage by muckraking journalists, urban reformers and social hygienists. In their critical account of it, the city was above all a place of display—of glittering shopwindows, cheap finery, racy theatrical entertainments. And to this kind of seduction, the thinking went, young women were particularly vulnerable. Department stores alone, warned Zola in *Au Bonheur des Dames,* "awakened in [their] flesh new desires," excited "the madness of fashion" to which eventually, fatally, they must succumb. "When a girl leaves her home at eighteen, she does one of two things," Dreiser wrote in *Sister Carrie,* which is, among other things, the apotheosis of these worries. "Either she falls into saving hands and becomes better, or she rapidly assumes

the cosmopolitan standard of virtue and becomes worse. . . .
The city has its cunning wiles, no less than the infinitely smaller
and more human tempter."

Bettie disappeared from the city in 1957. She missed the
pay-off. By the mid-1960s, the single girl in the city had herself
become fashionable. This new cohort had a manifesto (*Sex and
the Single Girl*), an anthem ("Downtown"), a tony fairy tale
(*Breakfast at Tiffany's*), and a television show ("That Girl"). It
included plenty of college graduates, shiny-haired Suzy Co-eds.
And it had numbers on its side: thousands of young, single
women were moving to the cities, expecting to meet a husband,
yes, but also to live on their own for a few years, to support
themselves (as secretaries, editorial assistants, models, stewardesses) and most scandalously of all, to have sex. After 1960,
these democratic adventuresses even had the Pill.

Magazines and newspapers took notice of single women,
and no longer seemed so worried about them. In 1961, an article in *Look* magazine—"Women without Men"—still described
them as an oddity, but not necessarily a source of social disrup-
tion. There were "signs everywhere that the unattached woman
feels she has the same right to a sexual life as a married
woman," the author reported, in tones of wonder. Held up for
befuddled scrutiny was a 19-year-old aspiring model from Cin-
cinnati who, even though she was "extremely pretty," blithely
asserted that "she wasn't ready for a husband yet and maybe
never would be." She worked as an usher at a theater and, in
her spare time, "walked around New York staring up at the
beautiful buildings and marveling that I'm here."

And just five years later *Look* was reporting on the single
life—"Young, Single, and a Stranger in New York"—as a certifi-
ably groovy phenomenon with any number of commercial possibilities (singles newspapers, bars, dating services). "The
habitat of the sophisticated single is the East Side, 50s through
80s, a vast honeycomb of new apartments, many of them with
just one bedroom." The Village was no longer chic; buildings
with a lot of stewardesses—"the single female"—were. Singles

parties had a "casual boy-meets-girl atmosphere . . . an exten-sion of informal campus attitudes." Nobody in this crowd was frenzied, or frantic—just fun, fun, fun. They were now part of a thriving singles "scene," which even a mainstream publication such as *Look* could portray as an acceptable antechamber to marriage, rather than a fundamental threat to the institution.

Bettie Page ran away to New York before the singles scene was chic. By Dreiserian standards, hers is a story of dissolution: the innocent girl with the heart-shaped face loses her soul to the fleshpots of Manhattan. Her own account of her life reads rather differently. For one thing, her youth in Nashville, where she was born in 1923, was not particularly innocent. Her father, Roy Page, was an itinerant mechanic and a lout, who molested Bettie when she was an adolescent, and bullied her mother. Bettie and her four brothers and sisters ended up in an orphan-age for a year, after her mother left Roy and couldn't support the kids. (Bettie used to entertain the other girls by mimicking the poses of movie stars and models in the fan magazines.) When she was 19, Bettie married a boy named Billy Neal, who had just been drafted into the army. He turned out to be a possessive type who accused her of acting "high and mighty" because she had graduated from teacher's college in Nashville.

Yet she was bright and venturesome, and seemed to thrive as long as she was on her own. When Billy was shipped out to the Pacific, she waited for him in San Francisco, where she modeled fur coats, won second prize (a $50 war bond) in a beauty contest judged by sailors, and got arrested for slugging a landlord who was mean to her sister. She worked in Nashville for the Office of Price Administration and in Port-au-Prince for an American couple who were selling off their mahogany busi-ness. And in 1947, now divorced, she decided to move to New York and try her hand at acting. The first job she snagged was as a secretary at the American Bread Company, but at least she was making her own way. Besides, it wasn't long before she had taken up with a handsome Peruvian student who taught her how to rhumba.

Her pin-up career was born one afternoon on the beach at

Coney Island, where she was discovered by an amateur photographer and New York City policeman named Jerry Tibbs. Tibbs put her in touch with some of the camera clubs, which were always on the lookout for young women willing to shed their clothes and their conventions. Tibbs was black, and many of the clubs were racially integrated, which made posing for them—especially if you were a white Southern woman in 1950—doubly risky. But Bettie Page seems to have been one of those holy idiots who don't so much transcend racial boundaries as never quite notice them.

From the beginning, she liked the work and was good at it. Once, when she was arrested for indecent exposure during a topless photo shoot near a highway, she pleaded not guilty, insisting, with some pride, that she "was not indecent and that the group was a legitimate camera club from New York City." She never dated the photographers, but she did pal around with them, teasing them about their predilections—"Oh, you and your lingerie"—that sort of thing. "From the first time I posed nude I wasn't embarrassed or anything," she told Essex and Swanson. And it certainly beat the clerical grind. "I never had any trouble getting a job back in those days," she says now. "But I didn't like sitting at a typewriter all day."

Even the story of her post pin-up life—she left New York and stopped modeling in 1957, when she was 34—is not exactly a story of renunciation, or creeping shame. In the '80s, as Page's cult status grew, so did the curiosity about what had ever become of her. Was she alive? Was she lonely? Was she married? Was she fat? Was she living in a trailer park or working at an Arby's? After all, plenty of other performers, some more gifted than she, had ended up poor, remorseful, dwelling furtively in the half-light of a vanished, minor fame, like so many low-rent Norma Desmonds. (There was, for example, the haute couture fashion model Dovima, of the elegant bones and the Givenchy gowns and the Avedon elephant photograph, who ended her days a few years ago as a hostess at a Two Guys Pizza in Florida.) Here and there, fans would claim that they had seen Bettie at a gun show, or slinging hash in a Texas diner. The mystery became her. Like Marilyn Monroe and James Dean, she was a '50s icon who had disappeared in her prime. But she hadn't died, as far as anyone knew. She had simply vanished.

When a reporter finally tracked Bettie Page down a few years ago, it turned out that she had not fallen into ruin. She had worked as a teacher, married a few times for love, gotten a Master's degree in English, traveled around. She had also gone to bible college and served as a counselor for the Billy Graham Crusades, but her newfound Christian beliefs had never convinced her that she had done anything wrong in her cheesecake years. She gives interviews now, but, to her credit in these days of epidemic exhibitionism, she won't appear on camera. She wants to be remembered as she was. There's nothing especially pathetic about her. She didn't end up as a parody of herself.

Some of Bettie Page's fans will tell you that the reason her photographs appeal to so many people today is that she was a woman more of our time than of hers, a sexual liberationist trapped in Ozzie-and-Harriet land. But in truth her pictures attract us precisely because they are so much of their time (erotically daring, but only within the context of the 1950s). Despite ourselves, we are nostalgic for a period that still retained a notion, and a realm, of the genuinely illicit—when sexually revealing photos were produced in dark corners and traded shyly, when porn skulked on the fringes, in a shadowland of desire. Now we have bondage motifs in our fashion advertising, and sex advice books that chirp about the dire effects of repression (and even reticence), and skin magazines that long ago won the battle to show pubic hair and are bored with it, and pop stars who do pseudo-serious picture books about their sexual fantasies, and chic writers who get big advances for books about their erotic humiliations, and regular people who go on talk shows to tell the world that they are foot fetishists or chronic masturbators or infantilists, and a computer network that can summon a pneumatic cyber-babe to your screen anytime you want her. In such a world, who could deny the power of a secret?

To look at these pictures, and others like them from the '50s and earlier, is to remember that there was a time when taking off your clothes was a potent gesture, when the mere fact of a naked woman, no matter how imperfect her body or coy her stance, could be thrilling. This is why almost all the old pin-ups have a kind of poignance. Most of them no longer arouse; the frontiers of the sexually explicit—the amount of flesh and of actual or simulated sex required to turn the viewer on—are always being pushed further. What was once erotic may now seem quaint or dumb. The Orientalist vamps of the 1910s and 1920s—Little Egypt ("See her dance the Hootchy-Kootchy. Anywhere else but in the ocean breezes of Coney Island she would be consumed by her own fire!") or the silent screen star Theda Bara (advertised as the woman who "Ruined 50 men, made 150 families suffer!")—look ridiculous now. Their faces are like masks, their bodies girded, gilded, unapproachable. Not only are they gone; so, too is the world in which they would have been found seductive. And the cycle moves ever more quickly. In her Gaultier bra, Madonna seems foolish and passé now. The anatomy never changes, but the body has a history.

Bettie Page still looks beautiful, and sexy too, but by today's standards even her bondage photographs are rather tame. Nobody is naked; nobody is pretending to have sex (or having it); there are no crotch shots. If we look closely at these pictures, we can still, barely, recover the feeling that they were scandalous. After all, when Irving Klaw was investigated by the Kefauver Commission, he was labeled "one of the largest distributors of obscene, lewd, and fetish photographs throughout the country by mail," a trafficker in "base emotions" and a contributor to juvenile delinquency.

In *Hardboiled America,* his elegant rumination on the fate of the pulp novel, Geoffrey O'Brien invokes the contemporary regard for '50s pulp writers such as Jim Thompson, who in their own day were commonly dismissed as cheap nihilists.

> What would once have been inconceivable was that Jim Thompson should seem, if not exactly a voice of reason, then at least a reassuring voice from down

home, a both-feet-on-the-ground messenger from a time and place where things looked just as cheap as they were. . . . If Thompson was supremely alienated, there had at least been a world for him to be alienated from. His industrial wastelands and hellish hotel rooms, his bus stations steeped in boredom and simmering disgust, represented some kind of geography, some minimal sense of location. He may have evoked it only to destroy it, but it had after all been there for him to destroy. His books spoke of a time when it was still unusual to feel the way his heroes felt, or at least to acknowledge the fact. It had become in retrospect a heroic period: gratuitous evil and affectless violence *meant* something back then.

The same could be said of the Bettie Page photographs. Finally they are tinged with pathos, since they are survivals of a time when fetishism and exhibitionism and ordinary sexual adventure really meant something, when their setting was the cheesy chiaroscuro world of roadside motels with linoleum floors and vinyl furniture, not the fake expensive world of fashion magazines and rock videos, a time before pseudoporn seeped into advertising and was made pleasant and normal. These images remind us what it was like when erotica was mostly hidden. There are many reasons to oppose repression, but in the universe of repression, one learned the twin arts of fantasy and mystery. Bettie Page always seemed so good when she was being so bad. It is a paradox made of distinctions that we have almost completely destroyed. Poor glutted smirking us. If we cannot be bad, how will we be good?

Norman Podhoretz

Lolita, My Mother-in-Law, the Marquis de Sade, and Larry Flynt

Not long ago, the Library of America put out a beautiful new three-volume edition of the novels and memoirs of Vladimir Nabokov,° and I decided to seize upon it as a convenient occasion for reacquainting myself with his work. Which explains why I happened to be reading *Lolita* on the very day a story by Nina Bernstein appeared on the front page of the *New York Times* that cast a horrifying new light on Nabokov's masterpiece. It also brought memories to the surface that had long been buried, and simultaneously forced me into rethinking a number of questions I had up till then considered fairly well resolved. As I was going through this difficult process, I was given a few more pushes by Milos Forman's movie, *The People vs. Larry Flynt,* and two recently published books, Roger Shattuck's *Forbidden Knowledge*°° and Rochelle Gurstein's *The Repeal of Reticence.*† By the time I was through, my peace of mind had been so

° Edited by Brian Boyd. Vol. I, *Novels and Memoirs 1941–1951,* 710 pp.; Vol. II, *Novels 1955–1962,* 904 pp.; Vol. III, *Novels 1969–1974,* 825 pp.; $35.00 each volume.
°° St. Martin's, 369 pp. $26.95. Reviewed by J. Bottum in Commentary, December 1996.
† Hill and Wang, 357 pp., $27.50.

disturbed that I was left wishing that those old memories and those settled questions had been allowed to remain in their contentedly slumberous state.

Nina Bernstein's story concerned the unearthing of a list of thousands of children "whose names were secretly compiled, annotated, and stored with a cache of child pornography on a computer used by a convicted pedophile in a Minnesota state prison" just north of Minneapolis. Minneapolis! The mere mention of it in this lurid context prodded the first of those long inert memories back to life. It featured my late mother-in-law, Rose Rosenthal, who in a sociologically unusual wrinkle of American Jewish history was born almost exactly a century ago in Minneapolis's "twin city," St. Paul, and lived there until her death in 1972.

A loyal Jew and a fierce Zionist, Rose Rosenthal was in all other respects so typical a Midwesterner that a character modeled on her would have been entirely at home in one of the novels of her fellow Minnesotan, Sinclair Lewis. Before meeting her, I had thought I understood—precisely from reading Lewis and many others—what the word "bourgeois" meant, but I soon began to realize that I had never known the half of it. After all, where would I—born and bred in a Brooklyn slum in the 1930's and then moving in the years after World War II from college and graduate school into the milieu of the New York intellectuals—ever have had a chance to encounter a true member of that much-derided species in the flesh?

Obviously I had run into many middle-class people, but such a battering had the "bourgeois" world view taken over the past several decades that they had either given up on it themselves or had lost the nerve to exhibit any of the traditional stigmata of their moral and cultural background. None of them, for example, would have risked appearing so unsophisticated as to condemn a movie star like Ingrid Bergman for flaunting an adulterous affair and then bearing a child out of wedlock. But my mother-in-law did, loudly, and with total confidence in the rightness of her judgment.

Intransigently provincial as she was, the only moral standards she recognized as valid were the rigidly puritanical standards prevailing in the St. Paul of her day. Any violations of those standards outraged her, and the more they were violated by the outside world, the more she felt confirmed in her commitment to them. So far as she was concerned, the rest of the country, and especially New York, was going to hell, while St. Paul, and the Midwest generally, remained an enclave of goodness and purity and rectitude. But surely, I would protest, the things that appalled her must be happening out there, too. "No," she would reply with a stubborn set of the jaw, "not in our part of the country."

Not in our part of the country: it was those words that started ringing in my head as I read the *Times* story about the inmate with "multiple convictions for child sexual assault" sitting in the Lino Lakes Correctional Facility, just a stone's throw away from St. Paul. There, in that prison, this monster had free and easy access to a state-of-the art computer and a modem, and using that equipment he had compiled a huge data base mostly of little girls between three and twelve for circulation on the Internet to other pedophiles.

The names came not from the Internet itself but from local newspapers all over Minnesota, to which he also had free and easy access through exchange subscriptions with a prison newspaper (founded, in a piquant detail, by members of the Jesse James gang in 1887 and still going strong). By combing through birthday announcements and such features as "Citizens of Tomorrow," he was able not only to collect names for his data base but also to embellish it with many helpful pointers.

Thus, the *Times* reports, the children "appear by age and location . . . in dated entries that . . . include personal details written as 'latchkey kids,' 'speech difficulties,' 'cute,' and 'Little Ms. pageant winner.'" Even more to the point of my ancient argument with my mother-in-law:

The towns where the children live are alphabetized and coded by map coordinates, as though on a road

atlas to the American Midwest. Most are hamlets in
northern Minnesota, places born of the railroad in the
last century and bypassed by the highway in this one.

Not in our part of the country indeed.

To be sure, even in the late 1950's, when I first met her,
my mother-in-law was wrong and I was right about life in places
like St. Paul. Premarital sex, adultery, illegitimacy, homosexuality, and—yes—pedophilia were by no means entirely unknown
there. (In the year of her death, the very pedophile who would
later use a computer to locate potential victims did the same
thing with the more primitive tool of a notebook, and was
caught and then convicted for the first time after breaking into a
home in St. Paul itself.) Such goings on, however, were sufficiently rare, or anyway well enough hidden, so that a novel like
Peyton Place could create a huge sensation merely by revealing
their presence in small-town America.

This revelation, like so many others before it in the literature and polemics emanating from the higher reaches of American culture, carried the additional satisfaction of confirming the
charge of hypocrisy that invariably accompanied attacks on the
moral professions of the middle class. But those who so loved to
yell "hypocrite" at the bourgeoisie always seemed to forget that
hypocrisy, being "the tribute vice pays to virtue," testifies to the
commanding power of the standards being violated, not to their
weakness or fraudulence.

As for my mother-in-law, I would bet my life that she was
no hypocrite and that she practiced what she preached. But she
was without any question a great denier, who simply refused to
see what she did not wish to see or to know what she did not
wish to know. In thus adopting what amounted to a private form
of censorship, she withheld even de-facto recognition from anyone or anything that disrupted or challenged the moral order in
which she believed with all her heart.

There were millions upon millions like her in America,
and their practice of private censorship was mirrored and rein-

forced by the law. And if this dual system did not work well enough to wall off their "part of the country" entirely from the "bad examples" being set by my part of the country, it did afford at least some measure of protection. Certainly it is hard to imagine the Minnesota of my mother-in-law's day becoming, of all things, the center of a network of child molesters.

Those walls, wherever they were built in America, have all long since been blasted to smithereens, as I first realized when, on a visit to Salt Lake City in the early 1970's, I discovered pornographic books and magazines being sold openly in a drugstore right across the street from the Mormon Temple. It amazed me that even a city dominated by Mormons had given up trying to defend itself against the tidal wave of pornography which had followed in the wake of a series of increasingly liberal court decisions. True, those decisions had still left a bit of room for restrictive local ordinances, but it had evidently become too troublesome and too expensive for local prosecutors to take advantage of them. For all practical purposes, then, the fight against censorship had already been won.

As a young literary critic and as an editor, I had taken part in that fight. It was not a very large part, consisting only in the writing and publishing of a few articles, the delivering of a few lectures, and on one occasion the giving of testimony in an obscenity trial. But this brings me to another cluster of long-dormant memories that rereading *Lolita* in conjunction with Nina Bernstein's story in the *Times* has prodded back to life.

One of these is of a talk I gave in defense of pornography at Bard College in the late 50's. In those days I never lectured from a prepared text and the notes on which I relied have gone the way of all notes, so that now, after nearly 40 years, I am a bit hazy as to what exactly I said. But as best as I can reconstruct it, the case I made in defense of pornography began with a literary analysis. Conceding that the purpose of pornography was to arouse lust, I argued that there was no reason why this should be considered any less legitimate than the arousal of such other emotions and passions as anger, sorrow, pity, and so on. Like any other literary genre, pornography could be well written or badly written, and the appeal to lustful thoughts and impulses could be artfully managed or unskillfully and crudely done.

I believe I then went on to claim that, aesthetic considerations apart, pornography had a value all its own. It represented a kind of utopian fantasy of pure sex, sex liberated from consequence and into unalloyed ecstasy ("pornotopia," as my old college friend, Steven Marcus of Columbia, would later call it in a book on pornography in the Victorian era). And this fantasy demanded and deserved recognition for the role it played in attacking—I cringe at the thought that such words ever came out of my mouth, even when I was young—the stifling proprieties and unhealthy repressions of bourgeois society.

The students in the audience at Bard (a "progressive" college, and as such already in tune with the spirit of the 60's to come) loved it. They applauded wildly when I was through, and their questions in the discussion period were all requests for more of the same. But then Professor Heinrich Blücher, whom I knew slightly through his wife Hannah Arendt, raised his hand. Though overshadowed by her growing fame as a political philosopher, this obscure German scholar was rumored to be working on a (never-to-be-completed) monumental History of Everything that would put her work to shame; and Hannah herself had told me more than once that he possessed one of the great minds of our age. With this reputation adding to the fearsomeness of his aristocratic Prussian bearing, he jumped to his feet and shouted at the top of his lungs in the heaviest possible German accent, "You are taking all the *fun* out of sex!"

I needed a small pause to shake off this stinging left hook, but after a second or two I recovered myself enough to counterpunch with the insistence that it was not necessary for sex to remain hidden in order to be fun. "But," he shot—or rather shouted—back, "don't you know that pornography soon becomes *boring?*" To this I replied that I knew no such thing, and that I was hard put to take people at face value who said they were bored by pornography. Embarrassed, yes; ashamed, yes; repelled, yes; disgusted, yes; but the claim of boredom seemed to me an affectation of superiority to something which only a saint could be superior to.

I now realize that Heinrich Blücher, who had probably grown sated with pornography as a young man steeped in the sexually unbridled culture of Weimar Germany, knew what he was talking about. But unlike the America of today—which has exceeded even Weimar in sexual license and licentiousness, and where pornography can be piped into any home at the click of a mouse or the flick of a television remote or the activation of a VCR°—in the America of the 50's there was still very little of it around. In the world in which I lived, it was easy enough to borrow copies of *Fanny Hill* or the novels of Henry Miller or a few other equally classy pornographic books that had been smuggled in from Paris by friends. But in general, getting hold of pornography was like trying to buy illegal drugs. One had to have a "connection," and one had to venture into seedy and possibly dangerous places to "score."

As it happened, I had such a connection in the unlikely person of an uncle of mine who was more like an older brother to me than an uncle. Unlike *his* brothers, who included my father and who all acted as if there was no such thing as sex, he made no bones about his obsession with it. But so far as I could tell, he indulged this obsession exclusively through the consumption of pornography. (That *acting* on it was not for him was something he discovered to his eternal regret when a friend told him that in order to participate in an orgy, he would have to do certain things that he did not think he could bring himself to do. "But can't I just do what I want?" he asked plaintively. "No," said his friend. "If you want to be a pervert, you have to act like a pervert.")

It was thanks to my uncle that I had seen a pornographic

° In 1996, according to a recent survey in *U.S. News & World Report*, the number of hard-core video rentals in this country reached a total of 665 million, almost all of them from "mom and pop video stores." Americans also spent an additional $150 million bringing "adult" films into their homes on pay-per-view TV, and yet another $175 million "to view porn in their rooms at major hotel chains such as Sheraton, Hilton, Hyatt, and Holiday Inn."

film starring a young woman named Candy Barr (a model who was reputed to be the "moll" of a famous gangster). The film was very short, hardly more than a five-minute clip, but the great beauty of the star and the apparent enthusiasm with which she performed had made it a classic and a collector's item among connoisseurs of hard-core pornography. They were right: even in a very bad print projected by a primitive camera onto a portable roll-down screen that resembled a cheap window shade, it was overwhelming—more so even than the few pornographic books I had read by then, and they were quite overwhelming enough.

Because I had actually seen a pornographic film, I was the envy of my circle, very few of whom had ever had this kind of first-hand experience (not that it stopped them from theorizing endlessly on the subject). And as the only one with a connection, I was under constant pressure to arrange a showing for them. At last I agreed, only to discover that my uncle's supplier had been arrested, and that he himself was very reluctant (justifiably, as it would turn out) to let his precious copy of the Candy Barr clip out of his hands. But when I explained that a group of distinguished writers and critics was eager to see the movie, he gave in out of deference to "educated people" whose readiness to lower themselves to his level simultaneously puzzled and pleased him.

The great event was scheduled for a party at the home of another old college friend, Jason Epstein, then a rising young book editor who would subsequently be active in the ultimately successful campaign to find an American publisher for *Lolita;* and among the many writers and critics who did indeed turn up was Susan Sontag, who would later deliver herself of a famously solemn essay in defense of pornography. By the time I arrived directly from Brooklyn with Candy Barr in the can and my uncle's projector and screen under my arm, the excitement, punctuated by many jokes, was intense. But the biggest and best joke of all was to come. First it emerged that not a single one of these "educated people" knew how to work a projector, and then the person who volunteered to try succeeded only in tangling the film and finally burning it in the heat of the projector's lamp. The sickening smell of smoldering celluloid pervaded the room, and when I thought of confronting my uncle, it sickened me even more. Everyone else was either deeply disappointed or convulsed with laughter at the fiasco which seemed to have a message hidden in it somewhere.

Not long afterward, I agreed to join another (though somewhat overlapping) group of distinguished writers and crit- ics in traveling to Provincetown, Massachusetts, to testify on behalf of a local bookseller. For stocking a novel by Hubert Selby, Jr. entitled *Last Exit to Brooklyn,* which was notorious for the graphic description it contained of a gang rape, this book- seller had been put on trial for violating the local law against the dissemination of obscene materials. But since the Supreme Court had exempted any work that, taken as a whole, possessed literary value, the defense in such cases usually consisted in summoning expert witnesses to grant the necessary certification.

I did not much like or admire Selby's unrelievedly grim novel, but there was no doubt that it was a serious piece of work by a talented writer. Hence I had no problem with testifying as to its literary merit when I was put on the stand. But then the judge, a local magistrate who had been scowling at all these interlopers from New York throughout the presentation of the case for the defense and who seemed to take an especially sour view of my testimony, suddenly decided to cross-examine me himself. "Do you have any children?" he demanded. "Yes," I said. "Any of them girls?" "Three," I replied. He grinned malev- olently. "Well, how would you like it if they read books like this?" The question took me by surprise, and I hesitated for a few seconds before coming up with an answer. "Your honor, there are hundreds and hundreds of books in my apartment. I don't forbid my daughters to read any of them, and I don't keep track of the ones they do." To which his honor snorted: "I'll bet."

Strictly speaking, I was telling the truth, but it was not the whole truth and nothing but the truth, given that the few specimens of hard-core pornography I owned were deliberately kept out of the reach of our kids by being placed on the top shelf of a very tall bookcase. Like Heinrich Blücher's charge that I was taking the fun out of sex, the judge's sarcastic remark stayed with me. Whenever I told the story, I would mock him with Menckenesque gusto, and so would my audience. But that "I'll bet" must have given me my first inkling that hypocrisy in these matters was no longer a monopoly of Mencken's "booboisie."

Though the pornographic books I kept up on that high shelf were all of the literate variety usually known as "erotica," they were still hard-core in the sense that their whole point was to provide highly explicit descriptions of sexual activity. To the extent that they made use of genuinely novelistic elements like a plot and carefully drawn characters, the purpose was to set off and heighten the impact of the dirty passages. (And "dirty" was the word that I and every other fighter for the legalization of pornography used in the privacy of our own minds, and indeed everywhere else except in a courtroom or when the politics of the issue required us to mouth the standard liberal pieties.) But a few other books that were not in the least pornographic in that sense were also up on that top shelf, and among them was the original edition of *Lolita,* published in Paris in 1955.

Nabokov had sent the manuscript to Paris with some re-luctance and only after numerous rejections had convinced him that he would never find an American publisher for it.* One of those rejections had come from Doubleday, where the fierce battle being waged for its acceptance by Jason Epstein had foundered on his superiors' quite reasonable fear of prosecu-tion. At any rate, it was from Epstein that I first heard of *Lolita,* and it was from him, if I remember rightly, that I got my copy of the cheaply bound and printed edition put out by the Olympia Press, a young company that specialized in erotica written, as *Lolita* was, in English.

English was not exactly a foreign language to Nabokov—

---

* He finally did in 1958, when Putnam put out the first American edition.

he had learned it as a child in czarist Russia from governesses and tutors—but it was still not his own in the way his beloved native Russian was. In fact, before venturing in his forties on a novel in English, he had already written many volumes both of fiction and poetry in Russian (most of them published in Europe after he had been driven into exile by the Bolshevik Revolution). And although he was not the only writer ever to have pulled off this trick of switching to English from a radically different native tongue, he outdid even his closest rival, the great Joseph Conrad, in his amazing mastery of the new language. More: in my judgment, to which I still hold today, he could even give James Joyce, born to English and its most spectacular contemporary virtuoso, a close run for his money.

But as I have now come to understand on rereading Nabokov in the new Library of America edition, there was something less admirable that went along with his linguistic genius and that he also had in common with Joyce: a contempt for his audience. I realize this is a very harsh charge, but how else can one honestly describe the attitude implicit in a style so in love with itself that it often loses sight of what it is supposed to be conveying, and so aesthetically narcissistic that it intransigently refuses to make any concessions whatsoever to the reader, even to the point of often requiring an editor's footnotes to decipher the pyrotechnical wordplay in which it so mischievously indulges?

Discussing this very issue in the course of deigning to engage in the "fatal fatuity" of explicating a series of such allusions, Nabokov was unusually frank about it. "It may be asked if it is really worth an author's while to devise and distribute these delicate markers whose very nature requires that they be not too conspicuous." Who, after all, will notice them or, having noticed, will be able to make sense of them without the help of footnotes? No matter. "In the long run, . . . it is only the author's private satisfaction that counts."

Far from being peculiar to Nabokov and Joyce, this attitude was shared by practically every novelist and poet associated with the modernist movement. In a manifesto issued in Paris in

1926, for instance, a large group of writers declared, among other things, that "The writer expresses. He does not communicate," and ended with "The plain reader be damned." It must further be acknowledged that in arrogant authorial indifference to the reasonable expectations of the reader, "plain" or fancy, Nabokov was a mild sinner when set alongside Joyce. Asked how he expected anyone to understand *Finnegans Wake*, Joyce once replied: "The demand that I make of my reader is that he should devote his whole life to reading my works." Nabokov never went that far either in theory or in practice (he admired *Ulysses* but not *Finnegans Wake*). Still, as a relentless player of what the editor of the Library of America edition calls "intricate games of deception and concealment" (meaning this, in accordance with good modernist doctrine, as a compliment), a sinner he was nevertheless.

Here *Lolita* is an exception among Nabokov's novels. It is relatively easy to follow, and the linguistic pyrotechnics, while still on display, are kept under unusually strict control. Yet if *Lolita* is more or less free of this species of modernist sin, it is just as driven as Nabokov's other novels by the radical modernist aestheticism of which their "intricate games of deception" and their stylistic excesses are only one symptom or expression. This kind of aestheticism was once summed up in the slogan "art for art's sake," which was to say, *not* for the sake of God or morality or ideology or society. Often for better (as a protection against the dictates of politics) and sometimes for worse (as an encouragement to mandarinism and hermeticism), the aestheticist creed thus represented a declaration of the artist's independence from any and all obligations other than those imposed by the laws of his art.

No more fanatical devotee of this creed existed than Vladimir Nabokov. There were only two things he cared about as a writer. One was capturing the exact feel and color and shading and texture of a perception or an emotion or a memory, and the other was fooling around with language for the sheer fun of exercising his enormous power over it. The subject matter of a novel was of little importance to him except as an occasion—I might almost say a pretext—for doing these things. Here is how he himself put it:

> For me a work of fiction exists only insofar as it affords me what I shall bluntly call aesthetic bliss, that is a sense of being somehow, somewhere, connected with other states of being where art (curiosity, tenderness, kindness, ecstasy) is the norm. . . . All the rest is either topical trash or what some call the Literature of Ideas. . . .

Whenever he could, Nabokov made sure to disabuse anyone who might be led by the subject matter of his own work to misinterpret it (even sympathetically) as belonging to either of those dread categories. A good example of how he did this was the introduction he provided to a later reissue of *Bend Sinister,* one of his earliest novels in English.

Set in a fictional country that has fallen under totalitarianism, and written by a man who had fled the Soviet regime and clearly hated it with all his heart, *Bend Sinister* was in danger of being taken by the innocent "plain reader" to be about Soviet Russia, much as George Orwell's roughly contemporaneous *Animal Farm* and *Nineteen Eighty-Four* were. But Nabokov repudiated any such reference. *Bend Sinister,* he insisted, had no kinship whatever with "Orwell's clichés" (which he clearly consigned to the category of "topical trash"):

> I have never been interested in what is called the literature of social comment. . . . I am neither a didacticist nor an allegorizer. Politics and economics, atomic bombs, primitive and abstract art forms, the entire Orient, symptoms of "thaw" in Soviet Russia, the Future of Mankind, and so on, leave me supremely indifferent. . . . Similarly, the influence of my epoch on *[Bend Sinister]* is as negligible as the influence of my books, or at least of this book, on my epoch.

In short, despite being interlarded "with bits of Lenin's speeches, and a chunk of the Soviet constitution, and gobs of Nazist pseudo-efficiency," *Bend Sinister* was "not really about life and death in a grotesque police state." Its main theme was the love of a father for his son, and what mattered most in it was certain recurrent images, such as a puddle that appeared at the very beginning and then reappeared at various points later on as an ink blot, an ink stain, spilled milk, and several other similarly interesting mutations.

As with politics, so with morality. *"Lolita,"* Nabokov declared of this novel about a pedophile (Humbert Humbert) who seduces his twelve-year-old stepdaughter (Lolita) and continues forcing himself on her until she runs away, "has no moral in tow." Indeed, those "gentle souls who would pronounce *Lolita* meaningless because it does not teach them anything" are more right than they know. For "the nerves of the novel, . . . the secret points, the subliminal coordinates by means of which the book is plotted" and through which it affords the discerning reader the "aesthetic bliss" whose achievement is the only purpose for which it exists, are not located in the story of a pedophile and his victim, let alone in any lessons that might flow from it. They lie, rather, in

> such images as Mr. Taxovich, or that class list of Ramsdale School, or Charlotte saying "waterproof," or Lolita in slow motion advancing toward Humbert's gifts, or the pictures decorating the stylized garret of Gaston Godin, or the Kasbeam barber . . . , or Lolita playing tennis, or the hospital at Elphinstone, or pale, pregnant, beloved, irretrievable Dolly Schiller dying in Gray Star (the capital town of the book), or the tinkling sounds of the valley town coming up the mountain trail. . . .

Now, Nabokov was undoubtedly right when he then proceeded to deny that *Lolita* was a work of pornography. While it did, in his words, "contain various allusions to the physiological urges of a pervert," it did not contain obscene language or explicit descriptions of sexual activity. The problem, then, as Nabokov recognized, was not with his treatment of the theme, but with the theme itself. It was, he wrote, one of three "which are utterly taboo as far as most American publishers are concerned," the other two being a successful interracial marriage and an "atheist who lives a happy and useful life, and dies in his sleep at the age of 106."

Yet here, for once, the snobbish sarcasm to which Nabokov was always given outraced his immense intelligence and trumped his normal passion for precision, since the other two themes were not remotely in the same class of the forbidden as the idea of adults molesting children. Nor did they inspire the same kind or degree of horror, assuming they even inspired it at all outside of certain restricted social circles. Hence in telling the story it told, *Lolita* was admitting something truly forbidden into public consciousness, and by doing so it was—whether Nabokov liked it or not—insidiously seducing its readers into "thinking about the unthinkable."

I have borrowed that phrase from the debates over nuclear war which were being conducted around the same time *Lolita* came out in an American edition. It was charged then that strategists like Herman Kahn who speculated about the waging of nuclear war were breaking the taboo against it and thereby making it more likely to happen. Could an analogous charge be lodged against Nabokov's novel about a pedophile? In the case of Kahn and the others, they defended themselves by saying that, on the contrary, they were making nuclear war less likely by teaching us how better to deter it. But no such defense was available to Nabokov. By his own account, he was not trying to teach us anything one way or the other about pedophilia. And while he did not hesitate to label pedophilia a perversion, the way he treated it was emphatically not calculated to deepen our horror over it. Just the opposite. And herein lies a paradox.

Because, as D. H. Lawrence said, the point of pornography is to "do dirt on sex," and because it also depends for its on the feeling that sex is dirty, a straightforwardly pornographic treatment of pedophilia would inevitably retain the sense of it as a taboo and would play on the horror attached to violating it. Not so with Nabokov. The very brilliance of his language, the very sharpness of his wit, the very artfulness of his treatment all help to shatter the taboo and thereby to rob pedophilia of its horror. In other words, in aestheticizing the hideous, Nabokov—as I can now clearly see—comes very close to prettifying it.

Worse yet, he comes very close to excusing it. Reviewing the first American edition of *Lolita* in 1958, my old teacher and mentor, Lionel Trilling, began with an acknowledgment of how shocking the book was, but then added:

> And we find ourselves the more shocked when we realize that, in the course of reading the novel, we have come virtually to condone the violation it presents, . . . to see the situation as less and less abstract and moral and horrible, and more and more as human and "understandable." Less and less, indeed, do we see a *situation;* what we become aware of is people. Humbert is perfectly willing to say that he is a monster; no doubt he is, but we find ourselves less and less eager to say so.

It is important to understand that Trilling was saying this not to bury *Lolita* but to praise it for fulfilling what he considered one of the primary *moral* duties of the novel, which was to deepen the reader's sense of the complexity of life. On this point I agreed enthusiastically, but I was also less ambivalent than Trilling about the smashing of taboos, from which—as it seemed to me at that age and at that time—only good could come.

Be that as it may, the sort of effect Trilling described never happens in reading pornography. There are no people to understand in pornography; there is only a succession of graphically represented sexual acts performed by faceless creatures who are driven by lust and nothing but lust. This may arouse the reader's own lustful urges, but at least it can be said that pornography never plunges him into a state of moral confusion—not even on those rare occasions when it tries to do just that.

The most notorious instance of a pornographer trying to sow moral confusion is to be found in the 18th century and in the person of the Marquis de Sade. "Evil, be thou my good," declares Satan in *Paradise Lost,* and Sade set out to follow that invocation into regions that would have been way beyond John Milton's most lurid antinomian imaginings. For this, Sade's books were banned in his own time. But in ours he has come to be hailed as a great writer, a great philosopher, and a great moralist—the "Divine Marquis," as his countryman, the early-20th-century avant-garde poet Guillaume Apollinaire, called him.

I was reminded of all this by the appearance of Roger Shattuck's *Forbidden Knowledge,* which spends many pages refuting the case for the rehabilitation and canonization of Sade. Shattuck does a very good job of it, but as I went through those learned and carefully nuanced pages with their earnest and respectful analyses of the arguments advanced by the (mostly French) intellectuals to whom Sade's work resembles (as one of them actually put it) "the sacred books of the great religions," I could not help thinking—again—of Orwell, and specifically of what he once said about certain obviously ridiculous ideas: "One has to belong to the intelligentsia to believe things like that; no ordinary man could be such a fool."

If Shattuck had been addressing the ordinary man, he could have won his case simply by juxtaposing the claims made by admirers of the "Divine Marquis" with the samples of Sade's own writings he quotes in *Forbidden Knowledge.* So disgusting are those writings that even today, when anything goes, it is daring of Shattuck to quote them, and even then he (or his publisher) must have thought it the better part of prudence to print a notice at the head of the book warning parents and teachers of material to come that is "inappropriate for children and minors," and still another notice in the chapter on Sade flagging "passages that many people will consider offensive and obscene in the extreme." Why then use them? Here is Shattuck's justification:

> Most writings on Sade and even some anthologies avoid such explicitness and limit their quotations to philosophical discussions of crime, passion, nature, freedom, and the like. To bowdlerize Sade in this fashion distorts him beyond recognition. The actions described in his works directly complement the ideas and probably surpass them in psychological impact.

Except for that "probably"—"most assuredly" or "infinitely" would have been more accurate—this is excellent, and it brings to mind the first time I finally read Sade himself after having read a number of the critics taken on by Shattuck. Encountering Sade in the flesh, so to speak, I was almost as shocked by the mendacity of those critics as by what I found in his books.

First of all, none of them had made clear that for Sade the supreme sexual act is buggery, both of men and of women, but of the latter mainly as an expression of revulsion for the female sexual organs so great that he could imagine—and actually describe with great relish—sewing them up. Though he does include plenty of the whipping and other forms of torture that have come to be associated with his name, buggery is by so wide a margin his favorite sexual activity that the term "sadist" might more precisely have been used as a synonym for sodomite.

I confess that I do not understand why the commentators I read some 35 or 40 years ago on Sade, who exalted him for his "unfaltering demand for the truth" (Jean Paulhan) and for "daring to look [his dangerous fantasies] in the eye" (Georges Bataille), were so prissily reticent about the homosexual content of those fantasies. Perhaps in passing lightly over the connection in Sade between homosexuality and a loathing of women—who are represented as foul in themselves and foul too because they breed (Sade, as Shattuck points out, regarded "propagation of the species as contrary to nature")—his apologists were being protective of homosexuality.°

Another possibility is that Sade's admirers were being protective of *him*, fearing that to call attention to his homosexuality would limit his allegedly universal relevance and compromise their claim that his fantasies are directly relevant to everyone. If so, this would be of a piece with the general bowdlerizing about which Shattuck complains, and which was the second source of my astonishment when I first read Sade after having read some of his defenders. Just as they glided so lightly over Sade's homosexuality that I was amazed to discover how blatantly pervasive it was in his books, so they also failed to convey a sense of what Sade's pornographic scenes were actually like.

Like Shattuck, I believe that the only way to convey such a sense is through quotation and paraphrase, and I now mean to borrow from *Forbidden Knowledge* in doing so. Being less nervy than he is, however, I will for the most part reproduce not Sade's own language but only a small segment of one of Shattuck's summaries, from which in addition I will omit a few details. Of course, even in this slightly cleaned-up version, the passage remains utterly revolting:

> After a bizarre double wedding ceremony in drag among members of the same sex, . . . the sons are forced to bugger the father, who imitates the shrieking behavior of a young virgin. Whippings begin, blood flows, breasts are ripped off, limbs are broken and dislocated, and eyes are torn out while Noirceuil sodomizes the victims. . . . Brought to extreme arousal by the excruciating torture to death of two female victims, Noirceuil buggers one of his sons while

° I learn from Shattuck that some critics are now finally acknowledging that "the central Sadean doctrine is the primacy of the act of sodomy." Shattuck himself agrees about "the all-pervasiveness of sodomy in Sade's writings," but interestingly enough, both he and the critics he cites, while talking easily about "anal intercourse" and perfectly willing to call it "buggery," still shy away from identifying it as a largely homosexual practice.

literally eating the boy's heart, which has been torn out of his body by Juliette.

Noirceuil then violently rapes Juliette's seven-year-old daughter ("this disgusting product of the sacred balls of your abominable husband"), after which, with the mother's enthusiastic assent, he throws the child naked into the flames. Sade writes, in Juliette's voice:

> I help him with a poker to arrest her natural compulsive responses to save herself. . . . Others are diddling us and buggering us. Marianne is roasting. She is consumed. Noirceuil discharges. I do the same.

One must indeed "belong to the intelligentsia"—or perhaps the *French* intelligentsia—to see moral value and wisdom in the abstract lectures about freedom and nature with which Sade surrounds such scenes and for which they are supposed to serve as concrete illustrations.

What Roger Shattuck does in discussing Sade is precisely what the director Milos Forman lacks the honesty and/or the guts to do in *The People vs. Larry Flynt.* As I have already indicated, I caught this movie while I was rethinking the issue of pornography, and quite apart from turning out to be wildly overrated as a work of cinematic art, it nudged me in exactly the opposite direction from the one it wanted me to go.

Flynt is the publisher of a magazine called *Hustler* whose stock-in-trade has been vividly described by Bob Herbert in his column in the *New York Times:*

> A photo of a man driving a jackhammer into the vagina of a naked woman was captioned: "A simple cure for frigidity." One of the magazine's covers showed a disembodied woman's head in a gift box. . . . [Another feature] showed four photographs of women's bodies in various stages of mutilation. The photos are attached

to what appears to be charred human skin. Razor blades are scattered about. Nipples and what appear to be clitorises are attached to the skin with fishhooks and safety pins. Some of the women in the photos have been decapitated, or have lost limbs. A dead woman, naked, is shown lying beside a toilet.

Not that you would guess any of this from Forman's movie, any more than you would suspect that a Justice Department report once calculated that children were shown as sexual objects in *Hustler* on an average of fourteen times per issue.

No doubt out of fear that seeing what *Hustler* is really like would alienate the audience's sympathy for Flynt (not to mention the fear of losing money by bringing an X rating down on his head), Forman bowdlerizes his subject much as, *mutatis mutandis,* the defenders of Sade used to do. Thus he conveys the impression that *Hustler* is nothing more than a downmarket version of *Playboy,* a bit raunchier perhaps but also more given to prankish humor and satirical high-jinks. In fact, a piece of satirical high-jinks is precisely how the movie characterizes the notorious *Hustler* cartoon that showed the evangelist Jerry Falwell committing incest with his mother in an outhouse. It was this cartoon which led to the libel suit whose resolution in Flynt's favor by the Supreme Court forms the triumphant climax of the movie.

Forman's cheerleaders—compounding his dishonesty with their own—make a big point of insisting that he never "glorifies" or even "whitewashes" Flynt himself. Yet the plain fact is that through the omission or misrepresentation of many damaging details about Flynt's life and career,° he too is bowdlerized—into a high-spirited and mischievous good old boy, a mixture of Huck Finn and Abbie Hoffman. Not only does this likable rogue mean no harm; he is actually a courageous fighter for freedom—sexual freedom and freedom of the press—

° In the February 17 issue of the *Weekly Standard,* Matt Labash digs up a host of such details.

against the puritanical hypocrites who wish to suppress both. Furthermore, never is there so much as a faint hint that there might exist other kinds of people with other grounds for objecting to the open circulation of a magazine like *Hustler*.

Prominent among these missing people and perspectives are feminists like Catharine MacKinnon and Andrea Dworkin who regard pornography as degrading to women and who are for that reason no less eager than the Christian Right to censor it.° Now I happen to disagree with these feminists about heterosexual pornography in general. In my opinion, what the critic Louis Menand observes about the mass-market pornography which emerged into full public view in the late 60's and early 70's—namely, that it was based on the idea "that women enjoyed sex as much as men, and in the same way as men were imagined to enjoy it—that is, actively, promiscuously, and without guilt"—has always been true of heterosexual pornography. This idea may be "just another male fantasy," and it may be false to the sexual nature of women, but it cannot be said to degrade them. (Of course Dworkin and MacKinnon believe that normal heterosexual intercourse, which they regard as almost always indistinguishable from rape, is just as degrading to women as the pornography that describes it.)

Where *Hustler* is concerned, however, I think these feminists have a point. If there is a case of heterosexual pornography that truly does degrade women, it is *Hustler,* in whose eyes they are all filthy sluts who deserve to be brutalized. Flynt, a kind of straight subliterate Sade, also forges the same "association of sexual gratification with malevolence, pain, torture, and murder" that Shattuck identifies as the distinctive mark of the "Divine Marquis."

° If in making his movie Forman was unaware that such feminists exist, he discovered after its release how influential they could be. A piece on the op-ed page of the *New York Times* by Gloria Steinem attacking Forman for glorifying Flynt was credited with damaging the movie's commercial fortunes, and feminist ire was also blamed for the film's failure to be nominated for an Academy Award even though it had been praised to the skies by all the leading reviewers (including the conservative John Simon writing in *National Review*).

❊   ❊   ❊

There is also another opposing perspective whose existence is not acknowledged either by Milos Forman himself or by the admirers of his movie. Less visible for the moment than the feminist argument but intellectually far more formidable, it is represented by the two recent books I mentioned at the outset. The first, Roger Shattuck's *Forbidden Knowledge,* I have already touched on in discussing Sade (though it covers much more ground). The second, Rochelle Gurstein's *The Repeal of Reticence,* carries the rather unwieldy subtitle "A History of America's Cultural and Legal Struggles Over Free Speech, Obscenity, Sexual Liberation, and Modern Art." Both these books—neither, by the way, written by a conservative—raise troubling questions about the price we have paid for what I myself once applauded: the shattering of all taboos (Shattuck) and the dragging of everything that was once private into full public display (Gurstein).

The great service Shattuck and Gurstein perform is to remind us forcibly that there is more—a great deal more—to say about the legalization of pornography than is dreamed of in the philosophy of the writers and artists for whom unrestrained freedom of expression is the supreme value and civil libertarians for whom the discussion begins and ends with the First Amendment. Here Gurstein is especially relevant. Reaching back to the late-19th and early-20th centuries, she revisits the writings of the mostly forgotten members of the "party of reticence" (among them the once well-known essayist Agnes Repplier, Professor Charles Eliot Norton of Harvard, and William Trufant Forster, the President of Reed College), and shows how much stronger and more intellectually sophisticated their arguments were than almost anyone remembers today.

Those arguments pointed to the deleterious effects of pornography on the moral and cultural environment, on standards of taste and judgment, and on sexual life itself. But the "party of exposure" (whose members included practically every prominent young literary figure of the age, along with sexual reformers like Margaret Sanger and political radicals of every stripe) managed to banish all such considerations from the debate. It did this first through the relentless Menckenesque campaign of ridicule that stigmatized them as hopelessly bourgeois and retrograde, and then by dragging the issue into the courts where, one by one, the objections to pornography registered by the "party of reticence" were ruled out as irrelevant, leaving the narrowly legal question of a given individual's constitutional rights as the only one that mattered.

One could scarcely dream up a more perfect epitome of this process than *The People vs. Larry Flynt*. To Milos Forman (and most of the reviewers of his movie), The People are all joyless troglodytes who have nothing to say that is worth hearing. As for Larry Flynt, he may not be to everyone's taste but everyone's freedom is nevertheless so inextricably implicated in his that when he wins his fight against Jerry Falwell in the Supreme Court, the ultimate guardian of all rights, he becomes an American hero.

Yet not even so great a victory can allow us any rest: the enemy is still there, and the fight goes on. Thus in a fawning piece, Frank Rich (whose opinion of *The People vs. Larry Flynt* is at the opposite pole from that of his fellow *New York Times* columnist Bob Herbert) writes of Forman's great anxiety over "the growing power of American cultural commissars on the secular and religious Right." "I spent my most sensitive years in two totalitarian regimes," Forman (who was born and raised in Czechoslovakia) tells Rich. "The Nazis and Communists began by attacking pornography, homosexuals—it always starts very innocently."

Never mind that neither the Nazis nor the Communists "began" in this way. (The original paramilitary unit of the Nazi party, the SA, was filled with homosexuals, including its commander, while in the early days of Communist rule in Russia, "free love" was elevated over marriage and the avant-garde dominated the arts.) Never mind that comparing "the secular and religious Right" in America to Nazis and Communists is a vile insult. Never mind that if we do have "cultural commissars" in this country, they are the very critics and reviewers who have cheered Milos Forman and pronounced his movie a great work of art.

Never mind all that, and never mind too that until only yesterday (as Gurstein demonstrates), no one ever imagined that the freedom of speech guaranteed by the First Amendment extended to pornography. So far as Forman and his admirers are concerned, anyone who opposes the likes of Larry Flynt is still backward or wicked or both, and the corrupting effects of pornography on our society and on our culture (if indeed there are any) are still a small price to pay (if indeed a price it is) for our most precious freedom.

I never knew until I read Rochelle Gurstein that one of the original and most influential authors of this line of reasoning, the famous civil-liberties lawyer Morris Ernst, came to have second thoughts about its validity. As far back as 1970, Ernst admitted that he was repelled by the "present display of sex and sadism on the streets" and "sodomy on the stage or masturbation in the public area." Surely, Gurstein comments,

> his lifelong project had miscarried when purveyors of pornography could claim they were completing the movement begun by his own brilliant defense of *Ulysses,* where, as he put it, he had "legitimatized a four-letter word." "I deeply resent the idea . . . that the lowest common denominator, the most tawdry magazine, pandering for profit, to use the Supreme Court's word, should be able to compete in the marketplace with no constraints."*

Here, then, we have a third perspective whose existence goes unacknowledged by Forman's movie and its admirers.

---

* Ernst was not the only leader of the "party of exposure" who later developed second thoughts. Even Mencken did to some degree, and others like Walter Lippmann and Joseph Wood Krutch also came to feel as they grew older that the complete rout of "the party of reticence" had brought with it unforeseen and unfortunate consequences.

*   *   *

Of the many points emerging from these varied perspectives, there are two that have hit me with special force. The first is the emphasis placed by the "party of reticence" on pollution. This is a word we now use only about the physical environment, having forgotten that we also live in a moral and cultural environment that is equally vulnerable to contamination. We have forgotten too that our minds and spirits, no less than our lungs, can be damaged when the air they breathe is fouled by pollutants. If we are willing to place restrictions on the manufacturers of material goods in order to protect ourselves against pollution of the physical environment, why should we not be willing to take measures that would offer protection against pollution of the moral and cultural environment?

The second point that has hit me hard has to do with the effect of pornography on sex itself. In this connection, Rochelle Gurstein leans heavily on a phrase that comes from Milos Forman's countryman and contemporary, Milan Kundera, who used it as the title of one of his novels: "the unbearable lightness of being." This phrase has long been one of my own favorites because it so wonderfully defines what life is like when the burdens of responsibility and consequence are lifted from it. These burdens may seem intolerably heavy, but it is the lightness experienced in casting them off that is really unbearable. And this is what has happened to sex in our time.

Listen to the testimony of Katie Roiphe in her new book *Last Night in Paradise.** A liberated young woman who talks openly and even boastfully about her many affairs, Roiphe has begun to understand on her own pulses what the unbearable lightness of being means:

> We find ourselves living without the pain, reassurance,
> and clarity of late-19th-century social censure. We are
> on our own . . . yearning for consequences. Meaning.
> A tiny ruffling of the social order. If an act has serious

---

* Little, Brown, 208 pp., $21.95.

social ramifications, . . . then it appears to have transcendent meaning as well. It matters. It changes
things. . . . The end of consequences has created a
new moral universe in which events such as Anna
Karenina's adulterous affair can seem formless and
weightless.

It was, I recognize, the sexual revolution, not pornography,
that created this state of affairs, but pornography helped trigger
that revolution and, accompanying it every inch down the slippery slope, also played an autonomous part of its own. Heinrich
Blücher, all those years ago, accused me of taking the fun out of
sex by defending pornography, but he might better have charged
me with turning it into something weightless. For sex without
consequence of any kind is precisely what pornography sells: sex
that is cut loose from morality, from love, from pregnancy, from
marriage, from jealousy, from hurt. In this "pornotopian" world,
sex thus liberated brings unalloyed ecstasy. In the real world, it
brings the unbearable lightness of being.

And so it is that I have fallen to wondering uneasily
whether, if we wish to clean up our moral and spiritual environment and at the same time put at least some of the weight back
into sex, we should consider a restoration of censorship. Roger
Shattuck provides all the materials needed to construct a case
for doing just that, but he answers No to Simone de Beauvoir's
question, "Must We Burn Sade?" (and *a fortiori* less extreme
variants of pornography). Rochelle Gurstein, after providing a
complementary set of materials, ends with a sympathetic account of a book by Harry Clor which forthrightly advocates cen-
sorhip, but she herself falls short of a ringing endorsement of it.

Daring, then, as Shattuck and Gurstein are in trying to
promote a return of the now-repressed arguments for respecting taboos and banishing obscenity from the public square, they
are not quite daring enough to drop the other shoe. Neither, if
truth be told, am I. This is not, as I have already indicated,
because I think that censoring pornography is the first step on

the road to totalitarianism. And it is not because I buy the specious historical and legal contention that the First Amendment applies no less to pornography than to political speech. No, the reason I hesitate to come out for censorship is that I cannot conceive of government bureaucrats I would trust to do the censoring. In the past, such officials could detect no difference between the likes of D. H. Lawrence and the likes of Larry Flynt; it seems unlikely that their successors would be any more discriminating.

And yet, having acknowledged that, I also ask myself whether the banning of some genuinely good books would be too high a price to pay for getting rid of the poisons in the moral and cultural air we breathe. Once upon a time, when I was a devotee of the religion of art and a leftist to boot, the very question would have struck me as nothing short of blasphemous. But I ask it of myself today because it is no longer all that obvious to me that my mother-in-law, who certainly would not have been able to tell the difference between *Lolita* and Larry Flynt, was wrong in trying to protect her "part of the country" from both. If we cannot have *Lolita* without taking Larry Flynt, or for that matter the Marquis de Sade, maybe we should refuse the whole package deal.

But what about *Lolita* itself? Must we have *Lolita?* I ask myself this even more blasphemous question because I can no longer dismiss out of hand the possibility that *Lolita* bears at least some share of the blame for the plague of pedophilia that has been raging through this country and that has now hit my mother-in-law's home state with a special vengeance. By helping to make pedophilia thinkable, may not Nabokov have to some indeterminate extent been responsible for the greater toleration that gradually came to be accorded what had previously been regarded as perhaps the most horrible of all crimes?[*]

---

[*] *Lolita* has by now sold more than fourteen million copies, and a new film version will soon be released. It will star a first-time actress in her early teens named Dominique Swain (whose saucy photograph recently adorned the covers of both *Esquire* and *Vanity Fair*). Unlike the relatively tame version done by Stanley Kubrick in the early 60's, or indeed the novel itself, the new Lolita will feature

Thankfully, not all the horror has been drained out of pedophilia. Child molesters are still excoriated, and the fear of them is still great enough to generate outbreaks of hysteria in which innocent parents and teachers are falsely accused by little children at the prompting of overzealous prosecutors and by grown women with "recovered memories" planted by quack psychotherapists. (I suspect, incidentally, that the credence given to these outbreaks is the displaced and distorted product of an uneasy conscience. After all, with so many little children being guiltily left in day-care centers, it is no wonder that lurid imaginings should arise of the dangers to which they are being abandoned; and it is also no wonder that an escape from guilt should then be sought in the idea that children are as much at risk from their own fathers at home as they are from custodians in nursery school. Even then, there is no escape from the guilt everyone surely feels over doing so little in general to protect the children of this country from the moral poisons in the air.)

In any event, even when the accusations of child molestation are true, these monsters are either sent for "help," which is what usually seems to happen to fathers who have committed incest with a child, or imprisoned with shorter sentences than they deserve. (If it were up to me, they would either be executed or put away for life without possibility of parole, instead of being released after a few years with nothing to stop them from preying again but a sadly ineffective Megan's Law.)

Nabokov's own fictional pedophile, Humbert Humbert, was not so gently let off by his creator, who arranged for him first to lose Lolita and then to die in prison (of a heart attack). But Nabokov stood at the top of this particular slippery slope, down which he did his part to push us. Now, after 40 years of sliding, we have landed in a region where the condition of being has become so light and so weightless that the only consequence suffered by a real-life Humbert Humbert like Woody Allen is a

---

explicit scenes of copulation in the nude. Miss Swain reportedly had no objection to appearing nude in those scenes herself, but to avoid running afoul of the kiddie-porn laws, a nineteen-year-old "body double" was used in her place.

short-lived scandal that does not even deprive him of his Lolita or leave him sufficiently disgraced to ruin his career.

Little did I ever expect that I would wind up on the edge of endorsing the censorship of pornography, and not in my wildest conservative dreams did I ever before entertain the thought that we might have been better off if even a masterpiece like *Lolita* had never been published. But such is the uncomfortable pass to which I have been driven by the dormant memories that were evoked and the settled questions that were reopened by that story about a ring of pedophiles in Minnesota which appeared in the paper just as I happened to be rereading what I now see as a dangerous book paradoxically made all the more dangerous by its dazzling virtues as a work of art.

Samuel Pickering

Satisfaction

"I want to live life to the fullest," the man said. "How can I make every moment meaningful? How can I be satisfied?" A stranger, the man telephoned at 8:30 in the evening. He called from Atlantic City, a town that panders to dissatisfaction. "Atlantic City," my friend Josh said, "the City of Dreams, most of which turn to sand and roulette." Although I stumbled through a paragraph, I didn't answer the man's questions. Instead of enriching days, meaning reduces, forcing happening into significance. Even asking if one is satisfied leads to dissatisfaction. Moreover, escaping malaise is difficult in a materialistic, goal-oriented society in which a person is measured by possessions. Perhaps the attempt to quantify the intangible, the use of words such as *measure* and *weigh,* contributes to melancholy. If people stopped setting goals, maybe they would enjoy life more. As soon as a child kicks diapers aside and totters into the sunny yard of life, counselors begin blowing like clouds across the heavens, darkening pleasure by asking, "What do you want to be?" When I was young, no one asked me such questions. Indeed no one has ever addressed that question to me. As I had no goals at ten, so I have none at fifty-five. Because I did not set goals, neither failure nor success has thrilled or disappointed me.

Instead of living a life throbbing with meaning, I have just lived. The day on which the man called was full. At eight-thirty Donna cleaned my teeth. Afterward I visited with Ellen and Roger at the Cup of Sun for twenty minutes. At ten o'clock George cut my hair. At eleven I went to the gymnasium and swam two kilometers. Early in the afternoon I mowed the yard. At five o'clock Edward finished baseball practice, and I fetched him from the middle school. From six to seven-thirty Eliza practiced soccer at Spring Hill, and I dropped her off and picked her up. The doings of a day are too frail and too strong to withstand dissection. A pop anatomologist could, I am sure, slice through life with a hammer, pounding hours and pleasure into razzleum-dazzleum absurdity. "There is a slight stretching of the onolas cellusis," an analysis might begin, "complicated by a chron-necrosis of the lamifuresis, resulting in some denusion of the malparium, in other words, to be plain, a blepharmedia mul-tipediti marginallis."

For the two days following the telephone call I gave exam-inations at eight o'clock in the morning. Although not the stuff of dissatisfaction, sitting examinations can bore, so I decided to "take inventory," as a student who worked behind stage at the university theater said. Thirty-two students took the first exami-nation, thirteen males and nineteen females. Six students were left-handed, two-thirds of them male. Seven females wore scrunchies. And while eight students wore baseball caps, the number was evenly split between male and female. Only one student, a female, wore a cap backward. Six students wore glasses, three of them sitting in the row of desks next to the window. The day was chilly, and only one boy wore short pants, while a single girl wore a skirt. The skirt was denim. In fact denim was popular as twenty-four students dressed in blue jeans. Eleven students wore sweat shirts. I tried to read inscrip-tions printed across the chests of the shirts. I was not successful. To read the print I would have been forced to lean over desks, making students behave unnaturally, thereby undermining the integrity of the inventory. Nevertheless I noted "EXP Jeans" stamped in green across the front of a gray sweat shirt. On another sweat shirt Tigger posed atop Winnie the Pooh. Under Pooh appeared a lumpy mound of words. I read the words, in the process unnerving the subject wearing the sweat shirt. "This is so embarrassing," she said. "I fell out of bed this morning and just grabbed clothes." Printed on the shirt was "Tigger chuckled. 'What's a Pooh?' 'You're sitting on one,' Pooh said."

Although the examination took place early in the morning, no student ate in the room. Two males did, however, drink liquids, the first coffee from a gray plastic mug on which was printed "DDS Mug. The Department of Dining Services. I have my DDS mug because it's the only cup that can leave the dining room." The second student sipped Fruitopia, a soda manufactured by Coca-Cola. Containing "10% Fruit Juice," the drink was a blend of water and jiggers of apple, passion fruit, and strawberry juices. Across the front of the label cavorted three plump strawberries, two apples breathless and red, and then a dizzy green swirl resembling a lollipop, this last spinning over a tepid blue sea. The boy did not finish his Fruitopia. "Too sweet," he said, placing the bottle in the waste can, "but this was all I could find before the test." In not purchasing a drink the previous night, the boy was an exception to the general run of students. The rest of the class came to the examination well-prepared. No one borrowed a pen from me, and sticking out of the backpack of another boy was a roll of toilet paper, the wrapping stripped away but the roll itself untouched.

I did not impose meaning upon the inventory. Still, the day was chilly, and temperature, I suspect, was part of the reason just one subject wore a short-sleeved shirt, to be specific, a T-shirt on which a yellow sunflower blossomed above the black earth. The inventory also helped me pass time, and only occasionally did I glance out the window. The sky resembled slate. While buds on a white ash by the parking lot had burst into green, new leaves on the silver maple beside Gilbert Road shook in the breeze like finely cut snowflakes. In part universities exist to ferret out meaning, and so in hopes of reaching conclusions, I repeated some sections of the inventory the following morning. A nap, I am afraid, prevented my being as thorough as I had been the previous day. Nevertheless in a class of thirty-seven students, fifteen of whom were male, I found four left-handed subjects, the number being evenly split between the sexes. Four females wore scrunchies, three of them on the backs of their heads and one on her right wrist. Three females also wore barrettes, this accounting for the difference between the number of scrunchies worn by members of the two classes. Four students wore baseball caps, all girls. Interestingly these four females were the first four students to complete the examination and leave the room. Although no conclusion ought to be teased from the observation, the odds of such an occurrence are one in 66,045, a statistic I find almost satisfying. When set beside this number, other facts pale, even the observation that in this second and larger class, three males rather than two consumed liquids, a fifty percent increase in the number of drinkers, all of them drinking coffee, two from cups with "DUNKIN' DONUTS" printed on them and one from a cup supplied by Lizzie, who operates the snack wagon parked outside the English department.

I doubt the caller from Atlantic City would find the results of my inventory entirely satisfying. Much as my professional career, as social scientists label teaching, has not soldered meaning to my days, so domestic life has not nurtured fulfillment like an aged orange nurtures fungus. Indeed the person who wants romance to generate satisfaction would do well to bypass the altar, hop on the Reading Railroad, and head for St. Charles Place, or if he has a deeper pocket, Ventnor or Pacific Avenue. Last week I received proof sheets for a new collection of essays. "I don't want to read my book," I moaned, thumbing the pages. "Nobody else does either," Vicki answered. Vicki thinks stories should probe truth and explain life. Rarely do tales in my essays mean anything. "Vicki is an idealist," Josh said, "and you are a nihilist. No wonder you get along so well together." Josh may be right. That aside, however, instead of sitting behind a desk pondering significance, lack of fulfillment gnawing at me like hunger, I wander aisles of students counting scrunchies.

Surroundings influence behavior. No matter how firmly a person anchors himself in the shallows, a current will eventually drag him toward midstream. I want Vicki to appreciate my writing, and so in hopes of improving the literary content of my stories I sometimes subject myself to a regimen of patented, improving reading. Two weeks ago I read the Riverside Edition of *The Writings of John Burroughs,* ten volumes published in 1895. Burroughs was a famous naturalist, and I read *The Writings* in order to make my descriptions of Nature poetical. I failed. I have aged into feeling diminished when I see a dead squirrel by the roadside. Burroughs admired and studied birds. Birds so intrigued him that he shot almost all he saw, even off their nests. Burroughs's pursuit of knowledge narrowed his vision and, for me, reduced his stature. Markings on the books themselves soon interested me more than Burroughs's learned observations, no matter their caliber. Inscribed on the title page of *Wake-Robin,* the first volume in the set, was "R. E. Dodge from Aunt Harriet and Aunt Mary, Christmas, 1895." On June 19, 1929, Dodge donated the set to the library of "Connecticut Agricultural College." Dodge owned the books for almost thirty-five years, and I wondered if he finally found Burroughs's readiness to kill repulsive. Had Dodge, like me, grown beyond goals that destroy not simply birds, but that, in aiming life like a gun, shrink a person's capacity to appreciate?

I did not spend much time pondering Dodge's motivation. In March Vicki, the children, and I visited Princeton. In the attic Vicki discovered a doll she owned as a child. Eliza named the doll Abigail and brought her back to Storrs. Over the years Abigail's clothes had vanished, and she made the trip clad in a worn shift. The day after I returned *The Writings* to the library, I drove Vicki and Eliza to Wal-Mart to buy the makings of a new wardrobe. Shopping for clothes tires me, and I remained outside the store, sitting on a red bench in an enclosed porch. For a while I watched a man stuff cans into a recycling machine manufactured by Tomra.

The man put twenty cans into the machine and received a chit for a dollar. The machine refused to accept one can and a plastic bottle, and the man dumped them into a gray trash barrel. Sitting on the porch was tedious, and I drifted toward the edge of dissatisfaction, once jerking myself back by studying the logo of the Tomra corporation—a blue bottle, from the neck of which three white lines circled the bottle, curving beneath its base then turning upward and ending in an arrow pointing at the other side of the neck. From a distance the logo resembled an eyeball. Because the image in the pupil never changed, I grew tired of staring at it, and for a while I listened to grocery carts jangling as employees fetched them from the parking lot and pushed them through the front door in trains. The longest train consisted of twenty-eight carts. The engineer was a sixteen-year-old boy who took great pride in not losing a single cart to derailment as the train thumped across the porch.

The porch was not a roundhouse of activity. After Vicki and Eliza had shopped for twenty-five minutes, I became impatient and, standing, peered inside the store. To the right of the door a large bald man with a black mustache sat behind a card table. He was Ox Baker, a retired professional wrestler, "The Ugly Hero," a poster stated. In order to raise money for an employee of Wal-Mart who was in the hospital, Mr. Baker was signing a glossy, eight-by-ten-inch photograph of himself. Ox loomed in the center of the picture, his hands curved like grapples. He did not wear a shirt, and hair rolled across his chest in heavy black waves. Jury-rigged around his left elbow was an elastic bandage. Tubes of tape supported three fingers on his left hand, and resembling a broken spar, a splint was strapped to his thumb. After Ox signed "To Eliza" on a photograph, we chatted. Ox had wrestled in Nashville, and when he mentioned Tex Riley and Jackie Fargo, a train of wrestling associations rattled through my mind—the Hippodrome the first cart, the fairgrounds the second. One night at the Hippodrome I watched the Mighty Jumbo wrestle five midgets. The last time he saw Jumbo, Ox recounted, Jumbo was working in a carnival in Florida. "I am sorry we took so long," Vicki said, suddenly appearing at my side. "I hope you weren't bored." "Not at all," I said, waving good-by to Ox. "We should shop here more often."

The caller from Atlantic City would probably turn down an invitation to sit on the porch outside Wal-Mart. Moreover, I suspect he would think the way I spent Memorial Day weekend remarkably unsatisfactory. Late in May a mallard nested in grass growing against the wall of the building that houses the English department. Secretaries supplied the duck with food and water. "The weekend is long, and I am worried," Helen said. "Since you live close to campus, would you mind feeding the duck? She is going to be a mommy soon." Not only did feedings impose structure on the weekend, but they provided pleasure and knowledge, this last obtained with bread rather than a shotgun. When I first approached the nest, the bird made a panting sound in hopes of frightening me away. Soon, though, the duck ate from my hand. On Saturday I fed her bread baked by a French bakery in Stafford Springs, a place popular with gourmands from Storrs. On Sunday I gave her Pepperidge Farm's Crunchy Grains Bread, made from "Whole Natural Grain." While one piece of the French bread was all the duck wanted, she quickly pecked through two slices of Crunchy Grains, then wagged her bill and begged for more. On Monday the duck celebrated the holiday with her favorite bread, snatching three slices of Arnold's stone ground Sprouted Wheat Bread out of my hand before I could soak them in water.

To put days on a sure thing a person ought to turn away from win and show and leap through place. As one wanders place, questions about meaning and fulfillment fray and slip from consciousness. Last week Eliza played softball at Hampton. The baseball field perches on the lip of a beech wood that slides smoothly into a valley like a cup into a saucer. At the end of the second inning vultures floated up from the valley and over the outfield like grounds swirling in tea. Just before dusk I roamed the wood. Two wood ducks paddled along a creek, and in the soft sun damp new leaves dangled from beeches, yellowing the air. The next morning I explored the university campus. Atop Golf Hill lupin glistened in blue spires. In low shade by the pharmacy building yellow lady's slippers bloomed, the two side petals spinning like halves of a mustache. I examined three flowers; on each blossom the side petals turned through four spirals. Near the Benton Museum red oak saplings poked through lilacs and drained away the sun. I dug two lilac suckers and planted them in the side yard, the first from a plant sudsy with white blossoms, the second from a lilac with purple flowers dark as evening.

Out of a crab apple I sliced a nest of tent caterpillars resembling a sock. To give my rambles the illusion of purpose, I toy with figures. At home I asked the children to guess the number of caterpillars in the nest. Edward guessed sixty-eight, and both Francis and Eliza, seventy-two. The nest contained three hundred and eighty-three caterpillars. Lest I be thought a modern John Burroughs wrecking havoc on the natural creation in the name of curiosity, let me say that I opened the nest near cherry trees bright with new leaves, the caterpillars' favorite munchies.

Years ago when I first explored the campus, flowers absorbed my attention. Now I notice trees. Unlike many flowers that vanish during winter, trees suffer the seasons, almost becoming emblems of endurance, something I admire more as I age and blight affects me trunk and bole. Many trees on campus seem companions, if not of daily life, at least of years. New growth seeped glowing down the branches of Norway spruce. Against a pillow of blue sky Austrian pines bristled like soldiers, old campaigners gray and hardy. In contrast tassels of yellow peas switched lightly on golden chaintrees. A cloud of small bees drifted over English hawthorn, the flowers, pats of white butter, petals melting from them and dripping to ground. Wider than tall, copper beeches loomed like pots in a pantry, one moment bronze and clean, the next purple and charred.

I am a compulsive walker. Once started, I don't stop until I have gamboled away my energy. I spent the next day roaming the university farm. Around the cornfield on Bean Hill highbush cranberry and autumn olive bloomed, white flowers on the olive aging yellow, dappling the edge of the woods. Cherry trees looked as if a steel brush had been rubbed through them, the teeth snagging and pulling crinkles of blossoms from the tips of limbs. Beside a stone wall rose a cushion of rye grass, spikelets shunting in and out of colors, blue, green, yellow, red, and then from flower scales fringes of silver blades. Barn swallows spun over a field, orange and blue streaming from their tails and lingering forked and ghostly in the air.

Under trees in the woods leaves of Canada mayflower jutted from the ground looking like spoons. Near laurel, lady's slippers swelled pink and inflamed. In the Ogushwitz meadow warmth radiated from Indian poke, the six stamens on each blossom resembling fragile yellow hearts. Cedar waxwings skittered through trees by the beaver pond. Along the edge of the pond yellow warblers circled, establishing territories. I followed Kessel Creek and climbed the ridge above the pond. False Solomon's seal bloomed in dirt atop a rock. I sat on the rock and noticed maidenhair and long beech ferns growing above the creek. Small beetles congregated in the flowers of false Solomon's seal, on each shaft a single long-horned beetle, then several brown throscid beetles.

The throscid beetles were minute. Even with a hand lens I could not see them clearly. I needed young eyes. The next day the children walked with me, Edward immediately spotting a ladybug the size of a freckle, then on a tree a jumping spider resembling a fleck of gray lichen. Later in Schoolhouse Brook Francis noticed a crayfish clinging to a stone. As a boy in Virginia I caught buckets of crayfish. I had not seen one in decades. My joints snap and creak when I bend over streams. Moreover, as I drive little at night because headlights weep through my eyes, so the light in creeks blears then staggers across bottoms, making objects drift like water. "How was the stroll?" Vicki asked when we returned home. "I saw a crayfish," I said, "the first since childhood. The day could not have been better. I broke the bank."

Jane Shapiro

This Is What You Need for a Happy Life

I want to be married to one man for life. So far this has eluded me—that's the way I think about it: *so far*. As if, after two marriages and two divorces and many quick, interesting years alone—during which years I've lived exactly as I wanted—it could still happen now. I'll be twenty-one and my sexy, considerate boyfriend and I will marry on a blue day, surrounded by an elaborate, loving, familial community that will ratify and then proceed to sustain our union, and he and I will live productively side by side for six decades, growing daily more tranquil and enmeshed. We'll move to a hot climate and sit in twin lawn chairs and telephone our many grown children. Our gold rings will wear and our fingers will shrink. We'll die married! Still this story seems so real to me.

One way I've been thinking about divorce these days has been in discussion with Raoul Lionel Felder, the famous New York divorce lawyer, whose matrimonial firm is the largest and most successful in the country.

Q: Do people first arrive in your office with great ambivalence about divorcing?

A: Not really. Because by the time they come here, they've been to the priest, the minister, psychiatrist, psychologist, the yenta next door—all these people. So while it's not a Rubicon beyond which they can't step back, the fact is they've usually played out all their hands.

Q: So you don't see people who aren't sure—

A: I see them. I see them. But that's not the profile of the majority of clients, no. Because even the people who say "I just want information"—they don't want information, they want to see if they can get up enough courage, or enough money, and so forth.

Q: Have you often thought "These two people should not get divorced"?

A: What I have seen is two misfits. Where you say "Jesus, they're made for each other in heaven! Why are these people ever getting divorced? Who would want to put up with either one of them?"

Fifteen years back in time, Ed's and my divorce is imminent. He phones, from a resort in South Carolina. "It's terrific here!" Ed cries, forgetting he and I are estranged. There are 125 tennis courts. There are lavish plants and lawns. Meanwhile I'm thinking: This guy owes me money. Ed has been my second husband—my real one, as I think of him; every divorced woman has had one real husband. Before the kids get to the phone, Ed has filled me in on the layout of his suite. Two giant bedrooms, a living room, a dining room, and an immaculate, gargantuan terrace now house my lonely future ex-husband as he struggles in South Carolina to get perspective on his confusing, tangled, ongoing life with me.

Divorce, like other traumatic events, causes time traveling—like me, many divorcing people, I imagine, find themselves vividly living in other time places: years ago, or years from now when all this will be over, when what is broken will be fixed. Or you feel like two people at once—an old woman who has lost everyone and a girl whose life is beginning at last.

I'm an ordinary divorcée, vivaciously mourning. I rise in

the morning peppy and sanguine; only hours later, a heaviness grows in my chest and I'm near sobbing. I weep for hours, fall asleep still snuffling, then wake in the night with tears running into my ears. The next day, I'm shaky and refreshed; at midnight, I can't sleep because I'm excited, planning my moves.

I call my friends to make crude jokes, talk urgently, over-explain and guffaw; I keep them on the phone too long and call again too soon. Daily, I have ideas! I impulsively introduce myself to new people, make plans to change careers or adopt some children or leave town, write sudden letters to friends from high school, sleep with wrong men: a merry widow, every day.

Ed takes the kids for the weekend. I can't bear two days without the kids. So I travel to Fire Island to see Benjy, my childhood friend, and his wife and their children—to visit them and their family-ness. On Ben and Alice's redwood deck, in hazy sun and wet air, I know I've been cast off the planet. How can I be among that vast company, the divorcing or divorced, and be so alone? Morosely, Ben introduces me to three sunburned couples: *"This lady is estranged, poor woman."*

All fall, when not working or cooking, I look at television. A week before our divorce is final, a Tuesday evening finds me intently watching the interviewing of some cover girls. Outside, it's darkening fast. The phone rings and I grab for it—could be my husband. But the line is dead. In pearly voices, the cover girls unanimously maintain that having your image appear in a magazine does not change your life.

I have never understood this construct: does not change your life. If these women are right, then divorce doesn't change your life either. I try saying this to myself, but with a convincing sense that my life is (for the second time, this being my second divorce) about to be over.

People who have gone from poverty and obscurity and struggle and despair to being famous movie actors and best-selling authors will say this too: It doesn't change your life. When patently it does. When anyone can see your life is changed beyond recognition.

❊   ❊   ❊

The imminence of Eddie's and my divorce brings back to me my old tormenting feeling of not belonging to any group, family, or clan. A raucous call from a divorced girlfriend reminds me I'll soon be joining a new family—that of women alone, making bawdy jokes, asserting their exhilaration at controlling their lives, and looking, wherever they want, whenever they choose, for fresh mates.

I want to steal some husbands.

I imagine some married women—my closest friends—dying. Right now they're young, lovely, strong. Suddenly they get painless illnesses and swiftly succumb. Their bereaved husbands and I, linked in shock and grief, begin having dinners together. Helpless, in extremis, each husband and I tell many truths. In a dignified way, we bond. At last, hesitantly, then robustly, he and I have brave, profound, elegiac, joyful sex; tears drop from our four over-informed eyes onto afternoon sheets. *Astonishing, life's bounty. We have found each other.* Except that the identity of the widower changes daily, my fantasy is almost pornographic in its extreme specificity: We take our several children to the Phoenix Garden, and then to the movies on Greenwich Avenue, where we chew jujubes and hold hands in the flickering dark and light. We borrow an eight-room condo at Sugarbush, ski hard and eat chili for lunch; at night the kids sleep curled together like pups.

I actually sit at married couples' tables around town, indefatigable in my frantic loneliness, accepting condolences and advice, and thinking, Do I want him? As if I might slip poisoned powder into my beloved girlfriends' Cabernets.

I see what this is: I don't want to have to begin again and set out and endure trial and error and finally make a husband out of an actual person loose in the world. I want someone who *already is* a husband.

I ask Raoul Felder if he has in mind a profile of the ideal client.

A: No, *I* don't. But generally a divorce lawyer would like a stupid rich woman. A stupid *compliant* rich woman. It doesn't mean the woman is going to be exploited. It means that there's enough money to get well paid, that the client isn't going to question you, and that the client will follow your advice. It's not pejorative, it doesn't mean you'll do something bad for your client—actually, it's the reverse, you'll do better for her; you'll just do your job and not be bothered. You can't blame a lawyer for wanting those three attributes.

Months pass and I am still thirty-eight—still young. While waiting for my best friends to die, I start dating.

When you first turn your attention from your husband, your judgment is wild and you can't tell potentially suitable people from entirely wrong ones. As we've learned, there are days almost any man (or woman) in the known world looks like a real possibility.

I find a man. I think he's a possibility. I support this idea with the contention that he and I are culturally similar. Our fathers both went (before the Second World War) to Harvard; the new man and I share a longing and admiration for our dead fathers, those darkly handsome, clever boys bucking the quota up there in foreign Cambridge so long ago. The correspondences between the new man and I are so unlikely as to appear significant: We are grandchildren of Latvian Jews who settled in Newark and sold rags until they got ideas and promptly made, in dental equipment and real estate respectively, two modest fortunes. The new man and I get stoned in his Jacuzzi and I make a fool of myself crying, *"From rags to riches!* I never understood what it meant!"

He's a surgeon and I'm ready for a lover; watching him cut a bite of steak is pretty much a sexual thing. We love meeting in the hospital lobby and rushing to a restaurant. All summer we sit on banquettes in chilled air, plates of pasta before us, trying to get to know each other, not too fast and not too much. We watch ourselves dialing for reservations, chatting at the theater, moving confidently through a lavish world, availing ourselves, without guilt or regret, of its pleasures—he and I share some romantic dream of being well-heeled grown-ups. This makes us appear to be in love.

The new man is great—competent, energetic, alternately solicitous and remote, well paid. After a couple of months, he suddenly appears distracted and says we are not the lovers I had assumed we had become. He needs to think. He wants time off. You are a passive-aggressive shit, I tell him, and our shared passion vanishes like day breaking.

I sob to a friend about our breakup. She says: "This always happens. This is a typical opening salvo: doesn't hit the target, just starts to define where it is."

My friend Ben, though married, knows many single men. When I beg him, he tries to think up a guy for me, suggesting in quick succession two rich, sentimental drug dealers and a never-married mathematician with a heart condition.

Not long after this, I stopped worrying about remarrying and promptly enjoyed fifteen interesting single years.

I ask Raoul Felder: is there a difference between a man's divorce and a woman's divorce?

A: The dynamics are different if you represent a man.

Q: There's probably more crying with a woman—?

A: More crying. There's more emotionality in a woman's divorce and less punching numbers in a computer. It's much harder when you represent a woman. Because today, in divorce in America, the business is at stake. If you represent a man, you're sitting with a party who has all the records, knows what he's doing, has the business accounts in his control. With a woman, you're outside knocking on the door, trying to get in.

Q: Has a woman ever come in to see you and not cried?

A: Oh, sure. *Sure.*

Q: Who? Women who are just completely fed up and finished?

A: [Looks at me sympathetically] Oh, there are fortune hunters and adventuresses in the world.

❊   ❊   ❊

Just this year—just this month—I woke early, in darkness, with the fully formed intention to talk to my first husband. Since our parting thirty years ago, I've laid eyes on him three times: twice, we spoke awhile; once, I happened to see him run past in the Boston Marathon (even before I recognized his face, I felt an access of pride: his legs were springy and he was breathing well). My first husband and I had never discussed our divorce, as we had never discussed our marriage—we've never mentioned what we were doing all those years ago. Recently, I gave him a call.

JANE: I have very little recollection of what happened when we got divorced. Do you?

DAVID: Well, I've always had three important recollections. I recall coming home from work one day and the apartment was cleared out: not only you and the baby but also furniture.

JANE: What furniture?

DAVID: Not a lot. We had some furniture. One of your father's trucks came for it.

JANE: I didn't take the furniture!

DAVID: The baby's furniture. And I remember a knock on the door about seven at night, I don't know what month. Two cops were there, and I remember the shine, the light reflecting off their leather jackets. And they handed me something—I think it was a court order.

JANE: It's not in your divorce folder?

DAVID: I couldn't find it. But I deduced that the court order was to pay child support of 125 dollars per—must've been a week.

JANE: Could've been a month. It was 1966.

DAVID: Yeah, it could've—

JANE: Sounds like a month.

DAVID: And I also remember going to New York and not being able to see the kids. Those are the three recollections that have stuck with me over the years.

JANE: Why couldn't you see the kids?

DAVID: One time you weren't there when you were supposed to be. And another time—

JANE: You mean I knew in advance you were coming?

DAVID: Oh yeah. In the folder I found a log, it was interesting, of when I went to see them. Strange pieces of paper, with dates. It says: "January: Jane to Europe. February: Jane asked to delay visitation because of her marriage." And then apparently I saw the kids March 22nd, 1969. And then: "April: Delayed because of death." I have no idea whose death it was—

JANE: My father's.

DAVID: That was your father's death, in sixty-nine?

JANE: Yeah, I got married in February and my father died in April.

DAVID: And then that May: "Not there." You weren't there. I remember knocking and there was no answer. And then in June: "Jane said no because of erratic behavior."

JANE: Whose? [laughing]

DAVID: Well, I don't know! I assume you had determined that my behavior was erratic—

JANE: Oh, this is terrible, this is—

DAVID: And then the visitation stops. I think you were still living then in Washington Square. And the Mexican divorce had been—

JANE: Yes, when was that? When *was* the Mexican divorce?

DAVID: I have a copy of it, so I assume you must have the original.

JANE: I don't have the original of anything.

DAVID: And I've also got all these papers from Ephraim London and all your high-powered—

JANE: He was a civil rights lawyer, I don't know why he—

DAVID: He was your attorney! You had all Park Avenue—

JANE: I know. London had an elegant office. I mainly remember the dresses I wore when I went to see him. I have a sartorial record of that time, nothing else—it's really embarrassing. But I went to Juárez, I had to fly to El Paso, so—

DAVID: I know that.

JANE: Well, when did—when was that?

DAVID: Hold on. I've got it here—

JANE: [laughing] I'm pretty excited about this—

DAVID: You're "excited." This is just like a reunion then, isn't it?

JANE: This is great!

DAVID: "This is *grreatt.*" Is it?

JANE: No, but it's—it's important, for me anyway, because who's going to be able to tell me about my life?

DAVID: I'll tell you about your life.

DAVID: Yeah, after reading these papers over the weekend, I had so many strange feelings. Okay. How do you want to proceed?

JANE: Well, we *are* proceeding. My memories from that time are so hazy. And one reason I don't remember much, I think, was that I'd been suddenly thrust into another, completely consuming life. Because of course when I left I had one baby and I was pregnant, and then soon I had two babies, and I moved alone to New York, where I got no sleep, I didn't have time to eat, I got up at five in the morning and took care of the babies and I went to school at night. So I was hurled out of the life I had lived with you, you know?

DAVID: Yes.

JANE: Into another life, all alone. I just don't remember a lot from that time. Do you recall anything about our marriage? I mean—how did we *decide* to get married? And who brought it up? And how did—

DAVID: You brought it up.

JANE: I did?

DAVID: You brought it up.

JANE: That's what I figured.

DAVID: One day, I think, you called and said Let's get married. So we did.

JANE: Sounds plausible.

DAVID: Late December.

JANE [gloomily]: I know we had anemone and ranunculus.

DAVID: Do you want the Hebrew date?

JANE: Yeah, I'd love that.

DAVID: The sixth of—either "Teves" or "Jeves."

JANE: Probably a *T,* don't you think?

DAVID: Rabbi Stanley Yedwab.

JANE: Doesn't Yedwab sound like one of those invented words, or like a name backwards?

DAVID: Absolutely.

JANE: "B-A-W-D-E-Y," it is, backwards.

DAVID: Bawdy. We said that at the time.

JANE: Oh! We did? At the time? So that was a memory, what I just said?

DAVID: It was a memory.

JANE: Now, do you remember anything about our marriage?

DAVID: Uhh. I—

JANE: I mean, did we have fights? Probably did.

DAVID: I don't remember fights.

JANE: I don't remember *any*.

DAVID: None. I remember feeling pressure from your father and, less so, from you: "What are you gonna do with your life?"

JANE: But you were in graduate school.

DAVID: No.

JANE: Oh.

DAVID: I was only in school when we first got married, in Ithaca.

JANE: Well, how long did we live in Ithaca?

DAVID: Two semesters. A calendar year.

JANE: I've often wondered. Well, what was our—did we have any relationship, that you recall? I know we did, but do you specifically recall anything about it?

DAVID: I remember a dock we used to walk to. On Cooper River.

JANE: Do you remember having discussions about anything, ever?

DAVID: About me: "What are you going to do that's respectable?"

JANE: That was scapegoating—it seems so now. It was neatly structured. I was sinking and dying. And nobody was saying to *me,* "What're you gonna do?" Also, when I got pregnant, nobody said "Gee, isn't it a little early?" In those days, y'know, it seemed sensible.

DAVID: Well, I don't recall if you were taking birth control pills. I think you were, weren't you?

JANE: Well, obviously at some point I must not've been.

DAVID: It was a conscious choice, therefore, not to continue with birth control. Okay.

DAVID: I would have to say I did not know the kind of turmoil you were going through. I had no idea of the psychological pain you felt.

JANE: Did I ever mention anything? I can imagine I didn't. I'm just wondering.

DAVID: I don't think so. But it could've been my insensitivity.

JANE: Oh no no no, I doubt I did mention it, actually. Did I talk much? I think I was silent.

DAVID: You were quiet.

JANE: Did I attack you? I can imagine that too.

DAVID: Attack me? Physically?

JANE: Emotionally. I mean did I get mad?

DAVID: I still don't recall *ever* having an argument.

JANE: Isn't that interesting. I don't either.

DAVID: And that was part of the difficulty I had in understanding why there was a breakup. I suppose retrospectively it seems our marriage was meant to be an escape for you.

JANE: Yes, it was.

DAVID: I was a way out.

JANE: Well, I didn't know what else to do with my life. I didn't *have anything* I could possibly do with my life. And I couldn't work, I couldn't study, I couldn't think. There was this blind pain in my head. For many years. And I guess—it was a desperate thing: "Okay, I'll get married, what else can I do. Because I can't think straight."

DAVID: It's a shame we have to have our conversation by phone. There's so much here, real and imagined. And maybe the prelude to your writing about our marriage and divorce is for us to—

JANE: Well, y'know, I'm not writing about *our* divorce. I'm doing a piece about divorce generally. Which is just one of those things in my professional life. And I could imagine our conversation might end up a paragraph, or a sentence. And I'll interview Raoul Felder, the big divorce lawyer, and that'll be another paragraph. And I'll write some very emotional thing about—maybe what I recall of Juárez (which is almost nothing).

But really, the main thing is, this is about thirty years later. Our lives are moving fast. I thought I'd like to—know what happened.

Q for Raoul Felder: What qualities make an excellent divorce lawyer?

A: Well, the field attracts a mixed bag. Some of them are good lawyers—very few—and some are just cesspool types. Some are control freaks and some are exploitation people. It attracts the worst. (And sometimes some of the best, but very few.) It's not a complicated area of law. I think it's fair to say of most divorce lawyers that you wouldn't want to have a cup of tea with them. And you wouldn't want to kiss them. There's just nobody home.

Q: So it attracts an unsavory group?

A: "Unsavory" is a strong word. A needy group of people. And when you marry need with mediocrity, you get an awful hybrid.

As David and I reminded ourselves, I secured our divorce in Juárez. At once, I forgot it; decades later when I tried to remember, what returned so strongly was an odd constellation of things—heat and pale sunlight and dust blowing, and a grim feeling of timelessness and urgency and sadness, and air-conditioning and the scent of martinis and whiskey sours transpiring from iced glasses. I remember the experience both vaguely and intensely, as if this divorce had been a childhood milestone, which of course it almost was—I was twenty-four.

My younger sister flew down with me to El Paso. (The family, I think, assigned her to do this; it's still astonishing to me that she was there. My sister must've stayed in a motel with me and the next morning ridden with me across the border along with the other charges of our local Mexican lawyer. Down in El Paso, we were this morning's bunch of New Yorkers about to be unhitched fast, in concert, in Spanish. We crossed and recrossed the border in a van, through clouds of dust that hung in Texan, then Mexican, then Texan air.

Later, I think our group drank cocktails in a freezing hotel bar in the middle of the afternoon, me and my sister and the other divorced people. Dark red glow of the bar's interior, relief and camaraderie and pain. The others were older than I and either hectically pleased to be unencumbered or despondent about it or both. In farewell, our lawyer said to my sister, who was twenty-one and engaged to be married: "I'll see you in a couple of years."

I ask Raoul Felder how many years he has been married.

A: Thirty—I don't know, thirty-one years, something like that.

Q: Could you imagine getting a divorce?

A: I'm not a divorce person myself. I'm not a divorcing kind of person. If people leave me alone, I leave them alone.

Q: But let's say yours and your wife's paths diverged?

A: Things don't bother me, I'm into my own head. I don't get bothered if somebody makes a lousy meal—so you eat out. You don't like the perfume—so you sniff other people's perfume. That's all. It's a simple life.

Q: Right. So why is it that other people are coming in this office, their paths have diverged and they've got to—

A: Because most of the time, I think, people are narrow intellectually; they've put too much investment in marriage. You put a lot of investment in marriage, it doesn't work out. You don't put a lot of investment, you roll with it as it comes.

Q: Like anything else. If your expectation is at the correct level, it's going to work?

A: That's right.

1 9 9 5

My Lover and his former wife still own together, for tax reasons, the house he lives in. When we met, this seemed okay—sensible and modern. But my lover sleeps on the futon they shared, under his wife's childhood counterpane; nearby sits her dressing table, holding makeup and combs and perfume; on his desk is a silver box with bracelets and earrings inside. The bathroom (dual sinks) is a gallery of photographs: They have no children, so over and over, in black-and-white and color, it's just them. She graduates from law school, he catches a fish. Every time you step out of the shower, you meet again the annoyingly fresh-faced couple at their wedding in 1978. One of the pictures is so prized that a duplicate appears in his study, pinned as if casually on the wall. They are splashing in the Caribbean sea! Enjoying honeymoon water play! My lover says: "That picture is not characteristic of us. I don't know who stuck it there. I never look at it." He says about her clothes in the closet: "I don't notice them."

"Well, do you notice when she's sleeping with you?"

This is a tough one. Sometimes she drives the two hours from the city and sleeps in their former bed at his side. It isn't often, but it does happen. They don't make love, or touch at all. (I believe this; they hadn't had wholehearted sex in years anyway; why would he need to invent this, after the amazing stuff he's cheerfully confessed?) They just lie there. Probably he clings to the futon's edge and immediately drops unconscious. Maybe she falls quickly into her own dreamless sleep and wakes wondering where she is. She walked out of this house, for somebody else, five years ago.

Well, it turns out they're not divorced yet—haven't gotten around to it. Almost every day, some of the mail that arrives is addressed to his wife. "Do you notice her mail?" I demand. "Not this again," he says. "No. I don't. It's an occasional piece of *mail*."

And of course she used to cook once in awhile, and his kitchen is still hung with her omelette pans, and her spices are lined up, alphabetized and fading, above the sink. One night while I'm standing under the copper-pot ceiling, the phone rings, and he cries, "Don't answer it!" I answer it. She asks for him: "This is his wife." When, midsentence, she realizes who I am, she hangs up. So is she gone?

He's sick of me. He says *Yes, sue me, I was sad when she left.* He says she left regretfully but irrevocably. He says their interdependence is the merest vestigial convenience, their emotional contact nil. (On alternate days, he says she's his best friend for life.) He says the distance between them is vast and unvarying and immutable and he's so fucking tired of being badgered. He says it means less than nothing that they're not divorced yet; not being divorced yet is fundamentally a clerical oversight; of course they plan to divorce, they can divorce any time.

"How about now?"

"Man, you make trouble, don't you?"

Anybody can see I'm stupid in romance and inclined to believe just about anything. We both want me to think my lover's story adds up. Still, I've learned a simple thing in my complicated travels: If you're not divorced yet, you're married.

DAVID: You gonna interview your second husband too?
JANE [puzzled]: Of course not. I know what happened with him.
I talk to him once a week.

Raoul Felder tells me: In the beginning when you married somebody you were twenty-five, all you did was pound away; you're two sweaty bodies—that's what the marriage is. And then you realize, "Why'd I marry this one?"

Q: So you meet someone else, or you just decide to leave.

A: And most of the time people end up marrying the same people. A little younger, or sexier, or richer, or this or that. But basically the same people again.

Q: Have clients come back to you repeatedly?

A: Of course! As many as four times—a man I talked to this morning, I've done three divorces for. [Pauses. Reflects.] Give 'em a nice divorce, they keep coming.

Q: That's very interesting—it makes the divorce sound nicer than the wedding.

A: It's more expensive but sometimes nicer. You're giving them freedom. At the wedding, they're selling themselves into bondage. With the divorce, you're giving them happiness, release, a chance to make a better life for themselves. How many times can you say to someone, "Here: This is what you need for a happy life. Go. [glumly] Have a happy life."

Divorce has left me high and dry. The other day, after, as I've said, many years of excellent single living, I surprised myself with that thought.

I tell my married friends: "I've changed my mind—I want to live with a man." They all say the same thing: "No you don't."

Whenever I have dinner with another single woman, after a decent interval we say what we want in a husband. We name popular qualities, always the same ones, as if men were truly commodities. Potent, we say. Rich, we say. We all claim to want to mate with independent, mature men, and later in the evening all claim to want younger, gentler, more passionate and malleable ones with beautiful arms and legs.

Everybody always says her cherished fantasy is to be *with* a man but to live in a separate house. Okay, maybe that's impossible. So everybody rushes to say she wants a man who is "very busy." This is a universal wish: busy. I am often the first to assert that I want a busy man—somebody who has his "own life," who doesn't "cling," who will leave me alone and so on. Who can sit nearby without leaning into the edge of my vision or even glancing my way. Of course we don't want to marry a cold or hard or distant man, but somebody as anomalous, fantastic, as a satyr or unicorn: so independent, so warm. And we'll live with him forever—we'll never divorce.

Rich, we say.

Let him live across town, we say.

We are hard-hearted hannahs. We laugh like maniacs and order more wine.

Nobody says: somebody to care for me alone in the world.

Vivian Gornick is the author, most recently, of *The End of the Novel of Love*, a collection of critical essays, *Fierce Attachments*, a memoir, and *Approaching Eye Level,* a collection of personal essays. She lives in New York City.

Thomas Lynch is the author of two volumes of poetry, *Heather Grace* and *Grimalkin & Other Poems*, and *The Undertaking: Life Stories from the Dismal Trade*, which was nominated for a 1997 National Book Award. He lives in Milford, Michigan.

Francine Prose is the author of nine novels, two story collections, and, most recently, a collection of novellas, *Guided Tours of Hell*. Her stories and essays have appeared in *The Atlantic Monthly, Harper's, The New York Times*, *The New York Observer*, and other publications. The winner of Guggenheim and Fulbright fellowships, two NEA grants, and a PEN translation prize, she has taught at the Iowa Writers' Workshop and the Bread Loaf and Sewanee writers' conferences. A film based on her novel *Household Saints* was released in 1993.

Stanley Fish, Arts and Sciences Professor of English at Duke University, was educated at the University of Pennsylvania and at Yale. He has taught at the University of California at Berkeley and at the John Hopkins University, where he was the Kenan Professor of English and Humanities. He has published work on subjects ranging from late medieval literature to John Milton to linguistics to legal theory, and is currently the Executive Director of the Duke University Press.

Mary Oliver has received both the Pulitzer Prize and the National Book Award for her poetry. She has also written two books of essays, *Blue Pastures* and *Winter Hours,* and two books on the process of writing. Mary Oliver is on the faculty of Bennington College.

Carlos Monsivais writes a weekly column for *La Jornada*, and articles and essays for *Proceso* and other magazines. He has published nine books of essays and chronicles, and a book of short stories (*Neuvo Catecismo para Indios Remisos*). His first book in English is *Mexican Postcards* (Verso).

Bert O. States was born and grew up in Punxsutawney, Pennsylvania, where most of "My Slight Stoop" takes place. He is a graduate of Penn State University and the Yale School of Drama. He has published eight books on dreaming and literature, and his essays have appeared in *American Scholar, Hudson Review, Georgia Review, Kenyon Review, Salmagundi,* and elsewhere. His most recent book is *Seeing in the Dark: Reflections on Dreams and Dreaming* (Yale University Press, 1997). He is currently finishing a book of personal essays. He has also written a *Field Guide to Birders* and an exotic detective novel which attempts to answer the question "What if James Bond were 300 pounds?" He lives and writes full-time in Santa Barbara.

Joseph Epstein is the author of *Once More Around the Block, Plausible Prejudices, The Middle of My Tether, Partial Payments, Familiar Territory, Ambition,* and *Divorced in America.* He lives in Evanston, Illinois.

William Maxwell was born in 1908, in Lincoln, Illinois. When he was fourteen, his family moved to Chicago and he continued his education there and at the University of Illinois. After a year of graduate work at Harvard, he went back to Urbana and taught freshman composition, and then turned to writing. He has published six novels, three collections of short fiction, a memoir, a collection of literary essays and reviews, and a book for children. For forty years he was a fiction editor at *The New Yorker.* From 1969 to 1972 he was president of the National Institute of Arts and Letters. He has received the Brandeis Creative Arts Award Medal, and, for *So Long, See You Tomorrow,* the American Book Award and the Howells Medal of the American Academy of Arts and Letters. He lives with his wife in New York City.

Emily Fox Gordon's essay "Mockingbird Years" was reprinted in the inaugural volume of *The Anchor Essay Annual*. She lives in Houston, where she continues to write and to teach workshops in the personal essay. Her essays and stories have appeared in a number of literary journals, and new work is forthcoming in *Boulevard* and *Salmagundi*.

Guy Davenport, Professor Emeritus of English at the University of Kentucky, has published three collections of essays, nine collections of short fiction, and two books of poetry. His *7 Greeks*, a book of translations, won both the PEN and American Academy of Poets translation prizes in 1997. His most recent books are *The Cardiff Team* (New Directions) and *Objects on a Table* (Counterpoint).

Gilles Deleuze (1925–1995) was professor of philosophy at the University of Paris, Vincennes–St. Denis. With Félix Guattari, he coauthored *Anti-Oedipus, A Thousand Plateaus,* and *Kafka.* He was also the author of *The Fold, Cinema 1, Cinema 2, Foucault,* and *Kant's Critical Philosophy.*

Lucy Grealy is an award-winning poet, and attended the Iowa Writers' Workshop. Born in Ireland, she grew up in New York and currently lives in New York City. She teaches writing at Sarah Lawrence and Amherst Colleges, and is the author of *Autobiography of a Face.*

David Lazar teaches creative writing at Ohio University. His essays and prose poems have appeared widely in journals such as *Chelsea, Southwest Review, The Prose Poem, Denver Quarterly,* and *Quarterly West,* and he has been cited three times by *Best American Essays* as having written one of the Notable Essays of the Year. His essay collection *The Body of Brooklyn* is forthcoming.

"The demands of tact frequently turn any autobiographical essay involving living subjects into something of a complicated love letter. The hidden formal machine of this essay is, in that sense, the epistle, written to self and father simultaneously, like the ultimate Janus image of the face at the end of *Persona*. Where do I end and you begin? The essay that doesn't attempt to penetrate the psychology of its *other* careers toward a form of narcissism. At the end, we are invariably left with ourselves, but the essay mustn't know what that might mean from where it starts."

J. B. Jackson (1909–1996) founded *Landscape* magazine in 1951, taught at Harvard University and the University of California at Berkeley, and wrote nearly two hundred essays and reviews during a long and distinguished career.

Luc Sante was born in Verviers, Belgium, and now lives in New York City. His work has appeared in *The New York Review of Books, Interview, The New Republic,* and *Harper's*. He was the recipient of a Whiting Award in 1989, and is the author of *Low Life* and *The Factory of Facts*.

Gerald Early has edited *My Soul's High Song: The Collected Writings of Countee Cullen, Voice of the Harlem Renaissance,* and *Speech and Power,* an anthology of African American essays. He is also the author of *Tuxedo Junction,* a collection of essays on American culture, *The Culture of Bruising: Essays on Prizefighting,* winner of the National Book Critics Circle Award, *Lure and Loathing,* and *One Nation Under a Groove*. He is the recipient of a Whiting Award and a General Electric Foundation Award and lives in St. Louis, Missouri.

Murray Kempton (1917–1997) was an editor of *The New Republic* and a contributor and columnist for *The New York Post, New York Newsday,* and *The New York Review of Books*. Winner of a 1985 Pulitzer Prize, he is the author of *Rebellions,*

Perversities, and Main Events; Part of Our Time; America Comes of Middle Age; and *The Briar Patch.*

André Aciman is the author of *Out of Egypt: A Memoir.*

Robert McLiam Wilson is the author of *Ripley Bogle* and *Eureka Street.* He lives in Belfast.

Hilary Masters was born and raised in Kansas City, Missouri. His eight novels include The Harlem Valley Trio—*Clemmons, Cooper,* and *Strickland. Home Is the Exile* was named a notable novel of 1996 by the *Dictionary of Literary Biography.* His essays and stories have appeared in the important literary journals, and his family memoir *Last Stands: Notes from Memory* has been called a classic of the genre. He is a member of the English Department at Carnegie Mellon University.

Edward W. Said is University Professor of English and Comparative Literature at Columbia University. He is the author of sixteen books (including *Orientalism, Culture and Imperialism,* and *Representations of the Intellectual: The 1993 Reith Lectures*), which have been translated into twenty-seven languages. Forthcoming in 1999 are a book on opera, to be published by Cambridge University Press, and *Not Quite Right: A Memoir,* to be published by Knopf.

Edward Hoagland's sixteenth book, *Tigers and Ice,* will be published in March of 1999, forty-five years after he sold his first. He has taught at ten colleges, including Bennington, Brown, Columbia, Beloit, the City College of New York, the University of Iowa, and the University of California at Davis. About one third of his titles are fiction, but for the last thirty years he has specialized in personal essays.

"Like Emerson, I've wanted to be 'a transparent eyeball . . . part or particle of God,' a rapturous witness to the glory we live with and seldom open our eyes wide enough to see. But another facet of me has been convinced by the view of, for example, visionary nature writers like Robinson Jeffers and Edward Abbey, who believed that man has gradually been metastasizing into a kind of fungus or skin cancer on the face of the earth. (I think Emerson himself might now agree.) This grim view grips me more often, however, in 'developed' countries such as the United States, where greed and solipsism are the destroyers, than in Africa or India, where people are merely trying to survive. Witnessing a famine in the southern Sudan, when hundreds of starving, bony, wobbling children ran toward me in hopes that I could save their lives, my heart of course went out in simple grief. *They* were not a fungus. Nor were they anything that Emerson had ever seen."

David Foster Wallace's most recent books are the novel *Infinite Jest* and the nonfiction *A Supposedly Fun Thing I'll Never Do Again.* He lives in Bloomington, Illinois.

Donald Barthelme (1931–1989) was a longtime contributor to *The New Yorker,* winner of a National Book Award, a director of PEN and the Authors Guild, and a member of the American Academy and Institute of Arts and Letters. His sixteen books— including *Snow White, The Dead Father,* and *City Life*—have earned him a place among the most influential and imitated authors of the last half-century.

Margaret Talbot is a Senior Editor at *The New Republic*, and has written for a number of other publications, including *The New Yorker* and *The New York Times Magazine.* She lives in Washington, D.C.

Norman Podhoretz was editor-in-chief of *Commentary* between 1960 and 1985, and is now editor-at-large of the magazine as well as a senior fellow at the Hudson Institute. He is the author of innumerable essays and seven books, the latest of which, *Ex-Friends,* will be published in early 1999 by the Free Press.

Sam Pickering is the author of several books, including *Trespassing, Living to Prowl, The Blue Caterpillar,* and *Still Life*.

Jane Shapiro's first novel, *After Moondog,* was a finalist for a *Los Angeles Times* Book Prize. Her story "Poltergeists," which originally appeared in *The New Yorker,* is included in *The Best American Short Stories 1993.* Her short fiction and journalism have been published in *The New Yorker, The New York Times, The Village Voice, Mirabella,* and many others. She has taught fiction writing at Rutgers University and lives in Princeton.

Phillip Lopate is the author of *Against Joie de Vivre, Bachelorhood, The Rug Merchant, Being with Children, Portrait of My Body,* and *Confessions of Summer.* He is the editor of the now classic *The Art of the Personal Essay* and is the series editor of *The Anchor Essay Annual.* His work has been included in *The Best American Essays* and the Pushcart Prize annuals. He lives in Brooklyn, New York.

ACKNOWLEDGMENTS

Grateful acknowledgment is made for permission to reprint copyrighted material as follows:

"The Princess and the Pea" by Vivian Gornick. Copyright © 1997 Vivan Gornick. First published in *The Threepenny Review*, Fall 1997.

Excerpt from *The Undertaking* by Thomas Lynch. Copyright © 1997 by Thomas Lynch. Reprinted with the permission of W. W. Norton and Company, Inc., New York. All rights reserved.

"The Old Morgue" by Francine Prose. Copyright © 1997 by Francine Prose. First published in *The Threepenny Review*, Fall 1997.

"Boutique Multiculturalism, or Why Liberals Are Incapable of Thinking About Hate Speech" by Stanley Fish. Copyright © 1997 by Stanley Fish. First published in *Critical Inquiry*.

"Sister Turtle" by Mary Oliver. Copyright © 1997 by Mary Oliver. First appeared in *The Ohio Review*. Used by permission of the Molly Malone Cook Literary Agency.

"Identity Hour, or What Photos Would You Take of the Endless City?" by Carlos Monsivais. Copyright © 1997 by Carlos Monsivais.

"My Slight Stoop: A Remembrance" by Bert O. States. Copyright © 1997 by Bert O. States. First published in *The Hudson Review*.

"Grow Up, Why Dontcha?" by Joseph Epstein. Copyright © 1997 by Joseph Epstein. First published in *The American Scholar*.